DATE DUE

MAR 8 1992	
APR 18 1993	
MAY 04 1993	
FEB - 3 1999	
SEP 2 8 2001	
JUN 1 0 2002	
JUN 1 4 2002	

BRODART, INC.   Cat. No. 23-221

THE GILDS AND COMPANIES
OF LONDON

CHEAPSIDE IN 1639

STANDS OF LIVERY COMPANIES AT THE RECEPTION OF MARY DE MEDICI

THE
GILDS AND COMPANIES OF LONDON

GEORGE UNWIN

WITH A NEW INTRODUCTION BY
William F. Kahl
Professor of History, Simmons College

FRANK CASS & CO. LTD.
1966

Published by Frank Cass & Co. Ltd.,
10 Woburn Walk, London W.C.1
by arrangement with George Allen & Unwin Ltd.

First edition	1908
Second edition	1925
Third edition	1938
Fourth edition	1963
Reprinted	1966

*This book has been printed in Great Britain by
Taylor Garnett Evans & Co. Ltd
Watford, Herts*

PREFACE

THE scope of this book, which is based on a study of all the printed and unprinted sources which have been accessible to me during a ten years' residence in London, has been largely determined by a definitely practical aim. I have sought to provide for students of social and economic history in general—and more especially for those interested in the Livery Companies—an outline of the continuous organic development of the gilds and companies of London from the days of Henry Plantagenet to those of Victoria, such as would serve as a starting-point for more particular investigations. Whilst not losing sight of individual peculiarities, I have endeavoured to lay the main stress on the significance which the gilds and companies as a whole have had for the constitutional history of the city, and for the social and economic development of the nation at large.

That an even wider aspect of the subject has not been neglected will be clear from the title of the opening chapter. The historical development of English gilds—still more that of Scottish gilds—cannot be adequately interpreted without reference to the contemporary development of the gilds in continental cities. It was indeed in pursuit of this clue that a young German scholar, Lujo Brentano, wrote in 1870 the brilliant essay which, in conjunction with Mr. Toulmin Smith's collection of ordinances, may be said to have inaugurated the scientific study of the English gild. In Professor Gross's

Gild Merchant, published in 1890, the note struck is rather that of contrast than of comparison, but the essential value of that work—the most scholarly of all contributions to British gild history—lies in the application of a mind fully stored with the results of continental learning to the interpretation of a wide range of English records. And in spite of much valuable work—above all, the work of the late Miss Mary Bateson—in the field of British municipal history, it is still to German scholars that we must turn for the largest body of suggestive theory and of scientifically ascertained and interpreted fact. Three books I would mention to which the serious student of gild history will find himself impelled continually to return with increasing profit to himself—Professor Otto Gierke's *Das deutsche Genossenschaftsrecht*, Professor Gustav Schmoller's *Strassburger Tucher und Weberzunft*, and Professor E. Gothein's *Wirthschaftsgeschichte des Schwarzwaldes*.

The desirability of providing such a broad historical approach, as has been here attempted, to the study of the London gilds was first suggested to me by the invitation in 1905 of the Committee of the Advanced Historical Teaching Fund to deliver a course of lectures on the subject at the London School of Economics.

The extent of my debt to the published records and histories of the companies will sufficiently appear in the references. I am likewise under deep obligations to the ruling bodies of the Clothworkers', Drapers', Leathersellers', Cordwainers', Haberdashers' and Feltmakers' Companies for kind permission to examine their records at first hand, and to the further courtesy of the Leathersellers', the Cordwainers' and the Merchant Tailors' Companies in connection with the illustrations.

Through the death of Miss Bateson my book early lost the keenest and most stimulating of its critics, but it has owed a great deal—including all the materials for the account of the Confederation of Rectors—to some papers of hers kindly placed at my disposal by her brother, Mr. W. Bateson, F.R.S., and Mr. W. Page, F.S.A., the general editor of the Victoria County Histories.

All writers who enter the great field of London history must tread in the footsteps and enter into the labours of Dr. Sharpe. Without his invaluable *Calendars* of the *Wills enrolled in the Court of Husting*, and of the *Letter Books of the Corporation*, this book could not have been written, and Dr. Sharpe has at all times been most generous in placing his store of unpublished learning at my disposal. To Professor Charles Gross, of Harvard, and to the Rev. Dr. Cox, the general editor of this series, I owe a number of valuable suggestions; but I must hasten to add that whatever errors and heresies are found in this book are exclusively my own. My chief debt is to my wife, who has given me unstinting help at every stage of composition and of publication.

G. U.

24, BUCCLEUCH PLACE
EDINBURGH
November, 1908

I take this opportunity of expressing my thanks to Mr. F. J. Fisher for his kindness in bringing the appendices up to date and seeing them through the press.

F. M. U.

August, 1938

CONTENTS

CHAPTER XIX

APPENDIX A

APPENDIX B

LIST OF ILLUSTRATIONS IN THE TEXT

LIST OF PLATES

INTRODUCTION TO THE FOURTH EDITION

BY

WILLIAM F. KAHL

Professor of History
Simmons College, Boston

B

IN the chapter devoted to craft fraternities, George Unwin described the annual feast of a fraternity of London merchants known as the *Feste du Pui*. The special features of this celebration, as it was held at the beginning of the fourteenth century, were a song contest and the election of a prince and twelve companions.* In a book, which at first glance, is merely a general history of London gilds, the story of the *Feste du Pui* is indicative of the kind of free fellowship which Unwin set forth as the essential nature of gilds. While historians have agreed generally upon the fraternal characteristics of gilds, Unwin's special contribution was to emphasize the fraternity as the creative element within the gilds. Nineteenth-century historians had attributed the phenomena of gild life to the social instincts of man, to the human impulse to work or worship in common. These were the germinal forces at work in all nations and centuries. Stubbs thought that institutions analogous to gilds could be found in any civilized nation in any age. For the Bishop of Oxford the ancient gild was " simply the club of modern manners."†

* George Unwin, *The gilds and companies of London* (London, 1938), pp. 98–9; *Munimenta Gildhallae Londoniensis*, II, Pt. I. Liber Custumarum (London, 1860), pp. 216–28.

† Unwin, *op. cit.*, 11–4; William Stubbs, *The constitutional history of England* (Oxford, 1903), I, p. 448.

However, fraternal association, according to Unwin, was more than a universal characteristic 'of gild organization. It constituted the dynamic spirit of social and political progress in Western history. The functions of voluntary associations, created by their founders to fulfil both personal and collective needs, exceeded the activities of mere private societies. Capable of growth, pliable, amenable to forces of change, flexible, and stronger than political authority, free fellowship was a formative energy in European society.*

By itself, however, free fellowship was insufficient to promote freedom. Voluntary association, Unwin pointed out, tended to be aimless and anarchic. To prevent chaos, society created the restrictive force of government. The interaction of voluntary associations of free individuals with authority was inevitable. Therefore, it was from the resolution of the " upward thrust of the new life and the downward pressure of the old formula " that the liberty of the individual developed.†

In Unwin's opinion, the institutions by which Western society wrested political liberty from the State took their foundations from the gilds. The earliest, continual inter-action between voluntary associations and political authority was the struggle of the gilds with urban government to obtain economic and political privileges for their members. Opportunity for such a conflict was inherent in the dualism of medieval society: the separation of secular and spiritual authority, the division of legislative from administrative functions of the State, and the distinction between the interests of the State and those of public opinion.

The inevitable consequence of these opposing jurisdictions was disorder. Society, therefore, instituted the State as a means of self-preservation and order. However, in the course of centralizing its authority, the State revealed its ability to oppress those who had created it. To contain the activities of the State, medieval men created unrestric-

---

* Unwin, *op. cit.*, 13–4, 23.   † *Ibid.*, 11–2.

ted, corporate associations. Moreover, such fraternal and mutual associations had the characteristic advantage of flexibility which the State lacked. Therefore, the gilds as voluntary and fraternal associations, constantly undergoing transformation by the free forces of change, became agencies of progress both within their municipal environment and the evolving national community.*

The question of the relation of gild organization and governmental authority has dominated much of the literature of gilds. Unwin made a unitary approach to the problem. His method contrasted with that of his predecessors of the nineteenth century who had developed an institutional analysis. They had speculated upon the origins of gilds. They had sought to isolate types of gilds, to study gild structure, and to evaluate the contribution of gild organization to municipal institutions. Unwin sought to study all aspects of the gilds in relation to the society as a whole.

This essay attempts to assess Unwin's position in the literature of gilds. Perforce, any summation made here of the work of gild historians must be both abridged and selective in treatment. The emphasis must reveal the contrast between the questions raised by earlier historians and those Unwin put forward. What answers did Unwin give to the most significant questions of the nineteenth-century historians ? How far did Unwin depart from previous conceptions of the functions of the gilds in European and English history ? To what extent did Unwin's work open new vistas and problems for successive generations of historians ?

* *Ibid.*, 108–9.

THE PROBLEMS OF GILD LITERATURE

I.

Origins

While historians have concurred that the character of gilds was fraternal, they have been unable to reach any general consensus with regard to the origins of gilds. The widest variety of explanations have been offered. These, to adopt a convenient order, are: (1) Sybel's theory that the gilds originated from the constitution of the Germanic tribes; (2) Sir Henry Maine's theory that gilds began with the primitive brotherhoods of co-villagers; (3) Winzer's theory that gilds arose from the Scandinavian confederacies for plunder; (4) Wilda's theory of gild origins in pagan sacrificial feasts and the Christian church; (5) Hartwig's theory that gilds developed from associations of priests in the Frankish kingdom; (6) Brentano's family theory; (7) the theory of Roman origins set forth by Coote, Pearson, Marquardsen and others. To review all these attempts to explain the origins of gilds will not be necessary. The summation and criticism of the earlier theories of Sybel, Wilda, and Hartwig by Brentano and the subsequent evaluation of Brentano's own view of gild origins made by Charles Gross need no recapitulation here. We need only note the tendency of nineteenth-century historians to seek simple origins for complex institutions. Searching in the shadows of prehistoric times, historians perceived the dim outlines of customs which bore resemblance to later gild life. The scant evidence forced scholars to elaborate speculation. And as a result, they constructed a variety of hypotheses which had little relation to the tenuous facts available.*

---

* Karl Heinrich von Sybel, *Entstehung des deutschen königthums* (Frankfurt a M., 1844), p. 19; Sir Henry Maine, *Early history of institutions*, 3d ed. (London, 1880), p. 232; J. Winzer, *Die deutschen brüderschaften des mittelalters* . . . (Giessen, 1859), p. 29; Wilhelm Eduard Wilda, *Das Gildenwesen im mittelalter* (Berlin,

Anglo-Saxon Gilds

The meagre information concerning Anglo-Saxon institutions induced historians to adopt an equally speculative approach toward English gilds. From the few available facts some writers have often deduced unwarranted assumptions while others have projected comprehensive theories of pre-conquest society. Inevitably, such conjecture has resulted either in greatly exaggerated interpretations or completely erroneous historical analyses.

The evidence for the existence and outlines of Anglo-Saxon gilds before the eleventh century lies in obscurity. No documents mention gilds prior to the ninth century. However, some continental and almost all English writers inferred from the use of the word *gegildan* in the laws of Ine (*c.* 690) and those of Alfred (*c.* 890) that there were fraternal associations of gild brethren (*gegildan*) in the seventh century.*

Historians also have looked upon the *Judicia civitatis Londoniæ* (Dooms of the City of London) as statutes of a London frith gild or peace gild during Æthelstan's reign (925–40). Taken together, the various enactments constituted rules of an organization for apprehending thieves.

n.d.), pp. 5, 28, 56–8, 130–47; O. Hartwig, " Untersuchungen über die ersten anfänge des gildewesens," *Forschungen zur deutschen geschichte* (Göttingen, 1862), I, pp. 148–9, 150–60; Lujo Brentano, " On the history and development of gilds." *English gilds*, Toulmin Smith, ed. (London, 1870), pp. lxviii–lxxi; Henry C. Coote, *The Romans of Britain* (London, 1878), pp. 383–96; Charles H. Pearson, *History of England during the early and middle ages* (London, 1867), I, pp. 274–5. Heinrich Marquardsen, *Über haft und bürgerschaft bei den angelsachsen* (Erlangen, 1852). For a summation and criticism of these and other theories of the origins of the gilds see Brentano, *op. cit.*, lxvii–lxxiii; Charles Gross, *The gild merchant* (Oxford, 1890), Appendix A. The literature of English gilds. Vide pp. 174–8; Edwin R. A. Seligman, *Two chapters on the mediaeval guilds of England.* Publications of the American economic association (Baltimore, 1887), p. 10; Cornelius Walford, *Gilds: their origin, constitution, objects, and later history* (London, 1888). Vide: Karl Hegel, *Städte und gilden der Germanischen völker im mittelalter* (Leipzig, 1891) pp. 15–9.

* Gross, *op. cit.*, Appendix B, Anglo-Saxon Gilds; Brentano, *op. cit.*, xcix; Unwin, *op. cit.*, 18–9; William Stubbs, *Select charters*, 9th ed. (Oxford, 1913), pp. 75–7; Sir Frank M. Stenton, *Anglo Saxon England* (Oxford, 1955), pp. 350–1.

Several provisions were similar to the regulations characteristic of all gilds. These were the rules requiring a common purse, a monthly feast for the members, charity for the poor, ceremonies to be performed upon the death of gild brethren, and a monthly meeting to transact business.*

There is conclusive evidence of Anglo-Saxon gilds only for the first half of the eleventh century. The oldest gild records extant reveal that social-religious fraternities flourished at Cambridge, Abbotsbury, Exeter, and Woodbury. There also seems to have been a cnihts' gild which, after the ninth century, existed in some of the principal cities of England. The most detailed account available to historians was that of the " Anglica cnihtene-gild " of London. It dissolved in 1125 at the very moment that the gilds typical of the later middle ages were emerging. The documents have provided little information about the functions of this fraternity. The cnihts of London were probably influential burgesses, but there is no indication that the brotherhood was associated in any way with town government.†

On the fragile evidence available, historians exaggerated the number and influence of Anglo-Saxon gilds. Many scholars found gild organization in any group which met to conduct mutual business, to worship in common, or to hold purely convivial gatherings.‡ Brentano asserted that England must have been the birthplace of all gilds. Moreover, Wilda and Brentano set forth the theory that the gild was the fertile germ from which the borough constitution

* Stubbs, *Select charters*, 175–7; Gross, *op. cit.*, Appendix B; Unwin, *op. cit.* 18–9.

† Gross, *op. cit.*, I, 183–8; Unwin, *op. cit.*, 23–7; Stenton, *op. cit.* See J. H. Round's *Commune of London* (London, 1899), pp. 103, 221 for a refutation of Loftie's view that the cnichten gild formed a part of the government of London in Anglo-Saxon and Norman times. W. J. Loftie, *A history of London* (London, 1883–4), I, 98.

‡ John M. Kemble, *The Saxons in England* (London, 1849), I, 238–45; II, 309–13, 332. Describes the gilds as ' frithborh.' However, he calls them in one case, private and voluntary associations, and in another place, public and compulsory unions. Gross, *op. cit.*, I, 190.

evolved. Lappenberg had suggested that landed proprietors upon or near whose estates towns arose became the patrician class of the town and eventually acquired the predominant influence in the town's government. In applying this theory, Brentano asserted that " a patrician aristocracy " gained complete domination over municipal government through an aristocratic fraternity, a " *collegium nobiliorum civium* " or a " *summum convivium.*" He believed that the London frith-gilds combined for the purpose of vindicating the privileges and interests of their brethren who had been excluded from influence by the original aristocratic gilds. He also proposed that the London cnihten gild may have been such a union of frith-gilds. Brentano shared with Wilda the conviction that the cnihten gild was the London Gild Merchant from which the constitution of the city developed. Finally, Brentano set forth a theory of a federation of frith-gilds opposing lordly oppressors throughout the entire kingdom and laying the foundations of urban government.*

As Charles Gross pointed out in his classic study, *The Gild Merchant,* none of these simple but comprehensive generalizations had any basis in fact. Brentano's thesis that a patrician aristocracy became the governing class in Anglo-Saxon boroughs through a fraternity of landowners rested upon the single example of the thane's gild of Canterbury. But Gross's scrutiny of the documents failed to confirm the existence of such a gild. He also pointed out that Brentano never substantiated his elaborate theory concerning the origins of the frith-gilds in the encroachments of rich landed magnates. Moreover, Brentano's conception of a system of frith-gilds throughout England battling throughout the ninth and tenth centuries against baronial suppression was, in Gross's opinion, merely a colourful

---

* Brentano, *op. cit.*, lvii, lxxvi, xcvi, xcviii, xcix, cv, cxcviii. J. M. Lappenberg. *A history of England under the Anglo-Saxon kings* (London, 1881), II, pp. 431-4; Wilda, *op. cit.*, 244, 248, 251.

account derived from the handful of facts available to its author.*

The Gild Merchant

Gross rejected as baseless the assertion that London had a Gild Merchant either before the Conquest or in the twelfth and thirteenth centuries. He could find no evidence for a general mercantile gild in the charters and chronicles of London. He thought, therefore, the gild first arose in the reign of William and was associated with towns other than London. Moreover, Gross believed that the historic roots of the gild were uncertain. He speculated that it may have arisen in one of three ways: (1) as an adaptation or reorganization of older gilds; (2) as a local adaptation of the gild idea to newly developed trade, or (3) as an entirely new institution imported directly from Normandy. Of these hypotheses Gross favoured the view that the gild migrated to England from Northern France and Flanders with the development of trade after the Conquest.†

Whatever the origins of the Gild Merchant in England may have been, Gross believed that it became the department of town administration which maintained and regulated a monopoly over trade. The gild obliged its members to share with their brethren at a common price all merchandise coming into town. By this rule the gild kept prices down and excluded the middleman. At the same time this practice enabled the gild to suppress those two offences so odious to the medieval townsman, regrating and forestalling.‡

The Gild Merchant conferred upon its gildsmen several privileges of the greatest importance to their business activities. In contrast to strangers or non-members, the brethren obtained both exemption from tolls upon their goods and favourable rates of toll. In those towns which

---

* Gross, *op. cit.*, Appendix B.
† *Ibid.*, Chapter I; See also Unwin's note on p. 60.   ‡ *Ibid.*, 43–50.

had a charter granting freedom from tolls throughout the kingdom, the gildsmen shared in this immunity. Furthermore, the gild denied foreigners and non-gildsmen the right to keep shop or to sell their goods by retail within the town. Both the stock and the transactions of merchant strangers were subject to scrutiny by the gild. Non-gildsmen could trade within a borough for forty days at a time. They could not sell under the protection of a gildsman's privileges nor enter into partnership with any of the brethren. Under the rules of the gild strangers could not purchase goods coming into town until the members had completed their buying.*

The question, therefore, which historians of gilds have had to ponder is whether the functions of the gild were those of a mercantile institution or those of an organ of municipal government. With regard to this issue there has been no unanimity. Historians have set forth essentially two important views which we must now consider. First, Merewether and Stephens asserted that the Gild Merchant was an ordinary mercantile association, a private society with nothing to do with the management of burghal business. Secondly, Brady and Thompson upheld the opposite view. The gild was identical with the borough constitution and was typical only of the larger towns in England. For these two historians the Gild Merchant was the essential characteristic of the "liber burgus" during the twelfth and thirteenth centuries. The one without the other was inconceivable. The gild, according to Brady, was the all-pervading, life-giving principle of the borough. Many of the continental historians concurred with this interpretation. Wilda and Brentano identified the grant of gild law with that of borough law. Brentano concluded that English kings recognized the constitution and liberties of towns by confirming their gilds.†

---

* *Idem.*

† Brentano, *op. cit.*, xciv, cxii; Wilda, *op. cit.*, 244, 250; Gross, *op. cit.*, Chapter V; Henry A. Merewether and Archibald J. Stephens, *The history of the boroughs and municipal corporations of the United Kingdom* (London, 1835), I,

Gross took issue with all these interpretations. Indeed, he condemned most of the generalizations concerning the influence of the Gild Merchant upon the municipal constitution for the lack of evidence. Fundamental to Gross's criticism was his distinction between gildship and burgess-ship. Gildship implied the ability to pay scot and lot while burgess-ship meant liability to perform watch and ward, office holding, and jury service. Gross, therefore, accused writers who described the Gild Merchant either as a mercantile body or as identical with town government of having confused the whole with the parts. Furthermore, the entire structure of urban government could never have arisen from the gild. No institution, endowed with such comprehensive powers as the Gild Merchant, would have yielded them peacefully to any single subordinate department of administration. Gross believed that such a contraction of authority could only have taken place by revolution. But he could find no evidence whatsoever of urban revolt during the twelfth and thirteenth centuries.*

Having dispatched the previous theories of the Gild Merchant as inaccurate, Gross formulated his own interpretation.. He found the gild to have been superimposed upon the civic constitution. It was " a separate growth, a powerful organism grafted upon the parent stem. . . . " It was not the " fertile germ " from which the town evolved. Gross found basis for this view in the subsidiary position of the gilds in urban government throughout the twelfth and thirteenth centuries. He further denied that the Gild Merchant had existed only in larger boroughs, as Thompson had believed. Early in the thirteenth century the gild had begun to play an important role in many mesne boroughs which lacked extensive liberties. Wherever a baron or

xiii, xvi, 117, 353, 437;   Robert Brady, *An historical treatise of cities and burghs,* 2d ed. (London, 1704), pp. 3, 20, 47, 49, 50, 77, 84;   James Thompson, *An essay on English municipal history* (London, 1867), 108–9, 119. As quoted in Gross, *op. cit.*, 37, 61, 86–7.
  * Gross, *op. cit.*, 61–3, 70–1, 84–5

prelate controlled the courts of a town through his bailiff, townsmen made the gild a centre of political action free from the lord's interference. The gild eventually became the symbol of independence, an instrument by which men of a dependent town might extend their franchises.[*]

Gross maintained that the influence of the Gild Merchant manifested itself not in the origin, but in the development of the civic constitution. Both Hegel and, less emphatically, von Below concurred with this view. The gild belonged to a class of " powerful affinities " which prepared the way in the towns for the notion of the community as an abstract personality. The concept of technical municipal incorporation was the basis of the " firma burgi " which implied the collective responsibility and action of the townsmen. The contribution of the Gild Merchant to the emergence of the corporate identity of the town arose from the traditional privilege of gildsmen to regulate all aspects of trade within a borough. Gildsmen also administered the affairs of the town. Unconsciously, they may have applied the outlook and methods of fraternal association to the problems of the entire borough. In Gross's opinion, however, the gild was not the sole element in the development of the urban community. The Gild Merchant was merely one of several cohesive forces at work in the transformation of a collection of tenants of the local lords into a corporate body of citizens.[†]

[*] *Ibid.*, 85, 90–3. For a discussion of various theories of the relation of gilds to the origins of municipal constitutions see: H. Pirenne, " L'origine des constitutions urbaines au moyen age," *Revue historique*, Vol. 53 (Paris, 1893) and Carl Stephenson, *Borough and town. A study of urban origins in England* (Cambridge, Mass., 1933), Chapter I, " The mediaeval town in historical literature." See also pp. 179–84 for London.

[†] Gross, *op. cit.*, 93–103; Karl Hegel, *Städte und gilden der Germanischen völker im mittelalter* (Leipzig, 1891), p. 111; Georg von Below, " Die bedeuten der gilden für die entstehung der deutschen stadtverfassung," *Jahrbücher für national-ökonomie*, Vol. LVIII (1892), (Jena, 1892), pp. 56–68.

The Gild Merchant and Craft Gilds

There was as little agreement among historians concerning the decline of the Gild Merchant as over its establishment as the most influential economic and political institution of the medieval town.   In England the diminishing influence of the gild accompanied the expansion of industrial production and foreign trade during the reigns of the three Edwards. Beginning with Henry I, gilds of craftsmen made their appearance and increased in number throughout the thirteenth and fourteenth centuries.   In the course of the next century, craft gilds had everywhere acquired the position of pre-eminence within those towns which were growing centres of trade.   Historians could reach general agreement concerning the formation of craft gilds because of the greater volume of evidence after the beginning of the twelfth century.   Controversy arose, however, over the role played by the craft misteries in the decay of the old mercantile gild.   Here, the principal point of contention was the relationship between the two institutions after the entrenchment of craft gilds in urban society.*

Brentano presented the earliest account of the origins of English craft gilds.   He asserted that the Gild Merchant admitted craftsmen from the first although merchants comprised the largest number of members.   However, in the course of the thirteenth and fourteenth centuries the increasing division between the trading and craft elements in industry widened the economic and social distinctions between merchants and craftsmen.   Entrepreneurs specialized in buying and selling raw materials and finished goods rather than in manufacturing.   The more extensive scope of the merchants' business resulted in far greater profits than those of handicraft shopkeepers.   Inevitably, the merchants' wealth enabled them to control the gild organization and to expel craftsmen from the old Gild Merchant.

* Gross, *op. cit.*, Chapter VII.

To protect their handicraft industries the free craftsmen formed associations in imitation of the constitutions of the Gild Merchant. According to Brentano, the relation of the craft gilds and the Gild Merchant throughout the fourteenth century was like that earlier contest which raged between the freemen who had united in the frith-gilds and the old patrician association. As in the earlier conflict, the merchant patricians heaped oppressive taxes upon the plebian craftsmen, withheld protection of the law, and appropriated to themselves the revenues of the town.

In the course of this struggle weavers were foremost among the free craftsmen. They formed a middle class between the patricians and unfree craftsmen. Weavers served an international market rather than the local demand. Their greater prosperity, therefore, made them champions of the craftsmen in the struggle with the patricians. In England the conflict which diminished the authority of the Gild Merchant and ultimately brought about its demise in many boroughs ended in the reign of Henry VII with the victory of the craft gilds.*

From these facts Brentano developed a simple thesis of industrial development. Merchant gilds arose because townsmen needed to protect their interests against the interference of the local lords. However, the Gild Merchant inevitably became exclusive, and, therefore, craftsmen formed their own gilds. Eventually, the craft gilds themselves became oppressive, and the journeymen formed fraternities for mutual support against their masters.†

Within the quarter-century after Brentano published his essay, many historians attacked his symmetrical theory as myth. They found his interpretation inaccurate and dependent upon continental analogies. Although Brentano had dramatically described the craft gilds as victors in their

---

* Brentano, *op. cit.*, cvii–cxxvi.
† Sir William J. Ashley, *An introduction to English economic history and theory* (London, 1919), I, p. 79.

clash with the old merchant gilds, Stubbs was cautious. He could find no exact parallel in England for the struggles in European cities between the patrician burghers and the plebian craftsmen. Gross, Cunningham, and Seligman were far more emphatic in their denial of Brentano's views. Gross altogether rejected Brentano's general account of the conflict between the Gild Merchant and craft gilds and of the resulting democratization of municipal government in England. Indeed, Gross pointed out that the changes in town government during the fourteenth and fifteenth centuries were exactly opposite to those portrayed by Brentano. Initiative in government in many towns passed from the citizens as a whole to a narrow group. This was principally the result of the citizens' dislike for assuming office and of the growth of the population. Ultimately, select bodies of citizens controlled many municipalities and inevitably became irresponsible. They levied taxes and administered city finances entirely from self-interest. Public protests were sometimes violent, but Gross could find no evidence for the alleged conflict between the crafts and the aristocratic Gild Merchant.*

Even though Brentano's followers outnumbered his critics,† Gross and Cunningham insisted that Brentano had erred in drawing an analogy between continental gilds and those of England. In Danish, German, and Belgian towns, merchants were in a position to oppress craftsmen. Indeed, fierce conflict developed between patricians and craftsmen in

---

* Gross, *op. cit.*, 109–14;   William Stubbs, *Constitutional history*, I, p. 474, William Cunningham, " Formation and decay of craft guilds," *Transactions of the Royal historical society*. New series, Vol. III, pt. I (London, 1885), p. 380; Edwin R. A. Seligman, *Two chapters on the mediaeval guilds of England* (Baltimore, 1887), pp. 54–71. For a cursory review of the literature on the rise of the craft gilds see: Stella Kramer, *The English craft gilds and the government* (New York, 1905), pp. 18–21.

† The following are among Brentano's followers: Walford, *op. cit.*; G. B. Salvioni, *Le gilde inglesi* (Firenzi, 1883); J. R. Green, *A short history of the English people* (London, 1888); W. J. Loftie, *A history of London*, 2 vols. (London, 1883–84); W. C. Hazlitt, *The livery companies of the city of London* (London, 1892); P. H. Ditchfield, *The city companies of London* (London, 1904).

the Netherlands, Switzerland, and Germany. But such class warfare was less likely to occur in English towns where the civic constitution was, in part, democratic. Like Stubbs before them, Gross, Cunningham, Seligman, and von Ochenkowski maintained that there could be no exact comparison between English towns of the fourteenth and fifteenth centuries and continental towns. Gross believed that the " Zunftrevolution " of Germany was not possible in a society where royalty was as powerful as in England. He concluded that it was " radically wrong to transplant certain prominent features of the burghal development on the continent to Great Britain, without other evidence than that of analogy."*

Moreover, Cunningham suggested that Brentano's exaggerations of the conflict between the Gild Merchant and the craft gilds arose from a second analogy. He pointed out that Brentano had proposed that both craft gilds and labour unions had arisen to enable workers to withstand the power of their employers. Cunningham absolutely denied this assertion. He maintained that the most cursory examination of gild and union records would indicate the two institutions developed from entirely different motives. Unions were based upon employees' opposition to their employers. However, both the avowed and real objects of the craft gilds were the regulation of industry and trade.†

Seligman did not reject out of hand Brentano's view that urban society had been disrupted by internal political upheavals during the fourteenth and fifteenth centuries. He regarded Brentano's theory of a contest for power between the aristocratic merchants and the plebian artisans as an exaggeration. But he believed that a clash had occurred between the entire citizenry, who did not compose a Gild

---

* Gross, *op. cit.*, 106; Cunningham, *op. cit.*, 380–1; Seligman, *op. cit.*, 54–71; W. von Ochenkowski, *Englands wirthschaftliche entwickelung im ausgange des mittelalters* (Jena, 1879), pp. 58–62, 74–9.

† Cunningham, *op. cit.*, 380–1; See also Cunningham's *Politics and economics* (London, 1885), pp. 98–9.

C

Merchant, and a " small collection of outsiders attempting
to arrogate to themselves illegitimate powers."*

William Ashley took a position between Brentano and
his critics. He advanced the theory that craft gilds came
into existence at the point in urban history when the
merchant gild had coalesced with town government, creating
a select political body which combined economic regulation
and political authority.   In opposing this municipal
oligarchy, weavers and fullers, followed by other craftsmen,
established gilds to obtain self regulation. Ashley, therefore,
suggested that the relations between the craft gilds and
borough authorities were far less harmonious than critics of
Brentano had suggested.†

Craft Gilds and the Civic Constitution

Having set forth the theory that craft gilds arose as a
result of class conflict, Ashley raised the question of the
relationship of crafts to the municipal government. He
suggested that two political issues arose in town politics
during the thirteenth and fourteenth centuries. The first
was whether gilds were to have an independent jurisdiction
over their members. The second raised the question whether
artisans were to come within the trading monopoly of the
Gild Merchant. Ashley maintained that these points of
contention between the municipal government and the craft
gilds could not be set forth precisely. He suggested that it
was impossible to describe exactly a quarrel over a jurisdiction for which the protagonists, themselves, had no specific
definition.‡

Ashley's account of urban politics led him to disagree
both with Brentano and his critics over the relation of the
craft gild to the civic constitution. He denied Brentano's
contention that the craft gilds were entirely independent in

* Seligman, *op. cit.*, 61.   † Ashley, *op. cit.*, 78–88.   ‡ *Ibid.*

supervising their members' work and trade practices. Gross had characterized this view as exceptional in the fourteenth century. But Ashley could not agree with Gross's assertion that although craftsmen were allowed to regulate their trades, they were subject to the general control of burghal magistrates. He was also critical of Cunningham's view that the craft gild was a " publicly recognized body for the regulation of some branch of industry." Equally unacceptable was von Ochenkowski's description of gild supervision as police work.*

In the last analysis, Ashley's account of the rise of the craft gilds and his concept of their jurisdiction was closer to Brentano's interpretation than to that of his critics. The craft gild, he believed, was the product of class struggles within the towns. Craftsmen formed their gilds to combat the dominant influence of a mercantile aristocracy over town government. Having won recognition, the craft gild exercised jurisdiction over its members, subject to " a vague but real authority " of the town fathers. Craftsmen, themselves, often drew up ordinances, but they were subject to the approval of the magistrates. Whenever the town gave its sanction to gild rules, it surrendered ordinary, detailed regulation of manufacturing processes and trade to the craftsmen.†

II.

London Craft Gilds

Brentano stated categorically that ". . . England must be regarded as the birthplace of gilds and London, perhaps, as their cradle. At least there is documentary evidence that

---

* Brentano, *op. cit.*, cxxiii; Gross, *op. cit.*, 113; Cunningham, *Formation and decay*, 372–3; Ashley, *op. cit.*, 84–5; von Ochenkowski, *op. cit.*, 63.

† Ashley, *op. cit.*, 85.

the constitution of the city was based upon a gild; and it served as a model for other English towns." Equally emphatic, Charles Gross wrote: " It is a mistake to consider London the type by which to judge of the general development of English municipal history. In many respects, the metropolis is, and for centuries has been, an anomaly among the towns of England."* These conflicting statements suggest the misconceptions, the myth, the distorted and inaccurate accounts of London Gilds which Gross and Unwin were obliged to clear away.

The first historian to write a comprehensive history of London gilds and Livery Companies completed his work more than thirty years before Brentano set forth his theories. Librarian of Guildhall Library from 1828 until 1845, William Herbert published his *History of the Twelve Great Livery Companies of London* in 1836–7. Whenever possible Herbert wrote from original sources. But obstacles to manuscript research were formidable in the nineteenth century. Among the companies there was a strong and ancient tradition of secrecy concerning records. Despite this hazard Herbert was able to compile a rich treasury of information. He began his work with an extended historical essay. This was at once a narrative and a functional analysis of the internal structure of the gilds and companies. It also included an account of the relation of the gilds to the government of London and to the Crown. The main body of Herbert's work, however, was devoted to individual studies of the Twelve Great Companies.†

Like the German historians who followed him, Herbert relied upon Madox for his authority on Anglo-Saxon gilds in London. He accepted the eighteenth-century historian's opinion that the town office of alderman was derived from the name for a chief officer of a secular gild. He also drew

---

* Brentano, *op. cit.*, xcviii, xcix; Gross, *op. cit.*, 80.
† William Herbert, *The history of the Twelve great livery companies* (London, 1837), 2 vols.

the erroneous conclusion from Madox that London had a Gild Merchant. As in the case of Wilda and Brentano, Herbert failed to note the qualification in Madox's statement, and, like them, he asserted conjecture for fact.*

Much of Herbert's general essay described the ceremonial of the Livery Companies, their election feasts, funeral customs, and Lord Mayors' shows. However, Herbert did not neglect the political aspect of the companies. He suggested that the weavers' gild held a dominant position in London and that the decline in its power was due to its quarrel with the burillers and the tightening of the city's jurisdiction over it after 1335. He also indicated the role played by the gilds in the civic unrest and open violence which marked London politics between 1376 and 1384. He suggested that the changes effected in electing civic officers resulted from contests among the greater gilds in the fourteenth century. Both in his general essay and his individual histories of the companies, Herbert emphasized the attempts of the gilds to obtain monopolistic control over their trades. Moreover, he described the companies as independent authorities in regulating trade and as co-operating organs of civic administration, in police work, defence, taxation, and, eventually, elections.†

Three other historical accounts of the Livery Companies must be mentioned: William C. Hazlitt's *The Livery companies of the city of London*, published in 1892, and P. H. Ditchfield's *The city companies of London*, issued in 1904, and Robert J. Blackham's *The soul of the city: London's Livery companies*, printed in 1931. All of these authors used Herbert's original scheme, a general essay followed by separate accounts of individual companies. However, only Hazlitt's work bears comparison with that of Herbert. In his general account of gilds Hazlitt drew heavily upon

---

* *Ibid.*, I, 8; Thomas Madox, *Firma burgi, or an historical essay concerning cities* (London, 1726), p. 30.

† *Ibid.*, 8, 17–21, 24–7, 36–70.

Brentano and Wilda. Consequently, he subscribed to Brentano's theories regarding the general development of gilds both on the continent and in England. With regard to the problem of the origins of gilds, the existence of a Gild Merchant in London, the struggle between a patrician aristocracy of merchants and a plebian class of craftsmen in the reigns of Edward I and Edward II, Hazlitt relied heavily upon Brentano. He reiterated the old hypothesis that gilds are the source of the municipality. With regard to the jurisdiction of the craft gilds in relation to the civic constitution and the Crown, Hazlitt described them as a " State department for the superintendence of the trade and manufactures of London."*

Unwin's Place in Gild Literature

While Herbert and Hazlitt focussed their attention on the individual Livery Companies, Unwin provided a general history. Throughout his study, Unwin sought to discuss the gilds and companies of London in relation to the economic and political history of both the city and the nation. He also emphasized those characteristics which provided the companies with continuity and enabled them to survive industrial and political change. Earlier studies had been limited. Some individual histories like Charles Matthew Clode's *The early history of the . . . merchant taylors* and Edward Jupp and William W. Pocock's *An historical account of the Worshipful company of carpenters* were domestic chronicles. Others such as Arthur J. Adams's *The history of the Worshipful company of blacksmiths* and Charles Welch's *History of the Worshipful company of pewterers* were largely collections of extracts from the companies' records. In

---

* William C. Hazlitt, *The Livery companies of the city of London* (London, 1892), p. 17; Peter H. Ditchfield, *The city companies of London . . .* (London, 1904); Robert J. Blackham, *The soul of the city: London's Livery companies* (London, 1931).

both cases the authors were bound by the limits of their companies' histories. They tended to concentrate on the customs, charities, government, and ceremonial of the companies. Unwin's intention was to give a more complete picture of the history of London gilds. He attempted to provide a starting-point for more specialized studies. At the same time he opened up for study a number of unexplored problems in the social and constitutional history of London.*

Unwin's talent for synthesis led him to reject the pursuit of the origins of gilds which had charmed his nineteenth-century predecessors. His interest was in the larger question, the contribution of gild organization to the growth of political liberty. To this end, he raised the question of why the gilds of the East were alive while those of Western Europe were dead. Unwin believed that the answer lay in the fact that the gilds of the West had long since performed their most useful function. They had built up a social structure which eventually superseded them. The gilds of the East were alive because they had not become the creative agencies of their society. " The gilds of the West expired in giving birth to progress, the gilds of the East are preserved and fostered in the interests of order."†

Unwin employed his pragmatic approach in his account of Anglo-Saxon gilds. Throughout his analysis of the frith-gilds, he emphasized those functions by which the gildsmen supplemented the limited powers of the government during the tenth century. In describing the character of the *Judicia civitatis Londoniæ*, he suggested that the vagueness in the distinction between the private association regulating its own affairs and the public authority preserving

---

* Charles M. Clode, *The early history of the . . . merchant taylors* (London, 1888), 2 vols.; Edward B. Jupp and William W. Pocock, *An historical account of the Worshipful company of carpenters* (London, 1887); Arthur J. Adams, *The history of the Worshipful company of blacksmiths* (London, 1937); Charles Welch, *History of the Worshipful company of pewterers* (London, 1902), 2 vols.

† Unwin, *op. cit.*, 4–9.

peace and order was peculiar to English gild history. " The gild," he wrote, " is constantly crossing, often unconsciously, the line that separates public functions from private, compulsory association from voluntary." In Unwin's opinion, the gilds shared these flexible and dynamic qualities with other English institutions. Indeed, the gilds and companies of London belonged to the same group of vital, social and political bodies as the Bank of England, the Universities, the Inns of Court, and the political parties.*

The concept that private, voluntary associations shared power with public authority led Unwin to study the gilds and companies of London in the light of interrelated social and economic forces of municipal and national politics. He believed that the development of the civic government and the gilds went hand in hand. Unwin recognized that his predecessors had distorted the role of gilds in urban history, and he concluded that their errors derived from a misconception of the word " craft."†

Brentano and other nineteenth-century scholars had thought of the craftsman as a manual worker. They had interpreted the " Zunftrevolution " of the fourteenth century, therefore, as the triumph of a democratic form of government. Unwin pointed out that the word craft like " art " or " mistery " meant generally a trade or calling. Goldsmiths or drapers were frequently well-to-do shopkeepers or tradesmen. Many master craftsmen were capitalists as well as traders. With the expansion of industry and commerce, masters became entrepreneurs, manufacturers or merchants. When prosperity enabled capitalist masters to rise in the social scale, they took their craft organization with them into what became an upper middle class. They left behind the small master craftsmen as a lower middle class to create new organizations for themselves.‡

The crafts made their first bid for power in London

* *Ibid.*, 18–23.   † *Ibid.*, 62.   ‡ *Idem.*

during the mayoralties of Fitz Thomas and Hervey at the close of Henry III's reign. The unrest of Edward II's reign provided the crafts with the opportunity to establish their position. By the charter of 1319 the crafts became the principal method of obtaining citizenship. This was not, as Brentano had claimed, the rise to power of a class of wage-earning handicraft workers. Moreover, it was not the victory of one class over another. It was, Unwin insisted, the ascendancy of voluntary association over the small aldermanic class which had previously dominated the city's political life.*

The subsequent history of the fourteenth century was filled with the conflict of the great crafts. The culminating period in the formation of the city constitution occurred during the national crisis of the reign of Richard II. Unwin described the years 1376–1384 as the most eventful in the history of London. Through revolution and counter-revolution, the crafts, fortified by the bonds of fraternal association, emerged as the dominant civic institution under the constitution.†

In the course of the 120 years of political struggle which marked the rise of crafts, they constituted the most creative energy in city politics. Unwin believed the gilds were " a force which shaped and reshaped the constitution, a force making for progress, or, at any rate for constant change and movement." He pointed out that Fitz Thomas and Hervey were not creating a new social impulse in the reign of Henry III. The two mayors were actually giving civic sanction to political agencies sufficiently assertive to have placed them in office. Unwin discovered from these crises two entirely different aspects of the crafts. (1) They were important instruments in effecting change in the civic constitution and (2) they exercised a subordinate authority delegated by the municipality.‡

* *Ibid.*, 70–1, 74–6.   † *Ibid.*, 127.
‡ *Ibid.*, 65–6.

Unwin perceived that the relationship between the gilds'
jurisdiction and that of the municipal authority and the
Crown was more complicated than nineteenth-century
historians had thought was generally true of English towns.
The king, mayor and aldermen, and elected craft officials
shared authority over the activities of the London business
community. The mayor derived from the king a direct
jurisdiction over all retailers of victuals. With the aldermen,
he possessed by custom the right of veto over private craft
legislation. Most of the crafts eventually obtained direct
authorization from the king. The gilds' purpose was not to
dispute supervision by the mayor and aldermen but to
procure certain advantages that were unobtainable in any
other way. Unwin tended to overemphasize the efforts of
the gilds to secure rights of supervision in the suburbs or at
fairs or the right to contest competition from other crafts
in the city. According to Sylvia Thrupp, Unwin's questionable interpretation arose from his unduly sensational account
of internal city conflicts.*

The story of the gilds and companies as told by Unwin
was the history of the growth of self-government in London.
But it was also an analysis of the fraternal associations which
became the driving energy of political change. Unwin's
description of the " Janus-like appearance of the gild, as a
craft on one side and as a fraternity on the other " gives us
the clue to his method. Nineteenth-century historians,
misled by the " Idol of Origins," had sought to find the
source of the gild phenomenon, to relate types of gilds, to
concentrate on fragments of gild history. However, Unwin,
as we have seen, saw gilds as dynamic forces in Western
civilization and, therefore, he adopted an organic method.
By using diverse approaches, he portrayed living institutions.
He studied the gilds as the essential political force in London,
the well-spring of craft organization, the cohesive bond in

* *Ibid.*, 79–81, 155–60; Sylvia L. Thrupp, *The merchant class of medieval
London, 1300–1500* (London, 1948), p. 93.

the religious, philanthropic, and convivial life of medieval Londoners.*

Unwin intended that his general account of the gilds and companies of London would raise specific questions for his successors to investigate. To a degree his purpose has been fulfilled by a number of excellent histories of individual Livery Companies and studies in the constitutional and social history of London. Unwin's insight into the importance for London's constitutional development of the national crises of the thirteenth and fourteenth centuries produced some remarkable research into the politics of the city. The most comprehensive work to follow Unwin's account was that of Martin Weinbaum. The viewpoint of his essay, *London unter Edward I und II*, is indicated in the title, " Die politischen Beziehungen zwischen Stadt und Königthum." He also published two specialized articles on London politics: *Das Londoner iter von 1341* and *Andreas Horn, ein Londoner stadtkämmerer*. The work of a second historian, Ruth Bird's *The turbulent London of Richard II*, was based upon important sources formerly unavailable. The author found that the centre of civic strife from 1376 to 1399 was not the conflict between the victualling and non-victualling traders, as Unwin had emphasized, but the clash between the oligarchic Court of Aldermen and the Common Council. To be sure, the economic cross-current was violent. However, the struggle did not originate in the city but in parliamentary attempts during the reign of Edward III to reduce the price of food at the expense of exclusive trading privileges in the boroughs generally.†

---

* Unwin, *op. cit.*, 108–9; Marc Bloch, *The historian's craft* (New York, 1961), pp. 29–35.

† Ruth Bird, *The turbulent London of Richard II* (London, 1949); Martin Weinbaum, " London unter Edward I und II." Band I: Untersuchungen. Band II: Texte Beihefte 28 und 29 zur *Vierteljahrschrift für sozial und wirtschaftsgeschichte* (Stuttgart, 1933); also his " Andreas Horn, ein Londoner stadtkämmerer " in *Festschrift. Albert Brackmann* (Weimar, 1931) and " Das Londoner iter von 1341." *Historical essays in honour of James Tait* (Manchester, 1933), pp. 399–404.

In social history, Miss Sylvia Thrupp's *The merchant class of medieval London, 1300–1500*, was an attempt to explore the environment in which London merchants carried on their business activities. The author did not intend her book to be a general economic or institutional history of the city. Miss Thrupp, therefore, went beyond the description of mercantile activity to consider class attitudes and ideals. As an analysis of the merchant class over two centuries, the book is an enormous compilation of new information. Although Unwin's influence is evident, particularly in the chapter on city government, the more direct inspiration for Miss Thrupp's work is undoubtedly that of Eileen Power.*

The most distinguished histories of individual Livery Companies followed the appearance of Unwin's *The gilds and companies. . . .* Aside from Arthur Henry Johnson's five-volume *The history of the Worshipful company of drapers*, Frederick J. Fisher's *A short history of the Worshipful company of horners*, Sylvia L. Thrupp's excellent *A short account of the Worshipful company of bakers of London*, Frances Consitt's first volume of *The London weavers' company*, Philip E. Jones's *The Worshipful company of poulters*, Theodore C. Barker's *The Girdlers' company*, and Cyprian Blagden's *The Stationers' company: a history, 1403–1959*, there are no other histories of Livery Companies written by scholars with a knowledge of contemporary social and economic trends.†

To be sure, not all subsequent histories of Livery Companies were based on Unwin's contributions. Many continued to be domestic chronicles of company traditions.

---

* Thrupp, *op. cit.*

† Arthur Henry Johnson, *The history of the Worshipful company of drapers* (London, 1914–22), 5 vols.; F. J. Fisher, *A short history of the Worshipful company of horners* . . . (London, 1936); Sylvia L. Thrupp, *A short history of the Worshipful company of bakers of London* (Croydon, 1933); Frances Consitt, *The London weavers' company* (Oxford, 1933), Vol. I. The second volume has never appeared; P. E. Jones, *The Worshipful company of poulters* . . . (London, 1939); T. C. Barker, *The Girdlers' company: A second history* (London, 1957); Cyprian Blagden, *The Stationers' company, 1403–1959* (London, 1960).

They described at length fraternal customs, the companies' feasts, halls, plate, their properties, and charities. To this category belongs George Elkington's *The coopers: company and craft*, which depends for its general observations upon Hazlitt's *Livery companies* and R. J. Blackham's *London Livery companies*. Much the same is true of Arthur Pearce's *The history of the Butcher's company* and William N. Hibbert's *History of the Worshipful company of founders*. A. C. Stanley-Stone's *The Worshipful company of turners* cites Unwin's work but fails to rise above the level of a domestic chronicle.*

A number of more specialized works appeared subsequent to Unwin's work. Theodore W. Moody's *The Londonderry plantation, 1609–41* was an impartial account of the relations between the city companies and the Crown in the establishment of the Ulster plantation. Recently, two scholars have contributed books on the printing industry and the porters of London. Taking its inspiration from Unwin's study of Elizabethan and Stuart monopolies both in *The Gilds and companies of London* and *Industrial organization in the sixteenth and seventeenth centuries*, Cyprian Blagden's *The Stationers' company* has provided at once a general history and a detailed account of the English stock. The author has described in great detail how the stock served as the means by which the company acquired a near monopoly over the most lucrative part of the trade and kept within a single corporation both capitalists and workers. Finally, Walter M. Stern has made in *The porters of London* a detailed study of what Unwin described in his final chapter as "Survivals: gilds of transport."

---

* George Elkington, *The coopers: company and craft* (London, 1933); Hazlitt, *op. cit.*; Blackham, *op. cit.*; Arthur Pearce, *The history of the Butchers' company* (London, 1929); William N. Hibbert, compiler, *History of the Worshipful company of founders* (London, 1925); A. C. Stanley-Stone, *The Worshipful company of turners of London* . . . (London, 1925). For further histories of individual Livery Companies which fall within the description, domestic chronicle, see: William F. Kahl, *The development of London livery companies, an historical essay and a select bibliography* (Boston, 1960).

Unwin concluded his book with the seventeenth century. In a revealing article, *The breakdown of gild and corporation control over the handicraft and retail trade in London,* J. R. Kellett has contributed a valuable supplement. Mr. Kellett has analysed the efforts of the companies to retain regulation of the City's trade and industry until the mid-nineteenth century. He has been able to indicate the pattern of the companies' endeavours to enforce the registration of apprentices and the enrolment of freemen throughout the the eighteenth century.*

The present account of recent historical research into London institutional history indicates that Unwin's influence has been fruitful of the sort of scholarship he envisioned. He was the good husbandman who took as much pleasure in ploughing and sowing as in the harvest. Through the reissue of this major work, he will continue to stimulate research into the history of urban institutions.

WILLIAM F. KAHL.

BOSTON, 1962.

---

* Theodore W. Moody, *The Londonderry plantation, 1609–41* (Belfast, 1939); Unwin, *op. cit.*; George Unwin, *Industrial organization in the sixteenth and seventeenth centuries* (London, 1904); Cyprian Blagden, *op. cit.*; Walter M. Stern, *The porters of London* (London, 1960); J. R. Kellett, " The breakdown of gild and corporation control over the handicraft and retail trade in London." *The Economic history review.* Second series, Vol. X, No. 3 (Utrecht, 1958), pp. 381–94.

THE GILDS AND COMPANIES
OF LONDON

CHAPTER I

THE PLACE OF THE GILD IN THE HISTORY OF WESTERN EUROPE

THROUGHOUT Western Europe till the close of the 18th century the control of trade and industry was largely, in some countries mainly, in the hands of the gilds. The attempt made by Turgot, in the same month in which Adam Smith published *The Wealth of Nations*, to abolish the privileges of the trade corporations in France, was one of the chief causes of his downfall. Fifteen years later, on March 17th, 1791, they were swept away by the Revolution, and the gilds of Belgium and of Holland shared the ame fate when those countries fell under the rule of France. The privileged associations of craftsmen and traders of Spain and Portugal were abolished during the revolutionary period of 1833–40 ; those of Austria and Germany in 1859–60 ; those of Italy in 1864. Attempts have been made in Austria and Germany to replace the old gilds (*Zünfte*) by associations (*Innungen*) under the complete control of the State, but the new institution, whatever useful purposes it may serve, can have little or nothing in common with the old. In many towns of Switzerland the old gilds (*Abbayes* or *Zünfte*) are still preserved, though they have lost their special privileges.*

* City of London Livery Companies Commission, Rep. 1, vol. v. pp. 365–396.

In England alone of the larger states of Western Europe there has been no legislative abolition of the gilds, since the confiscation of their religious endowments at the time of the Reformation. This is due to the fact that, while the English gilds (more especially those of London) have attained a much greater degree of wealth and social consideration than any continental gilds, their trading monopolies fell much earlier into desuetude. To this we owe that unique set of survivals, the Livery Companies of London, whose records and other antiquities have a value for English social history that can scarcely be over-estimated.

But the gild is not by any means an institution peculiar to the civilization of the Western world. Every thoughtful traveller in China is impressed with the number, strength, and importance of the gilds which are to be found all over that vast Empire. In all the crowded and busy cities that float their wares down the Yang-tse-kiang, and in the remotest parts of Manchuria, the halls of the gilds are not only as much renowned for their hospitality as are those of the London companies; they still preserve in full activity many of those economic functions of which the halls of the companies were the centre in the 15th and 16th centuries. And the Chinese gild is by no means a mere survival rooted in the soil. Wherever the ubiquitous Chinaman goes, he takes the gild with him. The laundry-man of San Francisco, the cabinet-maker of Melbourne or Sydney, preserves in his native organization a power of cohesion that enables him to smile at the ineffectual devices of the Western factory legislator with his notions of a minimum wage.

In India the trade castes assume all the forms of gild organization. Not only the wealthy cloth merchant who can afford to pay from £5 to £50 as an entrance fee, but also the poor potter or carpenter who has nothing to sell but his labour, is represented by them. In the Ahmedabad District they are especially strong. They fix piece-work rates, insist on

holidays, prohibit overtime, and devote their entrance fees and
fines to feasting and " friendly benefits." *

In Turkey, Bulgaria, and Servia most trades are controlled
by *Esnafs*, which in all probability may claim a continuous
descent from Byzantine gilds.   The Mohammedan tradition
indeed traces them back beyond the days of the Prophet
(who was himself a member of the Gild of Merchants), to the
time of Noah, the patron of carpenters and shipbuilders, and
of Adam, the patron of the bakers.   Eve presides over the
washerwomen, Cain over the butchers and the gravediggers,
Elijah over the furriers, Joseph over the watch and clockmakers, whilst sailors have their choice between the Seven
Sleepers of Ephesus and the prophet Jonah.   But what has
more claim on our attention is the fact that the Esnaf, in all
essentials but one, bears the closest resemblance to the
mediæval gild of Western Europe.   It has a governing body
and officers of its own choice, a common seal and corporate
funds sometimes enriched by endowment, its hierarchy of
grades beginning with apprenticeship, its written and unwritten
code, and its annual festival.   The shoemakers of Constantinople have a special privilege of jurisdiction, like that of the
14th-century fishmongers and weavers in London.   Some
of the Esnafs have apparently an organization of the younger
members corresponding to the " bachelors," or " yeomanry," of
the London company.†   The Watermen and the Fellowship
Porters of London, who throughout the 19th century still
preserved the essential features of mediæval industrial organization, have their counterparts in Constantinople.

Without going into further details as to the gilds of the
East, we may, I think, attempt to answer the question what it
is that distinguishes them fundamentally from the gilds of the
West.   The likeness is striking enough.   The traveller who
walks through the streets of the Montenegrin town has his or

* J. M. Lambert, *Two Thousand Years of Gild Life*, p. 52.
† L. M. J. Garnett, *Turkish Life in Town and Country*.

D

her mind inevitably carried back to the London of Chaucer and Piers Plowman, and the London Lackpenny. . Where lies the difference? In the first place, the gilds of the East are alive, whilst the gilds of the West are dead. This may not seem much in itself. We must, therefore, add that the gilds of the West are dead because they have performed the most useful of their functions; they have helped to build up a social structure by which they have been superseded. The gilds of the East are alive because they have not performed that function. The gilds of the West expired in giving birth to progress; the gilds of the East are preserved and fostered in the interests of order. The Western gilds were a dynamic force; the Eastern are a static force.

And yet, after all, this is a very incomplete way of putting the matter. We can only speak of the Western gild as dead if we confine the term "gild" to one particular form of organization. But if we are dealing with gilds in this strict sense of the term, we should not have to get much further than the end of the 13th century. Every century since then has seen the rise of different forms of organization to meet new conditions of social and economic life. In some cases the new form was gradually assumed by the old organization; in other cases both the body and the spirit were new, but the new was never so new as not to be very really connected with the old by conscious or unconscious emulation, imitation, adaptation. In this way the gild became the craft, the craft became the livery company, and the livery company became the corporation. At first sight it might seem as if these were mere changes of form, but a more careful consideration will show that this was not the case. The change of form indicates an inward growth, a social expansion of the deepest significance, both for the economic and the political development of the nation. In short, the Western gild, in its various forms and in its subsequent developments, has been one of the main instruments of what we call progress, the progress which distinguishes the West from the East.

But what meaning are we to attach to that much-abused word "progress"? Let us take a concrete instance. It has sometimes been thought that the break-up of the Roman Empire was a case of sheer retrogression. And at first sight the loss seems enormous. Out of a weltering chaos of barbarism and internecine war, the Romans had built up a nearly world-wide peace and a strong and unified administration; out of a mass of illogical and conflicting customs they had created an admirable system of law. They had worked out a clear and definite idea of the State, and an equally clear and definite idea of the individual, the like of which has not again been achieved till very recent years. Napoleon and William II. look back to Cæsar and to Justinian as their models. Are we to say that all the world has done and suffered in the interval, the feudal anarchy of the Dark Age, the motley incongruities of the Middle Age with its mad saints and heroes, the terrific uprisings of the Reformation and the Revolution with their wild illusions and their still more fatal disillusionings—are all these but a painful struggle to regain what was lost when the Roman Empire fell? Such a question is its own answer. The truth is that peace, and security of civil rights, and an administration even stronger, more able, and less corrupt than the Roman, is not too high a price to pay for liberty. And if the progress the world has achieved since that time is to be called by any one name, that name must be liberty. But a liberty which has to be won through such long and devious ways is no simple matter. It is based on deep and elaborate foundations. It is no mere casting off of fetters. It is the slow putting on of new habits and capacities, new sympathies, and new insight. It is a growth, the most gradual and most permanent of all growths, a psychological growth. In the achievement of progress and liberty in this sense, the lapse of twenty centuries is but a stage.

How can we best bring home to ourselves the nature of the advance which has been made by modern civilization over the civilization of antiquity ? It is not so much the result we need to consider as the means by which it has been secured. Briefly expressed, the difference between the modern constitutional State and the Roman Empire is that, whilst the modern State has attained to even more elaborate, far-reaching, and efficient administrative powers, there has at the same time been secured to the individual a far greater degree of liberty—not merely of speech, of publication, and of combination—but of the positive liberty which consists in equality of opportunity and the *carrière ouverte aux talents*. In the Roman Empire there was little or no protecting medium between the all-powerful State and the powerless individual, and the State by its very weight, even when moved by no oppressive intentions, crushed all spontaneous initiative out of the individual. At the present day there exist a great array of intermediate powers and agencies, offensive and defensive, which not only prevent the State from oppressing the individual, but actually enable individual initiative to gather power about itself and to bring pressure to bear on the State.

First of all, there is the element of restraint imposed upon the State by the character of the very agents whom it is bound to employ, the restraint that lies in the honourable *esprit de corps* and sense of social responsibility of the judicial and administrative functionaries who do its work. Secondly, there are the independent powers of local government (I am thinking especially of England) which are safeguarded from undue interference on the part of the State, and which have always served as the effectual basis of our parliamentary liberties. Thirdly, there is the power of and the capacity for voluntary association, exemplified in the fact that the direction of the State itself is always in the hands of the representatives of one of two great voluntary associations known as political parties. Students of constitutional history know that these three factors are each of very slow growth—the history of England is largely the story of their growth—and that in the absence of them mere formal stipulations and guarantees can give little assurance of political liberty. The enormous difficulties of the situation in Russia at the present moment, for example, arise from the fact that none of these essential bases of constitutional freedom can be conceived of as possessing any very effectual solidity. And it is in the direction of strengthening these natural pillars of the constitution that the instinct of the Russian reformer is rightly turned.

There are no doubt many historic reasons to be given for the constitutional weakness of Russia, but the most fundamental, perhaps, is to be found in the shortness of its history as a civilized people. When Russia came into the European system, the great formative process by which our Western civilization has been built up was all but accomplished. In that long and glorious work of social and political construction, which lasted from the 12th to the 17th centuries, Russia bore no effective part. During those six centuries Western Europe built up the town, and then on the basis of the town built up the nation. Without the town there could not have been the nation as we know it, because it was in the earlier centuries of town history that the three great essentials to a free national constitution already spoken of—a sense of professional responsibility, the experience of self-government, and a capacity for voluntary association—were painfully acquired. Russia has no towns in this historic sense of the word. She has, comparatively speaking, no middle class; that is why she has so many Jews. And her working class, such as it is, is not like our own, a working class inheriting largely the traditions and capacities of the middle class, but is composed of transplanted peasants of a social status resembling that of our own villeins in the days of Wat Tyler. It is for want of towns, and of those middle and working classes that only centuries of free town life can produce, that Russia finds it so hard to become a free nation.

This brings us to the point at which we were aiming. If the town may be said to have built up the nation, what built up the town? If we answer that it was the gild, we must safe-guard ourselves from the possible consequences of our rashness. There are many theories of the origin of the town, mostly German, and every theorist is naturally zealous for the purity of his doctrine. Let us take shelter behind the wisdom of Aristotle. Everything, according to that eminent sociologist, has at least four causes—the material, the efficient, the formal, and the final cause. If we give the town the benefit of all four, there is room for a number of theorists to live and let live. The final cause of the town—the end towards which it was unconsciously directed—was, according to the theory we have been setting forth, the free self-governing nation. The material cause—the stuff out of which the town was made—differed no doubt in different cases : sometimes it was a village, sometimes a market at a ford, sometimes a military post, some-times a deliberately planted colony. The formal cause—the legal title by virtue of which its special rights were exercised—this also varied in different cases, but is probably to be sought for in the creation of a separate and semi-independent juris-diction within a certain area. As to these causes we need not seek to dogmatize. What we are concerned with is the efficient cause or causes—the nature of the social force which, apart from mere material conditions or constitutional forms, served to bring it into existence and to make it what it became. The chief of these efficient causes was, I venture to think, the spirit of voluntary association, and that spirit found its most typical and widespread embodiment in the various forms of the gild.

But it may here be asked, has not a doubt been raised as to whether the gild itself was a voluntary association ? May it not have been an organ of public administration set up by the Crown or by the city, on the authority of the State, to regulate industry and commerce in accordance with a far-sighted State policy? No doubt it was, or became, such an organ, but it was at the same time, and to a still greater extent, a voluntary organization. The truth is that we cannot understand mediæval history without getting rid of some of our clear-cut modern conceptions. The State, the municipality, and the individual, as we know them, did not exist in mediæval times. They were each in a condition of becoming. They were helping each other to grow into their present definite shapes by constant interaction on each other. Each needed the counteracting influence of the other as a condition of healthy growth. If any of the three gained an undue predominance, it not only weakened the rest but prepared the way for its own overthrow. In mediæval Germany the municipal element had too much of its own way; it came to grief amidst the dynastic struggles of the 17th and 18th centuries. In the France of Louis XIV. the State crushed the initiative of the municipality and the individual, and by checking the flow of vital forces brought on a fit of paralysis. In the England of the early 19th century the individual overbore the commonwealth, until the factory inspector and the school inspector, with the newly created powers of self-government behind them, redressed the balance. But what has given the constitutional development of England its unique character is its exceptional continuity. The action and reaction which are absolutely necessary to growth have not taken violent forms. The State, the local community, and the voluntary association have grown up side by side, each recognizing the other spheres of action, and learning, however unwillingly, to co-operate for the general good.

To speak, therefore, as we did of the nation as having been built up out of the town, and of the town as having been built up out of the gild, is clearly a one-sided statement. In all the intricate processes of social construction, lordship has been

nearly as important a factor as fellowship.   From one point of
view—the legal point of view—it would almost be true to say
that the State built up the town and the town built up the
gild.   There have always been forces from above meeting and
co-operating with forces from below.   But the forces from
above have been mainly forces of formulation, whilst the forces
from below have been forces of germination.   The forces from
above have been mainly concerned in establishing and maintaining an equilibrium (which, indeed, is their natural function),
while the forces from below have been more often bent on
disturbing equilibrium in the interests of progress.

Of the evils that follow the ascendency of the former class
of influences, the decline and fall of the Roman Empire afford
the most striking example.   The first five centuries of the
Christian era, from Augustus to Justinian, culminating in the
great code which still dominates the legal mind of Europe,
constitute perhaps the greatest period of formulation that
the world has ever seen.   But the growth from below had
ceased, and the vital force of the body politic slowly ebbed
away.   In the formalism of the Byzantine Empire there is a
something that is almost Chinese, and the likeness would
undoubtedly have become greater if the pressure of outside
barbarism had not destroyed it.   If we want to be quite clear
that it was not the forces from above that called into existence
the town and the gild of the Middle Ages, we have only to
observe the influence of the all-powerful state on the similar
institutions of the Roman Empire.   Voluntary association and
the forms of local self-government were not wanting in the
earlier days of the Empire, but overwhelming pressure from
above gradually converted them into instruments of extortion
and servitude.   The trades and handicrafts which in the
Middle Ages we see emerging by their own free effort from
the bondage of custom, were under the Empire being steadily
forced by deliberate legislation into the position of hereditary
and semi-servile castes.   The town which in the Middle Ages

was the refuge from feudal oppression and the centre of a free upgrowth of new social forces, was so afflicted in the later days of the Empire, by the tax-collector and the official task-master, that its inhabitants had to be prohibited from fleeing into the country.*

Whence came the great change, the return to the upward movement, the budding morrow in the midnight of the dark ages ? Was it due to the infusion of German blood, or to the infusion of Christian doctrine, or to some other still more occult cause ? To use a convenient formula of M. Maeterlinck, " We cannot tell." We must leave these questions to the anthropologist or to the philosopher. Our sympathies may be on the side of the angels. We may look for the ultimate solution to the moral nature of man. But the secondary causes, with which we have to deal, are quite sufficiently important and quite insufficiently understood to deserve the fullest investigation. The greatest body of essential truth yet attained in this field is to be found in the great work of Professor Gierke, of Berlin, on the development of free association, with the ideas of which Professor Maitland has done so much to make us familiar. The early enthusiasts for the principle of free fellowship as a primary force in social evolu-tion no doubt left insufficient room for the operation of other causes, and those other causes, notably the Roman cause and the Feudal cause, have quite naturally of recent years found their champions. But the truth remains unshaken that free fellowship has been the most vitally essential element in social and political progress since the fall of the Roman Empire. When this is said, we may go on to admit that the element of

* Cunningham, *Essay on Modern Civilization--Ancient Times*, pp. 189-190 ; Waltzing, *Les corporations professionnelles chez les Romains*, II. pp. 476-484 ; Fagniez *Documents rel. à l'histoire de l'industrie et du commerce en France*, I. Nos. 50, 56, 71. An instructive comparison may be made between this aspect of Roman imperialism and the similar results of Russian policy under Peter and Catherine (see Sir D. M. Wallace's *Russia*, ch. xii.). Mr. A. Stead in his *Great Japan* describes a similar process now at work in that country.

lordship and of the formulating power from above are of the greatest possible importance to a sound development of human liberty. Free fellowship by itself may be an aimless and even anarchic social force.* In order to produce steady and coherent progress the upward thrust of the new life and the downward pressure of the old formula are both needed. But the upward thrust must be stronger than the downward pressure. Lordship is a good servant but a bad master. The study of mediæval social history is the study of the inter-action of upward and downward forces in which, as the upward forces on the whole prevail, the action of the down-ward forces may be, and often is, of a socially beneficent character.

This process of interaction can nowhere be studied to better advantage than in the birth, life, and development of the gild, and of those kindred organizations which have succeeded to its functions. We can there watch in all its successive phases that transformation of social forces into political forces which is the very essence of what we call progress. We see class after class constituting itself a social force by the act of self-organization. Then as the new social force gains political recognition, the voluntary association passes wholly or partly into an organ of public administration. As class power generates class privilege and exclusiveness, new social forces gather to a head and find expression for themselves in voluntary associations, which tend in their turn to be transformed as they are drawn into the vortex of political activity. This constantly recurring process is to be seen in the intimate relation of the Gild Merchant to the earliest constitution of our own towns and of many continental cities; and in the equally close relation which the craft organizations in many cases, more often on the continent than in England, bore to the more developed constitutions of the

* Mr. and Mrs. Webb, in *Industrial Democracy*, chap. i., give some admirable illustrations of this truth.

towns, just as it is to be seen to-day in the formation of a Labour Party on a Trade Union basis.

The main interest of the gild (using gild in a very broad sense so as to cover the whole of our present subject) lies in its having been an organ of social progress, the progress that distinguishes the West from the East. The progress of Society, like the progress of the individual, is a moral fact which cannot be ultimately derived from any cause outside of itself; but it rests on psychological conditions. The individual or the society must first acquire good habits of mind and will, and then learn to use these habits as an instrument for the achievement of higher ends, which gradually emerge when the individual mind or the social mind has become master of itself. The fundamental habits of the social will are embodied in the State. Society at first creates the State as an instrument of self-preservation and of inward order. But it may go on to use it as an instrument of self-advancement. There is always, however, the danger that the instrument may prove stronger than the user. We know that nine-tenths of mankind are the creatures of habit, that in nine-tenths of our lives we are the creatures of habit ourselves, and that salvation depends on the other tenth. It is not, therefore, in the least surprising that Society should tend to become the creature of the State, as it did under the Roman Empire. In the dark ages, the great instrument which had so long oppressed its maker was broken, and Society began the slow and painful task of building up its habits anew. The apparent inconsistencies, the endless dualism of the mediæval mind, are due to the instinctive efforts of Society to save itself from the domination of any one set of habits. In the broad features of Western civilization we see the results of these efforts: the separation of Church and State, the separation of legislation from administration, of local government from central government, and finally, the recognition by the State of the rival sovereignty of public opinion. The political liberty of Western

Europe has been secured by the building up of a system of voluntary organizations, strong enough to control the State, and yet flexible enough to be constantly remoulded by the free forces of change. It is hardly too much to say that the foundations of this system were laid in the gild. It was in the gild that voluntary association first came into a permanent relation with political power.

CHAPTER II

THE FRITH GILD AND THE CNIHTEN GILD

THE history of the gilds of London finds a natural beginning in the second half of the 12th century. From that time onwards the student may have solid ground under his feet. There is a natural but mistaken tendency in the human mind to seek simple origins for complex institutions, and in the twilight of prehistoric times this tendency finds free play. It is only when this simplicity, arising from the subjective interpretation of vague and shifting outlines, is disturbed by the unmistakable diversities of well-ascertained fact that history, properly speaking, begins. The gild, when we come to know it in detail, has many aspects, religious, social, economic, legal, and political, and its main interest as an institution or species of institutions lies in the interaction of these various elements, of which now one is predominant and now another, but of which, even in the simplest examples, there are always several to be found coexisting. Before the end of the 12th century all these aspects of the gild have come clearly to light, and thenceforward there is at our disposal a constantly increasing volume of facts about each of them. The subject still has an unity. Indeed, it now first possesses the true natural unity of life, unity in diversity.

There were, however, undoubtedly gilds in London before the 12th century. The English Gild of Knights, which dissolved itself in 1125, just as the earliest of the later gilds were beginning to form, claimed an origin in King Edgar's reign, and the Frith gilds of London are known to us through the *Judicia civitatis Londoniæ* embodied in the laws of Æthelstan. Both, therefore, take us back to about the middle of the 10th century, and both have been learnedly discussed by English and continental scholars. The one fact that emerges from the discussion is that no actual contact can be traced between these earlier cases of gild organization and the later ones with which definite history begins. The earlier gilds can, however, be brought into connection with the later through their relation to the feudal atmosphere in which both are enveloped.

The five centuries of Anglo-Saxon history represent a transition from a tribal to a territorial organization. The narrower bond of kinship was being gradually replaced by two wider principles of social union, lordship and fellowship. Lordship found its expression in feudalism. The transformation and enlargement of the idea of community by the principle of fellowship was achieved by such gentle and imperceptible stages that it is more difficult to realize, but the most easily recognizable form of it is to be found in the gild. Lordship and fellowship thus grew up side by side. But fellowship, having very much larger possibilities, was slower in developing them. There are thus two periods to be distinguished in the early history of fellowship, in the first of which it was overshadowed by the principle of lordship, whilst in the second it was learning how to displace it. In the first of these periods the legal forms of feudalism came to dominate society in almost every aspect, constitutional, religious, and economic. In the second period the community is found adopting the forms of feudalism in order that it may fight lordship with its own weapons. The gild first established its authority on a legal footing by assuming the position of a collective lordship. Only in that way could it acquire that power of independent growth which has enabled it, as we have seen, to build up the representative machinery of the modern State and the voluntary agencies which are the life-blood of modern society.

A law of Charlemagne of 779 decrees that no one shall presume to bind himself by mutual oaths in a gild (*geldonia*). A later decree of 821 warns the lords in Flanders and other maritime parts to restrain their serfs from sworn confederacies on pain of incurring a fine themselves. In 884, when France was suffering from the incursions of the Norsemen, the clergy and the local officials (*ministri comitis*) are required to instruct the villeins not to form the combination commonly called a gild (*gelda*) against those who rob them of anything, but to refer their case to that priest who is the bishop's representative and to the officials appointed for this purpose within the district. In each of these cases there is a clear indication of the spontaneous formation of a gild from below. Apart from the reference to a mutual oath, nothing is said of the religious character of these associations, but in that age the co-operation, official or unofficial, of the clergy was an almost indispensable element of any popular organization. We also know that by the middle of the 9th century the clergy of the diocese of Rheims were allowed to superintend the formation of religious gilds bearing essentially the same character as those which, throughout the Middle Ages, underlay every form of social and economic organization. It must also be remembered that the bishops were not, at this time, what in their political aspect they afterwards became on the continent, a mere part of the framework of feudalism. They supplied a vital link, not merely between the Church and the various States then only in the early stages of formation, but also between an imperial or royal authority of a very indeterminate character and the growing element of self-government in the towns. In this intermediate position lay their opportunity, and from it they drew their real authority, which was not derived exclusively from Pope, king, or people, but was itself an important factor in the development of all three.*

These facts and considerations ought to shed a little light on the much discussed question of the London Frith gilds of Æthelstan's reign (925–40). The existence of Anglo-Saxon gilds at an earlier period has been inferred from the use of the word *gegildan* in the laws of Ine (*c.* 690) and of Alfred (*c.* 890). *Gegildan* clearly means a group of persons larger than the family, who are mutually responsible for the payment of each other's fines. "If a man," says Alfred's law, " kinless of paternal relatives fight and slay a man, and then if he have maternal relatives, let them pay a third of the *wer ;* his *gegildan* a third part ; for a third part let him flee. If he have no maternal relatives, let his *gegildan* pay half, for half let him flee" (*i.e.* be himself responsible) ; and the law adds that, if a man without relatives is killed, half the fine shall be paid to the king and half to the man's *gegildan.* Dr. Stubbs † translated *gegildan* by "gild brethren," and the passage has been sometimes held to imply a widespread existence of gilds in King Alfred's day. On the other hand, it has been argued that the word *gegildan* does not necessarily point to a voluntary association, and might be equally used of persons grouped together in mutual responsibility by the public authorities. On one point the law leaves us in no doubt. There existed in England in the 9th century groups of persons formed to supplement the tie of kinship in the matter of mutual responsibility before the law.

The indisputable facts about the later London "Frith Gild" cover much more ground than this. An organization had been set up, including London and the district around it, with the main object of putting down theft. Its members were distributed in groups of ten, each with a leader of its own, and ten of these groups constituted a larger unit, of which the

---

* L. Brentano, *On the History and Development of Gilds*, pp. 12–18.
† *Select Charters*, p. 63.

ten leaders, presided over by a *hyndenman*, composed the executive who received the contributions of the members and administered the common fund. The executive met for business every month and feasted together, giving the remains to the poor. When a member died, his gild brethren were each to give a *gesufel* loaf for his soul, and to sing or get sung fifty masses within thirty days. The duties of members in regard to the pursuit of thieves were carefully defined. Those who had horses were to follow the track over the border for one riding, and those who had no horses were to work for the absent till their return. Members who had lost property and could show that it had been stolen, might claim compensation at a fixed rate (called the *ceapgild*) from the common fund. If a thief were caught and hanged, his goods were con-fiscated, and after the ceapgild had been deducted, half the surplus was given to his wife, and the other half was divided between the king and the fellowship.*

So far the facts are beyond dispute, and the question at issue lies in the interpretation of them. Are they to be taken as indicating the existence of a voluntary association or a group of such associations, or is the whole arrangement an elaborate police organization set up at the dictation of the authorities? To put the alternatives in this pointed way is at once to suggest a doubt as to the possibility of either of them. Could a purely voluntary association have had such important public functions assigned to it? And, on the other hand, could a purely police regulation, even in Anglo-Saxon times, have fixed the number of masses a man should sing for his gild brother? Let us examine the original document to see if it really impales us on either horn of this dilemma.

The *Judicia civitatis Londoniæ* (Dooms of the City of

* Thorpe, *Ancient Laws and Institutes of England*, pp. 97-103; Kemble, *Saxons in England*, II. pp. 521-527; F. Liebermann, *Gesetze der Angelsachsen*, I. pp. 173-83; Gross, *Gild Merchant*, I. pp. 178-181; G. L. Gomme, *The Governance of London*, pp. 122-134.

E

London) is embodied amongst the laws of Æthelstan as a
supplement to legislation already recommended at four
meetings of the Witan, and finally confirmed by the pledges
of all the representatives, two of whom were apparently from
London. This is stated in the tenth article of the *Judicia*,
which, seems to require reading along with the eleventh, as a
sort of displaced preamble to the previous articles.

ART. 10.—" [That] all the Witan gave their pledges all together to
the Archbishop at Thunresfeld when Ælfeah Stybb and Brithnoth
Oddas son came to meet the assembly by the kings command; that
each reeve should exact pledges in his own shire; that they should
all hold the frith as King Æthelstan and his Witan had counselled it,
first at Greatanlea, and again at Exeter, and afterwards at Feversham,
and a fourth time at Thunresfeld, before the archbishop, and all
the bishops, and his Witan whom the king himself named who were
thereat: that those dooms should be observed that were fixed
thereat."

The picture here presented of the action of the Witan is
not that of the organ of a fully developed State decreeing laws
with a conviction of its absolute sovereignty. Nor do the
Londoners accept the new law in this sense. " The bishops
and the reeves belonging to London" hold the frith as
required and take the pledges, but the law itself is partly
reformulated, and the machinery for carrying it out entirely
originated by them in consultation with the Londoners. The
result of their deliberations is set forth in Articles 1 and 12
of the *Judicia*, the general purport of which has already been
given. They are introduced as follows :—

" This is the ordinance which the bishops and reeves belonging to
London have ordained and confirmed with pledges among our
' frith gegildas' both nobles and freemen in addition to the dooms
which were fixed at Greatanlea and at Exeter and at Thunresfeld."

The first article states the law for the punishment of theft,
and whilst it contains several new provisions, designed to meet

the special needs of London, it is in the main a recapitulation of the dooms fixed at the national assemblies, since the longest paragraph of the article concludes with the words, "all as it was before ordained at Greatanlea, and at Exeter, and at Thunresfeld." Articles 2–9 are concerned with measures for enforcing the law. In substance they are police regulations ; but they have very largely the form and the spirit of ordinances passed by a voluntary association, except that they appear to represent the assent of all responsible householders. The wording is that of a series of resolutions passed by a large assembly. Thus Article 2 begins—

"That we have ordained that each of us should contribute four pence for our common use within twelve months and pay for the property which should be taken after we had contributed the money ; and that we should all have the search in common."

This does not sound like a police regulation dictated from above. It is the language of a community which is self-governing upon instinct. The Londoners have no notion of slighting the authority of the king or the Witan. They simply assume a natural right to amplify the law and to arrange for its particular application to themselves. They do this on their own initiative under the advice of bishops and reeves, but they remain open, as they conclude by saying, to further suggestions—

ART. 9.—"And let it not be denied nor concealed if our lord or any of our reeves should suggest to us any addition to the ordinances of our frith gilds that we will joyfully accept the same as it becomes us all and may be advantageous to us. But let us trust in God and our kingly lord if we fulfil all things thus that the affairs of all folk will be better with respect to theft than they before were. If however we slacken in the frith and the pledge which we have given and the king has command of us then may we expect or well know that these thieves will prevail yet more than they did before. But let us keep our pledges and the frith as is pleasing to our lord; it greatly behoves us that we devise that which he wills and if he order and instruct us more we shall be humbly ready."

There is a decided absence of formality in all this. It is not a bye-law of a "local authority" framed with a strict regard for constitutional limitations. And the amendment to the law subsequently made by the king and recorded in the twelfth article, is quite as remarkable for the informality of its procedure as for its humanitarian sentiments. The Witan of Exeter had declared that no thief should be spared over twelve years of age if caught stealing over sevenpence. The London ordinance had mercifully substituted a shilling for sevenpence. And it would seem that the influence of the clergy had been successfully used to temper the harshness of the law still further.

ART. 2.—" The king now again has ordained at his Witan a Witlanburh and has commanded it to be made known to the Archbishop by Bishop Theodred that it seemed to him too cruel that so young a man should be killed besides for so little as he has learned has somewhere been done. He then said that it seemed to him and to those who counselled with him that no younger person should be slain than 15 years except he should make resistance or flee and would not surrender himself. . . ." *

Now, this want of clear theoretical distinction between the functions of local and central government does not in the least imply that those functions had, in fact, no separate existence. On the contrary, this vagueness of the border-line between them was the natural condition of growth by mutual interaction. And precisely the same is true of the distinction between the sphere of voluntary association and that of public authority, whether local or central. If here and there the ordinances of the Frith gilds seem to indicate the activities of voluntary association, there is no reason for refusing to put

* A translation of the whole text has recently been made more accessible in Mr. Gomme's *Governance of London.*

this natural interpretation upon them. A document which is a mixture of national law, local police arrangements on a partly volunteer basis, and moral exhortation, may, without too great a strain on its consistency, have also embodied a record of charitable and religious agencies of a voluntary character designed to support a public effort for the preservation of peace and order.

This uncertain position of the Frith gilds, so far from being anomalous, strikes the very key-note of English gild history. The gild is constantly crossing, often unconsciously, the line that separates public functions from private, compulsory association from voluntary. In this respect it is a characteristically English institution, and can claim company with the Bank of England, the Inns of Court, the Universities, the political parties, and, indeed, most of the vital organs of our social and political life.

We hear no more of the London Frith gilds, and cannot therefore assume that the organization had a continued existence, or that it exercised any influence on the earliest constitution of London. But it is worth noting that the French institution called *La Paix*, or *La Commune de la paix*, which became very widespread in the course of the following century, had many points in common with the Frith gild. The bishops were the initiators of the movement which sprang out of conditions already described. Each diocese became the centre of a large association which embraced all classes, peasant and noble, cleric and layman, town and country. All members took an oath to pursue the violators of the peace, so that an armed force existed in each diocese, which the kings, as they grew more powerful, endeavoured to use for purposes anything but peaceful. The *Paix* had also courts of its own for the settlement of disputes.*

Concerning the English Cnihten Gild of London, the one thing that can be asserted with some degree of confidence is

---

* Luchaire, *Les Communes Françaises*, p. 39.

that it had a continuous existence for at least a century.   The
story of its origin as preserved amongst the records of Holy
Trinity Priory, which succeeded to the property of the gild, is
as follows :—

"In the times of King Canute (another version says King
Edgar) there were thirteen knights very well beloved both of King
and Kingdom.   These begged of the king a certain piece of land
in the east part of London which the inhabitants had lately forsaken
by reason of the hardship and service they stood charged withal.
The knights suit, for to have this land granted unto them for ever, with
the Liberty of a gild upon it, the king upon this condition granted
namely that every one of them should perform three combats, one
above the ground, and one beneath it and one in the water and
come off with victory, and that also upon a day appointed they
should run at tilt against all comers in the field which is now called
East Smithfield, all which they performed gloriously.   The king the
same day named the gild Cnihten gild appointing these boundaries
unto it.   First that it should reach from Ealdgate to the place where
the bars now are eastward on both sides of the road.   He extended
it another way towards Bishopgate, as far as the house of William
the priest. . . . To the southward the liberties of the gild reached so
far into the water of the Thames as a horseman riding into the river
at a dead low water could dart his spear from him.   So that all
East Smithfield with part of the right hand way, which stretcheth by
Doddings Pond into the Thames and also the Hospital of St.
Katherines with the mills (which hospital was founded in the reign
of King Stephen) together with the outer stone wall, and the new
ditch of the Tower, stand and are within the fee aforesaid." *

The earliest charter, however, in the possession of the gild,
that of Edward the Confessor, which gives them sac and soc
within burh and without over their men, carries back still
further the tradition of their origin by granting them to be
worthy of as good law as they were in King Edgar's days,

* Dr. Sharpe's Introduction to his Calendar to Letter Book, C, xvi.–xxvi.,
contains the latest and fullest discussion of the documents, of which the Letter
Book embodies a transcript (pp. 217–225).

"and in my father's day and Cnut's." After this the gild received a series of charters which prove its continuous existence until its dissolution in 1125. The fact that the knights' gild thus held in fee during such a troubled century the land commanding the eastern gate of London, taken together with the further fact that the gild, when it dissolved itself, had many aldermen within its ranks, has led to the not unnatural supposition that the gild had some large share in the control or government of the city. That it had some share is extremely likely, and in speculations as to the nature of that share, the meaning of the word "Cniht" becomes of vital importance, especially as that meaning had altered considerably between the days of the founding of the gild and its dissolution.

Originally it signified "boy, or servant," and though in the 10th century it had acquired some of its late meaning, it still conveyed the sense of a subordinate class. In the feudal hierarchy, then beginning to be formed, the cnicht was to the thane what in the later mediæval craft the journeyman was to the fully qualified master. He was part of his lord's household, not, indeed, as a mere page or servant, but as an armed retainer. He received grants of land in reward of faithful service, and his lord often mentioned him in his will along with his children.*

At a time when gilds were formed mainly of merchants and craftsmen a gild of knights would have a fine sound. But in a society predominantly feudal as it was in the 11th century, even in the boroughs, the gild of knights may well have borne much the same relation to the gild of thanes as the yeomanry or bachelors of a later London company bore to the livery. We know that at Cambridge and Exeter there were gilds whose membership embraced both classes, and that the knights were expected to bear themselves as junior members. These gilds had essentially the same social and religious features as the parish gilds of the 14th century, and

* Gross, *Gild Merchant*, I. p. 186.

differed only in the atmosphere of feudal violence in which their members lived, their superior social status, and the wider area from which they were drawn. Professor Maitland compared the Cambridge Gild of Thanes to a County Club.

It seems certain that part of the obligation under which the thanes in a county held their land was the keeping of one or more knights in the burh for its defence. These knights by their numbers and the cohesion that comes of a common life in close contact, may easily have become the strongest social element in the town—not, however, the highest element where, as in London, there were burh-thanes to whom the king addressed his writs. Neither knights nor thanes were merely professional soldiers. The law that a merchant might acquire thane-right by faring thrice over sea is well known. Just at this time the Italian cities were rising to commercial greatness, and their first social troubles arose from conflicts between classes resembling the thanes and the knights of England.

Such are the materials on which we may base speculations as to the character of the English Gild of Knights in London. That it had a social and religious element may be regarded as proved by the fact that in surrendering their land to Holy Trinity Priory on dissolution the members' chief motive was the maintenance of this element. That the grant of the land outside Aldgate was connected with obligations undertaken by the gild for the defence of the city is a hypothesis not unlikely, but not proven.* Corporations of knights connected with the defence of a city, and holding territory outside it, were not unknown on the continent. If the Cnihten gild possessed such a function, its constitutional importance would be great, but that it was ever the actual governing body of London is extremely improbable.

* This is the hypothesis of the late H. C. Coote. See *Trans. London and Midd. Arch. Soc.*, V. pp. 477-493.

It remains to notice briefly the manner of the gild's dissolution. It was a common thing for a gild to secure spiritual benefits by becoming affiliated to a religious house. In 1125 the surviving members of the Cnihten Gild determined to surrender their land to the newly founded Priory of Holy Trinity with this object. They assembled in the chapter-house and offered upon the altar there all their charters. After which act of consecration they went through the legally symbolic formality of handing over bodily to the Prior the church of St. Botolph as being the head of their land.* The king confirmed the gift, and the Prior " being admitted as one of the aldermen of London to govern the land and soke, did sit in court and rode with the Mayor and his brethren the aldermen as one of them in scarlet or other livery as they used " till the Reformation.†

---

* Round, *Commune of London*, p. 104, and *Geoffrey de Mandeville*, Appendices on " Gervase of Cornhill " and " Early Administration of London."
† Stow's *Survey*, pp. 147, 161.

CHAPTER III

THE COURTS OF THE BAKERS, FISHMONGERS, AND WEAVERS

THE central and distinctive feature of the London gild in its fully developed form of a Livery Company was a Court. This body, which became known in the course of the 16th century as the Court of Assistants, was not merely an executive committee like those to which all large societies are obliged in practice to entrust the management of their affairs. It was not a court merely in name. It had actual jurisdiction over its members, and even over outsiders who were engaged in the same trade. By its judgments unruly apprentices were whipped, journeymen on strike were imprisoned, and masters offending against regulations were fined. Members were forbidden to carry trade disputes before any other court, unless the court of their company had first been appealed to in vain. This element of trade autonomy was a recognized part of the civic constitution, and was supported, if need arose, by the authority of the Lord Mayor. This implied, of course, that it was exercised in due subordination to that authority, and that whatever power the court of a livery company possessed, was implicitly, if not explicitly, delegated to it by the city.

Yet even this limited degree of self-government requires to be accounted for, since it was not by any means universal. Some sort of religious and social organization indeed was possessed by practically all the leading trades in the larger towns and cities of the Middle Ages. But such organization did not carry with it the legal powers of a court. In most English towns it would seem that the municipal authorities were careful to keep even the primary jurisdiction in matters of trade in their own hands, and this was also the case in many continental cities, such as Nuremberg. Wherever we find the trade gilds exercising the powers of a court we may take it for granted that those powers were not won in the first instance without a struggle, and that their success in that struggle is a result that needs to be explained.

The first element of this explanation lies in the fact that in several important cases, the control of a trade had been exercised by its own members before it passed under the corporate authority of the city, and that this autonomous control was embodied in a court possessing exclusive rights of jurisdiction over the trade in question. For two centuries after the city had achieved a corporate existence these independent trade courts continued to exercise their powers, and they were not finally subordinated to the city's regulative authority without a severe conflict that shook the constitution to its foundations. In several of the greatest crises in the history of mediæval London the power based on the exercise of separate jurisdiction enabled the members of a single trade to play a dominating part in city politics ; and as it was just at this period that the courts of the larger livery companies were taking shape, it can hardly be supposed that the effect of so striking an example was entirely lost upon them. It is for this reason that the Weavers' Court and the Fishmongers' Hallmote claim so early a consideration in our study of the development of London gilds.

Of the various elements that went to make up the government of London, before the grant of the Mayor and Commune in 1191, the Folkmoot was the most primitive. It met three times in the year, at Michaelmas to hear who was sheriff and to receive his commandments, at Christmas to arrange for the special watch kept at that time, and at Midsummer to guard the city from fire. Any Londoner who neglected to attend the three Folkmoots incurred a fine of forty shillings to the king. A gathering of the same kind was common in German cities at this early period. It was known as the *ungebotene Ding* (Ding = thing = assembly), or the meeting that must be attended without summons, and there were generally three in the year. To the Folkmoot in later days some of the more solemn and legal functions, such as the proclaiming a man as an outlaw, continued to be reserved. But as the legal and administrative business of the city increased and became specialized, it passed largely into the hands of smaller assemblies held more frequently. The *Hus-Ting* (House-meeting = Hall-moot) met every week for legal and administrative business, and the same select body of landholders who pronounced the dooms there, presided in the several wards as aldermen over the wardmotes which localized the administration of order, cleanliness, public morality, and just dealing.

Among the duties of the king's representatives at the Folkmoot, or *ungebotene Ding*, was the elementary regulation of trade. As lord of the market the king claimed not only tolls on all goods brought for sale into it, but regular dues from the settled population of craftsmen or traders, and fines for the use of false weights and measures and the sale of noxious wares. Thus, at Hameln in the 13th century the Schultheiss at the three meetings of the Ding admitted new bakers, butchers, and weavers to the exercise of their callings on the payment of large entrance fees, and fined those who had sold bad food since the last meeting.* It was a natural result of the tendency to specialization that the king's representative should come to meet each trade separately. In Augsburg the Præfectus had three annual meetings with the bakers, three with the butchers, and two with the sausage

* F. Keutgen, *Urkunden zur städtischen Verfassungsgeschichte*, 149.

makers.* The same thing happened at London, where there were special hallmoots for the bakers and for the fishmongers. There were four principal hallmoots of the bakers, three of them being held at the time of the three Folkmoots, and another at Easter to provide for the king's arrival and that of the great men of his realm.† The fishmongers were obliged to attend two *Lag-halmotes*, one on St. Martin's Day, the other in Lent.‡

The next natural step in this process of devolution was that the king's representative should appoint deputies, or that the king or other lord should himself delegate the task of supervision. At Basel, for instance, the bishop, who was lord of the town, appointed, in the early part of the 13th century, separate masters or overseers to each of a number of trades.§ Where the feudal tendency was strong these offices, like that of the sheriff itself in England under Stephen, would tend to become hereditary fees. In Paris the lordship over a number of the chief trades was transmitted as an hereditary right to the descendants of the royal favourites, who first received the grants, and in some cases the trade did not buy its liberty till a late period.‖ There is no trace in London of any such complete feudalization of the control over trade and industry. The sheriffs appointed bailiffs to hold their courts and collect their tolls, and the control of the bailiff was in time reduced to a mere formality, by the gradual encroachment of the members of the trade forming themselves into open or concealed association for this purpose.

The actual emergence of a gild through this process can only be traced in a few cases, but the influence of the early methods of regulation and toll-taking in drawing together the members of trades and in fostering the spirit of voluntary

* F. Keutgen, *Urkunden*, 125.
† *Liber Albus*, translated by H. T. Riley, p. 310.
‡ *Ibid.*, p. 323.
§ F. Keutgen, *Aemter und Zünfte*, 158.
‖ R. Eberstadt, *Magisterium und Fraternitas*.

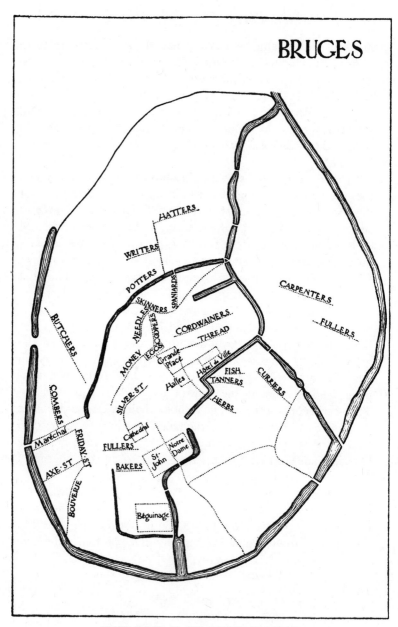

BRUGES

TRADE NAMES IN THE STREETS OF BRUGES

association must have been universal. There can be little
doubt that this was one of the main causes of that localization

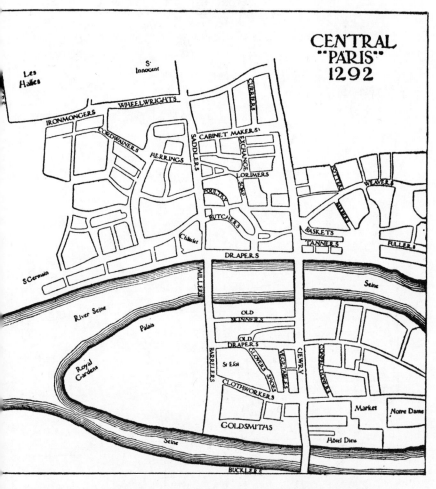

of trades in streets named after them, which is one of the most
striking features in the early topography of the mediæval city.
The most casual observer wandering through the streets of

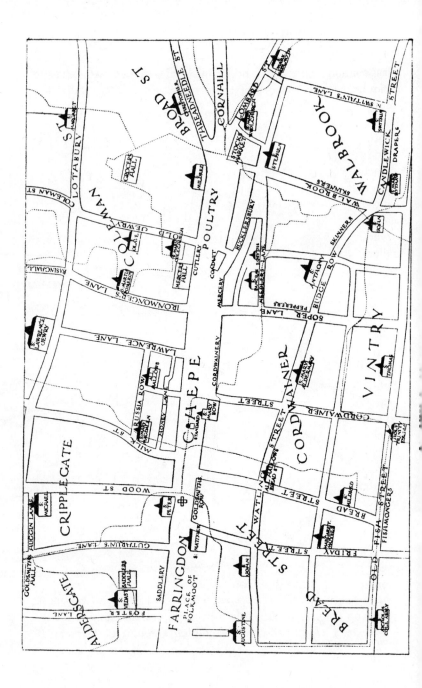

Bruges cannot fail to notice what a large number of them still bear the names of the trades once carried on within them. Many such names survive even in modern Paris, and when mediæval Paris is reconstructed from a tax roll of the 13th century, distinct evidence of two successive localizations of trade can be found—the first in the island Cité between the cathedral and the palace, and the second caused by a migration to larger quarters on the northern bank of the Seine.[*] In the 12th-century records of Cologne, the position of houses is indicated with reference to the localities occupied by the several trades—"amongst the shoemakers," "amongst the tailors," etc.[†] And if we look up amidst the roar and bustle of our own Cheapside, the signs of Wood Street, Bread Street, Friday Street, Milk Street, and Ironmonger Lane carry our minds back to the stalls and booths of a mediæval market.

Early market regulations were chiefly concerned with the tolls. Only in a few cases was there an attempt at inspection in the public interest. Foremost amongst these is that of the baker, who has always worked under the eye of a jealous public opinion and subjected to a kind of regularized lynch law. Bakers' associations were everywhere amongst the first to be formed, but the vigilance of public regulation held them in check and prevented their assuming the more autonomous powers of the fully developed craft-gild. Whilst, therefore, the bakers afford us the earliest clear evidence of the first stage of the development of the gild out of the hallmoot, we shall have to look for illustrations of the later stages in other trades.

An early document gives us the dues originally payable by the London bakers as the customs of the hallmoot. These were, a halfpenny or a farthing loaf, whichever he baked, from every baking, "and all those who baked three times a week or more, owed a penny a week."[‡]

[*] H. Geraud, *Paris sous Philippe le Bel.*
[†] F. Keutgen, *Aemter und Zünfte,* 141.
[‡] M. Bateson, "A London Municipal Collection" in *English Historical Review,* October, 1902.

F

Now, in the year 1155 we learn from the Pipe Roll that the bakers were paying into the Royal Exchequer £6 a year for their gild. That it was a large sum for them to pay may be inferred from the fact that in 1158 they were £4 10s. in arrears, and that for the next two years they paid apparently nothing at all and were £16 10s. in debt. Later on we find the gild struggling back into solvency, and in 1165 it was again paying £6 a year, and continued to do so regularly till 1178, after which the gild disappears. What did the bakers get in return for these large sums? It can scarcely have been the bare privilege of self-government, and it is questionable whether in the case of the bakers this privilege was to be bought at all. The only possible equivalent for such a payment was the removal of the tolls. If the gild had thirty members paying a penny each in tolls per week, it would make a slight profit on the transaction. The bakers were in fact securing for their own trade what the citizens had secured for London as a whole under Henry I., but had lost again in the interval of anarchy—the privilege of farming their own taxes. When the city regained the farm in 1191, the lesser farm of the bakers was probably merged in it. Under Edward III. we find the city bakers paying a toll of a halfpenny a day for each stand in the market towards the farm of the city,* and a bezant (2s.) to the sheriff on first entering the trade. The four meetings of the hallmoot continued to be held—the account already given of them is derived from an ordinance of Edward I.—but in course of time their practical functions were displaced by the Assize of Bread fixed yearly at the Guildhall, and by the regulation of bakers by the alderman in the wardmoot. In 1485 the hallmoot has become a solemn formality. It is the Holymot, the *Curia Sancti Motus* (Court of Holy Motion). The bakers are assembled yearly on the Sunday before the feast of St. Thomas the Apostle, to swear to things that "in times past have not been observed" and so

---

* Plea and Memoranda Rolls at Guildhall, A1 Roll 2 (1327).

"run into perjury to the great peril of their souls." * In the mean time what had become of the bakers' gild? In the sense of an association recognized by the king and responsible for the payment of a yearly farm to the Exchequer, it had disappeared. But associations of craftsmen have at all times existed long before they were officially recognized, and have continued to exist long after that recognition was withdrawn. It may be taken for granted that the tax-farming operations had been rendered possible by the earlier formation of a social and religious fraternity such as we know the bakers to have possessed in the 15th century. Throughout the 13th and 14th centuries the existence of the bakers as an organized community is continually manifested, though the civic authorities seem to have withheld from it, until 1496, most of the powers of self-regulation which were usually conferred on a " craft" or mistery.† Shortly after that date it succeeded, in advance of the majority of the crafts, in gaining incorporation as a livery company.‡

The bakers' gild seems to have openly taken over the most important functions of their hallmoot—its taxing functions, and to have held them for a score of years, after which they passed to the city. The fishmongers, without any public recognition as a gild, captured their hallmoot by silent permeation, and held it for at least a century and a half. And the fishmongers' hallmoot had much fuller powers than that of the bakers. It was known as the *Laghalmote* or *Leyhalmode*, and in addition to the two yearly meetings on St. Martin's Day and in Lent, which all members of the trade must attend on pain of a fine of 21 pence, its functions comprised

---

* Harl. MSS. 6811, fo. 121. An entry in Letter Book, H (p. 207 of Dr. Sharpe's Calendar) reveals an intermediate stage in the decay of the hallmoot. In 1382 the bakers complained of having to attend twice a year at the Halymotz held in St. Thomas Acres ; and obtained leave to be exempt from fine if they attended once.

† Letter Book, L, fo. 122.

‡ *Ibid.*, fo. 227b.

the holding of a court which sat once a week to settle disputes amongst the London fishmongers, and might go on sitting from day to day in cases in which foreign fishmongers were involved. The fishmongers were not craftsmen like the bakers, but merchants, and their court was in part a court of the "law merchant."   Now the "law merchant" was administered in the 13th century at the Guildhall in the Court of Husting ; yet any case affecting the fishmongers could be withdrawn from the Husting by their bailiff and taken before the hallmoot in Bridge Street.   In short, a separation of the lesser hallmoot from the Husting had taken place exactly parallel to the separation of the larger hallmoot from the Folkmoot.   Both courts were under the nominal presidency of the sheriff, and it is not clear what motive produced the separation.   It may have taken place when the right kind of law was not to be had at the Husting.   Or the sheriff may, at a time when his own office was tending to become an hereditary fee, have created a subtenancy in the fishmongers' hallmoot.   But whatever the original motive, the ultimate effect was to pave the way for the fishmongers' independence.   By the end of Henry III.'s reign the courts of hallmoot, though nominally held by the sheriff's representative, were actually administered by the fishmongers, who paid two marks a year for the privilege.   This is their own account of the matter—

"Also the men of the said trade give unto their Bailiff two marks per annum . . . the same in farthings, halfpennies, and pennies, according as their collectors may collect.   And they so pay these two marks, because if anyone belonging to the Hallmote is impleaded in the Husting, it is the duty of the Bailiff to withdraw him from the Husting into the Hallmoot in Bridge St., that they may distrain upon their own debtors or do that which justice shall demand." *

Now, there can be no doubt that by this time the fishmongers were one of the wealthiest and best organized bodies

* *Liber Albus*, p. 323.

of tradesmen in the city. One of the chief accusations made by the aldermanic party against Walter Hervey, the popularly elected Mayor of 1271–2, was that he had received an annual fee from the community of the fishmongers to support their causes, whether just or unjust.* A list of eighty-nine of them paid the enormous sum of five hundred marks in 1290 to purchase pardon for all illicit transactions, forestalling, and other trespasses.† The first name in this list was that of Adam de Fulham, who was afterwards Alderman of Bridge Ward and became Sheriff in 1298, being at that time in possession of Botolph's Quay ; ‡ and the second name was that of Richard de Chigwell, a leading wool exporter, and owner of one of the three ships with which the city furnished Edward I. for his navy. From the time Edward II. ascended the throne the fishmongers began to play a leading part in city politics. Their young men did battle with the armed retinue of Edward's foreign favourites in the streets of the city. When the Londoners received the joyful news of Isabel's safe delivery of the young prince who was afterwards Edward III., and " did little for the greater part of a week but go in carols throughout the city with great glare of torches and with trumpets and other minstrelsies," the fishmongers determined to celebrate the event with a noble pageant.

" They caused a boat to be fitted out in guise of a great ship, with all manner of tackle that belongs to a ship, and it sailed through Chepe as far as Westminster, where the Fishmongers came, well mounted and costumed very richly, and presented the ship to the Queen. And on the same day the Queen took her departure for Canterbury on pilgrimage, whereupon the Fishmongers all thus costumed escorted her through the city." §

Finally, the growing power of the trade reached its culmination in the election of Hamo de Chigwell, one of the most

* *Chronicles of the Mayors and Sheriffs*, translated by H. T. Riley, p. 175.
† Calendar of Patent Rolls, 1290, p. 377.
‡ Calendar of Letter Book, B, p. 218.
§ Riley, *Memorials of London*, p. 106.

notable Mayors of London, who, by the support of the middle class, the king's favour, and his own adroitness, managed to retain office, with the exception of two brief intervals, from 1318 till the calamitous close of Edward's reign in 1326.

All this social prestige and political influence had their economic basis in the enjoyment of a certain degree of monopoly in what was, after bread, the first necessity of life in the Middle Ages. Such a monopoly implied not only a strong organization, but sufficient capital and mercantile ability to give control of the sources of import. In early times London fishmongers had estates on the Thames and the Lea, and owned the small river craft that brought in the fish; later on they were not only the chief shipowners, but rode out in companies to bargain for the fish in the Norfolk and Suffolk ports. The trade therefore included every degree of wealth from the merchant prince to the costermonger, and class divisions sprang up inevitably within its ranks. The strongest body of fishmongers, the well-to-do shopkeepers who had places in the three authorized fish-markets in Bridge Street, Old Fish Street, and the "Stocks," insisted on all fish passing through these markets before it was retailed elsewhere. The poorer dealers, who made a living by carrying the fish on barrows to the doors of the craftsmen in the suburbs, wanted to buy their stocks direct from three large fishmongers who had places on Fish Wharf. The dispute ran high, and blood had already been shed in the quarrel, when the free trade party appealed to Parliament. The king ordered an inquiry, and this, being held by the mayor Hamo de Chigwell, himself a fishmonger, declared against the free traders, who appealed against the decision. Then the king's justices discover that the whole power of the monopoly rests on the Hallmoot.

"We understand," says their new writ, "that certain ordinances have lately been made by certain fishmongers of London and confirmed by oath amongst themselves, as to the sale of fish, that it shall be sold exclusively through their hands at a higher price than it otherwise would be . . . and that they hold a certain court amongst themselves for their own purposes which they call Halimot in which they have enacted such ordinances as aforesaid and have conspired to maintain and defend them contrary to the regulations made for the common good of the city."

The justices ask by what warrant the fishmongers hold this illegal assembly. The fishmongers indignantly reply that no such illegal assembly has been held. The two yearly courts to which the title of Halimot properly belongs have been held since time immemorial by the sheriffs or their bailiffs to regulate the trade and punish offenders, and a weekly court is also held under the same authority to decide disputes in the fish-market. All fines inflicted go to the city.

While this cause was still pending, during the famous *Iter* of 1321, Hamo de Chigwell, who had been replaced in the mayoralty a few months previously by a political opponent, was suddenly restored to power and the hallmoot was saved. Edward III. confirmed its powers by a charter of 1363, which makes no secret of the monopoly conferred thereby on the fishmongers. During the ten years of continual revolution which commenced just before the accession of Richard II., the fishmongers' privileges were the main question at issue between the two city parties. In 1379 nearly a third of the aldermen elected were fishmongers. It was the fishmongers or some of them who opened the gate to Wat Tyler. The year after John of Northampton—elected mayor for that very purpose—got the fish monopoly abolished by Parliament, only to find himself hurled from power and his policy reversed in 1383. The fishmongers though restored to power did not venture to re-establish the hallmoot immediately. One of the last acts of Richard was to bestow on his friends the fishmongers a new charter with all their original privileges,* but with the

* *Liber Custumarum,* I. 385–405; Herbert, *Twelve Great Livery Companies,* II. 118; Calendar of Letter Books of Corporation, H, Introduction.

arrival of Bolingbroke this grant lost its value, and the hallmoot never regained the exercise of its distinctive immunities.

Though we may not be able to follow in detail the process by which the fishmongers first acquired their privileges of jurisdiction nor the manner in which they exploited them, the general significance of the hallmoot is sufficiently clear. It was a court of public law transferred into private hands. In fact if not in form it presented an almost exact parallel to the private jurisdiction in the hands of lords temporal and spiritual which constituted so great a part of local government in the Middle Ages. More than a score of such seignorial immunities existed in London and were being challenged by the king's justices at the same time as the hallmoot. Many of these, like the "liberties" of St. Martin and of Blackfriars, long survived the Reformation. On the grounds of this similarity we may venture to apply to the fishmongers' hallmoot the expressive phrase coined by a French historian and to call it a *seigneurie collective*, a collective lordship. The author of this phrase, M. Luchaire, points out that the towns themselves first won the right of self-government under this form. They gained a collective right of immunity from the public law of the county, and a collective right of quasi-private jurisdiction within their own boundaries.

The power of the fishmongers is probably to be explained by the fact that they had got a good grasp of their special immunity before the city had thoroughly consolidated its powers of self-government, and were therefore able to resist absorption for a long time.

What the fishmongers may be said to have won by stealth, the weavers secured at an early date by the open grant of charter. Like the bakers they gained the privilege of farming their own taxes. But they secured it much earlier (before 1130), and continued to hold it till Tudor times. The position of the weavers amongst London trades was in this respect unique, but in the 12th century there were gilds of weavers enjoying similar privileges at Lincoln, Oxford, York, Winchester, Huntingdon, and Nottingham, as well as a gild of fullers at Winchester. A century later many of these gilds are found to be engaged in a struggle with the newly constituted municipal authorities, who refuse them the rights of freemen. It has been suggested that the weavers were foreigners. This is not improbable, but the explanation of the antagonism may be sought on the more general grounds, already suggested in the case of the fishmongers.

The weavers of London gained their first charter from Henry I. about the same time as the city received its charter. But, as Dr. Round has conclusively shown, the essential points of the grant to the citizens, the farm of London and Middlesex at £300 and the election of sheriff and justiciar, were lost a few years later, and not regained till the grant of Mayor and Commune in 1191, whilst the weavers retained their farm and the rights of self-government involved in it throughout the century.* Moreover, the citizens of London to whom Henry I. made his grant were a community still enveloped in a feudal atmosphere, a community whose rights and powers were closely restricted by the privileges of its individual members, as well as by those of non-members dwelling in its midst. The charter itself reveals this clearly in its famous ninth clause, " that the churches and barons and citizens may have and hold quietly and in peace their sokes with all their customs . . . and that the guest who shall be tarrying in the sokes shall pay custom to no other than him to whom such soke shall belong or to his bailiff." † And even a century later we find the king's sheriff, elected by the citizens, compelled to lie in wait in the highway for debtors or offenders against the peace, since he may not attach them in the soke of a baron.‡

---

* J. II. Round, *Geoffrey de Mandeville*, Appendix.   † *Liber Albus*, p. 115.
‡ M. Bateson, "A London Municipal Collection," in *English Historical Review*, July, 1902, p. 8.

Now, the effect of the charter granted to the weavers was to place them collectively on a level in this matter with the barons and religious houses that possessed sokes in London. The grant of a gild gave them a private jurisdiction, a soke, a collective lordship over their trade. In the great *Iter* of 1321, when the king's justices were challenging the feudal immunities held by barons and churches in London, they not only called in question the fishmongers' halimot but the weavers' gild. The weavers cite their charters conferring a gild, and say that by virtue of their gild they claim to have " their court from week to week concerning all matters touching their gild, . . . and if any one of their gild is impleaded elsewhere than in their gild, viz. in a plea of debt, contract, agreement, or small transgression, they ought to claim him from Court and have him before the Court of their Gild." An unfriendly jury of Londoners who have many objections to raise to the way in which the weavers exercise their powers, admit the legality of the court itself, and they further find that since the grant of their first charter the weavers have had a gild in the city by right of which they have chosen bailiffs from themselves from year to year.* In the course of an earlier dispute the weavers were allowed to have the right to hold a yearly gild in the church of St. Nicholas Hacoun on St. Edmund's Day, to which all of the mistery must come on pain of a fine of threepence.†

In its yearly meeting, its weekly court, and its right of withdrawing pleas from the sheriff, the weavers' gild presents a fairly close likeness to the fishmongers' halimot. Both are in effect feudal immunities, but the legal basis in the one case is entirely different from that in the other. The fishmongers boldly claim that their halimot is a public court. The weavers claim a private court by charter. The charter indeed says nothing of a court. Henry II. grants the weavers their gild with all the liberties and customs which they had in the days

---

* Liber Custumarum, I. 420–422.   † *Ibid.*, I. 122.

of his grandfather, and that none shall meddle with their craft within the city or in Southwark or other places pertaining to London except through them and unless he belong to their gild. In return for which they are to pay yearly two marks of gold (£12); and no one is to do them wrong on these points on pain of a fine of £10.* This grant of exclusive control of their trade seems to have implied jurisdiction over it. In a similar charter which Henry II. gave to the tanners of Rouen conveying all the customs and rights of their gild, the concluding words are "that none shall vex nor disturb them nor implead them concerning their craft except before me." † When such an exemption from a local court of first instance was granted, the recipients of the grant always appear to have assumed the right to exercise this lower jurisdiction themselves.

But there was another important difference between the case of the weavers and that of the fishmongers. The privileges of the fishmongers grew up out of obscure beginnings, and were at their height when they were abolished. The exceptional position of the weavers, based on explicit royal charters and confronted only by a half-formed municipal government, was strong at first, but became weaker as the city grew stronger, and was at last so ineffectual as not to be worth while abolishing. The first weavers were not mere craftsmen. Their ability to purchase a charter, the amount of their farm, which was twice that of the bakers, and their possession of a court of merchant law, all point to their having a body of well-to-do traders amongst them. During the 12th century, however, a body of influential citizens grew up outside the ranks of the weavers, who were interested in the cloth trade and had an unchartered gild of their own. Hence the attempt of the city soon after the grant of the Mayor and Commune to destroy the privileges of the weavers. The citizens offered to pay yearly farm of 20

* Liber Custumarum, I. p. 418.   † Fagniez, *Documents*, 115.

marks in place of the 18 marks paid by the weavers, and to give a further sum down of 60 marks if the gild were abolished and not again restored. The offer was accepted; yet a few years later the weavers were reinstalled on condition of paying the higher farm, and in Henry III.'s reign they deposited their charter with the Exchequer for safety. A century of economic development rendered these legal safeguards useless. In 1300 most of the weavers were employed by burrellers and other capitalists engaged in the cloth trade. They could only retain their gild and their bailiffs by submitting to an appeal from their court to the mayor and by allowing the burrellers to assist in revising their ordinances. The only use of their court was to protect their status as craftsmen. In 1321 the citizens accused them of passing ordinances to shorten their hours and raise their wages. In 1335 the city court set aside the exclusive rights of the weavers by declaring it lawful for all freemen to set up looms and to sell cloth as long as the king received his yearly farm.* After that, though the independent position of the weavers was in form retained, their relative importance steadily declined, till the introduction of silk-weaving under the Tudors gave their gild a new lease of life.

* Unwin, *Industrial Organization*, pp. 29, 30.

CHAPTER IV

THE ADULTERINE GILDS

THE gilds for which the weavers and the bakers paid a yearly farm to the Exchequer of Henry II. were not the only institutions of that name in the 12th century. We are confronted on the very threshold of gild history, with the problem of the unlicensed or "adulterine" gilds. The data for our study of them are few and simple. They consist of eighteen entries in the Pipe Roll of 1179–80 recording fines inflicted by the king upon as many gilds for having come into existence without licence. The fines vary in amount from half a mark (6s. 8d.) to 45 marks (£30), and the total is just under £120, which sum is recorded in subsequent Pipe Rolls as being still unpaid even in part. The fines seem to have been given up for a bad debt and the entry consequently dropped, but it suddenly recurs, perhaps under the stress of pecuniary embarrassment, towards the end of the reign of John, long after London had got its Mayor and Commune.

The interest which the entries of 1180 have for the student of London history is undoubtedly very great. Occurring as they do only eleven years before the extortion of the Commune, and presenting, as they also do, unmistakable evidence of a widespread system of organization among all classes of Londoners, which is viewed with suspicion by the Government, they suggest the almost irresistible conclusion that the gilds must have had some connection with the revolution that happened as soon as the pressure of the great administrator's hand was removed. Translated and rearranged the entries run :—

The gild of Goldsmiths of which Ralph Flael is alderman owes	45 marks
The gild of which Goscelin is alderman owes . .	30 ,,
The gild of St. Lazarus of which Ralph le Barre is alderman owes	25 ,,
The gild of Pepperers of which Edward is alderman owes	16 ,,
The gild of Bridge of which Aylwin Finke is alderman owes	15 ,,
The gild of Bridge of which Peter Fitz Alan is alderman owes	15 ,,
The gild of Bridge of which Robert de Bosco is alderman owes	10 ,,
The gild of which William de Haverhill is alderman owes	10 ,,
The gild of strangers of which Warner le Turner is alderman owes	40 shillings
The gild of which Richard Thedr is alderman owes .	2 marks
The gild of Haliwell of which Henry Fitz Godron is alderman owes	20 shillings
The gild of Bridge of which Thomas Cook is alderman owes	1 mark
The gild of Bridge of which Walter Cuparis alderman owes	1 ,,
The gild of clothworkers (*parariorum*) of which John Maur is alderman owes	1 ,,
The gild of butchers of which Lafeite is alderman owes	1 ,,
The gild of which Rochefolet is alderman owes	1 ,,
The gild of which John White is alderman owes .	1 ,,
The gild of which Odo Vigil is alderman owes . .	½ ,,

The first comment which this list suggests is the enormous difference in the amount of the several fines which must have had some reference to the wealth of the offenders. The gilds clearly represented some of the poorest as well as some of the richest of the citizens. Not only so, but the cleavage between the two classes is wide. Eight of the gilds are fined only a mark each, whilst another eight pay sums varying from 10 marks to 45 ; and whereas the aldermen of the poorer gilds bear in several cases plebeian names like Cook and Cooper, those of the richer gilds have amongst them some of the leading citizens of the time. William de Haverhill was to be one of London's first sheriffs under the new constitution of 1191. He bore a name that takes a distinguished place in the annals of the city both before and after his time. Aylwin Finke was one of the king's minters. He appears on the Pipe Rolls as paying feudal aids to the king, and there can be little doubt that he was of the family from which St. Benet Fink derives its name. The alderman Edward evidently required no other name, and it is therefore likely that he is identical with Edward the Reeve who figures prominently in the Pipe Rolls at this time. Peter Fitz Alan was not improbably a nephew of the famous Gervase of Cornhill, the Justiciar of whose family Dr. Round has given such an interesting account. Goscelin appears again in the Pipe Roll of 1191-2 as one of two " by whose view Holeburn bridge is repaired."

Whatever uncertainty may exist as to the identification of individual names, there can be little doubt as to the general conclusion that the eight gilds with the fines of 10 marks and upwards represented in their membership the aldermanic class into whose hands the practical control of the constitution of 1191 fell ; and that the eight gilds which were fined a mark or less indicate the beginnings of an organization in that larger mass of citizens who had no effective share in that constitution, and whose discontent gave the rising of William Fitz Osbert in 1196 its serious aspect. We can hardly be wrong, therefore, either in taking the appearance of the adulterine gilds as a whole as evidence of the growth of organized civic opinion that led to the grant of the Commune, or in finding in the social cleavage, which is so marked a feature of the gilds in

1180, an explanation of the disturbances that followed so soon upon the erection of a new form of oligarchic rule with a popular name.

When we turn from these general considerations to consider the gilds more particularly, we are at once struck with the fact that no less than five, three of the wealthier class and two of the poorer class, bear a common designation as gilds of bridge. This has been supposed to indicate an element of localization in the gilds.   Now, the bridge no doubt has always been the centre of London trade and traffic, so that not only the cooks or the coopers, but the fishmongers, the vintners, or the wool-mongers, would have been justified in calling their gild after it. But this is not exactly localization, nor is it very likely that five trades any more than five localities would adopt or receive the same name for their association unless for a special reason. And this special reason existed.   Only four years before the adulterine gilds were fined, the great work of replacing the old wooden bridge, so often destroyed by assault or fire or flood, by the stone bridge which became the pride of the Londoner and one of the marvels of Europe, had been commenced.   It was regarded as a religious work.   Peter of St. Mary Cole-church began it, the Archbishop of Canterbury is said to have given a thousand marks towards its construction, and the bridge-chapel wherein masses were daily celebrated was dedicated to St. Thomas of Canterbury.   When it first began to need repair, Edward I. not only imposed an extra toll for the purpose, but sent an appeal through the clergy for the pious aids of the devout.   The chapel on the bridge preserved a list of such benefactors "in a table fair written for posterity."

It can scarcely be thought that during the thirty-three years in which this great undertaking on which the prosperity of London trade so largely depended was going forward, there was an entire absence of voluntary organization in its support Religious associations for this purpose were common in the

Middle Ages. The repair of bridges and roads was among the objects of the gild of Holy Cross at Birmingham. At the very time when London Bridge was building, a special religious order of Bridge Brothers was spreading over Europe, and the celebrated bridge of Avignon over the Rhone, four arches of which are preserved in the modern structure, was their work.* Although, therefore, we have no more positive evidence than is contained in their name, it is at least a plausible hypothesis that the five gilds of bridge were so called because, amongst their other religious and social objects, they gave special prominence to the regular contribution of alms to this common purpose.

But, it may be asked at this point, are we justified in taking it for granted that the adulterine gilds existed mainly or even partly for religious and social purposes ? Only two of them bear names that suggest a religious dedication, and four of them bear names of trades. May not the majority of the eighteen have been the forerunners of the later craft-gilds and not religious fraternities at all ? It is well to raise this question thus early in order to get rid of a confusion that has been created by a misunderstanding of the royal inquiry into gilds and crafts in 1389. It is often supposed that of the two writs which were then issued, one asked for particulars of all existing religious gilds, and the other for similar parti-culars of all craft-gilds. This is quite a mistake. The inquiry made in the first writ related to gilds and fraternities generally, and included in its scope the gilds or fraternities connected with crafts, as the returns extant for London, which include the certificates of the Drapers', Cutlers', Barbers', Glovers', and Whittawyers' fraternities, sufficiently show ; and the ordinances of these fraternities differed in no essential respect from those of the parish gilds. The other writ required the produc-tion of all royal charters granting special privileges to crafts and misteries. Very few crafts and misteries possessed such

* J. J. Jusserand, *English Wayfaring Life in the Middle Ages*, pp. 38-42, 48-49.

G

royal charters, as the great majority owed their constitution as crafts or misteries entirely to the authority deputed to them by the city.* But in neither case did the "fraternity of the craft" owe its origin or its constitution to these grants of royal or civic authority. The fraternities existed before the charters and the civic ordinances. Indeed, they procured the grant of them and supplied the social force that made them effective. The craft or mistery element and the fraternity or gild element became ultimately so intermingled in the livery company that the combination of both elements was sometimes expressed by any one of these terms. Some of the companies, and these were the earlier cases, were incorporated as gilds or fraternities, others were incorporated as misteries, whilst in a few cases the relation between the two elements is made quite clear by the terms of the charter; but in all cases of incorporation the fraternity element underlay the mistery element.

In order to make the interaction of these various factors clear a separate chapter must be devoted to the discussion of each. But it is necessary at the outset to emphasize two points : (1) that in the complex structure of the later livery company the fraternity or gild element supplied the nucleus round which the rest was formed ; and (2) that these fraternities among members of the same trade were of essentially the same character as other fraternities, such as the parish gilds.

If we may take these points for granted, the difficulties raised about the adulterine gilds largely disappear. They were none of them crafts or misteries because they were not organs of deputed authority. The Crown disowned them. The municipality did not yet exist. They did not pay like the weavers' gild a yearly farm to the Exchequer. The only remaining sense in which they can have been gilds at all is as voluntary associations for social and religious purposes.

* The writs are given in Toulmin Smith's *English Gilds* (Early English Text Society).

The gild in this sense existed, as we have seen, in the 10th century, if not earlier, and it continued to exist in the same sense down to the Reformation. The broad features of the institution changed remarkably little. We find them serving as a social bond between the turbulent feudal society of the Saxon shire, between the knights who were gradually being withdrawn from feudalism behind the walls of a borough, and between the Londoners, noble and simple, who were making a common effort to replace feudalism by a settled civic security. And we find them, four centuries later, a little elaborated but essentially the same, providing a social basis for a clique of wealthy merchants bent on monopoly, for a body of journeymen plotting to raise their wages, and for a band of peasants who are being encouraged by their parson to consult Domesday Book and cast off all servile obligations to their lord. The oath of initiation, the entrance fee in money or in kind, the annual feast and mass, the meetings three or four times a year for gild business, the obligation to attend all funerals of members, to bear the body if need be from a distance, and to provide masses for the soul ; the duty of friendly help in cases of sickness, imprisonment, house-burning, shipwreck, or robbery, the rules for decent behaviour at meetings and provisions for settling disputes without recourse to the law,—all these features have their precedents in Saxon gilds, and they constitute the essential ordinances of the fraternity down to the Reformation, and indeed long after it.

We may assume, therefore, with some confidence that all the adulterine gilds belonged to this general type. And the only details we possess of the inner life of a London gild of this period lend weight to this conclusion. These are contained in an agreement between the Fraternity of Saddlers and the canons of St. Martins-le-Grand, which dates from about the end of the 12th century. The saddlers had their shops at that time, as later, at the north-west corner of Chepe, near the ends of Foster Lane and Gutter Lane, close to the site of their present hall, and they had formed a religious connection with the neighbouring collegiate church, of a kind that became very common later between the fraternities of crafts and the various religious houses.   On the feast of St. Martin they attended mass together and made an offering of alms and tapers.   The funeral obsequies of deceased members were also held in St. Martin's church and 8d. was paid for tolling of the bell. In consideration of the dues that fell in this and other ways to the canons, the saddlers were admitted to be partakers of all benefits with the church of St. Martin's, both by night and by day, in masses, psalms, prayers and watches ; moreover, they were all to be separately prayed for by name, on appointed days during Holy Week, in two masses, one for the living, the other for the dead.   The presiding officer in the Saddlers' gild as in the adulterine gilds was called an alderman, and he was supported by four echevins, who fill the same place as the four wardens who are met with later. Of the purely social side of this fraternity the agreement naturally tells us nothing.*

Now, the Saddlers possessed, during the 14th century, one of the most powerful organizations in London.   They were one of the half-dozen who secured special privileges by royal charter, and they were incorporated before the close of the 14th century.   And it is a most significant fact that the only misteries of which we can say the same, *i.e.* the Goldsmiths, the Merchant Tailors, the Skinners, and the Mercers, are all known to have had strong fraternity organizations early in the 14th century, some of which can be traced back into the 13th century.   With this important evidence of continuity before our minds, we may turn for a last glance at the adulterine gilds.

Four of the gilds are definitely connected with trades. The goldsmiths head the list with a fine of 45 marks, and

* W. Herbert, *History of Twelve Great Livery Companies*, I. 16 ; J. W. Sherwell, *History of the Guild of Saddlers*.

the pepperers are assessed at 16 marks, whilst the butchers and another of the humbler crafts are only fined a mark apiece, which is the amount likewise paid by Thomas Cook's gild and Walter Cooper's gild. The distance between merchant and craftsman is here unmistakable. In later times there is no such yawning gulf dividing the greater from the lesser companies. It is a mere historical accident that has placed the Salters or the Clothworkers amongst the greater companies and the Leathersellers amongst the minor companies. The difference in wealth and power between the greatest and least of the livery companies in the 15th century was considerable, but it shaded off into intermediate degrees. Why should the distinction between rich merchant and poor craftsman have been most marked when the total wealth of the city was smallest ?

The answer is that in the 12th and 13th centuries this distinction was not produced mainly by economic forces, but was due to the existence of social and political barriers which were not removed by the new constitution of 1191. On the contrary, the aldermanic class under a mayor of its own choice consolidated its power, and the name of commune only served to stimulate the discontent of the outsiders. This ruling class was not one of merchants in the modern sense of the word. That honourable profession had not yet come into existence. The aldermen were, in the first place, landholders, the thanes and knights of former days, and this was the basis of their political privileges. But by the end of the 12th century they had become also a class of royal officials—the king's minters, his chamberlain, his takers of wines, his farmers of taxes. There was scarcely a mayor, sheriff, or alderman of London in the 13th century but held at one time or another one or more of these offices. This official position was the source, or at any rate the essential condition, of their mercantile success. The profits of honest merchandise were small in the 13th century. The Jews, indeed, grew enormously rich by

money-lending, but they were the king's chattels, and had no
security for life or property. To the Italians who succeeded
them, merchandise and even money-lending were subsidiary
to the farming of taxes and even to the exploitation of real
estate. The aldermen, many of whom were of Jewish, Italian,
or Gascon descent, were in the closest relations with the
foreign financiers, and acquired their wealth by the same
means, except that they had a more solid stake in the country
and controlled the city courts. Their wealth was largely
invested in real property, and they sat in judgment on pleas
concerning land. In times of social disturbance, the popular
party suspended the aldermanic land court and went about
with crowbars reclaiming the aldermanic encroachments.*

As aldermen the ruling class assessed the king's taxes,
and they were constantly accused of oppressing the poor and
obtaining exemption for themselves.† As sheriffs and
chamberlains they were the purveyors to the royal household,
and it was said that they paid the king's debts in bad money
and stockfish. It would be unjust to accept the truth of
these charges as applying to the whole class. But it is at
least clear that the mercantile operations of the aldermen were
closely connected with the exercise of official power.

The two most influential citizens of London at the end of
the 13th century, Henry le Waleys and Gregory Rokesley,
will serve as ready examples. One was the alderman of
Cordwainer Ward and the other of Dowgate, and between
them they held the office of Mayor from 1273 to 1284. Henry
le Waleys held a great number of tenements in the city. He
is found disputing the right to a bakehouse; administering
the house-property of the Archbishop of Canterbury; acquiring a widow's land in Boston. When the city sends him in
1297 to Scotland to appease the king's wrath, he gets a grant
of a quay and houses in Berwick which have fallen into the

* Riley, *Chronicles of Old London,* pp. 59, 164.
† Rot. Hund. for London, *passim.*

king's hands. He is constantly going to Gascony on the king's business, and while there he deals largely in wines on behalf of the king's butler.* Rokesley, too, was interested in land, and held a mortgage over the Bishop of Ely's property. Moreover, he was, in conjunction with one Italian, the buyer of the king's wines; in conjunction with another, a farmer of taxes; whilst with a third he administered the king's Exchange; and at a later date was associated with a fourth in reforming the coinage (it was he who was accused of paying in bad pennies and stockfish). At the end of his long official career we find the king seizing his goods.†

Henry le Waleys and Gregory Rokesley were typical members of a small class which was almost acquiring the character of an hereditary caste, based on the descent of landed property and strengthened by intermarriages. Its hereditary character is shown by the repetition of the same family names in the list of sheriffs—the Blunds, the Buckerels, the Basings, the Aswys, the Cornhills—and the intermarriages are proved by their wills. This class has left many marks on London topography, in names like Bassishaw and Farringdon Wards, Bucklersbury and Cosin Lane, names that have become rooted in the soil because of its association with them for generations. How far can we connect this class with any form of the gild?

A large number of its members were probably included in the wealthier adulterine gilds. The Basings, Blunds, and Buckerels were not only mayors and sheriffs, but goldsmiths, *i.e.* financiers and minters; and though the goldsmith lost some of his relative predominance, it is not unlikely that the gild of 1180 was the same fraternity of St. Dunstan which we find in existence in 1272,‡ and which supplied a basis for the

---

* Calendar of Patent Rolls, 1277, p. 242; 1280, p. 421; 1299, p. 408; and Calendar of Close Rolls, 1274, pp. 73, 114, 126.

† Calendar of Patent Rolls, 1275-9, pp. 15, 95, 126, 236, 240, 278, 301, 421; Calendar of Close Rolls, 1289, pp. 9, 95, 212.

‡ Sharpe, *Calendar of Wills*, vol. i. p. 14 *n.*

later livery company. The 14th-century fraternity of Pepperers, which afterwards became the Grocers' Company,
cannot claim formal continuity with the Pepperers' gild of
1180, because its own records contain an account of a distinctly
fresh start made in 1345. Other links between the later
fraternities and the earlier gilds are extremely conjectural.
The fraternities of three crafts that were strongly organized
before the close of the 13th century—the Tailors' fraternity of
St. John the Baptist, the Skinners' fraternity of Corpus Christi,
and the fraternity of the Mercery—had probably been in
existence since the early part of the century, and it is likely
that each of them had members in the aldermanic class.
The early sheriffs and chamberlains dealt largely in skins for
the royal wardrobe ; Serle the Mercer was twice mayor, and
Philip le Taylur was the aldermanic candidate when the
populace elected Walter Hervey in 1271. We might perhaps
be justified, therefore, in assuming that the fraternities
mentioned along with others connected with such flourish-
ing branches of merchandise as the wine and the wool trades,
were taking the place of, if they did not actually arise from,
the eight wealthier gilds of 1180. But on the whole we hear
less than we should naturally expect of their influence and
activity.

A possible explanation of this gap in gild history may
be suggested. Amongst the leading citizens of London
there was very little specialization in trade till the 14th
century. Most of the aldermen were woolmongers, vintners,
skinners, and grocers by turns, or carried on all these branches
of commerce at once. The social affinities which found
expression in the gilds of 1180 were of a semi-feudal character.
The political aims which were not improbably the strongest
motive for their formation, found satisfaction in the grant
of Mayor and Commune. After appropriating the new
constitution to its own purposes, the aldermanic class had
less need of minor organizations as long as it held together.

But the history of oligarchies is always the same. As their numbers increase their ranks close, and those who are excluded place themselves at the head of those who have always been outside, and lead an attack on the citadel of privilege. This situation had grown up in London during the first half of the 13th century, and the king fostered the divisions in the city for his own purposes by coquetting with the anti-aldermanic party. The national crisis of 1262-3 further complicated matters. The Barons also made bids for popular support. The aldermen who joined Simon de Montfort's party found themselves obliged to lead a mob. Under the command of a Buckerel, as Marshal, the citizens marched out to burn manor-houses and pillage fishponds.* The list of those proscribed as rebels in 1269 shows a strange mixture. It contains two or three of the oldest names in the city, and side by side with goldsmiths, mercers, and drapers there are fishmongers, barbers, butchers, tailors, and armourers.† It is clear that, from a variety of causes—inward as well as outward and political as well as economic—the oligarchy is beginning to break up. And amongst the agencies that are tending to produce this result there is the struggle of the organized trades, some of which now emerge into the light of history for the first time. In 1267, when the embers of the recent civil war were still smouldering, an armed conflict took place in the streets of London between some of the goldsmiths' craft and some of the tailors'. The clothworkers and the cordwainers also joined in the fray on either side. Over five hundred were said to have been engaged, and many were wounded and some slain. Geoffrey de Beverley, a clothworker, and twelve others who had taken part on either side, were hanged.‡ The crafts taking part in this struggle were amongst the very earliest to gain special privileges from the Crown or the city, but as they had not yet obtained these, their organization

---

* H. T. Riley, *Chronicles of the Mayors and Sheriffs*, p. 65.
† *Ibid.*, pp. 125-127.　　　　　　　　　　　‡ *Ibid.*, p. 104.

was without any public authority.   We may, therefore, assume that the belligerents were members of fraternities, and,
indeed, in three out of the four trades, private associations are
known to have existed before the close of the century.   But the
special significance of this incident is that the main issue of city
politics is shifting.   For a century it has been chiefly a struggle
between the aldermen and the outsiders, or between two sets
of aldermen inside.   Now it is between two sets of crafts.
The meaning of this new phase of civic life must be reserved
for a subsequent chapter.

NOTE.—A mercantile oligarchy such as that above described might not
unnaturally have been expected to find its appropriate legal form in the Gild
Merchant, an institution of all but universal prevalence in English towns at this
time, and for this reason the existence of a Gild Merchant in London was generally taken for granted by historians until recent years.   When, however, the
subject came to be scientifically and exhaustively dealt with by Professor C. Gross
in the *Gild Merchant* (1890), it was shown that there was no evidence to
warrant the assumption, as not a single reference to such an institution had been
found in the records of London.   This conclusion remains unshaken, in spite
of the discovery (*English Historical Review*, April, 1903), by Mr. C. G. Crump,
of a document in which the needed reference is explicitly made.   This consists of a
charter granted by the king at Windsor in 1252 to a Florentine merchant, conferring on him and his heirs, all the liberties and free customs of London, among
which are the right to buy and sell as freely as any citizen, and to be in the Gild
Merchant of that city.   But as Mr. Crump very justly observes, "a chancery clerk
endeavouring to convert a Florentine merchant into a citizen of London might
well have thought fit to mention a gild merchant as a matter of mere form."
What, however, is of special interest in this document is that the Florentine
is not to be tallaged at more than one mark of silver.   This was a privilege which
many of the aldermanic class had been procuring for themselves individually by
charter.   This avoidance of the full incidence of the property tax was one of the
chief grievances of the citizens against the oligarchy as recorded in the Hundred
Rolls.   It may be added that the city of London possessed all the rights that
would have been conferred by a grant of gild merchant.

CHAPTER V

THE CRAFTS AND THE CONSTITUTION

IN that great development of civic life in which lay the main contribution of the Middle Ages to the cause of Western progress, and which reached its culmination about the middle of the 14th century, the organized power of the crafts was undoubtedly the most striking feature. From one end of Western Europe to the other, from Lubeck to Florence, and from Bristol to Vienna, this new social force was to be found under every variety of external circumstance, working out a political revolution, sometimes by a quiet series of compromises, but in other cases with a violence that foreshadowed the worst days of the reign of terror. In many of the largest cities of Europe—in Paris, in Florence, in Ghent, in Cologne, in London—and in a great number of smaller ones, the crafts wielded, for a time at least, the whole power of municipal government.

In contrast with this period, the centuries that follow down to the 19th are apt to seem a time of sheer reaction, both in municipal life and in the organization of trade and industry. Cities and towns settle down under the rule of oligarchical councils, and the wealthy companies which have replaced the crafts are constituted upon the same oligarchical model. It looks as if the bright promise of municipal democracy was cruelly cut off when it was on the very verge of fulfilment, and the best hopes of human progress deferred for five long centuries.

Such a catastrophic view of history is based on a misconception both of the revolutionary age and of that which succeeded it. The forces so noisily at work in the 14th century were quietly pursuing the same task in the 15th century—the task of building up an enduring social and political organization for the middle classes. The 14th century had been a time of social growth—a growth rapid, indeed, and luxuriant, but irregular and anarchical, and unconscious of the common principles in which it was rooted. It was the work of the 15th century to give effect to those principles, to prune away excrescences, to harmonize conflicting tendencies, and to produce a working compromise. Out of the number of brilliant but ephemeral sketches it had to make a lasting work of art. In this way the fraternity and the craft were absorbed into the livery company, but the process involved no break with the past, either of the form or of the spirit.

It is chiefly around the word "craft" that the misconception above alluded to is apt to gather. The craftsman is thought of as a manual worker, and a revolution wrought by the crafts seems to involve the rise of an extremely democratic form of government. But the word "craft," like "art" or "mistery," with which it is largely synonymous, had no such limited meaning in the Middle Ages. It signified a trade or calling generally, and the typical member of a craft was a well-to-do shopkeeper, a tradesman. Often, it is true, he had gone through an apprenticeship to the manual side of his craft, and this fact was of the greatest importance as it brought manual labour under the influence of the professional spirit. But the full master of a craft was from the first always a trader, and as trade and industry developed and gave more scope for the ability to organize and direct, and more opportunities for the employment of capital, the master rose in the social scale. He became a merchant or a manufacturer, and he carried his "craft" organization along with him into what was now an upper middle class, leaving the small master of the lower middle class to build up a new organization for himself on the same model, and it is not till comparatively recent times that the manual worker proper—the wage-earner—secured a permanent professional organization for his own class. In the Middle Ages the manual worker as such was not an important factor in social or political development. He fought the battles of contending factions, and in times of disturbance he might try to strike a blow for himself, but his desires and his grievances were not among the forces that moulded social history.

The story of the relation of the London crafts to the city constitution opens suddenly in a most dramatic fashion. Shortly before his final struggle with Simon de Montfort, Henry III. had been bidding for the support of the London populace by appealing to them in their almost obsolete general assembly, the Folkmoot, against the authority of the aldermen. As soon as civil war broke out the barons also made bids for the adhesion of the Londoners. The path of revolution was thus made comparatively smooth. For nearly a century the government of the city had been in the hands of the aldermen with the mayor as presiding officer. FitzThomas, the mayor now elected by the popular party, was enabled by the king's example to ignore the aldermen, and to make the Commune a reality, by submitting all large questions to a general assembly. "In all he did," says the aldermanic chronicler, "he acted and determined through them, saying, 'Is it your will that so it should be?' and if they answered 'Ya Ya,' so it was done." A popular organization which may have been helped into existence by some vague traditions of the old frith gild, though its spirit and aims were entirely different, was formed to support the mayor. "The people leagued themselves together by oath, by the hundred, and by the thousand under a sort of colour of keeping the peace." Strong in their sense of this new union, they went about reclaiming public land which had been encroached upon by the aldermen. The mounted watch, which represented the feudal traditions of the ruling class, was swamped by a crowd of armed men on foot eager to find a pretence for harrying the Jews and other alien capitalists.

It was in a London thus imbued with the revolutionary spirit that the crafts first appear. FitzThomas, after a little temporizing and diplomacy, had decided for the barons, and the barons in return had offered to extort from the king any additional liberties which the Londoners might desire. This great opportunity, says the aldermanic chronicler, was entirely lost. Instead of strengthening the existing constitution against the king as the aldermen would have done, the mayor proceeded to open the floodgates of revolution.

"He had all the populace of the city summoned, telling them that the men of each craft must make such provisions as should be to their own advantage and he himself would have the same proclaimed throughout the city and strictly observed. Accordingly after this, from day to day individuals of every craft of themselves made new statutes and provisions—or rather, what might be styled abominations—and that solely for their own advantage and to the intolerable loss of all merchants coming to London and visiting the fairs of England and the exceeding injury of all persons in the realm." *

The mayoralty of FitzThomas ended with the defeat of Earl Simon three years later, and the regulative powers of the crafts no doubt disappeared with the revolutionary constitution of which they formed a part. But in 1271, when Henry III. was on his death-bed and the future king was in Palestine, the craftsmen again succeeded in getting a mayor elected to represent their interests. The aldermen and more discreet men of the city wished to elect Philip le Taylur, but the populace made a great tumult in the king's hall so that the noise reached his lordship the king in bed, continually crying aloud,

* *Liber de Antiquis Legibus*, translated by H. T. Riley, pp. 58–60.

" We are the Commune. We ought to elect the Mayor. We want Hervey to be Mayor. Hervey is our man." The aldermen, to prevent something worse happening, consented in the end to Hervey's election, and contented themselves with calling him to account after his term of office had expired. Amongst other charges made against him it was alleged that he had levied a voluntary contribution on his adherents for the defence of their interests ; that he had taken a regular yearly fee from the fishmongers on the understanding that he should support them in their causes whether just or unjust ; that he had taken bribes from the bakers to connive at short weight ; that he allowed the brewers to sell ale below the assize ; and that for a great sum of money received from certain trades he had set a part of the seal of the community which was in his keeping to new statutes which they had made solely for their own advantage without the consent of the aldermen. The ordinances he had made were disallowed, he was degraded from his aldermanry, and excluded for ever from the councils of the city.*

These two crises in London history afford us a brief but vivid glimpse into the working of the forces that were re-moulding the constitution of the city. It is not merely a case of a mayor setting up a new kind of craft organization. It is still more a case of the craft organizations setting up a new kind of mayor. FitzThomas and Hervey were not creating a new social force ; they were merely giving a public sanction to the exercise of a force already active enough to have placed them in office. It is necessary, therefore, to distinguish carefully two different aspects of the craft : (1) It was one of the main agencies in the transformation of the civic constitution ; (2) it exercised a subordinate authority delegated to it by the constitution.

Nearly everywhere in Western Europe at this time the social and political life of cities was exhibiting the same form

* *Liber de Antiquis Legibus*, translated by Riley, pp. 174-175.

of development—in Flanders, along the Rhine, in North and South Germany, in Italy. A court of magistrates (Aldermen, Schöffen, Echevins), whose semi-hereditary privileges were connected with the ownership of land, was being transformed into a council representative of mercantile interests, and this council was being invaded by the crafts. Beginning at first perhaps with some indirect share in electing the council, the crafts during the first two or three decades of the 14th century secured in many councils half or more than half of the representation, and finally, after further struggles, the whole of it. And in proportion as the crafts gained the predominant power in the council, the main interest of city politics passed from the conflict between them and the previously ruling class, and centred in the party struggles of the crafts themselves.

Throughout the 14th century, then, the crafts furnished the strongest creative force in city politics—a force which shaped and reshaped the constitution; a force making for progress, or at any rate for constant change and movement; a dynamic force working from below. But in the ordinances granted to the crafts by the city we naturally see little or nothing of this. In them the crafts appear as mere instruments of order and authority, as exercising a static force directed from above. To realize the other side of their activity we should require another kind of record that has seldom been preserved, a full account of election contests and a report of the debates in the city council. As it is we have to content ourselves with glimpses vouchsafed us by the chroniclers in times of crisis and revolution.

At such times the secret of the craft's political achievements are revealed. We see it acting as a well-organized voluntary association, meeting frequently to devise plans of concerted action, and levying contributions on its members to furnish a war-chest. Such activity could not be effectual without permanent organs, and we shall not expect to find these amongst the official machinery of trade regulation sanctioned by the authorities. Whenever a line of policy is persistently followed by a craft, it proves the existence of a social bond more intimate, binding, and secret than the one furnished by the civic ordinances, and the universal form of establishing such a bond was in the Middle Ages a Fraternity or Gild. We have already taken a glance at the essential features of gild organization, and shall consider them in detail in a later chapter. For a moment we can take the gild for granted as the living force behind the craft-movement, and proceed to take a brief survey of that movement in its two closely related aspects, (1) the growth of the influence of the crafts on the civic constitution, and (2) the development of the powers delegated to them for the regulation of trade and industry.

Between the defeat of the crafts under the leadership of Walter Hervey and their next decisive advance lies an interval of fifty years, a time of economic progress and, except for the last ten years, of comparative political rest in the city. In order to assuage the violence of faction (which had led to the hanging of Lawrence Ducket in Bow Church at midnight), Edward I. had suspended the mayoralty for thirteen years, and restored the city's liberties only on condition that the foreigners, who were the chief victims of every disturbance and who supplied him with loans and the city with capital, should enjoy freedom of trade and security. The anarchy of Edward II.'s reign left parties in the city once more free to settle accounts with each other. But parties had in the mean time changed their character. The struggle was no longer one between the aldermen and the crafts. The leading crafts had prospered and had now aldermen in their ranks. The ruling class no longer identified their economic interests with those of the foreign capitalist. A new capitalistic interest had grown up connected with the trades and industries of the city. When, therefore, the popular mayor reappears, he is no longer dependent on the support of the irregular Folkmoot or the

H̄

levies of illegal fraternities. Not only has he a new middle
class behind him, but he leads a party of aldermen, and
remoulds the constitution from within. It is instructive to
compare the position of Hervey with that of Richer de
Reffham (1310–11), who was the next reforming mayor. We
are told that he caused the ancient customs and liberties
recorded in the rolls and books of the city to be examined,
and having gathered the wiser and more powerful citizens
along with the aldermen he had them read in their presence,
and then spoke to this effect, " Dear fellow citizens. These
are the ancient customs of the city which have been neglected
through frequent changes of mayor and sheriffs. Do you
wish them to be firmly maintained ? " Whereupon all those
present cried " We do." Richer de Reffham also went about
as FitzThomas had done reclaiming public land from encroachment.* But this time it was not a mob that the mayor
led behind him, but a solemn procession of aldermen clothed
in all the pomp and circumstance of civic authority. We find
the same mayor granting, with the assent of the court of aldermen, a set of ordinances to the Cappers, which gave them power
to restrict foreign competition, and conferring powers of self-
regulation on a number of other crafts (*e.g.* Turners, Dyers,
Whittawyers, and Ironmongers).†

John de Gisors, his successor, was a mayor of the same
type. When Edward II. fled to the North in his last effort
to save Gaveston, and the city was left to defend itself, the
popular party took the opportunity to demand certain constitutional reforms. No alien was to be admitted to the
freedom, and no public obligations were to be incurred, without
consent of the commonalty, and three of the six keys to the
chest in which the common seal was kept were to be in the
possession of the commonalty. These changes John de Gisors
persuaded a quorum of the aldermen, after some consideration,

* *Chronicles of Edward I. and II.* (Rolls Series), I. 175.
† Calendar of Letter Book, D 240 271 ; Riley, *Memorials*, pp. 78, 85.

to accept, together with an article by which the commonalty agreed to give the mayor £40 for his expenses out of a sum of £43 then in the city treasury.* Here we have the illegal popular levy of Hervey's case turned into a constitutional grant, and this precedent was followed in the case of the third revolutionary mayor of this period, Hamo de Chigwell, a few years later. All that was needed to complete the parallel was the demand of the crafts for a share in the constitution, and this too was not wanting. At the end of the same year (1312), after Gaveston's execution and the re-election of Gisors, the mayor and aldermen received at the Guildhall a deputation of the good men of the commonalty of every mistery to treat of certain articles for the commonalty. The deputation asked, among other things, that "the statutes and ordinances regulating the various trades and handicrafts be duly enrolled on a register and that once or twice a year they be read in public assembly, and copies be delivered to such as desire them"; and that "forasmuch as the City ought always to be governed by the aid of men engaged in trades and handicrafts, and whereas it was anciently accustomed that no stranger, native or foreign, whose position and character were unknown, should be admitted to the freedom of the city until the merchants and craftsmen, whose business he wished to enter, had previously certified the Mayor and Aldermen of his condition and trustworthiness, the whole Commonalty pray that such observance may be strictly kept for the future as regards the wholesale trades and the handicrafts (*grossiora officia et operabilia*)." †

What came of this meeting is not stated, but party feeling continued to run high, and there were many cross-currents. The issue between the commonalty and the remnant of the oligarchy was confused by the intermingling of other issues, such as that between the victuallers and the other trades, and the national cleavage between the king's party and the

---

* Calendar of Letter Book, D, 283.   † *Ibid.*, E, 13.

Lancastrians. In 1315 the situation of 1263 and 1270 seems to be repeated. "The common people and plebeians are conspiring among themselves and holding clandestine meetings in private places and have of their own accord without being summoned thrust themselves into the election of mayor." * This time, however, they are on the eve of a decisive advance, if not of complete victory. In 1319, when the city obtained a new charter confirming its existing liberties, a number of articles were added which embodied all the concessions made to the commonalty of recent years, and others which, if duly observed, would have revolutionized the government of the city. These articles, we are told, were obtained much against the will of the mayor, yet the mayor and aldermen appear as petitioning the king for them, and they cost the city £1000.† In one important respect, therefore, the revolution was complete. The mayor and aldermen have become the instruments (and, what is more significant, the unwilling instruments) in carrying out a popular demand.

Some of the more vital articles of this charter, more especially those which made the office of alderman as well as that of mayor subject to annual election, and forbade the holding of either office by the same person two years together, were not afterwards observed. But there is no doubt that the provision that most concerns us here became a really operative part of the constitution. "No man of English birth and especially no English merchant, who followed any specific mistery or craft, was to be admitted to the freedom of the city except on the security of six reputable men of that mistery or craft." ‡ This article of the city's charter, in conjunction with a complementary article which each craft got subsequently inserted in its own ordinances, that no one should exercise that craft if he were not free of the city, served not only to give the

---

* Calendar of Letter Book, D, 25.
† *The French Chronicle of London*, translated by H. T. Riley, p. 252.
‡ Liber Custumarum, I. 268.

crafts as a whole a hold on the constitution, but also to give each craft the power of drawing all who exercised the trade in question into the ranks of its organization, and thus placing them under its control. On this power (which the Germans call *Zunftzwang*), all the later political achievements of the crafts were based. No wonder, then, that the victory of 1319 was felt to open a new era of civic life, and that the feudalism which had lingered in cities seemed already a thing of the past. " In this year (1319)," says the chronicler, " swords were forbidden . . . by reason of which many swords were taken and hung up beneath Ludgate within and without. At this time many of the people of the trades of London were arrayed in livery and a good time was about to begin." *

* *The French Chronicle of London*, translated by H. T. Riley, p. 253.

CHAPTER VI

THE GREATER MISTERIES

THE class interest whose growing strength of organization produced the political results recorded in the last chapter, was not a simple or a uniform force. It was composed of many and divers elements which might be momentarily united as outsiders in the common object of securing a share in the constitution, but which would immediately fall asunder as soon as that object was even partially secured. Nor was it essentially a democratic force, though it won its victories in the name of the commonalty and of the crafts. Such permanent unity as it possessed was that of a new middle class, which while it attacked the position of the privileged few was equally concerned in guarding its own status, and in holding back the encroachments of a still lower class. Its leaders were wealthy merchants like Hamo de Chigwell the fishmonger, and its main body consisted of well-to-do shopkeepers, the masters of the more prosperous crafts. But these two sections, the wholesale trades and the handicrafts, the *grossiora officia* and the *operabilia*, did not comprise between them the whole population of the city. Nominally the *operabilia* ought to have included all the working population, but, effectually, the term only covered a select number of the crafts whose wealth or efficient organization gave them political power. The crafts that carried the day against the aldermanic oligarchy were largely officered and controlled by rich traders and employers of poorer craftsmen.

Clear signs of this intermediate position of the crafts are not wanting from the first. The charters granted by Walter Hervey are said by the chronicler to be "solely made for the benefit of the wealthy men of the trades to which they were granted; and to the loss and undoing of the poor men of those trades, as also to the loss and undoing of all the other citizens and of the whole realm." And when the charters were annulled the men of the several trades were said to be at liberty to follow their crafts "at such hours and such places as they should think proper, and to carry their wares to sell within the city and without, wherever they might think proper." The charters had evidently aimed at restricting the operations of the itinerant tradesman, who then as now supplied a considerable part of the needs of the poorer population. To put down "Eveschepings," street markets and hawkers, was one of the main objects of the policy of the crafts throughout the Middle Ages. In part, these street vendors were from outside districts—like the bakers of Stratford and the butchers of Stepney—but many of them were the poorer craftsmen of the city who could not afford to rent a shop in the main streets, and who therefore had either to hawk their wares or sell them to the shopkeepers. To establish themselves as the middlemen between these poorer craftsmen and the market was the natural aim of the craftsmen who had shops. The saddlers, who had their shops round St. Vedast's, at the end of Foster Lane, employed lorimers, painters, and joiners who lived around Cripplegate, and tried to prevent their selling to any one else.* The fishmongers, who had stalls in the authorized markets, insisted on the itinerant trader buying his stock through them and not on Fish Wharf.† In the same way the burillers acted as middlemen to the weavers, the skinners employed the tawyers, the cutlers gave out work to the sheathers and blademakers. And it is noteworthy that most of the

* See below, p. 86.   † See above, p. 40.

ordinances actually confirmed by the city down to the end of Edward II.'s reign were not for the regulation of a single craft, but for settling the relations between two or more crafts —sometimes fixing the prices at which one craft shall sell its work to the other.   Even when only a single craft is concerned the two classes are discernible within it, as in the ordinances granted to the brass potters in 1316, when four dealers and four founders are appointed to make a joint assay.*

Now, this appearance of a class of middlemen in a number of separate industries was due to an expansion of the market. London produced articles of luxury—the wares of the goldsmith, the skinner, the tailor, the girdler and the saddler, for sale in all the great fairs of the kingdom.   Hence the outcry of the chronicler against the ordinances granted by Fitz-Thomas to the crafts, that they would be " to the intolerable loss of all merchants coming to London and visiting the fairs of England."   If a body of traders connected with each of the leading industries of London were to be clothed with special privileges of search, the monopoly which such powers would enable them to exercise would seriously restrict the operations of the class of general merchants to which the foreign traders and many of the aldermen belonged.   Although the aldermen held a political monopoly which gave them great economic advantages, their commercial interest, at that time, lay in the maintenance of a free general trade.   But as has been already explained, there had been a great change in this situation between the first failure of the craft movement in 1265 and its first success in 1319.   At the later date practically all the aldermen belonged to one or other of the wealthier crafts or misteries, and had become interested in some specialized form of trade.   Of these trades some, like those of the mercer, the grocer, the vintner, and the woolmonger, were merely so many branches of the general import and export trade which had

* Riley, *Memorials*, p. 118.

been carried on by the Aldermen in the 13th century ; whilst
others, like those of the goldsmith, the skinner, the draper, the
tailor, the saddler, and the girdler, represented an increasing
investment of capital in the industries of London, or rather in
trading operations of a national scope based on those
industries.

The subsidy roll of 1319 contains ample evidence of this
change. The amount of taxation at which citizens were
assessed varies from 6¾d. to £5. Nearly thirty of them are
assessed at sums of £4 and upwards. In half of these cases
the trade of the taxpayer is ascertainable, and this wealthiest
class is found to consist of drapers, mercers, pepperers or grocers,
fishmongers, woolmongers, skinners, and goldsmiths. The class
next below this, containing about a hundred and thirty citizens
who paid £1 and upwards, consisted chiefly of members of
the same trades, along with a few vintners and girdlers and a
saddler. The poorer members of the mercantile crafts and
the wealthier members of the industrial crafts paid sums
varying from 6s. 8d. to 13s. 4d. ; the general body of shopkeeping craftsmen and retailers paid from 1s. to 5s. ; and the
craftsmen without a shop who worked for a middleman paid
6¾d., 8d., 10d.*

These figures sufficiently show how mistaken it would be
to suppose that the members of the various crafts or misteries
were upon anything like a footing of economic or social
equality. And it is clear that what has been described as the
victory of the crafts must not be interpreted as the capture of
the constitution by a class of wage-earning handicraftsmen.
It was in fact the victory, not of one class over another,
but of a new form of social and political organization over an
old one, and one of the main causes of the victory was that
the ruling class had gradually transferred itself from the old
form to the new one. The importance of the victory lay
in the fact that the new form contained much more room for

* Subsidy Roll for London, 1319, in Record Office.

social expansion than the old. It could be adapted to the several needs of all that widening range of classes which was growing up within the mediæval city, and it enabled each class in varying degree to share or to aim at sharing in the civic constitution. In this sense the fruits of victory were partly enjoyed even by the humbler craftsman who had played the part of a henchman in the fray; but the battle had been directed by the larger interests of the leading crafts.

Before the middle of the 14th century these had already begun to form themselves into that select group which afterwards became known as the Twelve Great Livery Companies, and from one of which it was customary to select the Lord Mayor. This distinction between greater and lesser crafts was common to many of the leading cities of Europe. In Paris the privileged *Corps de Metier* were only six in number; there were seven *Arti Maggiori* in Florence; and many German cities divided their *Zünfte* into two ranks in the same way. The old oligarchical spirit thus found a new form, but a form that was much wider and more flexible. In London, at least, there was no rigid line drawn between the greater and lesser companies. It was not till the middle of the 16th century that it was finally decided which were to be the Twelve, and the rule about the selection of the Lord Mayor has not been strictly adhered to. It was, moreover, a common practice for a citizen to get himself transferred from a lesser company to a greater if he seemed to be on the high-road to civic honours.*

The occasion of the first appearance of this select group of crafts was noteworthy in another respect. It marked a fresh stage in the process we have been tracing by which the crafts worked their way into the constitution of the city. By the charter of 1319 the crafts had been made the main—almost the exclusive—avenue to citizenship. In 1351 an attempt was made to give the leading crafts the power to elect the

* Unwin, *Industrial Organization in the 16th and 17th Centuries*, p. 74.

Common Council. The Court of Aldermen was still the body by which the regular work of civic administration was carried on, but on special occasions, when the assent of the Commonalty was deemed necessary, a Common Council was summoned through election in the wards. In 1351 a summons of this kind was issued to the thirteen chief misteries, in consequence of which the Grocers, Mercers, and Fishmongers each elected six members ; the Drapers, Goldsmiths, Woolmongers, Vintners, Skinners, Saddlers, Tailors, Cordwainers, and Butchers each four members; and the Ironmongers two members, to form a Common Council.* A similar summons was issued in the following year, but after that the election of the Common Council reverted to the wards for a quarter of a century. When, in 1376, the misteries once more assumed electoral functions, there were some fifty of them in a position to demand a share in the privilege. During the interval, the lesser crafts had been building up their fraternity organizations, modelled largely upon those of the select crafts that had already attained political influence. A clear understanding of the constitution of the thirteen misteries of 1351 will, therefore, supply the clue to the development of the rest.

In the first place, it will be noticed that of the thirteen misteries above mentioned, eight have been already referred to in a previous chapter as possessing fraternity organizations, some of which had been in existence since the end of the 12th century ; and it is extremely probable that the influence of the other five rested on a similar basis. In the extant records of the Mercers', the Goldsmiths', and the Grocers' fraternities, which take us back to the first half of the 14th century, we see them acting as powerful voluntary associations which had come into existence independently of the civic authorities, and which exercised control over their several trades largely at their own discretion. The Commons complained to Parliament in 1363 that merchants called

* Calendar of Letter Book, F, 237, 238.

Grocers engrossed all manner of vendible goods, " and those who have the merchandise raise the price suddenly by a covin (combination) called a fraternity and by counsel and assent keep the goods for sale till they are dearer." * And the poor commons of the mistery of Goldsmiths sought protection in 1377 from Parliament against the great and rich Goldsmiths of their Company, who compelled them to seal divers obligations to the effect that they would not sell to any mercer, cutler, jeweller, upholder, etc., any of their work except at treble the price, "and those who refuse are taken and imprisoned and in peril of death by grievous menace till they seal the bond as their poor companions have done before." †

Secondly, it is significant that we do not, as a rule, find these wealthy mercantile bodies coming, like the lesser crafts, before the Mayor and Aldermen with a petition that they may be constituted as authorized misteries by the grant of a full set of ordinances.   From the time when the records of the city, properly speaking, begin, in the reign of Edward I., they are constantly appearing before the Court of Aldermen as recognized bodies of traders, whose right to a certain amount of self-government is taken for granted.   Most frequently these entries are connected with the election by the several trades of brokers, who are to oversee the bargains made by their members with foreign merchants.   The city records at the end of the 13th century are full of the acknowledgments of debts owed by London merchants to foreigners.   It is quite clear that the mercantile crafts were at that time largely dependent on foreign capital and upon foreign shipping. The alien merchant had partners among the city magnates ; he supplied the city trader with goods on credit ; and he advanced the king ready money on the security of the taxes. He might be unpopular, but he was indispensable.   By the middle of Edward III.'s reign the situation had greatly changed.

* Rolls of Parliament, II. 277.   † *Ibid.*, III. 9.

The English capitalist was gradually replacing the foreigner. English grocers farmed the taxes. English mercers, drapers, and vintners traded overseas on their own account, and the fishmongers of London equipped vessels for the royal navy. The very class of aldermen who used to be hand-in-glove with the foreigner were now ready to foster the outcry against him for their own purposes ; and at their instigation a Genoese merchant was, in 1379, stabbed to the heart in front of his London lodging.

With this change is connected the third source of the power exercised by the greater crafts. Before the close of the 14th century, most of them came to hold charters from the king, conferring upon them special powers for the regulation of their several trades, not only in London, but in some cases throughout England. These charters were granted to the Goldsmiths, the Skinners, the Tailors, and the Girdlers in 1327, and to the Drapers, the Vintners, and the Fishmongers in 1363-4. The charter of the Goldsmiths states in its preamble that—

" it had been ordained that all who were of the Goldsmiths' trade were to sit in their shops in the high street of Cheap, and that no silver in plate, nor vessel of gold or silver ought to be sold in the city of London except at our Exchange or in Cheap, among the Goldsmiths, and that publicly, to the end that the persons of the said trade might inform themselves whether the seller came lawfully by such vessel or not. But that now of late merchants as well private as strangers, do bring from foreign lands into this land counterfeit sterling whereof the pound is not worth above sixteen shillings of the right sterling, and of this money none can know the true value but by melting it down. And also that many of the said trade of Goldsmiths keep shops in obscure turnings and bylanes of the streets, and do buy vessels of gold and silver secretly without enquiring if such vessel were stolen or lawfully come by, and immediately melting it down do make it into plate and sell it to merchants trading beyond the sea . . . and make false work of gold and silver . . . and that the cutlers in their workhouses cover tin with silver so subtly and with such sleight that the same cannot be discerned and severed from the tin."

And the king proceeds to enact, with the assent of the Lords Spiritual and Temporal and the Commons—

"That henceforth no merchant . . . shall bring into this land any sort of money but only plate of fine silver, . . . and that no gold or silver work wrought by Goldsmiths or any plate of silver be sold to the merchant to sell again and to be carried out of the kingdom ; but shall be sold at our Exchange or openly among the Goldsmiths for private use only, and that none that pretend to be of the same trade shall keep any shop but in Cheap, that it may be seen that their work is good and right. And that those of the said trade may by virtue of these presents elect honest lawful and sufficient men best skilled in trade to enquire of the matters aforesaid ; and that they so chosen may upon due consideration of the said craft reform what defects they shall find therein, and thereupon inflict due punishment upon the offenders and by the help and assistance of the Mayor and sheriffs if need be. And that in all trading cities and towns in England where goldsmiths reside the same ordinance be observed as in London and that one or two of every such city or town for the rest of that trade, shall come to London to be ascertained of their Touch of gold, and to receive the puncheon with the leopard's head to mark their work." *

Although the goldsmiths, owing to their connection with the coinage and the foreign exchanges, stood a little apart from other crafts, the leading features of the situation indicated in their charter were common to most of the greater companies : (1) Their leading members were rich merchants, their main body was composed of well-to-do shopkeepers, and they had a substratum of working craftsmen ; (2) they showed a tendency to extend their control over other crafts ; (3) the powers and the monopoly conferred on them were national in character ; (4) they brought to the regulation of London trade and industry an authority derived, not from the Mayor and

* Herbert, *Twelve Great Livery Companies*, II. 289.

Aldermen, but from King and Parliament. The first three of these points will be amplified in a later chapter, and it is the fourth that calls for special notice here.

By virtue of the royal grants, and of the powerful bond of private association which enabled them to secure and enforce those grants, the greater companies each exercised a kind of *imperium in imperio* within the city. They were never at any time mere branches of civic administration as the lesser crafts tended to be. As a rule no doubt they paid every deference to the authority of mayor and aldermen, as was natural enough when they themselves supplied the motive power that worked the constitution. The true nature of the situation was revealed when the companies quarrelled amongst themselves, or split into two factions on some vital issue. Each company then armed its retainers like the feudal magnates whose great houses had become their halls, and did battle in the streets of the city. London mediæval history is full of such conflicts. There was the struggle of the Goldsmiths and the Tailors in 1268 already described, and that of the Skinners and the Fishmongers in 1339; in each case attended with bloodshed and followed by executions.* The Pepperers and the Goldsmiths came to blows in 1378 over the Wycliffe question in St. Paul's Churchyard.† In 1440 the Tailors and the Drapers disputed over the election of Mayor in the Guildhall itself with such violence that some of the defeated party suffered long imprisonment. Most notable of all was the great conflict between the manufacturing and the victualling crafts, which lasted through the first ten years of Richard II.'s reign, the story of which will require a chapter to itself. And in both these two last cases the real cause of the struggle is clearly revealed. It lay in that exercise of special powers over trade with which one of the more powerful companies had been invested by the Crown, and which was disputed by one or more of the others. ‡

* Riley, *Memorials*, p. 210.　　　　　† *Ibid.*, p. 415.
‡ *Fabyan's Chronicle for* 1440.

CHAPTER VII

THE LESSER MISTERIES

THE greater companies cannot, therefore, be considered as the creatures of the civic constitution, since during the latter half of the 14th century they made the constitution the battle-ground of their special interests. And in this respect they set the tone to the lesser crafts. These might have to content themselves at the outset with accepting such ordinances as the Mayor and Aldermen would grant them, but the natural ambition of each was to become a livery company and then a chartered corporation, and in this a certain number of them were destined to succeed. The spirit of an institution, like that of an individual person, is to be measured much less by what it actually is than by what it is tending to become—by the often silent direction of its aims. And for this reason it was desirable to approach the study of the lesser crafts through some general understanding of the position of the greater crafts.

The best link between the two groups is afforded by several crafts that lay on the margin and belonged at different times to both. The Cordwainers, the Saddlers, and the Girdlers were among the earliest to receive charters of special privileges and grants of incorporation. The Saddlers and the Cordwainers were included in the thirteen misteries which sent members to the Common Council in 1351, but none of the three was ultimately included in the Twelve Great Companies. Each of them embraced from the first a mercantile element that tended to bring it on a level with the wealthier crafts, but the industrial element in them remained predominant, and they were displaced from their leading position by newer mercantile combinations like the Haberdashers and the Salters.

Both the Girdlers and the Cordwainers were among the crafts that received ordinances from Walter Hervey in 1271, and in these ordinances of the Cordwainers which have been preserved and are almost the earliest evidences of craft organization extant, we find all the leading features of that organization, which a century later had become common to all the handicrafts of London, already fully developed. There were two branches of the craft, the cordwainers proper (*alutarii*) and the workers in "bazen" (*basanarii*), and the worker in each was confined to his own branch, except that the cordwainer might use bazen for particular purposes. The cofferers who worked in cow-hide were forbidden to meddle with either branch, though both branches might work in cow-hide. An apprentice to either branch must be admitted before the Mayor and shown to be of good character; he must pay 2s. to the city, and 2s. to the poor-box of the craft, besides 40s. if a cordwainer, or 20s. if a worker in bazen, as a premium. A stranger who wished to enter the trade must pay the same fees. The premium was a high one, and only the sons of well-to-do parents who were going to be set up in business can have paid it. The majority of the workers in the trade must never have been regularly apprenticed at all, and therefore must never have qualified as masters. This indeed would follow from two other ordinances, one forbidding a master to have above eight servants and the other forbidding a servant to have apprentices under him, whilst a third, which forbids a master to give out work to servants in their homes, strengthens the supposition. It was from this body of servants without prospect of a regular mastership that a class of hawkers would naturally arise.

I

Hence we find that the selling of shoes in the streets is forbidden elsewhere than in the recognized shoe-market in Cheap between Cordwainer Street and Soper Lane (see map), as also the hawking of shoes in the country around London within twenty leagues. And in some additional ordinances as early as 1300 the serving men of the cordwainers are forbidden to form combinations or make agreements to the prejudice of their masters.

From the very first, then, the trading masters seem to have

A CORDWAINER'S SHOP

formed a separate class. Their interests were those of traders rather than those of craftsmen, and their policy was directed towards controlling the market. The outsider who imported shoes might do so if he sold his stock wholesale to them, but he must not sell to the public direct. As between full members, the craft cherished an ideal of equality. If any member managed to secure a stock of material from a foreign merchant, any other member might claim to share the bargain.*

We know, indeed, from the record of the Letter Books that

---

* Liber Horn, fo. cccxxxixb, Guildhall MS. 108, Vol. I. fo. 393.

groups of cordwainers were in the constant habit of sharing, by previous agreement, bargains with various Spanish merchants, and of thus getting credit by joint guarantee. The joint purchases of leather made by a dozen cordwainers, in varying groups of from two to seven, over a period of less than three years (1276–9), amounted to nearly £1000, or about £80 apiece.* So that each of the dozen was on the average accustomed to lay out an amount equivalent to three or four hundred pounds, in present values, on leather every year. In those days of small capital, therefore, he was a trader of very respectable standing, even though he had to combine with his fellows to obtain credit.

On the whole the ordinances of the Cordwainers leave us with a decided impression that they constituted an aristocracy in their profession, and were mainly concerned in keeping the ranks beneath them—the workers in bazen, the workers in cow-hide, and their own servants—each in its proper place. In this respect the Saddlers afford an interesting parallel. The Saddlers themselves possessed, as we have seen, a fraternity of very old standing, and it is the subordinate branches of their trade, the lorimers, the painters, and the fusters or joiners, whom we find first applying for ordinances to the Mayor. The ordinances of the Lorimers, which are earlier than those of any other craft, except the Cappers, having been procured in 1269, are tinged with a surviving element of feudalism.† They are granted by the Mayor and other Barons of London, and the Lorimers are to do annual service for them by presenting an "honourable and seemly bridle and bit" every Easter. No apprentice is to be taken for less than ten years, or with less than 30s. premium. No stranger is to keep house or forge until he has given half a mark to the Commune of London and 2s. to the alms-box of the mistery for the benefit of members who fall into poverty, and has put himself in frank-pledge

---

* Letter Book, A, *passim.*   † Liber Cust., I. 78.

and sworn to obey the ordinances. In 1283 the Painters, whose chief occupation was painting saddle-bows, obtained a similar grant of ordinances,* and the Joiners who made the saddle-bows were recognized as an independent craft in 1307.† The Saddlers had been obliged to acquiesce in the formation of these independent organizations, and to content themselves with getting provisions inserted to prevent the crafts working for "false saddlers," i.e. non-members of their gild. In 1320 they took advantage of a period of revolution to persuade Hamo de Chigwell to burn the Lorimers' ordinances publicly in Cheap.‡ But no sooner had Chigwell's long mayoralty come to its disastrous end than we find the joiners, the painters, and the lorimers in iron and copper up in arms against the saddlers. At the moment when one king had just been deposed and his boy successor was not yet safely seated on the throne, London was startled by the outbreak of a fierce conflict in Cheapside and Wood Street in which several were slain and many wounded. The allied crafts declared that the battle had been begun by the saddlers, who wanted to compel the craftsmen to deal exclusively with themselves, who already owed the various members of the four crafts nearly three hundred pounds, and who insulted and maltreated those who dared to ask for their money. The saddlers on their part complained that the allied crafts had come to a joint agreement to stop work simultaneously if any member of one of them had a dispute with the saddlers, that the lorimers had made an ordinance out of their own heads not to receive any outside workmen until he had taken an oath to conceal their misdeeds, and that the painters and joiners set every point of their trade at a fixed price by reason whereof they were making themselves kings of the land. The allies replied that they had a perfect right to swear in new-comers to their ordinances. They were freemen of the

---

* Liber Horn, fo. 341b.   † Liber Cust., I. 80.
‡ Liber Cust., Introduction, lix.

city, householders, and taxpayers, and their crafts had been recognized by the Mayor and Aldermen. They claim, in short, to be as "equals and commoners" * on the same footing as the saddlers, although in order to be a match for them the four crafts have to act in combination.

The tendency to fall into groups like those already examined was common to all the industrial crafts. The clothing crafts—the weavers, dyers, fullers, and shearmen—which came to be headed by the drapers, made one such group; the skinners, whittawyers, and curriers, another; the leathersellers, glovers, pursers, and pouchmakers, a third; the cutlers, bladesmiths, and sheathers, a fourth. And in all su·h groups one or more of the crafts tended to assume the position of employers and middlemen to the others. Yet it would be a great mistake to conceive of the member of the poorer craft as bearing the same kind of relation to the member of the wealthier craft as the modern wage-earner bears to the modern employer. The full members of the smaller crafts were generally shopkeepers and small capitalists. The joiner bought his own wood, the painter his colours, the lorimer his metal. They dealt in goods and not in labour, and they gave credit. Their privileges were the same in kind, and as strictly guarded as those of the greater crafts, and only a select number of their workmen could enter by the strait gate of apprenticeship.

It is the spread of the craft or mistery type of organization amongst the small traders of this class that supplies the key to the social and political development of the city in the 14th century. With the few exceptions that have been already indicated the movement did not begin till the accession of Edward III. A list drawn up in 1328 of twenty-five misteries authorized to elect officers for their own "government and instruction" consists almost entirely of the mercantile crafts, and of the wealthy manufacturing crafts which had obtained royal charters or were shortly to do so. Only about half a

* Riley, *Memorials*, pp. 156–162.

dozen lesser crafts are included ; *i.e.* the Cutlers, Cofferers, Beaders, Hosiers, Fusters, and Painters.* By the end of Edward III.'s reign at least thirty-five other crafts had obtained ordinances and become recognized as separate misteries. To the leather crafts were added the Pursers (1327), the Pouchmakers (1339), the Whittawyers (1344), the Glovers (1349), and the Leathersellers (1372) ; to the metalworkers the Armourers (1322), the Spurriers (1344), the Pewterers (1348), the Pinners and Cardmakers (1356), the Plumbers (1365), the Blacksmiths (1372), the Sheathers (1375), and in 1389 the Founders; to the textile crafts the Tapicers (1331), the Shearmen (1350), the Flemish weavers (1366), and the Fullers (1376) ; and besides these there were the Hatters (1347), the Furbishers (1350), and the Upholders (1360), the Surgeons (1353), and the Farriers (1356), the Waxchandlers (1358), the Taverners (1370), and the Cooks (1379), the Braelers (1355), the Verrers (1364), the Bowyers and the Fletchers (1371), the Scriveners (1373), and a little later the Horners (1391), and the Coopers (1396).† In 1377 fifty-one misteries took part in the election of a Common Council. That election represents the highest political achievement of the lesser crafts, but their numbers continued to increase. In the earliest volume of the Brewers' records there is inserted under the date of 1422 a list of all the crafts (*artium*) then exercised in London to the number of one hundred and eleven. And as the Brewers used the list as a guide for the letting of their hall, it is likely that all these crafts possessed some form of organization, though not all had received the self-governing powers of a mistery from the city.

It remains to consider very briefly in what these powers of self-government consisted. As a rule the ordinances were drafted by the men of the trade themselves, who presented

* Calendar of Letter Book, E, pp. 232–234.

† Riley, *Memorials, passim ;* and Calendar of Letter Book, G, pp. 187–188 (Verrers = Glassmakers).

them for approval, with the request that they might be permitted to elect overseers or wardens who should be sworn to see the ordinances enforced. The number so elected was sometimes as many as twelve and sometimes only two, but more often six or four. Apart from technical articles directed against special abuses or intended to subserve special interests in particular trades, the ordinances of nearly all the crafts conform to a common type which may be represented by a brief *résumé* of the Hatters' ordinances in 1348. (1) Six lawful men to be sworn to rule the trade. (2) None but freemen to make or sell hats. (3) None to be apprenticed for less than seven years. (4) None to take apprentices but freemen. (5) Wardens to search as often as need be with power to take defective hats before Mayor and Aldermen. (5) No night work. (6) None of trade to be made free of city or to be allowed to work if not attested by wardens. (7) None to receive another's apprentices or servant if not properly dismissed, or (8) who is in debt to previous master. (9) No stranger to sell hats by retail, but only wholesale and to freemen.* The amount of control over their own trade which the grant of such ordinances conferred upon the members of a craft was clearly very great. Though they were not directly constituted as a court for the settlement of their trade disputes, as in the case of the weavers and fishmongers, the Mayor, when appeal was made to him by the men of a trade, generally called together a jury of the craft to settle the question. The growth of this autonomy of the craft may be observed by comparing the Cutlers' ordinances of 1344 with those of 1380. In the former a provision was made that all those who did not wish to be judged by the wardens were to present their names to the Mayor and Aldermen in order to be judged by them, whilst the later ordinances state emphatically that no one shall be permitted to follow the trade if he will not stand by the rule of the overseers.†

* Riley, *Memorials*, p. 239.   † *Ibid.*, pp. 217, 438.

There were three ways in which a craft could turn its powers of self-government to economic account, (1) by controlling the import and export of wares, (2) by limiting its own numbers, and (3) by a secret agreement about prices. The power to seize defective goods could easily be turned into a weapon against the foreign competitor.[*] Defective foreign caps, gloves, and pouches were solemnly consigned to the flames in Cheap opposite the end of Soper Lane. The carcases of two bullocks said to have died of disease were burnt under the nose of the pilloried foreign butcher (a native of West Ham) in the Stocks Market.[†] If the foreigner attempted to sell by retail his goods could be seized without any pretence of their being defective. In 1298 before there is any record of ordinances granted to them, the cutlers seized a hundred and a half of knives belonging to Hugh of Limerick as being foreign knives.[‡] In 1341 the mercers were empowered to seize the silk kerchiefs, the Aylsham thread, the linen cloth exposed for sale by the men of Norfolk.[§] And the articles granted to a craft often included one to the effect that any wares of that trade must be sold wholesale to freemen, *i.e.* to themselves. An ordinance is also sometimes found giving a craft control of the export trade—as that of the Pewterers in 1348 that " no one shall make privily vessels of lead or of false alloy for sending out of the city to fairs, etc., but let the things be shown that be so sent to the wardens before they go out," [‖] and a similar ordinance of the Cutlers in 1380.[¶] The object of this oversight was to prevent the growing class of small masters who had no outlet for sale in the city from producing for outside markets through the agency of middlemen who were not of the craft.

The limitation in the number of full freemen in their trade who alone had the legal right to produce wares on their own

---

[*] Riley, *Memorials*, pp. 249, 529.   [†] Calendar of Letter Book, E, p. 110.
[‡] Riley, 39.   § Plea and Memoranda Rolls, A3, m22.
[‖] Riley, p. 243.   [¶] Riley, p. 441.

account or to sell them by retail was effected by restricting the number of apprentices, and by subsequently placing difficulties in the way of an apprentice attaining his freedom. It has sometimes been assumed that all journeymen or servingmen had passed through the stage of apprenticeship, but the language of the ordinances, carefully interpreted, seems to imply the recognition of a class of workmen who had not been apprenticed. Evidence of this has already been noticed in the case of the Cordwainers as early as 1270. The Cutlers' ordinances of 1380 provide that "no journeyman who is not free, or who has not been apprenticed in the trade . . . or otherwise served seven years in the city in such trade shall be admitted to work . . . if he have not first been tried by the overseers . . . to ascertain how much he is deserving to take." * And the Bladesmiths' ordinances of 1408 provide that no one shall teach his journeyman the secrets of his trade as he would his apprentice.†

But apprenticeship, even when faithfully served, did not always lead to the enjoyment of the freedom of the city. Masters often took apprentices without legally registering them, and when they came out of their time, neglected to present them for the freedom. The apprentice on completing his term seems often to have been in debt to his master, and it was provided by the Heaumers' ordinances in 1347 that in such cases the apprentice shall thenceforth serve no other person than his master till he has given satisfaction for the debt.‡ In 1364 the Commons petitioned the Mayor and Aldermen that Gild-days might be held once a month at which persons might be admitted to the freedom after serving in the same mistery for at least seven years, and on payment of 60s. or more at the discretion of those present. "For it were better that those unable to pay this sum should continue to serve others either as apprentices or hired servants than

* Riley, *Memorials*, p. 440.   † *Ibid.*, p. 566.
‡ *Ibid.*, p. 236.

that the number of masters should be unduly increased." *
Subsequently it became usual in most companies to interpose
a period of three years between the completion of apprenticeship and full mastership, and to require the aspirant to prove
that his means were sufficient to enable him to set up for himself.   In many cases the making of an expensive masterpiece
was required.†

The third use which a craft might make of its powers was
an indirect and illegal one.   The members of the craft had no
right to fix the prices of their wares by mutual agreement, and
the wardens could not openly countenance such action.   But
if the trade in some other organized capacity contrived to
effect such an agreement, the powers conferred on the craft
could, by the collusion of the wardens, be easily used in
support of it.   And as we have seen, it was of the very essence
of a powerful craft that another organization, the fraternity,
lay behind it and was available for any form of common action
that could not be openly avowed.   The part played by the
Goldsmiths' and Grocers' fraternities in fixing prices has been
already referred to ; and a most interesting parallel is forthcoming in one of the minor crafts.   In 1344 a purser lodged
a complaint before the Husting against a number of his fellow-
craftsmen, alleging that they had bound him by oath not to
sell his wares below a certain price, and that when he broke
his oath they summoned him before a Court Christian in the
church of St. Benet Fink as a perjurer.‡   The oath was
condemned as illegal, and there can be little doubt that it
had been administered in a fraternity.   It is to the fraternity,
not merely as supplying the force for the operation of craft
machinery but as an independent institution which filled a
large place in the social life of the 14th and 15th centuries
that we must now turn.

* Calendar of Letter Book, G, p. 179 ; cf. p. 211.
† Unwin, *Industrial Organization in 16th and 17th Centuries*, pp. 48, 56.
‡ Plea and Memoranda Rolls, Guildhall, A4, m7 (Dr. Sharpe's MS.
Calendar).

CHAPTER VIII

THE FRATERNITIES OF CRAFTS

I N dealing with the craft we have very largely taken the fraternity for granted, for reasons already explained. The only conceivable cause of the revolution effected by the crafts was the growth of private associations, and for such a growth the fraternity under the protection of the Church was the only practicable form in the Middle Ages. Moreover, we know that the fraternity had been adapted to various social and political purposes from the 10th century onwards.

On the other hand, it must be confessed that, with the exception of the valuable glimpses afforded by the rules of the Anglo-Saxon gilds, we know very little about the inner life of the fraternity before the middle of the 14th century, and that before that date the crafts appear in the records almost entirely on their secular side. So much indeed is this the case that it has been held by eminent authorities that the earliest trade associations were entirely secular in character, and there is no positive proof that this view is not correct. The early records that tell us of the Weavers' and Bakers' gilds, and of the Fishmongers' Halimot, do not speak of any religious side to those organizations, but there is no reason why they should do so, as they are concerned with the public financial obligations of the craftsmen, and not with their private arrangements. It is quite possible, of course, that a collective interest might spring up under the pressure of

common regulation and common burdens without the aid
of a religious motive.   But it is difficult to think of such an
interest finding a steady expression, or developing sufficient
public spirit for persistent common action, without all those
aids and sanctions to abiding fellowship which the Church
alone could supply.

This line of reasoning derives additional support from the
account which a recently published Patent Roll gives of the
Weavers' gild of Lincoln, which, like that of London, received
a charter from Henry II.   At the time of the immigration
of Flemish weavers in Edward III.'s reign, the original
weavers' gild had fallen into decay, and the farm had not
been paid since 1321, but it was recorded that in the time
of Henry II. there had been more than two hundred wealthy
and influential members, and that no one could exercise the
craft within twelve miles of the city unless he belonged to
the Gild of the Weavers of Lincoln, *which was constituted
in the name of the Holy Cross.**   As nearly all the craft gilds
of which we have any record in England before the 13th
century were weavers' gilds, constituted, as far as our knowledge goes, on the same lines as the weavers of Lincoln, there
is good reason for inferring the existence of a fraternity in
the other cases.

As to the fishmongers, they were the most orthodox of
trades.   The monastic chroniclers are strong partisans of their
cause.   Their Mayor, Hamo de Chigwell, was discovered, at
a moment of extreme peril, to be in orders, and was taken
under the protection of the bishop ; and a long series of early
wills show them to have been the most munificent donors to
religious objects of all the citizens of London.   Half a dozen
riverside churches were endowed and rebuilt by their bequests
for the maintenance of chantries, and the difficulty at a later
date is to decide, not whether they had a fraternity, but
which of several fraternities was most identified with the

* Calendar of Patent Rolls, 1348, p. 120.

mistery. Moreover, the fishmongers took a leading part at an early date in the production of pageants—one of the especial functions of the fraternity.

"In 1293," says Stow, "for victory obtained by Edward I. against the Scots, every citizen, according to their several trade, made their several show, but especially the Fishmongers which in a solemn procession passed through the city, having, amongst other pageants and shows, four sturgeons gilt, carried on four horses; then four salmons of silver on four horses, and after them six and forty armed knights riding on horses made like luces of the sea; and then one representing St. Magnus, because it was upon St. Magnus' day." *

St. Magnus' was at that time the central church of the fishmongers, and later on we shall find one of their fraternities there.

In the case of the other early organizations of traders or craftsmen in London we hear of the fraternity aspect first. Leaving the adulterine gilds aside, there is the Saddlers' fraternity, whose religious compact with St. Martin's-le-Grand has been already given; the Goldsmiths' fraternity of St. Dunstan, to whose wardens a bequest was made in 1272 for the maintenance of a chantry; † the Tailors' fraternity of St. John the Baptist, which, according to Stow (who was a member of it), received royal confirmation as early as 1300, and chose a certain Henry de Ryall to go on a vicarious pilgrimage for all its members in the same year; ‡ and the fraternity of the Mercery, which is mentioned in deeds of the 13th century. The Grocers' fraternity of St. Anthony, and the Drapers' fraternity of St. Mary of Bethlehem, were in existence before those companies received their charters, and there is a strong presumption that the same is true of the Skinners' fraternity of Corpus Christi. As far as the

---

* Stow, *Survey*, edit. H. Morley, p. 121.
† Sharpe, *Calendar of Wills*, I. 14.
‡ Stow, *Survey*, p. 193.

greater crafts go, then, there is little reason to doubt that the privileges they procured from the king, and the influence they acquired in the city, were due to the strength of fraternity organizations acting in their names.

But what of the lesser crafts which made their first appearance at the time of FitzThomas and Hervey? We have only one piece of evidence, but it recurs with cumulative force in the three sets of ordinances which have been preserved from that period. The apprentice to a cordwainer, it will be remembered, had to pay 2s. to the poor of the craft who had no means of livelihood.* The stranger who entered the lorimers' craft must pay 2s. to the alms-box, which was to be collected by the wardens of the mistery "for the relief of the good men of the mistery who were impoverished." † Now, an alms-box was so much the central feature of the fraternity that money left to the Goldsmiths' fraternity was often said to be bequeathed to the "Alms of St. Dunstan." But in the case of the Painters' ordinances we are left in no further doubt. The new-comer is to give to the *confrarie* of the mistery 2s. to support the poor of the mistery. Offences are punished by a fine of half a mark to the city and 2s. to the *confrarie;* "and every one who keeps house by himself is to give each year to the *confrarie* 8d. in four quarterly payments, each serving man who takes 18s. or more a year is to give 4d., and each worker by the piece 4d., to be collected by the wardens of the mistery, and spent by them and the other good men of the mistery in whatever way they deem best for the honour of God and of the mistery." ‡ We are therefore safe in concluding that the Painters' fraternity of St. Luke, held in St. Giles', Cripplegate, the later ordinances of which have been preserved,§ already existed in 1283 ; that it procured the grant of the craft ordinances, and that it supplied the means of maintaining the struggle with the Saddlers in

* Liber Horn, fo. 339b.　† Liber Custumarum, I. 79.
‡ Liber Horn, fo. 341b.　§ Add. MSS. in British Museum, 15664, fo. 106.

1327. But as the lorimers and joiners took an equal part in that struggle, and as each of them had secured craft ordinances in face of strong opposition from the Saddlers' gild, it is a natural inference that they too were backed by fraternity organizations.

The later ordinances granted to the crafts by the Mayor and Aldermen in the reign of Edward III. generally make no mention of the fraternity aspect of the crafts. When they do so it is for a special reason. Thus the Braelars' ordinances in 1355,[*] and the Verrers' ordinances in 1364,[†] both contain the provision that if a servant who has behaved himself well should fall into illness or poverty, the mistery will maintain him ; but this is inserted as a set-off against the next clause, that a servant who behaves ill shall be punished by the Mayor. The Whittawyers' is the only craft that we find bringing a full set of fraternity ordinances to be sanctioned by the Mayor and Aldermen, and the reason for their doing so probably was that they were pieceworkers to the Skinners, and that unless they got authorization for their fraternity, it would be liable to denunciation as an unlawful combination. [‡]

It is not always sufficiently realized that the Fraternity was essentially a secret association, which had every reason for withdrawing its existence and its regulations as much as possible from public notice. Even after they attained a fully authorized position as livery companies, the trade fraternities were extremely jealous of the secrecy of their proceedings. Of the unchartered fraternities we should have known practically nothing if it had not been for the chance preservation of the fragmentary results of a Government inquiry provoked by their revolutionary activity, and though the returns then made give a most valuable picture of the formal aspect of the fraternities, they show us nothing of

---

[*] Riley, *Memorials*, p. 277.
[†] Calendar of Letter Book, G, p. 188.
[‡] Riley, *Memorials*, p. 232.

the constructive or destructive part those organizations were playing in the social and political development of the time. Yet there can be no manner of doubt that society in the 14th and 15th centuries was literally honeycombed with fraternities in every direction. Kings and princes, barons and knights, cathedral canons, rectors of churches, curates, parish clerks, lawyers, wealthy merchants, comfortable shop-keepers, poor journeymen, peasants, and football players were bound together for the pursuit of their special class interests under similar social and religious forms and sanctions. That of this great mass of social activity we should know so little is simply due to the secretive nature of the facts. When, therefore, at the beginning of the 14th century, the records emerge for our study, we must not assume that they represent an entirely new social development. The fraternity was far from being a new thing. Nearly every feature of it was centuries old. What was new was the almost universal pre-valence of the institution, and the desire in some cases to keep a regular record of it.

On the very threshold of the 14th century we meet with one of the fullest and most interesting sets of fraternity ordinances in existence—those of the *Feste du Pui*. The form of fellowship that bore this name seems to have originated in Puy in Auvergne, and to have spread through France and Flanders in cities to which merchants resorted. Its objects were convivial and musical, and its membership tended to have an international character. The *Feste du Pui* belongs to that period of London history when the city's import and export trade was largely in the hands of foreigners, and when many of the ruling class were of foreign extraction, so that the mayor of Bordeaux in 1275 could become mayor of London in 1280. And this same mayor, Henry le Waleys, was a member and benefactor of the *Feste du Pui*, which was founded to the " honour of God, of Madame Saint Mary and all Saints of both sexes, and to the honour of

THE RESIDENCE OF THE CONSULS OF THE GILD OF INNKEEPERS AT FLORENCE

THE SHIELDS BEAR THE ARMS OF (1) FLORENCE, (2) THE PEOPLE, (3) THE ' PARTE GUELFA '
(4) THE GILD

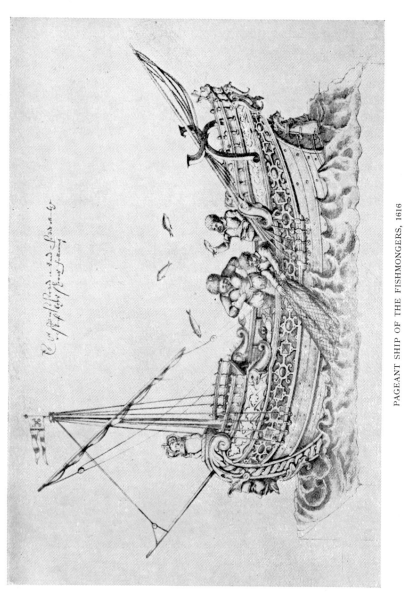

PAGEANT SHIP OF THE FISHMONGERS, 1616

our Lord the King and of all the Barons of the Land, for the safeguarding of loyal friendship and to the end that the City of London may be renowned for all good things in all places, and that good fellowship, peace, honour, gentleness, cheerful mirth and kindly affection may be duly maintained." The special feature of the fraternity was its yearly feast, when a prince and twelve companions were elected, and a crown was awarded to the best song, a copy of which was to be attached to the blazon of the new prince's arms in the hall. The body of the hall was to be simply decorated with leaves and rushes, and upon the seat of the singers alone was cloth of gold to be bestowed. The old prince accompanied by his companions was to march through the hall singing and bearing on his head the crown, and in his hands a gilded cup of wine, which he was to bestow upon the new prince in sign of their choice. No gluttony was to be tolerated at the feast. Each com- panion was to be served with " good bread, good ale, good wine, and then with potage, and one course of solid meat, and after that with double roast in a dish, and cheese, and no more." After this simple repast the members were to mount their horses and ride through the city, the poet laureate for the year riding between the old prince and the new, and having escorted the new prince to his own house, they were to dismount and have a dance by way of hearty good-bye, after which they were to take one drink and depart each to his own house on foot. Ladies were excluded from the feast in order that the companions " might learn to honour, cherish and commend all ladies as much in their absence as in their presence." *

If this were all we knew of the *Feste du Pui* we might have felt some scruples at attributing to so light-hearted a company all the more serious elements of the fraternity organization, merely because they were known as a *confrarie*. And it is a striking proof of the fixity which the conception of

* Liber Custumarum, I. 216-228.

J

the fraternity had attained, that we should find every feature of the religious and social gild represented in the ordinances of the Feste: the yearly mass in St. Helen's Priory, the maintenance of a light in St. Martin-le-Grand, the common box with several keys, the provision for poor members, the payment of a special chaplain to sing masses for the souls of members deceased, and finally, when funds were forthcoming, the building of a chapel for this purpose, the Guildhall Chapel of St. Mary.

On this side, the *Feste du Pui* belonged to the same category as the "Secret Confederation of London Rectors," which existed about the same time. But the ordinances drawn up by the Rectors between 1306 and 1317 exhibit a zealous pursuit of their professional interests which is entirely wanting in the Feste ordinances, and which gives them a very close similarity to the ordinances of a Craft. As, however, the Rectors' gild was of a purely voluntary character, it is to be compared rather with the trade fraternities in their earlier form, than with the misteries which had become in part the organs of public authority. Its main objects were to protect the interests of its members as beneficed clergy against the dishonesty or negligence of their curates (who also possessed a gild), against the greed of apparitors, the injustice of Archdeacons, the encroachments of the Friars, and the evil effects of slanderous charges and of their own internal dissensions. In 1317 the confederates numbered twenty-two. Their four wardens (*conservatores*) for that year were Thomas of St. Nicholas Cold Abbey, Nicholas of Grasschurch, John of St. Nicholas Olave, and John of St. Martin's Vintry ; their two chamberlains were John of Mokewell (St. Olave, Silver Street) and Nicholas of St. Margaret Pattens ; their treasurer, John of St. Bartholomew the Less, and their Referendarius, John of St. Edmund Grasschurch.*

* The rectors of St. John Zachary, St. Magnus', St. Mary Somerset, St. Bride's, All Hallows-the-Less, St. Peter Wood Street, St. Margaret Moses', St.

Like most other fraternities they had four ordinary meetings a year. On Thursday before Christmas they met at St. Bartholomew-the-Less ; on Thursday before Palm Sunday at St. Olave, Silver Street ; on the Thursday before St. John's Day at St. Margaret Pattens ; and on Thursday before Michaelmas at St. Andrew, Cornhill. Their proceedings were strictly private. Any member who revealed their secrets was liable to be expelled and to be held as a perjurer, since he had broken the solemn oath administered to him on entering. The gild had a common box, with various keys, to which each member contributed a penny a week, and from which the wardens assisted poor members at their discretion, but what was left over each year was divided among the members. There was the usual provision for attendance at the funeral and for supplying lights, and each rector was to say thirty masses for the deceased member. On the festival of the Saint to which each member's church was dedicated, all the other members were to attend that church, unless their own festival were on the same day, and each was to make an offering of not less than a penny. No chaplain or parish clerk who had left one of the members on bad terms was to be installed by one of the others, and the oath tendered to a chaplain on taking service bound him under conditions as strict as those laid upon a journeyman in a craft. In a typical case of the year 1304, the chaplain was to have 20s. a year and whatever legacies he could get out of the parishioners, but he was not to keep back any of the oblations or wax-money. His hours of attendance were carefully defined. If he happened to be out of the parish when curfew sounded, he must hasten back with all speed and sleep there at night. He must not stir up strife against the rector, and must report all he saw or heard that might turn to his rector's disadvantage. It is in the

Michael's Cornhill, St. Alban's Wood Street, All Hallows' Honey Lane, St. George's (Eastcheap ?), St. James' (Garlickhithe ?), St. Andrew's Cornhill, and St. Michael's Queenhithe, were the ordinary members.

dictation of these conditions to their chaplains that the rectors approached most nearly to the position of the authorized craft. We find them in 1309 petitioning the " Official " or Archdeacon for authority to impose such conditions by oath, just as we find the crafts asking the Mayor for authority to coerce their journeymen. The Confederation of Rectors remained, however, essentially a voluntary fraternity, and before we leave it, two important features should be noticed, which are found recurring in the ordinances of nearly all subsequent fraternities. The members were not to go to law with each other, but to submit all disputes to the wardens. And upon all solemn occasions of meeting they were to be habited in a seemly dress—an overgarment of white fur and a black undergarment—that they might be distinguished from non-members, as the sheep from the goats.*

The list of rectors is dated 1317, and it is in 1319 that we find the chronicler recording that " at this time many of the people of the trades of London were arrayed in livery and a good time was about to begin." Probably only the rich mercantile crafts are here referred to ; since in 1312, when in celebration of the birth of Edward III., the Mayor was richly costumed and the Aldermen arrayed in like suits of robes, we hear only of the Drapers, Mercers, Vintners, and Fishmongers as being also in costume. It had long been the custom for the wealthier citizens to wear a special costume on great occasions. In 1236, when they rode out to meet Henry III. and Queen Eleanor, they were clothed in " long garments embroidered about with gold, and silk in divers colours, their horses finely trapped, to the number of three hundred and sixty." In 1300, when Margaret, the child-wife of Edward I., was brought to London, six hundred citizens are said to have ridden " in one livery of red and white, with the cognisances of their misteries embroidered upon their sleeves." †

* MS. in Cambridge University Library, gg. 432, fo. 108 *et seq.*
† Stow, *Survey*, edit. H. Morley, p. 444. These numbers are probably

Only the ruling class can have afforded to make this display, and a change from a general livery to special costumes was an outward symbol of that specialization of trade organization already referred to. That such special liveries indicated the existence of as many fraternities there can be little doubt. In all subsequent cases of trade wearing distinctive liveries, the other characteristics of the fraternity—the yearly mass, the friendly benefits, etc.—are likewise found. Sometimes, indeed, the word "mistery" is used so as to include the fraternity element, but this implies that the fraternity has come to be identified with the trade. This was the case with the Mercers, whose records begin in 1344, though their fraternity was, as we have seen, much older. In 1347 an assembly of all the good people of the Mercery of London made a set of ordinances "for the cherishing of unity and good love among them, and for the common profit of the mistery, among which is one to the effect that all those of the said mistery shall be clothed of one suit once a year at the feast of Easter . . . and that no charge be put upon the said clothing beyond the first cost, *except only for the priest* and the common servant." The mention of the priest confirms the identity of the mistery with that Fraternity of the Mercery which we know to have been long in existence.

A clearer case of a fraternity absorbing a mistery is that of the Grocers' Company. Within a year of the Mercers' ordinances, twenty-two pepperers of Soper Lane determined to found a fraternity in honour of St. Antonin, and the Grocers' records open with an account of their procedure.

"Mem. That all the brethren of the fraternity dined the first time together at the house of the Abbot of Bury on the 12th June, 1345, at which dinner each paid 12 pence, and the whole was expended and 23 pence besides by the Warden. At which dinner

exaggerated, as the whole of the tax-paying householders at this time numbered less than a thousand.

* *London and Middlesex Arch. Trans.*, **IV.** p. 119.

we had a surcoat to be of one livery, for which each paid his
proportion. The same day after dinner ended, it was decreed by
common consent to take and hire a priest at the Nativity of St. John
next, to come to chant and pray for the members of the said
company and for all Christians, and to maintain the said priest each
one of the fraternity consented to give a penny a week, which
amounts to 4s. 4d. to pay now for the year.

"Mem. The priest commenced to sing July 3rd, and to receive
each week 15d. It was agreed that none should be of the fraternity
if he were not of good condition and of their mistery, that is to say
a pepperer of Soper Lane, or a canvasser of the Ropery, or a spicer
of Cheap, or other man of their mistery wherever he might dwell." *

A new member was to pay at least 13s. 4d., and with
loyal heart, in token of his obedience, to greet all those who
were already members with a kiss.

As might be anticipated from this opening the first
ordinances are entirely those of a fraternity. There is not
a single article, except perhaps that relating to the entrance
fees of apprentices, to which a parallel cannot be found in
the ordinances of fraternities that had no connection with
trade ; although in the provision for the relief of poor
members special mention is made (as also in the Mercers'
ordinances) of those who have become bankrupt, "by hazard
of the sea or by hazard of dear merchandise." The cost of
the annual dinner was to be 2s. 6d. per head (in the Mercers'
case it was 2s.), and after dinner the retiring wardens signified
their choice of successors in the manner of the *Feste du Pui*,
by placing garlands on their heads. The members were
exhorted to remember the fraternity in their wills, and in
1350 William de Grantham bequeathed £5 in maintenance
and aid of the fraternity on condition that they kept his
obit. Previous to this, in 1346, Lawrence de Halywell gave
them a chalice with pater of silver weighing 12 ozs., and a
vestment, amice, alb, stole, and chasuble, together with the

* Kingdon, *Facsimile and Transcript of Grocers' Records*, I. p. 8.

corporal and a small missal, on condition of their placing his father on their register to have his soul in the prayers of those who shall be maintained or assisted by the fraternity.

At first the fraternity was recognized as a distinctly private association within the mistery. In 1348 it was found that some members of the mistery who did not belong to the fraternity had been receiving its livery, and this was forbidden for the future.* But as the fraternity increased in numbers its membership came to be identified with that of the mistery of Grocers. In 1373 the members numbered 124. In 1376 new ordinances, " for enhancing the honour of God and of Holy Church and increasing works of charity," were issued in the name of the Grocers of London, and the members were called the " companions of the mistery."† In 1386 it was ordained by the masters and companions that every man who keeps a shop of spicery shall be under the government of the masters, whether he wear the livery or not.‡ But by this time the power of the Grocers extended far beyond the limits of their own trade. In 1376 and 1377 they elected six members to the Common Council. In 1384 nine aldermen out of the twenty-six were Grocers. Nicholas Brembre, who ruled the city with despotic power from 1384 to 1386, being at the same time one of the king's chief advisers and financiers, was a Grocer. Yet at this time, and for long after, the Grocers possessed no charter from the king, nor had their power been called into existence by civic authority. It had arisen out of the expansion of a voluntary association, the Fraternity of St. Anthony.

The same is true of the Skinners. They had, it is true, acquired a royal charter in 1327, and had both before and after that date regulated their trade as a mistery by the grant of ordinances from the city. But when these powers and privileges come to be consolidated by incorporation in

---

* Kingdon, *Facsimile and Transcript of Grocers' Records*, p. 17.
† *Ibid.*, p. 18.   ‡ *Ibid.*, p. 66.

1393, the social personality round which they are centred is the fraternity or gild in honour of Corpus Christi; whose procession, says Stow, passed once a year "through the principal streets of the city, wherein was borne more than one hundred torches of wax, costly garnished, burning light, and above two hundred clerks and priests, in surplices and copes, singing. After the which were the sheriffs' servants, the clerks of the Compters, chaplains for the sheriffs, the mayor's serjeants, the council of the city, the mayor and aldermen in scarlet, and then the Skinners in their best liveries." Stow likewise tells us that the Skinners' fraternity was formed out of two brotherhoods of Corpus Christi, one at St. Mary Spital and the other at St. Mary Bethlem; * and possibly these may have represented the two localities in which the Skinners were chiefly found, *i.e.* the region of St. Mary Axe, which was once called St. Mary Pellipers after them, and the neighbourhood of Wallbrook and Budge Row.

There were several fraternities specially connected with the Drapers in the 14th century. It seems likely that the drapers' craft grew out of that of the "bureller," or cloth-worker. In 1345 a certain John de Aylesham made a bequest to the Fraternity of Burellers of Candlewick Street, along with a similar bequest to the Fraternity of Tailors.† In 1356 two burellers made bequests to the Fraternity of the Blessed Virgin Mary of St. Mary Abchurch, and as that church was in Candlewick Street, this would appear to have been the Burellers' gild.‡ From about this time onwards we hear no more of the burellers' craft, but in 1361 a draper mentions the Fraternity of Candlewick Street in his will.§ There was also a fraternity of drapers in St. Mary Bow, to which the famous John of Northampton made a bequest in 1397.‖ But the gild out of which the Drapers' Company

---

* Stow, *Survey*, edit. H. Morley, p. 232.
† Sharpe, *Calendar of Wills*, I. 483.   ‡ *Ibid.*, I. 693.
§ *Ibid.*, II. 30.   ‖ *Ibid.*, II. 333.

grew was that founded in the Hospital of Our Lady of Bethlehem, in 1361, by the Drapers of Cornhill and other good men and women, for the amendment of their lives, in honour of St. Mary of Bethlehem: " in which most holy place," says the preamble to their ordinances, "our Lord Jesus Christ was born for the salvation of all his people, and the star appeared to the shepherds, and gave and shewed light to the three Kings of Cologne, who offered in the said place of Bethlehem their gifts, to wit, gold and myrrh and incense." *

Other fraternities which are known to have existed in definite connection with crafts in the 14th century, are that of the Glovers, dedicated to the Assumption of Our Lady, in Newchurchhaw † (1354); that of the Cordwainers, to which a bequest was made in 1354,‡ and which is referred to in 1372 as that of St. Mary in the church of the Carmelites ; § that of the Brewers, in All Hallows', London Wall (1361) ; ‖ that of the Cutlers in the Charterhouse (1372) ; ¶ that of the Painters, dedicated to St. Luke in St. Giles', Cripplegate ; ** that of the Pouchmakers (1380) ; †† that of the Whittawyers or Curriers in the Carmelites ; the Fraternity of the Barbers,‡‡ and that of the Weavers.§§   To these, on rather less direct evidence, may be added the Girdlers' fraternity of St. Lawrence, in St. Lawrence Jewry (1332) ; ‖‖ the Salters' fraternity of Corpus Christi, in All Hallows', Bread Street (1349) ; ¶¶ the Blacksmiths' fraternity of St. Eloy,*** and the Pewterers' fraternity.†††
With the 'half-dozen already fully dealt with, this accounts for

---

* Gild Certificate in the Public Record Office.
† *Lond. and Midd. Arch. Soc. Trans.*, IV. p. 28.
‡ Sharpe, *Calendar of Wills*, I. 689.   § *Ibid.*, II. 153.
‖ *Ibid.*, II. 26.   ¶ Gild Certificates of 1389, 215.
** Add. MS. in British Museum.
†† Sharpe, *Calendar of Wills*, II. 223 ; *and Certificate*, 463.
‡‡ S. Young, *Barber-Surgeons*.
§§ Facsimile of Weavers' Ancient Book.
‖‖ *Calendar of Wills*, I. 383.   ¶¶ *Ibid.*, I. 547.
*** *Lond. and Midd. Arch. Soc. Trans.*, IV.
††† C. Welch, *History of Pewterers*, vol. I.

more than half of the trades which are known to have been recognized as crafts or misteries by the grant of charters or ordinances, and there is the strongest presumption that most of the other crafts had similar fraternity organizations.

It was not merely a matter of sentiment, nor even of the satisfaction of the social instinct, though both these motives were strong.   There were sound practical reasons of policy for forming a fraternity.   The right of pursuing economic ends by voluntary association was not recognized in the mediæval city.   Association always needed a sanction, and the less an association of craftsmen could rely on the tacit sanction of the civic authorities, the more it needed the shelter and the sanction of the Church, which was rarely refused in some form or other, even to bodies of rebellious journeymen.   We have already had a case of a craftsman being indicted in a spiritual court for breach of sworn agreement with his fellows ; and the jealousy with which the State regarded the fraternities is to some extent explained when we find that fraternities were in the habit of registering their ordinances in the court of the Commissary of London, in order to secure their enforcement by the spiritual arm.   The Glovers' ordinances of 1354 were registered in this way.   Those who broke the rules or got behind with their quarterage were to be summoned before the Official (*i.e.* a spiritual court), and the fines imposed were to be divided between the old work of St. Paul's and the fraternity, just as the Tailors in 1371 proposed to divide their fines with the city.   Even the Water-bearers of London, the poorest class of labourers, had the ordinances of their fraternity confirmed before the Commissary in Austin Friars in 1496, and the observance of them enforced by penalties varying from two pounds of wax to " the great curse." *

The Janus-like appearance of the gild, as a craft on one side and as a fraternity on the other, and the difficulty we find in clearly separating these aspects, were not the result of a mere

* *Lond. and Midd. Arch. Soc. Trans.*, IV. 54.

confusion in the mediæval mind. It was a more or less conscious device for securing liberty of action. It was the consequence of that division of authority between Church and State without which the principle of free voluntary association would never have grown strong enough to assert its own rights against either.

CHAPTER IX

THE PARISH FRATERNITIES

WHEN Chaucer in the Prologue to his *Canterbury Tales*
speaks of

> " An Haberdasher and a Carpenter
> A Webbe, a Deyer, and a Tapiser,"

as being all

> " Clothed in oo liveree
> Of a solempne and greet fraternitee,"

he has sometimes been supposed to have drawn his burgesses
from a smaller place than London, where several trades were
associated in one gild. But Chaucer was a Londoner born
and bred, and the picture he draws of the five craftsmen and
their ladies could hardly have been realized outside the
capital.

> "Well seemed ech of them a fair burgeys,
> To sitten in a yeldhall on a deys.
> Everich for the wisdom that he can
> Was shaply for to ben an alderman.
> For catel hadde they y-nogh and rente,
> And eek hir wives wolde it wel assente ;
> And elles certein were they to blame.
> It is ful fair to been yclept ' ma dame '
> And goon to vigilyes al bifore,
> And have a mantel royalliche y-bore."

And, as a matter of fact, the liveried fraternities of London
in Chaucer's day were not by any means all craft-gilds. The
poet's five craftsmen may very well have been brethren of one

of the local or parish fraternities which began to be founded before the middle of the 14th century, and which were established in half the churches of London at the time the *Canterbury Tales* were being written.

The fraternity has been aptly described as a co-operative chantry, and the description applies, as we have already seen, to the craft-gilds, though it does not express their permanent essence. It applies still more exactly to the parish fraternities, which had their origin in chantries, and were so intimately associated with them that they shared their fate at the Reformation. The part occupied by the chantries, co-operative or otherwise, in the religious life of the Middle Ages was greater than can be easily realized. The majority of the persons ordained, says Bishop Stubbs, speaking of the later Middle Ages, " had neither cure of souls nor duty of preaching ; their spiritual work was simply to say masses for the dead."* Nor was this less true of an earlier time. Chantries had no doubt multiplied as wealth increased, and the spirit of association enabled all classes to share in their foundation, but the development of parochial life had at the same time been gradually displacing what had previously been the chaplaincies and chantries of great magnates. That many of the parish churches in London had an origin of this kind is clear from the survival of such names as St. Benet Fink, St. Mary Woolnoth, St. Margaret Moses, St. Mary Mounthaunt, St. Benet Sherehog, and St. Martin Orgar.†

Some of the facts recorded about the last-named of these churches indicate the importance of the chantry element in the " manorial parish." Towards the end of the reign of Henry II. John Bucuinte and Dionysia his wife brought a suit against the Canons of St. Paul's before the King's Justice for the possession of the churches of St. Martin of Candlewick Street and St. Botolph, Billingsgate, which they claimed as an

---

* Stubbs, *Constitutional History*, III. 386.
† Bateson, *Mediæval England*, p. 46.

inheritance from Orgar, who has given his name to St. Martin's Church. The Canons produced a charter which showed that they held the churches by the gift of Orgar and his sons, and of Christina the mother of Dionysia; and John Bucuinte and his wife thereupon renounced their claim on condition that the anniversary services for Orgar's soul were faithfully observed, and that their own names were added to the list of those for whom such masses were sung.*

The extension and rebuilding of churches which were constantly going on throughout the 14th and 15th centuries in London as elsewhere were largely supported by the foundation of chantries. The feudal magnates who had held the churches in early days were replaced by wealthy drapers, fishmongers, vintners, and mercers, who not only acquired their great houses but adopted their social traditions, and who sought to found a family in a spiritual sense by making permanent provision for themselves, their ancestors, and their posterity. Within a stone's cast of St. Martin Orgar on either side lay the churches of St. Lawrence Poultney and St. Michael, Crooked Lane. The first of these derived its name from Sir John Poultney, Draper and Mayor of London, who died in 1348. Sir John dwelt in the great mansion of Cold Harbour, which came into his hands from those of the Bigods and passed afterwards into those of the Bohuns, a house in which princes were lodged and kings feasted, and by his will he left to the Bishop of London " his finest ring with a red stone called a ruby," and to the Earl of Huntingdon "a beautiful ring with two stones called diamonds," on condition that they would see after the establishment of chantries in St. Paul's, which the Mayor, Recorder, Sheriffs, Common Pleader, and their servants were to be rewarded for attending, and the endowment of St. Lawrence as a collegiate church with a master and seven chaplains to sing masses for the dead.†

* Ninth Report of Hist. MSS. Com., Pt. I. p. 16.
† Sharpe, *Calendar of Wills*, I. 609.

In the same way St. Michael's, Crooked Lane, was rebuilt by John Lovekyn, Stockfishmonger, and four times Mayor, who was buried there in the choir under a fair tomb with the images of him and his wife in alabaster, was increased with a new choir and side chapels by Sir William Walworth, Stockfishmonger and Mayor, sometime servant to John Lovekyn, and finally, was endowed as a college for a master and nine chaplains by Sir William, who was buried there in 1385.*

The College with which Richard Whittington endowed St. Michael Paternoster Royal, where he was "three times buried," and which has given its name to College Hill, included along with its Master and chaplains an alms-house for twelve poor men and women under the rule of a tutor, who every day when they rose from their beds were to kneel upon their knees and say a Paternoster and an Ave with special and hearty recommendation of Whittington and his wife to God and Our Blessed Maiden Mary, and at other times of the day when they might best have leisure thrice seven Aves fifteen Paternosters and three Credos. But if prevented by feebleness from carrying out this duty, they were to come together once in the day at least about Whittington's tomb, "and they that can shall say the Psalm *De Profundis* and they that can shall say three Psalms, three Aves and one Credo. And after this done the Tutor or eldest of them shall say openly in English, 'God have mercy on our Founders' souls and on all Christians.' And they that stand about shall answer and say, 'Amen.'" †

Instances might be multiplied at any length to show how the great merchants of London bequeathed their wealth in the spirit of the feudal magnate with a view to securing the spiritual welfare and permanent commemoration of their families. The amount bestowed with a direct regard for the good of a wider community remained even down to the eve of the Reformation inconsiderable as compared with the

* Stow, *Survey*, p. 223.   † Strype, *Stow*, III. 4.

constant stream of bequests great and small for the benefit
of the souls of testators and of their immediate kin.   But the
student of mediæval wills finds a more liberal spirit gradually
spreading abroad in the course of the 14th century.   In part it
is stimulated by a self-regarding motive.   The testator wishes
to have a permanent guarantee that the spiritual benefits he
is paying for will not be withheld through the slackness of his
beneficiaries.

Thus John de Holegh, Hosier, whose many bequests in
1351 were mostly made with a view to his own spiritual
welfare, desired that his testament might remain in the custody
of four honest parishioners of St. Mary Bow, and that a copy
of it might be written in a missal which was to be used at the
high altar in that church, for the purchase of which he left £5.
He left also £3 for an image of the Virgin to be placed in the
choir with a crown on her head and with a copy of his will on
a tablet at her feet.*

Soon after the accession of Edward III., and just at the
time that the majority of the crafts were attaining recognition,
the work of extending the parish churches and of enriching
their services began to be undertaken in a much worthier way
than by the gifts of the dead.   The leading parishioners
united in an effort to meet the spiritual needs of the parish,
and invited their poorer neighbours to co-operate with them
by giving small regular contributions.

" In the tenth year before the great Pestilence," says one of the
gild certificates of 1389, " Geoffrey Wynchecombe and Roger Compis,
parishioners of the church of Our Lady of Colechurch in London,
seeing that the said church was too small and narrow to receive
the parishioners, of their great goodness and for the easement of
the people added a chapel to the honour of . . . St. Katherine to
the said church, and afterwards the said Geoffrey and others commenced of their great devotion a company or fraternity of the people
of the same parish to furnish and sustain five candles to burn in the

---

* Sharpe, *Calendar of Wills*, I. 656.

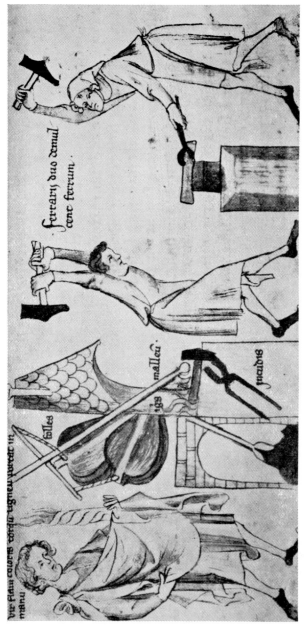

BLACKSMITHS AND THEIR TOOLS

EARLY FOURTEENTH CENTURY

LEATHER-SELLERS' ELECTION GARLANDS

said chapel in honour of God, Our Lady, . . . St. Katherine and all the saints of paradise, and to find a chaplain to sing in the said chapel for our Lord the King, our Lady the Queen, their progenitors and their posterity, and for all those living or dead who are were or shall be of the said company." *

"In the 17th year of King Edward the third," says another certificate, "Ralph Capeleyn, Bailiff, William Double, Fishmonger, Roger Clonyll, Chandler, Henry Boseworth, Vintner, Stephen Lucas, Stockfishmonger and others of the better sort of the parish of St. Magnus near London Bridge . . . commenced and caused to be sung an anthem of Our Lady called *Salve Regina* at every Vesper and ordained candles to burn at the time of the said anthem in honour and reverence of the five principal joys of Our Lady, and to excite the people to devotion. . . . Whereupon several other good people of the same parish seeing the great seemliness of this service and devotion proffered to be aiders and partners in sustaining the lights and the anthem, by paying each person every week a halfpenny and soon after with the people gave to the light and anthem they commenced to find a chaplain to sing in the said church for all the benefactors of the light and anthem."

There had likewise been a fraternity, the certificate proceeds to say, of St. Thomas the Martyr in the chapel on the bridge, whose members belonged to St. Magnus parish, but in view of the fact that the parish church was old and ruinous, besides being too small, the two fraternities determined to become one, to have the anthem of St. Thomas after the *Salve Regina*, and to devote their united resources to enlarging of St. Magnus' Church. "So that they have no chattels at present but are in debt £20 13s. 4d. on the above account."

The Fraternity of St. Giles, which was one of half a dozen fraternities founded in the church of St. Giles', Cripplegate,

---

* It will save further references to state that the materials for the rest of this chapter are derived from the Gild Certificates of 1389 in the Public Record Office. In many cases recourse has been had to the originals, but full use has also been made of the transcript and translation which is to be found in the Guildhall MS. No. 142 ; and of Miss Toulmin Smith's *English Gilds*, which contains three sets of ordinances.

had its origin in the building of a chapel as an enlargement of the church in 1333, by Guy Clerk, citizen of London.   In this chapel of St. Giles' the members of the fraternity maintained thirty-one lights (afterwards forty-three) by the weekly payment of a farthing apiece.   In all these cases the regular contributions were supplemented by gifts and bequests.   Each of the four founders of the *Salve Regina* at St. Magnus' remembered the fraternity in his will, and thus laid the foundation of a considerable endowment.   Such bequests were, however, usually burdened with the obligation of saying masses for the donor's soul.   The Fraternity of St. Mary in All Hallows, London Wall, founded in 1342, had for its principal benefactor a certain John de Enfield, blader, a parishioner of St. Owen's, Newgate, who in 1361 left the gild some property in Smithfield on condition of their establishing a chantry in St. Owen's ; and if this condition were not performed, two residentiary canons of St. Paul's were authorized to admonish the gild once, twice and thrice, and then to take possession of the land for the same purpose.   The fraternity, by way of showing their zeal, made the parson of St. Owen's an ex-officio brother of their gild.

Regarded merely as a co-operative chantry for souls, the fraternity marks a great advance in social development. Voluntary co-operation for such a purpose is a sign of the displacement of the tie of kinship by the tie of neighbourhood.   Something of the same kind had happened in the ancient city state.   The religious bond which originally united only those of the same kin, was widened as the city expanded and outgrew this narrow ancestral worship, by the formation of artificial tribes within which room could be found for all free sharers in the civic life.   The substitution of the parish gild for the family chantry served the same end, but a still more beautiful example of this transition is furnished by the foundation of the Fraternity of all Christian souls in the chapel of the charnel of St. Paul's churchyard.   This chapel had been

originally endowed by one or more of the great families of the
city for the performance of their chantries, but as, in the
chances and changes of time, the families had died out or had
left the city, the chapel had fallen into decay, its windows were
broken, its very altars full of rubbish and ordure, so that
masses could no longer be sung there. This sad spectacle
met the gaze of all those who came to worship in the cathedral,
and the Archbishop of Canterbury when preaching there seized
on the opportunity to stir up the Christian zeal of his hearers.
He offered a full pardon to all who would share in the work
of repairing the chapel, and of furnishing it with the means of
renewing its services. The members of the new brotherhood,
who contributed 3*d.* a quarter for this object, would at
the same time be providing for the due performance of their
own obsequies and making a contingent provision for old age
or poverty. But the lesson of the decayed chantries was not
to be lost. Once a year they were to realize for themselves
and to bring home to others the need for the devout fellowship
of all Christian souls. On All Souls' Day they were to
assemble at Holy Trinity Priory and go in solemn procession
to St. Paul's, "with modest steps offering secret orisons as they
passed with a cordial countenance."

On the chantry side most of the parish fraternities followed
the same course of development, though some had more means
to dispose of than others. They began by offering lights, sometimes only a single light, but more often five or even seven, on
their high feast, and two on other feasts to burn on the altar
of their patron saint; but their ambition was always to pay
for a chaplain as soon as they could afford it. In one case,
the Fraternity of St. Katherine in St. Sepulchre, the provision
of a chaplain for daily service by "the poor people of the
parish" seems to have been the sole object. The brethren
met four times a year to collect the priest's salary, and all
contributed equally. They imposed no oaths, wore no livery,
possessed no chattels.

The attendance at mass on the feast day of their saint, and the offering of a penny, a halfpenny, or a farthing, seems to have been universal.   At a member's funeral, tapers were provided, generally five, and four torches.   If the member died outside the city within ten miles the body was met and carried in.   All members must attend in livery at the dirge on the day before and at the mass on the day of the funeral on pain of a fine, generally a pound of wax.   Thirty masses, and in some cases as many as three trentals, were commonly paid for out of the common box for the soul of the deceased member.

Apart from these observances, which were common to nearly all fraternities, the proportion which religious objects bore to social or charitable objects varied considerably.   Sometimes a religious note is sounded in the preamble to the ordinances.   Thus the brotherhood of the Holy Cross in St. Lawrence Jewry commence their return with the following pious invocation :—

" In the name of the Holy and Undivided Trinity, the Father, the Son and the Holy Spirit, Amen.   On the Saturday in the Feast of the Exaltation of the Holy Cross in the year of our Lord 1370 the Brethren and Sisters in Christ whose names are written in a certain paper (and may they be written in the Book of Life), by the inspiration of the Holy Spirit by unanimous assent agreed and out of devotion and reverence and honour to Our Lord Jesus Christ crucified, and to his Holy Cross on which our same Lord Jesus Christ was exalted for sinners, nailed by the hands and feet, his side pierced with a lance, his bleeding body fed with gall, his thirst assuaged with vinegar, commending his spirit to the Father and so dying, resolved upon the article written within."

And one or two at least of the fraternities cherished ideals of a missionary order.   The Gild of Holy Trinity at St. Botolph, Aldersgate, which began by supplying thirteen tapers at Easter, went on four years later to establish a chaplain to celebrate daily at daybreak for the benefit of workmen, and the Fraternity of Our Lady in St. Dunstan's in Tower Street undertook to provide a similar early mass for the benefit of the common people. Several fraternities state the amendment of their members' lives to be one of their main objects.

In the majority of cases, however, what may be called the social and benevolent activities of the gilds receive as much emphasis as their moral and religious aims. The Gild of Holy Trinity of Coleman Street puts them first. "This brotherhood was begun in London of good men of Coleman Street in nourishing of love and of charity amongst them and in help to him that falleth in poverty . . . through the hand of God, and also in other deeds of charity." The men of Coleman Street were in humble circumstances. Their quarterly sub-scription was only 1*d.*, and they could only offer 6½*d.* a week to sick or unfortunate members. As a rule, when the quarter-age was 3*d.*, the fraternity offered 14*d.* a week, which is equivalent to an offer by a modern Friendly Society of 14*s.* a week "sick-pay," in addition to a funeral benefit, for a payment of 3*d.* a week. To a non-expert this seems a generous offer, especially as the conditions are often some-what loosely stated. The Fraternity of St. Stephen in St. Sepulchre's Church ordains that "if any brother or sister fall into poverty by way of robbery or accident of fire or by any other misfortune, not through his own fault, and he have not wherewith to live or help himself he shall every week have fourteen pence." And if any member is imprisoned un-justly, he or she is to have the same and to be visited weekly by one of the masters. Generally, however, a member must have paid his subscription seven years before he became eligible for relief. This was the case in the Fraternity of St. Mary at All Hallows, London Wall, and in the Fraternity of St. Augustine in St. Augustine's, Paul's Gate, though in the ordinances of the latter the rule is softened by the addition, " and if any of the company fall into poverty within the seven

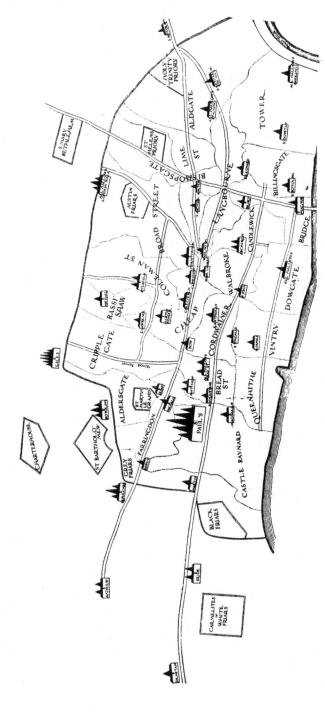

PARISH FRATERNITIES OF LONDON C. 1400

(The gilds have been indicated by imaginary steeples)

years we will help him to the best of our power by a contribution from our private purses." The financial responsibility of
the fraternity was, of course, lessened by the fact that the
"sick benefits" were not supposed to be paid to all sick or
aged members, but only to those who actually needed it.
Nevertheless, it may be doubted whether the common box
can always have been equal to the demands made upon it.
The prosperous fraternity of St. Giles in St. Giles' stated, when
making its return in 1389, that 10½*d.* a week was paid to poor
members as long as the common box had the means of doing
so, but that for the moment there was only 15½*d.* in the box.

Other assistance of various kinds was offered by different
fraternities to their members. St. Katherine's fraternity in
St. Botolph's, Aldersgate, made loans to those in need of
small advances. The Gild of St. Fabian and St. Sebastian in
the same church assisted its young members to find work.
The Fraternity of St. Mary in All Hallows', London Wall,
offered to give legal or charitable assistance to any member
whose son or daughter had been unjustly treated by the
master to whom he or she had been apprenticed. But the
most universal and perhaps the most valuable of all the social
services rendered by the fraternity to its members, lay in the
settlement of disputes between them without recourse to the
law.

"If any of the brethren," runs the ordinance of the Gild of the
Assumption in the Church of the Friars Preachers, "be at discord,
which God forbid, then the plaintiff shall make the plaint to the
masters of the Brotherhood, and if the masters cannot agree the
plaintiff should go to two or four of their other brethren, and if all
these cannot make them agree then it shall be well and lawful for
him to go to Common Law, and if the plaintiff act contrary to this
ordinance he shall pay to the box for his trespass two shillings."

Such being the advantages offered, it remains to consider
briefly the conditions of membership of the fraternity, its inner
life and its methods of self-government. Towards the end of

the 14th century any citizen wishing to join such a society would have found one, if not in his own, at any rate in the next parish, and though most of the gilds were founded in connection with a parish church, they were not confined to the residents in the parish. But the entrance fee might prove prohibitive, although it was never as high in the parish fraternities as the fee of 20s. demanded by the Mercers or Drapers. The Gild of St. Katherine in St. Mary Colechurch levied 13s. 4d., that of St. Fabian and St. Sebastian and that of St. James Garlickhithe 6s. 8d., on their new members. The Gild of St. Magnus left the member to pay according to his means. "Some give five marks, some forty shillings, some twenty, some nothing." In many cases no entrance fee is referred to, but the assent of all the members was generally required, and sometimes inquiry was made as to the candidate's character before admission. On being accepted he took an oath to obey the rules, and was saluted by each member with a fraternal kiss.

The first obligation of membership, apart from the attendance at funerals, was the observance of the annual feast of the patron saint. The members attended mass together and made an offering, after which they had a dinner or a drinking, or a revel. Those who failed to attend must equally share in the common expense. At this feast were elected the officers for the ensuing year, " four men of the best and most discreet of their fellowship . . . who for the year following shall have power and custody over all goods and chattels belonging to the fraternity . . . and give a reasonable account of all the profits, gains, mises and expenses thereof." In the Fraternity of St. Mary at All Hallows', London Wall, four under-masters were also chosen to assist the four principal masters and to be jointly responsible with them. At the yearly feast of St. Katherine's gild in St. Mary Colechurch, the ordinances were expressly rehearsed and read in the English language " so as to have them in better memory," and they were then openly discussed by the members so that any of them might be amended, if necessary, by common consent.

In the majority of fraternities a livery appears to have been worn at the annual feast, at funerals, and on other solemn or great occasions. The livery was generally made under the direction of the wardens and paid for by the members at cost price. If complete it consisted of both hood and gown, but sometimes the hood was allowed to suffice. Members were generally forbidden to sell or give away their livery within two years. Besides the annual feast there were usually four quarterly meetings for the payment of contributions and the transaction of other business. The Gild of St. Stephen in St. Sepulchre had a summoner who called the brethren to meetings, and who received 6d. from the common box for every day spent on going his rounds. In all cases a member might be expelled for bad conduct. The ordinance of St. Stephen's gild expresses the common usage.

" If any one of them be a common brawler or given to quarrel or be a vagabond or night-wanderer or use dice or brothels or be guilty of any crime whereby the brethren or sisters may incur scandal . . . he shall be admonished once, twice or thrice, and if he be delinquent the fourth time he shall be wholly expelled from the brotherhood."

As to the property of the fraternities, most of them must have possessed a stock of wax, levied on the members as fines, to be made into tapers, and the four torches used at funerals. Many owned a mass-book, vestment, and chalice for the use of their chaplain. The Fraternity of Salve Regina in St. Magnus' had two chalices, one principal vestment and two others, a white and a blue, besides napkins, towels, and altar furniture. The missal, vestment, and chalice of St. Katherine's fraternity in St. Botolph's were valued at 10 marks. The common box, which was a universal feature of the fraternity, seems to have had often very little in it, if the certificates are to be credited, but the Fraternity of St. Mary in the Carmelites' admitted to

the possession of 100*s*. But the chief source of income of
the wealthier gilds lay in rents of land bequeathed to them
or purchased by means of bequests, and some device had
to be adopted to evade the laws against the alienation of land
to religious purposes. The land was generally made over to
several trustees on the understanding that they would pay
the rents to the gild. Thus the Fraternity of St. Katherine in
St. Paul's, after declaring that it holds no property in land,
adds that two of its members have purchased tenements, "to
have to them and their heirs and assigns of the capital heads
of the fee by the services due and accustomed for ever, with
the intention to put them at mortmain for the maintenance of
a chantry priest if they can obtain license from the king."
And the Gild of St. Fabian and St. Sebastian acknowledges
an arrangement whereby certain tenements are left in the
hands of feoffees, "until hereafter by license of the king it may
be put at mortmain for the use of the gild, and the feoffees
when it shall please them pay the rent . . . in aid of the
maintenance of the light and for the amendment of vestments
and in other divine works." In 1370 the Gild of Salve Regina
in St. Magnus' paid the king £40 for a licence to hold in
mortmain messuages and rents of the yearly value of
£14 7*s*. 6*d*., which they professed they had deferred to enter
or receive until they got the licence, and soon afterwards the
annual value of the property was increased to £24 by further
bequests. The licensing of property in mortmain was
evidently a valuable source of income to the Crown, and one
of the motives of the inquiry into the gilds instituted in 1389
must have been the desire to force more of them to pay for
the licence, as many of them soon afterwards did.

It will be easier to appreciate the force of the more political
motives for the inquiry after a consideration of the events of
the early part of Richard's reign to be given in the next
chapter. In the mean time the facts may be briefly stated.
In the Parliament of 1389 the Commons had petitioned

against the wearing of livery given by lords, " and also that no
livery shall be given under colour of gild fraternity or any
other association . . . but that all shall be put down within
ten months after this Parliament. And that if any take livery
contrary to this ordinance he shall be imprisoned for a year
without redemption and besides this the said gilds and
fraternities shall lose their franchises and those gilds and
fraternities which have no franchises shall forfeit £100 to the
king." Although the king's assent which would have converted this Bill into an Act was not granted, the threat created
much alarm amongst the members of fraternities, and the
receipt of the royal writ of inquiry made them feel they were
on their trial. Those that possessed no land, gave out no
livery and imposed no oath, made the most of the absence of
these suspected elements, and where these features could not
be denied, it was earnestly insisted that they had no political
significance. The warders of the Gild of St. Bride in St.
Bride's, Fleet Street, nervously admitted that there had been
something in the nature of a livery, but urged that it was " not
out of any wicked intention of maintaining a confederacy. . . .
They had no oaths, congregations, conventions, meetings, or
assemblies." They had no box and no rents, nothing but
wax made into tapers, and they were 6 marks in arrears
with the salary of their chaplain. Some of their original
members were dead, others had withdrawn, and the remainder,
after they heard the news and the ordinance of the last Parliament, wholly refused to pay their quarterage, so that unless
the Government did something to reassure them, the gild's
religious work would cease, " perchance to the peril of many
souls."

It is extremely unlikely that all the parish fraternities were
as innocent of political intentions as they would have had the
Government believe. Although there is no positive proof of
their intervention in politics, it is significant that they were
spreading most rapidly precisely at the time when party

feeling in the city was running highest. Besides the score whose certificates have come down to us, another fifty are mentioned in wills, nearly all before the close of the 14th century; and the period just before the rising of 1381 saw the establishment of a great number both in London and in the country. It is significant that, at the very moment when the issue was being decided whether the Common Council should be elected on a basis of localities or of trades, the local gilds should spread rapidly over the whole city, so as for the time to rival if not to surpass the trade gilds both in number and in wealth.

CHAPTER X

THE RULE OF THE MISTERIES, 1376–1384 *

THE first ten years of the reign of Richard II. were the most eventful ten years in the history of London, not excepting even the first ten years of Richard I., or the last ten of Henry III. Revolution was twice followed by counter-revolution, and then, after a lengthened period of unrest, the constitution of the city settled down in what proved to be its final shape. But the records of this time are a labyrinth to which there is no single clue. The struggle in London cannot be interpreted simply as the working out of an issue in municipal development. Intermingled with the crisis in civic affairs, there was a still more important national crisis. And the national crisis itself presented no simple political issue. The ordinary landmarks of constitutional conflict had been for the moment swept away by a tumultuous flood of social and economic discontent, which had long been angrily chafing the restraining banks of custom and tradition. And behind all lay the brooding spirit of religious reformation, which, though it had taken logical shape in the minds of but a few, had weakened the allegiance of many, and loosened the hold of authority upon all.

* The main authority for the whole of this chapter is Dr. Sharpe's recently published Calendar of Letter Book H, which, with the editor's valuable introduction, is the most important contribution to London constitutional history since the publication of Liber Albus, Liber Custumarum, etc. As the references are so numerous they are indicated merely by the letter H.

Of all these mingling elements of revolution, London was the natural focus. It was at London, in St. Paul's or at Lambeth, that Wycliffe and his accusers were brought face to face, each backed by a noisy mob of citizens, most of whom knew little and cared less about the real questions at stake. It was in London, or close outside its walls if the citizens shut their gates in time, that the factious nobility—in whose eyes national politics wore the aspect of a family feud—menaced each other with rival armies of retainers, and sought to over-bear the deliberations of Parliament. And it was towards London that the revolted peasants from north and south directed their march, when they had determined to square accounts with the lawyers and to make trial of the good will of the boy-king.

But though the stage is full of notable actions, that draw away our eyes as they must have drawn the eyes and the thoughts of contemporaries, our concern is with the gilds. And London by this time was full of gilds of the most diverse kinds; different in origin, in interest, in wealth, in social status, but all resting on the similar basis of a fraternity organization. In the *mêlée* of class and party interests that ensued, the fraternity was a weapon common to all. It was a pike to those who fought on foot. But it was a lance to those who were mounted and wore the armour of privilege. We have already seen something of the special powers with which the stronger class interests had armed themselves for the struggle. The Fishmongers had their Halimot, which placed them for some purposes outside the ordinary jurisdiction of the city, and thus gave them a powerful leverage by means of which they had at times effectively controlled the constitution. The greater crafts secured a similar leverage by acquiring royal charters. The lesser crafts used the powers of regulation granted them by the city to exclude competition and restrict their numbers. There is reason to think that some of the victualling crafts which were not entrusted with powers of self-regulation, exercised a special influence on some of the parish fraternities. Only the poor journeyman or small master was reduced to dependence on the single resource afforded by voluntary association with his mates, and even this was declared in his case to be illegal combination.

The impending conflict was not a simple two-sided one. There were wheels within wheels; secret compacts between unlikely allies. It will be well, therefore, to glance for a moment at the various elements of antagonism which we know to have existed, out of which, by a chemical process not always traceable, the explosive mixture must have been compounded.

In the first place, there was the cleavage between the governing oligarchy and the general mass of the citizens. The charter of 1319 had provided that the aldermen should vacate office at the end of the year, and that an entirely fresh set should be elected. But this rule must have been ignored almost from the first, and the aldermen were still holding office for life in 1376. And as the Common Council was only called when the aldermen thought fit, and was elected by the wards under the presidency of the aldermen, it furnished no adequate representation of the will of the citizens.

In the next place, there was the bitter rivalry between native and foreign merchants. By this time the control of national finance had passed almost entirely into the hands of English merchants who were citizens of London. But in the larger operations of the import and export trade the competition of Italians was still a serious grievance. In 1383 we read of an Italian vessel—which had put in with a rich cargo at Sandwich—being bribed to leave for Flanders by London traders who had a stock, no longer fresh, of fruits of all kinds, oil, etc., and did not want its value to be diminished.

Thirdly, there was the opposition of interest between the importers and the exporters, between the dealers in food and heavy produce who wished to control the channels of the city's supply, and were specially hostile to aliens, and the manufacturing exporters who wished to keep down the price of food and raw material, and were, therefore, in favour of free trade in imports.

Fourthly, there was the conflict between those who had a large national interest in manufacture and those who had a small local interest. The drapers wanted to make London a depôt for all kinds of English cloth, whilst the weavers wanted to discriminate by special trade-marks against all cloth not made in London. The drapers were glad of the influx of Flemish weavers, whose competition the English weavers in London regarded with bitter hostility.

And lastly, there was the widening breach in a number of trades between the master craftsmen and the journeymen, who were now excluded from the benefits of the craft organization, and were bent on forming fraternities of their own.

In the summer of 1376 London was strongly stirred by the recent revelations of the Good Parliament. Three of its aldermen had been using their power in the city, and their influence as Government financiers, to enrich themselves by dishonest transactions. Richard Lyons and John Peche had been fined and imprisoned, and had only escaped severer penalties through the protection of friends at court. Adam de Bury had fled the country. But the scandal did not stop here. Peche had been accused of obtaining a monopoly in sweet wines, and had asserted in defence that the Mayor and fifteen aldermen were fully cognisant of his action.* More than half the aldermanic bench, therefore, were involved in the imputation of corruption, and the time was clearly come for the reformers to strike their blow. Their proposal was to destroy the monopoly of power enjoyed by the Court of Aldermen by creating an independent Common Council,

* H, iii-v.

elected not from the wards but from the companies, and by compelling the aldermen to call it regularly and to act by its advice. While this measure was being fiercely debated, the king sent a message threatening to intervene in case of disturbance. To prevent the suspension of the city's liberties, the mayor determined to act on the advice of the reformers— of whom there were only five among the aldermen—and to call a large Common Council on the new plan, by election of the misteries. At the meeting of this assembly on August 1st, in which forty-one crafts were represented, the three aldermen were discharged from their offices, the new Common Council was made a regular part of the constitution (it was to meet twice a quarter and its members were to elect the Mayor and Sheriffs), and a message was sent to the king that the constitutional crisis was now at an end. Later in the year the reformers obtained authority from the Crown for insisting on the annual election of aldermen, in accordance with the articles of 1319.*

With these men the reform of the civic constitution was only a means to an end. It will not be misleading to call them the party of manufacturing free traders, as long as too much credit is not given them for purity of doctrine. But it would be a mistake to regard them as, in practice, an ultra-democratic party. Undoubtedly they were the party of ideas, the progressive party. Many of them shared in the anti-clerical feeling which was then beginning to take a strong root in the trading classes, and which found political support in the powerful but unpopular John of Gaunt. They were the spiritual ancestors of the Puritans and the Whigs, democratic more by theoretical conviction than by social sympathy. By temperament, indeed, they were aristocrats, but they were driven by political exigencies and by the logic of their principles to appeal for popular support, which, as is often the case with an earnest minority, they might secure and

* H, 35-42.

L

utilize for a brief revolutionary period, but could not permanently retain. Their class interests separated them from the rank and file of their fellow-citizens. Their leaders belonged to the wealthy misteries which had procured exclusive rights by charter from the Crown, and which jealously guarded their privileges by the exaction of large entrance fees ; so that it was possible for their opponents, as soon as they came into power again, to pose as the really democratic party by calling in all the special charters enjoyed by crafts, and by lowering the financial barriers to citizenship. The victuallers had not only more command than the manufacturers over the ordinary sources of popularity—the love of display and of festive self-indulgence ; they could also appeal successfully to the lower industrial population, who bore the employing capitalists no good will.

The leader of the party that had carried through this revolution, John of Northampton, alderman first of Cordwainer ward and afterwards of Dowgate, was one of the most striking personalities in London history.

"He was a man," says the monastic chronicler, who viewed his doings with no friendly eye, "of unflinching purpose and great astuteness, elated by his wealth, and so proud that he could neither get on with his inferiors nor be deterred by the suggestions or warnings of his superiors from striving to carry out his drastic ideas to the bitter end." *

He was a draper, and had his warehouse and dwelling on the south side of Thames Street in the part then called the Ropery, between the Steelyard and the church of All Hallows the Great, most of which is now covered by Cannon Street Station. Behind his " Inn with broad gates " he had a brewhouse and a dyehouse, and owned much property in the lanes running down to the Thames, as well as shops in other parts of the city. Later on he acquired the

---

* Thomas Walsingham, *Historia*, II. 65.

manor of Shoreditch from John, Lord Nevill, and entered into some of the riverside property of the fallen Richard Lyons.* His more immediate followers were John More and Richard Norbury, mercers, William Essex, draper, John Willarby, tailor, and Nicholas Twyford, goldsmith ; and he had many supporters amongst the saddlers, cordwainers, haberdashers, and in the lesser crafts.

The reformers lost no time in getting to work. They got a committee appointed with authority to revise the city ordinances, especially those relating to the sale of victuals, and the result of their labours—the Jubilee Book, probably so called from the year of the king's jubilee, in which it was compiled—became an object of detestation to the victualling trades.† But they soon began to find power slipping from their grasp, and to realize the truth that those who set up a new constitution cannot always rely upon it to serve the purposes for which they designed it. The other party had no hesitation in appealing to the new constituencies, and had already set about improving its own organization. The Fraternity of St. Anthony, which had by this time drawn within its ranks most of the great importing merchants of dry goods, assumed its new form as the Grocers' Company within a month of Northampton's revolution ; and with the Grocers were closely allied the Fishmongers, whose unique and powerful organization had been recently sanctioned by royal letters patent. These two bodies represented a large part of the mercantile capital of the city, and, as events proved, they had influence enough to secure the election of a majority of aldermen belonging to their party. ‡

Political ambitions, which destined him to a tragic end,

---

* Calendar of Patent Rolls, 1384, 462–463, 468, 516, 524, 531, 562, 569, 573, 581 ; 1385, 18, 50, 100.

† H, 41.

‡ The Rev. A. B. Beaven has contributed a most interesting analysis of the list of Aldermen for those years to the *English Historical Review* for October, 1907.

were soon to place the leadership of this party in the hands of Nicholas Brembre, Grocer, but for the moment two more cautious and fortunate politicians, William Walworth and John Philipot, were equally prominent in it. The deed that immortalized Walworth lay still in the future, but Philipot was soon to win golden opinions from the London populace by fitting out a victorious fleet against the pirates, which led nobles to call him in derision the "King of London." * A still solider claim to popularity lay in their championship of the cause of the freemen of London against the foreigner. This outcry against the alien so often raised in times of disturbance, united for the moment many interests which had nothing else in common—the wealthy skinner or vintner, who wished to prevent the Eastland or the Gascon merchant from dealing direct with the consumer or with the country trader ; the native weaver, eager to suppress his Flemish competitor or to compel him to contribute to his "farm" ; the shopkeeping fishmonger or butcher, whose life was embittered by the thought of the foreigner from Kent or Norfolk trading as freely in London market as a citizen who was "at scot and lot."

The victuallers, headed by the Fishmongers, had one supreme object of policy—to control the avenues of the food supply. Amongst these the foremost in importance was the Bridge, because it had a permanent depôt at the other end of it. Hence the eagerness of the London victuallers to draw Southwark under the jurisdiction of the city. Edward III. at the beginning of his reign had indeed made a grant of the vill of Southwark to the city ; but this was restricted within very small limits by the existence of other jurisdictions, foremost among them being that of the King's Marshal. Whilst John of Northampton's committee were compiling the Jubilee Book with a view to ensuring free trade in food, the other party were drawing up a petition to the Parliament

* *Chron. Angliæ*, p. 121.

about to assemble asking to have the city's control of Southwark renewed and extended.

" Many bakers and other victuallers and false workers at divers
trades . . . who eschew the punishments of the city, repair to the
vill of Southwark, where the city officials cannot arrest and punish
them because the Court of the Marshalsea will not suffer them to
exercise any jurisdiction there." *

The Government were not prepared to grant this request.
Indeed, at that very moment they were considering a scheme
for extending the powers of the Marshal so as to act as a
check on the London victuallers.† It had long been made a
matter of complaint by the Commons outside London that
the Mayor, Sheriffs, and Aldermen connived at monoply and
were judges in their own cases ; and the Government had
threatened to remove the jurisdiction in such matters into
the more impartial hands of the county justices or of the
Constable of the Tower. Some such measure was recommended by John of Gaunt in the spring of 1377, and may
possibly have been suggested by the city reformers, who were
just beginning to feel themselves overborne by reaction. The
appearance of Wycliffe to answer his accusers, in St. Paul's, on
February 19th, 1377, was the signal for an outburst of party
feeling in the city which had little relation to the religious
issue, but was more concerned with the price of fish. When
John of Gaunt and Earl Percy the Marshal, who was then in
alliance with him, entered the cathedral as the protectors of
Wycliffe, they had to pass through an angry crowd of orthodox
fishmongers who had just got wind of the threatened Bill ; and
an unseemly scuffle was followed by a bitter altercation
between the Bishop of London and the Duke. After the
party had passed into the Lady Chapel the dispute continued,
and when the citizens outside began to hear high words
passing into threats of violence, they could no longer be

* Rolls of Parliament, II. 366.   † H, 56.

restrained from rushing in—one party to protect the Bishop
from the Duke, the other party to rescue Wycliffe from the
Bishop.*

But the news of the proposed Bill had turned the tide of
popular feeling against the reformers. And when next day
a meeting of citizens was suddenly informed that Earl Percy
had commenced the exercise of his jurisdiction by imprisoning
a citizen in his house—probably Northumberland House just
within Aldersgate—a rush was made to the rescue. Percy
was not found at home or it might have fared ill with him,
and the mob poured out of the city to the Savoy, which was
John of Gaunt's town house.   Meanwhile one of John's
knights hastened to inform his master and Percy, who
happened to be dining in the Vintry, that unless they took
great heed that day would be their last.

" With which words the duke leapt so hastily from his oysters
that he hurt both his legs against the form.   Wine was offered, but
he could not drink it for haste and so fled with his fellow Henry
Percy out at a back gate, and entering the Thames never stayed
rowing till they came to Kennington." †

The Savoy was saved by the intervention of the Bishop, but
the Duke's friends had to keep within doors, and the arms
of Lancaster, which one of the Duke's city supporters had
displayed over his shop in Cheapside, were reversed by the
mob.

The elections of new aldermen, carried through a few
weeks later under stress of the civic patriotism thus generated,
gave the victuallers a competent majority, no less than eight
of the new aldermen being fishmongers ; and a week afterwards the mayor, Adam Stable, was removed by royal writ,
and Nicholas Brembre took his place.‡   On May 27th, 1377,
the counter-revolution was completed by the expulsion from

* *Chron. Angliæ*, pp. 120-121 ; Trevelyan, *England in the Age of Wycliffe*, p. 45.
† Stow, *Survey*, p. 246.   ‡ II, 58, 61.

the Common Council, which then represented fifty-one misteries, of the five principal supporters of John of Northampton, who were accused of betraying the secrets of the Council.*

Thenceforward, till after the rising of 1381, the victuallers retained their dominance in the city,† which was closely connected with the financial aid rendered by the great merchants of the party to the Government of the young king. John Philipot, John Hadley, and William Walworth, who succeeded Brembre in the mayoralty in 1378, 1379, and 1380, were called to a Council at Westminster in July, 1377, and Walworth and Philipot along with two fishmonger aldermen, Carlille and Sibille, were the city's representatives in Parliament in the following October. It was the same group of merchant princes who headed a loan of £10,000 to the king, and when the Commons demanded the appointment of wardens who should be responsible for the proper application of supplies, Richard appointed Walworth and Philipot.‡

In return for these important services Brembre's party procured from the king the grant of a charter, which gave to the citizens a monopoly of retail trade by forbidding all foreigners except the merchants of Acquitaine to traffic among themselves. This was claimed by the citizens who were in favour of it as the restoration of an old city custom which had of late years been infringed by the free trade policy of Edward III. The charter, which also declared the citizens free from the Marshal's jurisdiction, was proclaimed through the streets by order of the Mayor, and the party in power proceeded to carry its principles into effect.

* H, 64.

† It is true that the other party managed to elect Nicholas Twyford as one of the Sheriffs in the autumn of 1377, but when in the following March he attempted to protect one of his party who had been engaged in a second Wycliffe riot, he was removed from office till he made submission to the mayor.

‡ H, xii–xiv.

Merchant strangers were informed that they could not continue to keep house on their own account, but must take steps to board and lodge with some free hosteler, and must sell their merchandise within forty days of their arrival;[*] and precept was sent to the eight mercantile misteries of Grocers, Mercers, Drapers, Fishmongers, Goldsmiths, Skinners, Ironmongers, and Vintners to elect searchers who were to see these orders carried out.[†] All classes of aliens soon began to feel the effects of this change of policy. The merchants of the German Steelyard found the liberties they had enjoyed for many generations suddenly suspended and themselves roughly handled, so that letters were received from the headquarters of the Hanseatic League in the Baltic threatening to break off intercourse with England unless better treatment were accorded to their merchants.[‡]

But the great merchants and the victuallers were not alone in their hatred of the foreigner. The English weavers had perhaps the most solid grievance of all. They were the oldest chartered craft in the city, and though the monopoly conferred by their charter had long been lost, they still had to pay their yearly farm to the king, to which the Flemings and Brabanters whom Edward III. had invited over did not contribute. It was not to the interest of the drapers and clothworkers of the city to allow the English weavers to control the aliens, since the latter furnished an important addition to the supply of labour. Whilst insisting, therefore, that the aliens should adopt the same rules (as to night work, etc.) as the native weavers, the authorities had permitted them to choose bailiffs of their own. The Flemings and Brabanters belonged to hostile races that could not agree even in exile, but fell to blows when they met to offer themselves for hire. Separate churchyards were therefore assigned to them, St. Lawrence Pountney for the Flemings and St. Mary Somerset for the Brabanters, and each race was to have its own officers.

* H, xiii, 86.   † H, 90.   ‡ H, 101.

This arrangement was still in force when Brembre took office as mayor.*

In the summer of 1378, when the anti-alien movement was at its full height, the English weavers naturally thought the auspicious moment for action had come. But they could not hope to achieve anything with divided ranks, and they had a large number of journeymen amongst them who, if left out of account, could soon have learnt methods of organization from the Flemings. They therefore started their campaign by setting up a fraternity that would include and equally represent both householders and journeymen, each class having two of the four wardens assigned to it. Apart from this unique feature, the new organization has a special interest as illustrating the relations of the fraternity to the craft. If its ordinances had not been registered in the Weavers' Ancient Book we should not have had any evidence to connect it with the craft, as the weavers are not once mentioned. The fraternity is said to have been begun by certain young men and women in the worship of the Assumption of our Lady, and the ordinances are in almost every point identical with those of a parish gild. But it is distinctly provided that the members are not to be bound to a particular parish. They are to hear mass at St. Lawrence Pountney or at any other place ordained by the assent of all the brotherhood, "so that they bind them nought to that place." In this way they obtained the protection of the Church with the minimum loss of independence. But their motive in forming a religious fraternity was to obtain, not merely protection, but sanction, *i.e.* coercive authority. Each brother or sister was to swear to obey the ordinances, and that if summoned by the wardens *before his Ordinary* or any other judge, he would appear and submit to judgment.†

* Calendar of Letter Book, G, 16, 157, 175, 204, 214, 235, 255, 265, etc.
† Facsimile of Weavers' Ancient Book.

The first annual meeting of the new fraternity was to take place in the middle of August, 1378, and at the end of July the free weavers sent a petition to a special Committee appointed by the Common Council to hear grievances, asking that the aliens, " being for the most part exiled from their own country as notorious malefactors," should be compelled to place themselves under the rule of free weavers, who were to regulate the price of their labour. This request put the dominant party in a difficulty. They could not refuse to grant the same "protection" to the weavers which they had been conferring on the victuallers and the wholesale merchants, and they were willing enough to annoy the drapers who employed the aliens, but it was difficult to wipe out all the royal privileges conferred on the Flemish weavers without some show of law. They therefore advised the free weavers to watch the foreigners till they found them guilty of some default or deceit in trade, which would be a reasonable excuse for doing what was desired.* With this threat hanging over them the foreigners thought it best to come to terms, and in March, 1380, they signed an agreement to join the free weavers in an annual search and to pay their proportion of the farm.†

Down to the autumn of 1378 the dominant party in the city had succeeded in carrying out its policy without a check, even where large national interests were concerned. But it had as its opponent the most powerful man in the kingdom, who had not exhausted all his moves in the game. In October, 1378, John of Gaunt made an attempt to remove the national government from the pressure exercised by the great London merchants, who for the moment had the populace of the city behind them. A Parliament was held at Gloucester in which the monopoly granted to the citizens by the charter of the previous year was withdrawn, the privileges of the German Hanse were restored, and the

* H, 94-95.　　　　　† H, 151.

management of the subsidy was taken out of the hands of Walworth and Philipot. To the majority of city tradesmen, however, the reversal of Brembre's policy may well have seemed a less serious blow than the removal of Parliament from London, and the serious loss of custom involved in the absence of the great lords who lodged in the city when the Houses were sitting at Westminster. If this were repeated in subsequent years, ruin would soon stare hundreds of London shopkeepers and victuallers in the face. Meetings were called by the mayor to discuss the best way of preventing this calamity. It was resolved to make a large present to the lords with a view to recovering their favour. The mayor laid down £10, and over £350 was raised by a loan, "and thanks be to God," adds the record, "a good accord was effected between the lords of the realm and the city" The next two Parliaments were held at Westminster.*

But this alarm had scarcely subsided before another serious cause of dissension arose between the Londoners and the Government. A rumour sprang up that it was intended to solve the difficulties created by the city's hostility to foreigners by making another port the seat of foreign trade. It was said that a wealthy Genoese merchant then staying in London had offered to make Southampton the greatest port in Western Europe, if the king would grant him the use of a castle there as his depôt. The indignation of the extremists in the anti-alien party at this prospect passed all bounds, and the unfortunate Italian was struck down in the open street before his inn by the hand of an assassin named Kirkeby. Feeling ran so high in London that it was impossible to bring the murderer to trial there, and as the Government were determined he should not escape, the Parliament of 1380, the Parliament which enacted the fatal Poll-tax, was held at Northampton. Kirkeby was convicted and executed, says the chronicler, with all London looking on.†

* H, xv–xvi. † Walsingham, I. 407.

The eventful story of the four days of June, 1381, when the rebels were in London has been admirably told by two recent historians, and need not be repeated.* But the account that has been given above of the relation of parties within London during the six years that preceded the rising, should help to explain some of the dealings of influential Londoners with the rebels. Historians have not unnaturally been puzzled to account for the fact that the aldermen who were afterwards charged with having sympathetically parleyed with the peasants and invited them within the walls, and who were in fact responsible for the gates that were opened to admit them, were members, not of the reforming party, but of the party of victuallers whose leader, William Walworth, afterwards aimed the decisive stroke that put an end to the rising. Now, there can be little doubt that Walworth himself had no wish to admit the rebels, but there is such a thing as a man leading a party that he is unable to control, and the presence of the rebels offered a temptation to the extremists which they proved unable to resist. Their party had been dominant in the city for over four years and, as events proved, its lease of power was running out. The early triumphs of Brembre's mayoralty had been reversed. The hated foreigner had been reinstated in all his privileges and the monopoly of the city retailer withdrawn ; Parliament had been again removed, and with it all the season's trade, to a provincial town ; the one man who had dared to strike a blow for their liberties had been hanged as a criminal, and John of Gaunt, the author of all these calamities, had still the leading influence in the national councils. If they could use the force of popular discontent—much of which was already directed against their great enemy—to strike a decisive blow at the Duke, to settle old scores with the Marshalsea, to make an end of the foreigner, and to place their leaders in the position they were

* G. M. Trevelyan, *England in the Age of Wycliffe* ; Oman, *The Great Revolt of* 1381.

naturally qualified to occupy of confidential advisers to the young king, a little interval of disturbance would be a small price to pay for so many advantages.

These considerations supply an adequate motive for the action of Alderman John Horn in advising the peasants on Blackheath to " come to London since we are all your friends," and in giving them a royal standard to march under. They account for the scarcely concealed satisfaction with which Alderman Walter Sibille, who was in charge of London Bridge, looked upon the destruction of the Marshalsea, and for his replying to the expostulations of the citizens, " These men of Kent are our friends and the king's." They explain, too, why the cry of " To the Savoy " should have been raised as soon as the rebels had crossed the bridge, and why the labourers and weavers' journeymen should have turned to the loot and slaughter of the aliens ; but, above all, they account for the strange anxiety manifested by a mob of peasants, most of whom had never seen London before, to find and destroy the Jubilee Book.[*]

As far as paying off old scores went, the plot of the extremists succeeded. But as a means of furthering their constructive designs it was a failure. In the autumn following the rising John of Northampton was elected mayor and remained in office two years. Of the methods by which he maintained himself in power we have a picture that is startlingly modern. It is drawn by no friendly hand, and forms, indeed, part of an indictment for treason, but the treason of that day has become the political commonplace of this, so that with a little necessary modification the charges may be accepted as true without greatly lowering our opinion of John of Northampton. In the first place, he was guilty, says the indictment, of the crime of organizing a party.

" When he was mayor he and his friends . . . sought to draw to

[*] Oman, *The Great Revolt*, pp. 187-213 ; Trevelyan, pp. 230-8.

themselves many men of diverse misteries and a great number of the middle class (*mediocrem populum*) who were entirely ignorant of good government, and by a system of public meetings carefully organized beforehand, they proposed to maintain their false and evil schemes with a strong hand, under cover of talk about the common good ; and they were always urging the people to be in readiness to stand by them."

On the basis of the party thus formed he had set up a still more modern organization—a Caucus.

" He caused at diverse times a meeting to be held at the tavern of John Willingham in the Bowe, of one or two men from each of twenty misteries, viz., Armourers, Girdlers, Lorimers, Pinners, Wire-drawers, Cardmakers, Curriers, Horners, Tilers, Smiths, Dyers, Fullers, Shearmen, Haberdashers, Cordwainers and other small misteries, who held by him and had been elected through him to the Common Council. And there were present at such meetings along with him John More, Mercer, Richard Norbury, Mercer, William Essex, Draper, and also Thomas Usk, Scrivener, to write out their resolutions. And there they discussed various matters . . . so that those who were present might vote together unanimously at the meeting of the Common Council. And so by this method he and his friends introduced whatever proposals they pleased and had them registered at the Guildhall."

And finally, if we are to believe the indictment, this early master of the art of politics proceeded to "gerrymander" the constituencies.

" And because William Walworth, Knight, and others were of a contrary opinion it was agreed . . . that John of Northampton while he was mayor could call to his counsel those whom he pleased . . . and that of every mistery that held against him no more than two members should come and even those must be presented by those of that mistery who agreed with John in opinion, whilst the misteries that were on his side could send as many as they chose. And so he secured a sufficient majority in every Council."

But even a unanimous Council would not be omnipotent

if all its permanent officials were active members of the opposition.

" And seeing that the old officials, viz., the Recorder, the Chamberlain of the Guildhall, the Common Clerk and other officials would not consent to the opinions of the party but held the contrary view, John Northampton and his supporters conspired in March, 1382, to remove them in process of time and to fill their places with such men as would maintain their opinions." *

Having thus carefully armed himself for the combat the Mayor commenced his great duel with the fish monopoly. The first great blow was struck at Midsummer, 1382, when a number of articles were published by the authority of the Mayor, Aldermen, and the whole Common Council, which purported to have been collected from various royal charters and ancient ordinances of mayors and commons. No fish-monger was to go to forestall fish by land or water or to take any alien fishmonger into his house or to form a partnership with him. All strangers bringing salt-fish, red herring or other victuals that would keep, were to offer it for sale three days to the public before disposing of it to city tradesmen. Strangers bringing fresh fish of the sea might sell it on their ships or in Cornhill or Cheapside, and city fishmongers were limited to two hours a day for retailing such fish. Sweet-water fish was to be sold direct to consumers by those who caught it or their wives and servants.†

Throughout the following three months a continuous struggle went on about the execution of these ordinances. The wealthy fishmongers who had depôts at Yarmouth and Gorleston, continued to " embrace fish at the sea coast," and sell it for consumption in the country so as to keep up the London price. The Bailiff of Southwark was bribed to delay the disembarkation of foreign fish on the south side of the river so as to make it too late for the

* Powell and Trevelyan, *Documents*, pp. 27-9.　　† H, 190.

market.* The foreigners who stood in Cheapside were not allowed to sell their fish in peace. On the 8th of August Adam Carlille, one of the aldermen who had been responsible for letting in the peasants, came to the Stocks market, "and in a haughty and spiteful manner cursed the said strangers, saying aloud in the hearing of all that he did not care who heard it or knew of it, but that it was a great mockery and badly ordained that such ribalds as those should be selling their fish within the city . . . and that he would be better pleased that a fishmonger who was his neighbour in the city should make 20 shillings by him than such a ribald 20 pence." The Common Council petitioned the Mayor and Aldermen that they would not lightly allow this roguery and malignity to pass, and Adam was declared incapable for the future of holding office.†

When Parliament met at Michaelmas the conflict was transferred to Westminster. Under the influence of Northampton and his party a number of measures had been introduced which gave a national sanction to his policy. Already in the spring an Act had been passed confirming the liberties of merchant strangers, and it was now proposed to give aliens full power to sell victuals wholesale or retail; to forbid London fishmongers to buy fish, except eels, luces, and pike, to sell again; and to enact that no victualler should hold judicial office in any city or borough unless no other sufficient person could be found, in which case he was to abstain from victualling during his term of office. All these measures passed into law, but not without strenuous opposition from the fishmongers. Nicholas Exton, their leader, who appeared before Parliament as a witness or a petitioner, told the knights of the shire assembled in the refectory of the Abbey that " if he had been found at home the previous night he would have been arrested and led through the midst of Cheap like a robber and a cut purse." He declared that if the Bills passed

* H, 192–193.   † Riley, *Memorials*, p. 468.

HALL OF HOLY TRINITY GILD
NEAR ST. BOTOLPH, ALDERSGATE

WOMEN WORKERS IN WOOL

FIFTEENTH CENTURY

the fishmongers would be in peril of their lives, and prayed that the king might take them under his protection; and Walter Sibille, another fishmonger, having obtained leave to speak, "began to crow that these devices were not exhibited for any good zeal" to the commonwealth, but for mere malice borne to the fishmongers who had been the means of getting several of the promoters imprisoned in Edward III.'s time. Whereupon John More, who was at that time M.P. for the city, replied that there was no intention on their side of breaking the peace, "unless," he added significantly, "they [the fishmongers] went about to let into the city the rebels of Kent and Essex as Walter himself and others did lately." *

These mutual recriminations of the party leaders had immediately found an echo in humbler quarters. As three or four fishmongers of Queenhithe sat talking with a few neighbours, heated words arose between them on the crisis in the city. "It seems to me," said one, "that the Mayor is taking the bread out of our mouths." "Yes," said another, "and you and I and all the other fishmongers are bound to put our hands beneath the feet of Nicholas Exton for his good deeds and words on our behalf." "That may be," broke in a neighbour, "but I wouldn't have been in his place at the last Common Council for a house full of gold." This timorous sentiment roused another fishmonger to fury. "For half a house full," said he, "I would call the Mayor a scoundrel. I should like to have it out with him in a stand-up fight on Horse Down." †

A few days before this talk took place, John Northampton had been re-elected for a second year of office. To accomplish this without too gross a breach of consistency had been a delicate matter. The new civic constitution was based on the principle of annual changes of Mayor and Aldermen. But principles had to be subordinated to political necessities. To

* H, xxix ; Rolls of Parliament, III. 141-143.
† Riley, *Memorials*, p. 473.

M

abandon office at that moment was to risk losing all the ground
he had gained, and Northampton had no such intention.   If
we are to believe the indictment already quoted, a meeting
had been held at Goldsmiths' Hall to take measures for his re-
election, a special Common Council had been packed, and
friendly non-voters were to be at hand with physical support.
Nevertheless two writs from the king, dictated no doubt by
friends at court, were needed to overcome Northampton's
scruples.   The first informed the Sheriffs, Aldermen and
Commons that the king had no intention of interfering, but
if they should elect John of Northampton it would be agree-
able to him.   The offer to re-elect Northampton was then
made and declined.   But on receipt of another letter addressed
to himself, praying him to accept office if elected, the revolutionary leader agreed to serve " on account of his reverence
for the king." *

The second year of his mayoralty must have been one of
declining popularity.   At first, the chronicler tells us, he
pleased everybody by his regulation of the fish trade ; but
when he went on to call other trades to account for their
transgressions and began to set up as a reformer of evil
customs generally, he soon made more enemies than friends.†
And the records prove that John Northampton was a very
Calvin in restless zeal and unbending thoroughness.   His
hand was felt everywhere.   Brewers and bakers were to make
farthingsworths for the poor, and, to leave them without
excuse, a supply of farthings and of farthing measures was to
be had at the Guildhall.   And the same rule was applied to
the supply of spiritual needs.   No priest was to charge more
than a farthing for a mass.   If he said he had no change the
parishioner might leave without paying.‡   But it is in administration rather than in legislation that the true vigour of
reform is revealed, and the scrutiny of the mayor seemed to
penetrate every hole and corner in the city.   The quack who

* H, xxxii.   † Higden, *Polychron*, p. 29.   ‡ H, 183.

sold nonsensical Latin charms for fevers, the fortune-teller who professed to discover stolen goods by an act of divination with balls of clay, the sharper who played with an uneven draught-board or false dice, the begging impostor who displayed imaginary wounds and spread false reports about the war in Flanders, were one and all exalted in the pillory. There was a grim humour or a grim pedantry in the mayor's penal methods. An offender who had slandered both the mayor and an alderman must appear in the pillory with two symbolical whetstones hung about his neck, a larger one for the mayor and a smaller one for the alderman. An alderman who appeared on the Feast of Pentecost without the proper taffeta lining to his green cloak, must provide a dinner to the whole aldermanic bench free of charge.*

A mayor of such a temper was not likely to be long popular either with the aldermen or the crowd, and the natural swing of the pendulum might have been trusted to bring his opponents back into power. But both sides now felt too strongly to leave events to their natural course. When the election day came round again arrangements for packing the Guildhall were made on either side, but Nicholas Brembre was chosen mayor, according to the statement of the defeated party, "with strong hand and against the peace." Northampton was not disposed to accept his defeat quietly. There was still a fortnight of office left him. On the day of the election he discussed the situation with three friends over dinner at John More's house near St. Mary Bow. They resolved to call together the caucus at Goldsmiths' Hall next day, and in the mean time they dispatched a messenger to John of Gaunt asking that a royal writ might be sent ordering a new election.

At the party meeting the mayor eloquently denounced the methods of his opponents. "If," said he, "we suffer this mockery of an election to hold good, we shall be little better

* Riley, *Memorials*, pp. 455-480.

than slaves. I for my part do not intend to suffer it. Let us all die at once rather than put up with such an indignity." Loud cries of assent and demands for a new election followed this outburst, and, according to the hostile account of the indictment, the mayor was on the point of appealing to force when the calmer counsels of the aldermen restrained him. Perhaps also he may have been discouraged by John of Gaunt's reply, which told him that no royal intervention could be expected.

But though the new mayor was allowed to take office the activity of the opposition did not cease. The leaders met almost daily, sometimes at More's house, sometimes at St. Paul's, at Grey Friars' or Austin Friars', and conspired against the Mayor and Aldermen so that a great part of the people appeared by divers signs of voice and countenance to be rebels against the mayor. In January, 1384, Brembre complained to the king, and Northampton was bound over to keep the peace. Early in February, however, as the mayor was dining in Wood Street with Sir Richard Waldegrave and a number of aldermen, he received tidings that Northampton was marching at the head of five hundred followers through Cheap in the direction of Ludgate. He dispatched a messenger to bid them halt, and hurried after with the sheriffs. Twice Northampton ignored the messenger, but when on passing Fleet Bridge he looked back and saw Brembre in pursuit, he called a halt, and parting his men to right and left, waited to receive him. The zeal of the mayor had outrun the discretion of his followers, and, turning round, he found himself alone in the midst of his enemies and looking rather ridiculous. Once, twice, thrice by word and by gesture he bade them follow him. Not a man stirred. Thus, says the record, did John Northampton show himself a rebel and make himself the equal of his mayor. At last the ex-mayor led the way to the church of the Carmelites, where, it seems, it had been their peaceful intention to hear a mass for the soul of the

Earl of Nottingham's brother, and having thus proved at once his innocence and his power, he allowed Brembre to arrest him and to imprison him in the mayoral residence.

Four days later the discontent of the leaderless party broke into open revolt. The shops in Cheapside, Budge Row, Fleet Street, and elsewhere were suddenly closed, and a crowd assembled before the mayor's house demanding the release of his prisoner.* Brembre at once proclaimed martial law, and seizing on a cordwainer named Constantine, who was said to have been the first to put up his shutters, he ordered him off to instant execution.† Northampton, More, and Norbury were tried in the autumn and condemned to death, but their sentence was immediately commuted to one of ten years' imprisonment. Norbury was sent to Corfe Castle, More to Nottingham, Northampton to Tintagel,‡ but two years later they were released on giving security not to come within eighty miles of the city.

With the election of Brembre the victuallers gained a new lease of power, which was to run, as it proved, for five years, and the whole policy of Northampton was immediately reversed. The representatives sent by the city to the Parliament then sitting were all of Brembre's party. The Act of the previous year limiting the operations of fishmongers was at once repealed, and a new charter was granted to the city restoring to its freemen the monopoly of retail trade, and once more limiting merchant strangers to a forty days' stay with a host. The mayor, indeed, found it necessary to contradict rumours to the effect that foreign traders were not to be allowed to bring victuals to London market at all.§ Northampton's book of ordinances naturally fell into abeyance, but it was not till three or four years later that the famous Jubilee Book, which had been the occasion of so much violent party

* Powell and Trevelyan, *Documents*, p. 35.
† Riley, *Memorials*, p. 482.
‡ H, xxxvii–xxxix.   § H 222, 226.

feeling, was solemnly committed to the flames by Brembre's successor, Nicholas Exton.*

The overthrow of the new constitution introduced by Northampton, based on the exercise of electoral functions by the misteries, was equally complete. It cannot, indeed, be said to have justified its existence by its smooth operation in practice. The discretion left to the mayor as to which misteries should be called upon to elect representatives was obviously open to be abused in the interests of party. At the end of Hadley's mayoralty in 1380 the compromise was tried of electing a Council partly from the misteries and partly from the wards, and Walworth opened his mayoralty a month later by instructing the aldermen to consult their wardmotes as to whether it were best for the election to be made from the misteries, from the wards, or from both. If they decided in favour of making the election themselves, they were to proceed to act on their self-conferred powers. What their decision was is not recorded, and it is not quite clear how the Common Council was elected for the rest of Walworth's year of office. On one important occasion it was certainly chosen from the wards. With the election of Northampton in 1381 the misteries regained their political functions, but their exercise of them during the next two years had a revolutionary character, and did not afford any prospect of permanence.

Soon after Brembre became mayor in 1383 a committee was appointed to draw up a new constitution for the Common Council, " where," it was said, " matters had of late been carried rather by clamour than by reason and sometimes by members not qualified to sit," and a week before Northampton's arrest their proposals were laid before an immense Commonalty of honest and discreet men for their consideration. They were to the effect that the elections should be given back to the wards. Every year, within a fortnight of their own election, the aldermen were to summon

* Riley, *Memorials*, p. 494.

their wards and charge them to elect four persons, qualified by means and understanding, regardless of any office they might have held before, to be of the Common Council for the year ensuing, but if the mayor found that more than eight persons from any one mistery had been chosen by the whole city, he was to select, with the advice of the aldermen, eight of the best, and have new ones chosen in place of the others. This recommendation, with the modification that some of the larger wards were to elect six members and some of the lesser ones only two, was afterwards adopted, and proved to be the final settlement of the question.* The annual election of aldermen, which had been the other part of Northampton's constitution, was allowed to remain till 1394, when an Act of Parliament declared that the aldermen should remain in office " till they be removed for just or reasonable cause."†

The subsequent career of Brembre belongs rather to national than to civic history. He threw in his lot with the fortunes of the small party that was beginning to assist and direct the absolutist aims of the youthful king.‡ Brembre's position in the city was one of the main supports of this new policy, and his connection with the Court enabled him, on the other hand, to hold the mayoralty " as it were of conquest or maistery." " He made," says a later petition, of the mercers, " divers enarmings by day and by night and destroyed the king's true lieges, some with open slaughter, some with false imprisonment, and some fled the city for fear." At the next election he laid an ambush of armed men in the Guildhall, who sprang out on the electors crying with loud voice, " Slay ! Slay ! " If any grudged or complained of any wrong he was held untrue to the king.§ Another petition speaks of a number of prisoners whom Brembre had secretly conveyed out of the city for execution by martial law in Kent.||

* H, Introduction, vi–vii.   † *Ibid.*, ix.
‡ Stubbs, *Constitutional History*, II. 486–504.
§ Rolls of Parliament, III. 25. || *Ibid.*, III. 231.

This reign of terror ended when Parliament impeached the king's friends as traitors, and Brembre was hanged in 1388. Two years later the sentences of the exiled leaders of the other party were reversed and their property restored. Northampton's political career had ended, but the old rivalry between himself and Brembre still dominated the imagination of their fellow-citizens and supplied their parties with catchwords, so that it was found necessary as late as 1394 to forbid the mention of their names. Northampton died in the full odour of sanctity in 1398. It would seem that the unbending austerity of his reforming days had been softened by his misfortunes. By his will he made provision that every Lent each monk in the Charterhouse should have a pound of dates, a pound of figs, and a pound of raisins beyond his usual allowance.*

* Sharpe, *Calendar of Wills*, II. 334.

CHAPTER XI

THE INCORPORATED LIVERY COMPANY

W E are now better able to appreciate the significance of the inquiry instituted in 1389 into the constitution and property of the fraternities, and into the privileges of the chartered crafts. A glance at the Rolls of Parliament will show that that inquiry was no isolated fact. The nation was beginning to take stock of the social forces that had begun by building it up, and might end by tearing it asunder.

The central characteristic of the Middle Ages was unconscious growth, the development, side by side, of social forces not fully aware of their mutual antagonism. With the middle of the 14th century there commenced a period of climax ; the forces began to realize their antagonism, and their first instinct was to give it free play. The experience of anarchy and revolution thus produced brought into fuller consciousness the wider and deeper common interests that had been growing up behind the antagonisms. The larger communities, the city and the nation, began to assert their rights over the partial interests of family or trade or class, and to demand that these should cast off the devices of feudal faction and subordinate their differences to the rule of a common authority.

In this object the city, as was natural, succeeded in advance of the nation. The struggle of factions in London was a kind of rehearsal on a small scale of that larger conflict in which the feudal privileges of the nobility were to batter themselves to pieces on the fields of Towton and Bosworth. Each side began by attacking the privileges of the other and ended by surrendering a good deal of its own.   Northampton's party insisted that the victuallers should be under the rule of the mayor, and struck a death-blow at the feudal immunity embodied in the fishmongers' halimot.   As soon as Brembre came into power he demanded that all the royal charters held by the wealthy manufacturing crafts, the Drapers, the Goldsmiths, the Girdlers, the Saddlers, Tapicers and Cordwainers, should be brought in to the mayor in sign of submission to his authority.*   The Saddlers refused at first, and only submitted when Brembre threatened to drive them out at the point of the sword and cause the whole city to rise against them.†   Later on, in Northampton's mayoralty, the misteries that had given up their charters complained that the Fishmongers had kept back the most essential documents, and it was resolved that these also must be handed over to the mayor.   The Fishmongers, like most of the other victuallers, had never exercised the powers of self-government which it had become usual to confer on a craft, so that to deprive them of their special privileges was to reduce them to a position below the level of other trades.

"He compelled the fishmongers to acknowledge," says the chronicler in his hostile account of Northampton's mayoralty, "that the craft they had hitherto exercised was not a craft at all and was not to be reckoned or named as such amongst the other crafts of the city, and thus he brought it about that those who were before superiors were now scarcely admitted amongst the inferiors."

In Brembre's second mayoralty the victuallers had to content themselves with removing the disabilities that had been imposed on them, and with re-establishing the rights of

---

* Calendar of Letter Book, H, 193.   † Sherwell, *Saddlers*, p. 41.

free citizens generally as against foreigners. The halimot was not to be restored, and "no one of any mistery or estate whatsoever was to enforce his franchise without leave of the Mayor and Aldermen." Conventicles and assemblies were forbidden by proclamation. The political activity which had centred in the halls of the greater crafts was suppressed. The powers which the lesser crafts and the journeymen had been exercising, by means of a fraternity organization backed by the sanction of the Church, were declared illegal. And the inquiry of 1389 was merely the culmination of a movement which had long been in progress, and which had been helped forward by the action of both the leading parties, towards placing all lesser franchises and all the powers of private association under the control of the public authorities, whether civic or national.

But at the moment when civic feudalism in its more direct political forms was passing away, the social influence of the feudal ideal on city life was taking a shape that has survived to this day—that of the incorporated livery company. The livery company did not fully achieve its typical and permanent form till about a century later, and the elements of which it was composed had each of them been in existence a century earlier, but it was at the end of the 14th century that those elements began to blend into a new organic whole, a new type that was to dominate the social organization of the city for four centuries. The fraternity, the court of halimot, the chartered trading body, the craft or mistery, each contributed important features to the livery company, but each element thus contributed was modified or transformed as it passed into the life of the new organization. The livery company was perhaps most closely akin to the fraternity, but the fraternity element embodied in the livery company was from the first largely free from ecclesiastical dominance, and its religious functions became so subordinated to its social activities that they could be entirely transformed at the

Reformation without causing any serious break in the continuity of the company's existence. Each fully developed livery company had its court in which trade disputes were settled and by whose authority members could be fined and even imprisoned, but while this jurisdiction was a real and effectual one, and sharply distinguishes the livery company from the craft or mistery in its earlier form, it was not an immunity jurisdiction like the court of the Weavers or of the Fishmongers, but was exercised under the authority of the mayor. Similarly, each company based its existence on the possession of a royal charter, but this charter was not necessarily a grant of exclusive trading privileges like the earlier ones granted by Edward III. to the Goldsmiths, the Skinners, the Drapers, and the rest ; the essential point of it was that it conferred the immortal collective personality of a corporation.

It was not until the corporate existence of the livery company had been invested with the security of legal sanction that the type could definitely form itself and begin to spread by the process of open imitation. And the necessity of such a sanction had been made sufficiently clear by the events related in the last two chapters. All the rights hitherto enjoyed by the great trading fraternities had been recently called in question. The mayor had suppressed their right of assembly, Parliament had demanded the suppression of their liveries, the Commission of 1389 had required the return of their charters, and had revealed the illegality of their landed possessions. Immediately after the inquiry, therefore, the older trade fraternities began to place themselves on a firmer footing. The Tailors, who procured their new charter as early as 1390, contented themselves with obtaining a confirmation of all the rights previously enjoyed—to hold their gild of St. John Baptist, to make a livery, to hold their assemblies and their annual feast at midsummer, and to make ordinances— with the sole addition of a clause providing for the election of

a master and four wardens.* But in the charters granted to
the Goldsmiths,† to the Mercers in 1394,‡ and to the Saddlers
in 1395,§ there is an entirely new departure. Each of these
misteries asks for and obtains the right to have a perpetual
commonalty of themselves, and to have a licence to hold lands
in mortmain to the value of £20. The connection between
these two grants is made clear by the petition of the Goldsmiths, who state that they had previously held a licence in
mortmain from Edward III., but that it had not yet been
executed because " no person capable " was named therein.
The Skinners, who obtained in 1393 a similar licence to hold
lands in mortmain, seem to have thought they had acquired
an adequate personality by procuring a grant at the same
time " to hold for ever their fraternity or gild in honour of
Corpus Christi and to increase it " ; ‖ but subsequent charters
betray an increasing sense of the need of a definite grant of
incorporation. The Tailors' charter of 1408 constitutes them
" a sound perpetual and corporate fraternity," which is to have
a common seal, may plead and be impleaded, may have and
hold lands, etc.

In all these early cases of incorporation it is to be noted
that while the grant is addressed to the men of the trade in
general—the skinners of London, the men of the mistery of
goldsmiths, of mercers or saddlers—the body endowed with
legal personality is a fraternity. Not only had fraternities
existed in all the trades in question from an early date ; it is
the need of strengthening the social and religious activities of
these fraternities that supplies the justification for the grant.

" Our well beloved liege men of the mistery of Saddlers," runs
the charter of that company, "have besought us that whereas many
men of the mistery . . . by old age, feebleness and other infirmities
. . . come to poverty and need, our said lieges piously sympathizing

---

* Calendar of Patent Rolls, 1390, p. 321.   † Ibid., 1393, p. 219.
‡ Ibid., 1394, p. 425.   § Ibid., 1395, p. 560.   ‖ Ibid., 1393, p. 286.

with the estate of such . . . purpose to acquire lands for the sustenation of the said poor and of one chaplain," etc.

In the same way, in addition to providing a chaplain, the Mercers propose to relieve those who have suffered through shipwreck and other misfortunes, and the Goldsmiths " those who by fire and the smoke of quicksilver have lost their sight."

In giving such prominence to religious and benevolent objects as the motives for their incorporation, the fraternities were following the natural line of least resistance. To maintain their control over their respective trades was, no doubt, a more important object than the relief of their poor. But theoretically their right to exercise this control had never been called in question, whilst in practice it was only effectual in proportion to their political influence, and their political influence largely depended on the maintenance of their social prestige. It was with a view to establishing permanent organs for the accumulation of social prestige that the livery companies were incorporated.

For nearly half a century incorporation remained an exceptional privilege, even amongst the wealthy fraternities whose members constituted the ruling class of citizens. The next batch of charters—those granted by Henry VI.—turned the exception into the rule, and by so doing effected a change in the significance of incorporation. It included the four great victualling misteries, the Grocers (1428),* the Fishmongers (1433),† the Vintners (1436),‡ and the Brewers (1437),§ as well as five leading manufacturing misteries, i.e. the Drapers (1438),‖ the Cordwainers (1439),¶ the Leathersellers (1444),** the Haberdashers (1447),†† and the Armourers (1452).‡‡

---

* Herbert, *Twelve Great Livery Companies*, I. 320-321.
† *Ibid.*, II. 24.   ‡ *Ibid.*, II. 632.
§ Calendar of Patent Rolls, 1437, p. 142.   ‖ *Ibid.*, 1438, p. 244.
¶ *Ibid.*, 1439, p. 308.   ** W. H. Black, *Leathersellers*.
†† Herbert, II. 536-537.   ‡‡ Guildhall MSS., No. 110, I. fo. 179.

The Parish Clerks were also incorporated in 1442, and the Cutlers had received a charter from Henry V. Incorporation thus became the established rule amongst the greater misteries, and an object of legitimate ambition to all the rest.

The effect of this movement is seen in the wording of the charters. Although the basis for incorporation was still supplied in most, probably in all, cases by a fraternity organization, the government of the mistery gradually comes to the front as the main object. The Drapers' charter of 1438 clearly indicates the point of transition. The men of the mistery of drapers are authorized "to erect a gild in honour of the Virgin Mary and to hold it and enjoy it to all future times." The men of the gild may annually elect a master and four wardens, who must be drapers and freemen, to manage the business both of the mistery and of the gild; and the master, wardens, brethren, and sisters of the gild are to be one body and a perpetual community, with a common seal " for the business as well of the mistery as of the gild and fraternity." A year later the charter of the Cordwainers gives them authority to choose yearly a master and four wardens " to survey, rule and govern the mistery . . . and all men and works pertaining thereto and all workers and works in tanned hides . . . and of all new shoes sold or exposed for sale in the city or for two miles round."

That this openly avowed incorporation of the misteries by royal charter was creating a new situation that called for vigorous action on the part of the municipal authorities, is shown by an Act of Parliament passed in 1437. The preamble to the Act states that "masters, wardens and people of gilds, fraternities and other companies corporate . . . oftentimes by colour of rule and governance and other terms in general words to them granted . . . by charters . . . of divers kings, made among themselves many unlawful and unreasonable ordinances as well in prices of wares and other things for their own singular profit," and the Act requires all such incorporated fraternities or companies to bring their charters to be registered by the chief governors of cities, boroughs, and towns.* The city of London had evidently been foremost in procuring this legislation, and immediately began to put it into operation. The charters recently obtained by the Brewers and the Cordwainers were called in question. The Brewers declared their obedience to the Mayor and Aldermen, and promised to renew the declaration when called upon to do so. The Cordwainers were enjoined to renounce before the Lord Chancellor all benefit of their new charter, and after taking time for consideration, they submitted to the authority of the Court of Aldermen.†

Disputes about the validity of royal charters would seem to have formed the main staple of city politics at this period. The Drapers' charter of 1438 aroused the jealousy of the Tailors, who had been fully incorporated in 1408, and led them to procure another charter in 1439, giving them some exclusive rights of search over the cloth trade. In 1440 the two candidates for the mayoralty were Robert Clopton, Draper, and Ralph Holland, Tailor.

" When the Tailors in the Guildhall saw that Clopton was chosen they cried, 'Nay, Nay, not this, but Ralph Holland' . . . and incensed others of low fellowships of the city to take their part . . . and would not cease for speech of the Mayor nor Oyez made by the Sergeant of Arms. Wherefore . . . twelve or sixteen of them were sent into Newgate, some fined and some long imprisoned."

At the instance of the new mayor the powers granted to the Tailors were recalled by the king.‡

No doubt the opposition thus shown by the city to any diminution of its control over the crafts explains the reversion

---

* 15 Hen. VI. c. 6.   † Guildhall MSS., No. 110, Vol. I. fo. 154.
‡ Herbert, *Twelve Great Livery Companies*, II. 413–414 ; *Fabyan's Chronicle*, p. 615 ; Clode, *Early History of Merchant Taylors*, I. 135.

INITIAL LETTER OF HENRY VI'S CHARTER TO LEATHER-SELLERS

DYEING AND DYERS

END OF FIFTEENTH CENTURY

to the earlier formula in the incorporation of the Haberdashers (1447) and of the Armourers (1452). In both these cases the usual corporate rights of perpetual succession, the possession of a common seal, the power to hold lands and to plead, are conferred on fraternities, the one in honour of St. Katherine, the other in honour of St. George, and nothing is said of the regulation of trade. The Armourers' charter is indeed almost unique in the prominence given to religious objects, which was no doubt meant to appeal to the pious feelings of Henry VI.*

(A new epoch opened with the accession of Edward IV. One of the earliest acts passed in his reign prohibited the importation of a long list of foreign manufactures with a view to encouraging native industries.† This policy was strongly supported by some of the London crafts. The Cutlers took a leading part in getting the Act passed, and were backed by the contributions of lesser crafts like the Pinners, who paid 10s. to obtain an exemplification of the Act in the form of a mandate to the Mayor to enforce it.‡ In 1464 the Horners obtained an Act forbidding the export of the raw materials of their industry, and giving them powers of search for a distance of twenty-four miles round London.§) The charters granted by Edward IV. were part of the same policy. He incorporated the Tallowchandlers (1462), the Barbers (1462), the Ironmongers (1463), the Pewterers (1468), the Dyers (1471), the Musicians (1472), the Parish Clerks (1475), the Carpenters (1477), the Fullers (1480), and the Cooks (1482). By these incorporations—and those of the Waxchandlers (1484), the Plasterers (1501), the Coopers (1501), the Poulterers (1504), the Bakers (1509), and the Innholders (1515)—the middle class in the city was invested with the same social status as the upper class represented by the membership of the greater companies.

---

* Guildhall MSS., No. 110, Vol. I. fo. 179.   † 3 Edw. IV. cap. 1.
‡ Egerton MSS. in British Museum, 1142.   § 4 Edw. IV. cap. 8.

The records of the Pewterers enable us to follow, in what was no doubt a typical case, the process by which they secured the object of their ambition.* In 1452 they paid a clerk of Chancery 5s. to assist two of their members "to search for statutes and other things to the intent to labour to the Parliament for a charter for the craft to have search through England." The outbreak of civil war seems to have put a stop to their effort for a time, but with the accession of Edward IV. it was renewed. Counsel's opinion was taken and another Bill prepared for Parliament, the cost of which, together with "expenses done on such as shall put it up," amounted to the modest sum of 10s. 8d. A deputation entrusted with 8d. to bestow in drinks went to Cutlers' Hall to ask the advice of the officials there, and another person of experience or influence was interviewed in the Mitre in Cheap, at a cost of 16d. for bread and wine. The Pewterers seem to have been advised that incorporation was a costly affair, and that they had better put more money in their purse before attempting it. Another ten years was to elapse before their final and successful effort. In 1467 a sum of £80 which had been accumulated was placed in the hands of one of the wardens "for purchacing of our lyvelihood." In 1471 and 1472, sums of £7 4s. and £2 3s. 4d. are entered as legal expenses "on divers persons learned and writings for the speed and purchasing of the corporation," and in 1473 a final sum of £41 18s. 8d., for the provision of which a special levy had to be made on all the householders of the craft, thirty-nine of whom contributed amounts varying from 2s. to £3.

As soon as the charter was granted the new corporation proceeded to equip itself with a seal, which cost 10s. 5d. for silver and 6s. 8d. for graving, with a great book with two clasps, and "a coffin" for the "corporation" to lie in, and several copies of the charter in English. These last

* C. Welch, *Pewterers*, Vol. I. 18, 34-76.

were for the purpose of enforcing the rights of search which they had now acquired over country pewterers and over pewter sold at fairs, and which soon proved to be a valuable source of income. The searchers authorized by the craft seem to have covered the greater part of England, and during the following year they brought in over £20. Thirty-two country pewterers, braziers, and bell-founders had been induced to enroll themselves and to pay entrance fees varying from 3s. 4d. to £1, and no doubt much defective metal had been seized.

Hitherto the Pewterers had held their meetings at Austin Friars, where they had rented a hall and other rooms for festive and business purposes, but with such a prospect of extended resources they began to think of having a roof of their own over their heads. A year after the charter had been granted, the senior warden was authorized to seek a hall, and spent 8d. in tips. A hall in Coleman Street was viewed by a deputation, but the place finally decided upon was part of the estate of the Nevilles in Lime Street. Here they entered into occupation of some existing premises as tenants, but soon after they began to build, and in 1485 they acquired the site, after much negotiation at the Mitre, the Salutation, the Pope's Head and St. Paul's, and the consequent expenditure of half a dozen six-and-eightpences in lawyers' fees and as many twopences in drinks. The site itself cost £120, towards which the Master gave £6 13s. 4d. Another £45 was raised amongst seventy-five members. These sacrifices soon began to bear fruits. The possession of a charter and a hall gave the company an effectual hold on the imagination of its members. Gifts and bequests began to flow in for the endowment of the new collective personality—glass windows, furniture, linen, plate and towels for the hall, a fair banner with the arms of the craft for its pageants, and a gorgeous cloth of gold to serve as a pall at the funerals of members. The Pewterers were rapidly climbing the ladder of social advancement. In the mayoralty of Sir Henry Colet (1488), they held the fourteenth place in a list of sixty-five crafts, and may well have indulged hopes of being soon within the magic circle of the twelve great companies.

The case of the Pewterers may be taken as fairly representative of the dozen companies incorporated by Edward IV. But success of this kind could not be universal. It implied a degree of wealth unattainable to a body of mere craftsmen or small traders. The money that bought the charters and built the halls was supplied mainly by well-to-do employers and merchants. In the new organization these claimed a share of influence proportionate to their wealth, and soon came to form a class apart from the working craftsmen. In the fraternity of the 14th century, the livery had been worn by all members alike, but most of the incorporated livery companies of the 15th century contained from the first a number of members who were householders and paid quarterage but were " out of the livery," and who were frequently grouped in a separate organization known as the Yeomanry, and the more prosperous members of the Yeomanry were advanced from time to time into the Livery. Unless a craft could produce a class of capitalists and retain them within its own ranks, it could not support the expense involved in achieving the new type of organization.

Hence arose a struggle for existence, in the course of which a considerable number of the hundred and eleven crafts which we know to have been in existence in 1423 disappeared, or were absorbed by their more successful rivals. The formation of the Leathersellers Company furnishes the most striking example of this process of amalgamation. Throughout the 15th century they had maintained a constant struggle as to rights of search with the various crafts working in leather, the Glovers, the Pursers, the Whittawyers, and the Pouchmakers. In 1451 they arranged for a joint annual search with the Glovers, which did not, however, prove to be a

A LIST OF THE CRAFTS OF LONDON IN 1422

From the Brewers' Records.   See Appendix A II., p. 370

permanent settlement. In 1479 their records state that "we had much trouble with the Pursers and also with the Glovers and with much and great labour had of them our intent . . . according to right. Also the craft of Tawyers came to us to be of the craft of Leathersellers and took their clothing with us and brought in their book." In 1498 the Pursers and the Glovers petitioned the Mayor and Aldermen that they might be united as Glover-Pursers, on the ground that both crafts were sore decayed both in number of persons and in substance of goods ; and four years later the new amalgamation was " by the good and virtuous mediation of the Mayor " united to the Leathersellers. And finally, in 1517, the Pouchmakers besought the mayor "to annex, knit and make in unison " their craft with that of the Leathersellers, to continue in one fellowship, one name, one assembly and one body.

In the same way the Armourers absorbed first the Bladesmiths and then the Brasiers ; the Spurriers were united to the Blacksmiths ; the Hatters and Cappers fell under the control of the Haberdashers ; the Pinners and Wiresellers, after vainly uniting their forces, became subordinate members of the Girdlers' Company. In other cases the amalgamation was on more equal terms, as in that of the Barber-Surgeons, that of the Painter-Stainers, and in that of the Clothworkers' Company, which arose out of a union of the Fullers with the Shearmen. The last case is a specially interesting one. The Fullers and the Shearmen had each contrived, in spite of strong opposition from the Drapers and the Tailors, to obtain separate grants of incorporation, yet they still found their wealthier members being drawn away from them by the superior attractions of the Drapers' Company. Accordingly, they joined hands in 1528, and by this stroke of policy just managed to secure the last place amongst the Twelve Great Companies.*

But the prevalence of the new type is not to be measured

---

* Unwin, *Industrial Organization*, pp. 44, 108.

by the number of crafts that had achieved legal incorporation. Of the sixty crafts that had a place at the mayor's feast at the Guildhall in 1531 not more than half were incorporated, but at least a dozen of the remainder were organized in the same fashion. Many of these, like the Butchers, the Curriers, and the Tilers, had long possessed halls, and the royal charters ultimately granted to them by Elizabeth or James I. merely confirmed them in the exercise of powers they had enjoyed for a century or more. Legal incorporation was needed to consolidate the new type of association whilst it was still in process of formation, but when the type had become firmly established by the incorporation of a score of the leading companies, its features might easily be copied by companies that were not incorporated. That this actually happened may be seen by comparing the ordinances granted by the Mayor and Aldermen to the crafts in the reigns of Edward IV. and Henry VII. with those granted in the reigns of Edward III. and Richard II. The set of articles for the regulation of their calling which the men of a mistery presented to the civic authorities in the earlier period were almost entirely silent as to the social machinery by means of which the regulations were to be enforced. The rules about the length of apprenticeship, the entrance to a trade, the search of workshops, the seizure of defective wares or materials, were sufficient to give the craftsmen a fairly complete control of their trade if they were well enough organized to take advantage of them. But no such organization was directly authorized by the city. From the strictly constitutional point of view the wardens or overseers of a trade, though elected by the craftsmen, were the sworn officers of the municipality, and could only enforce their authority by a direct appeal to the Mayor and Aldermen. They were not authorized to hold courts of the craft or to levy quarterage upon its members. The whole social machinery by which the " craft " secured an effective control of trade—the annual and quarterly meetings, the common dress, the entrance fees, quarterly subscriptions and fines, the authority to settle disputes between members, the religious and charitable functions which gave the association its binding force —belonged not to the craft as such but to the fraternity; and the fraternity, whilst it might need the toleration of the civic authorities, derived its sanction from the Church.

The royal charters of incorporation effected a twofold change in this situation. They replaced the ecclesiastical sanction upon which the trade fraternities had rested by the secular sanction of the State, whilst at the same time they preserved for the livery companies a basis of voluntary association independent of the civic authority. Spontaneous growth from below was thus left much freer than it would have been if the companies had been the mere creations of the mayor and aldermen, but, on the other hand, there was serious danger of civic anarchy if the larger companies became too independent of the municipal government. It was in order to safeguard itself from this peril that the city promoted the Act of 1437, and insisted on the charters granted to the companies being presented for approval and enrolment to the Mayor and Aldermen.

Such was the situation in the middle of the 15th century. Each of the dozen livery companies that had secured incorporation had a history of its own, but the general type was formed by a mixture of the "mistery," or organ of municipal administration, and the fraternity. The charter might lay all or most of the stress on one of these elements, but in each case both elements co-existed and were beginning to blend into a new whole. During the reign of Edward IV., as we have already seen, this type of organization was rapidly spreading among the lesser misteries. The civic authorities opposed the movement to the best of their power, but if a craft could collect sufficient funds they could not prevent it from buying a grant of incorporation from the king. In the end they found it wiser to compete with the king by offering similar advantages at a cheaper rate. In the reigns of Edward IV. and Henry VII. more than a dozen sets of ordinances were granted to the lesser crafts, in which all the features of the livery company except legal incorporation were outlined and authorized by the city. The ground covered by these ordinances corresponds much less with that covered by the old articles granted to the crafts, than it does with that covered by the rules of the religious fraternities as returned in 1389. They provide not only for the election of wardens but for annual mass and feast. They empower the wardens not only to search for defective goods and to divide the fines imposed upon offences with the city, but also to collect quarterage for religious and charitable objects, to hold courts for the settlement of disputes, and to appoint a livery. They lay upon members the obligation of attending the court on the summons of the beadle, of accepting office when elected, and even of following the funeral and bearing the body of a departed brother of the fraternity. Thus, in the cases of the Blade-smiths (1463),* the Painters (1466),† the Bakers (1476),‡ the Masons (1481),§ the Hurers (1489),‖ the Bowyers (1489),¶ the Lorimers (1489),** the Founders (1490),†† the Saddlers (1490),‡‡ the Weavers (1492),§§ the Pastelers (1495),‖‖ the Wiresellers (1497),¶¶ and the Upholders (1498),*** the whole of the gild organization became a matter of civic ordinance. In some instances at least the city would appear to have exercised pressure upon the fraternities in this direction. The fraternity or organization of the Saddlers is the oldest of which we have any record, and it had been incorporated by Richard II. The Saddlers had fallen out of the ranks of the greater companies, and perhaps they had neglected to have

---

* Letter Book, L, fo. 16.   † L, 43.   ‡ L, 122.
§ L, 165.   ‖ L, 266.   ¶ L, 261b.
** L, 270.   †† L, 278b.   ‡‡ L, 280.
§§ L, 295.   ‖‖ L, 318.   ¶¶ L, 329.   *** M, 56.

their charter enrolled. In 1490 they were commanded to bring in their book containing all the ordinances "which their predecessors had long afore this time made and which they had peaceably enjoyed," but which "had not been authorized within the city." These were straightway cancelled and a fresh set of ordinances dealing with their religious observances, their livery, the appointment of assistants, the holding of courts, the election of officers and the auditing of accounts, were issued on the authority of the Mayor and Aldermen.

If all the city companies had come to exercise their functions as voluntary associations under the direct sanction of the municipal government, their most vital characteristics would have been effected. The influence of the incorporated companies prevented this result. It was in them that the type had been first formed, and their semi-independent position served as an example to the rest. Most of the crafts that first took shape as livery companies by virtue of a municipal grant of ordinances, contrived at a later date to establish themselves on a corporate footing by grant of a royal charter, or were absorbed into other companies more successful in this respect than themselves.

Nevertheless, it would be a great mistake to regard the legal formalities of incorporation as in any way essential to the corporate spirit. That spirit had become universal amongst all classes of dwellers in cities before the end of the 15th century. The clergy, regular and secular, of all grades ; the legal, medical, and teaching professions ; the merchant, the shopkeeper, and the craftsman ; the persecuted alien and the despised waterbearer—were all entrenched behind the bulwarks of professional association. Even the Labourers of London looked back at a later date to the golden age of Henry VII. and Henry VIII., when their interests had been protected by some form of recognized corporate activity.

Nor was the corporate spirit by any means a purely selfish one. The jealous spirit of professional honour which is recognized as one of the most important contributions to modern civilization, was an essential part of it. This chapter may fittingly close with a glance at two documents from different ends of the 15th century, which may serve at once to illustrate the wide range of corporate activity and the best spirit of professionalism at this period of London history.

In the first year of the reign of Henry VI. Gilbert Kymer, Master of Arts, Doctor of Medicine, and Rector of Medicine in the city of London, appeared with the two Surveyors of the Faculty of Physic and the two Masters of the Craft of Surgery before the Mayor, to ask for the authorization of their professional organization. Their rules were meant to ensure that all practitioners in both branches should be duly qualified, if possible, by a University training, and they sought to provide a hall where reading and disputation in Philosophy and medicine could be regularly carried on. No physician was to receive upon himself any cure, "desperate or deadly," without showing it within two or three days to the Rector or one of the Surveyors in order that a professional consultation might be held, and no surgeon was to make any cutting or cauterization which might result in death or maiming without similar notice. Any sick man in need of professional help but too poor to pay for it, might have it by applying to the Rector. In other cases the physician was not to charge excessive fees, but to fix them in accordance with the power of the sick man, and "measurably after the deserving of his labour." A body composed of two physicians, two surgeons, and two apothecaries, was to search all shops for "false or sophisticated medicines," and to pour all quack remedies into the gutter.*

If we turn from the higher ranks of the medical profession to the lowlier agents of the law, we find a similar sense of serious responsibility. The Fellowship of the Yeomen Officers of the City, who served under the Sheriff's Serjeants and were

* Letter Book, K, 6.

the police constables of their day, introduce an enumeration of the rules of their profession with this preamble—

" In the name of God, Amen.   Forasmuch as among all things pleasant to our Lord God in this transitory life after due love had unto him, is the love, amity and good concord to be had among all Christian people, and in especial among them that be daily associates together, and like as their continual conversation by reason of their dealing must daily be had and accustomed, so may they be knit together in very true amity, charitable and kindly dealing. Of the which ever groweth not only such pleasure to God, but also the commonwealth, and prosperity of all them that in such wise deal. So always that their said dealing be put and set under due and good ordinary rule."

The rules require that " every Yeoman shall well and honestly behave himself in the House of the Sheriffs, and in the presence of the Master Sheriff and my Mistress, and diligently shall do him service upon the waiting days ; that he shall courteously behave himself to the head officers and ministers of courts as to Masters and Under Sheriffs, the Secondaries and all the Clerks, and them in all lawful commandments to obey, and to attend to do the services of Mrs. Sheriffs " ; they forbid him to miscall any serjeant or misuse any of his fellows or to disobey his wardens, " and forasmuch as by the will of God and ordinance of Holy Church every one that sweareth or blasphemeth is holden accursed, therefore it is ordained that whoso he be that sweareth by God our Heavenly Father or by His blessed Son Jesus, or by His bitter Passion which He suffered for mankind or by His precious blood which He shed for the sins of the whole world, or by His Blessed Mother St. Mary shall forfeit and pay sixpence or else a pound of wax to the light," maintained by the gild in Austin Friars. But the chivalry and the piety of the Yeoman were not to unfit him for the stern performance of his professional duties.

" Whereas," says another rule, " as at many suddens a yeoman is called to lead a Prisoner before a Justice or to the Gaol of Newgate, and the manifold dangers by the way considered, as the Sanctuary of St. Martin's, the Grey Friars' and other places of danger, it is ordered that every yeoman shall have always in readiness one good and comely slip to lead Prisoners in, either of tape or leather with a buckle or strong button and he that is found without to forfeit and pay as aforesaid."

Undoubtedly, however, the most interesting feature of this singular professional fraternity was its survival till the close of the 18th century. Established as a religious fraternity in the church of Austin Friars, it escaped destruction at the Reformation, as is evident from a new arrangement made in 1581 for collecting quarterage for charitable uses, and from an ordinance made apparently about the same time fixing a fine of 3s. 4d. upon the offence of going out before the sermon when in attendance on the Sheriffs at St. Paul's.

" Forasmuch as the word of God which is the food of the soul is to be desired before all other things, and that the Rt. Hon. the Lord Mayor and the Rt. Worshipful Aldermen his brethren and the Rt. Worshipful our master the Sheriff do every Sunday resort to St. Paul's to hear the sermon . . . and some of us have not abiden the sermon till the end but have had more regard to our own wills than to our duties towards God and our master."

The book in which these ordinances are fairly copied contains a record of the meetings of the Yeomen's Gild from 1710 till 1767, so that there is every reason to suppose that the association had a continuous existence for nearly three centuries.*

* Guildhall MSS. 508.

CHAPTER XII

HALLS, LIVERIES, AND FEASTS

IN the middle of the reign of Richard II. there were probably not more than two or three of the livery companies that possessed halls of their own. In the reign of Richard III. the halls numbered twenty-eight, and others were in course of being built. Some of them were of baronial extent and magnificence. The banqueting-hall of the Merchant Tailors was spacious enough to hold a couple of hundred guests, and splendid enough for the entertainment of the company's royal members. The windows were enriched with the best Flemish glass ; its walls were decked with scenes wrought in tapestry from the life of St. John the Baptist, whose gilded image must have often looked down from its gilded tabernacle on a spectacle that presented a remarkable contrast to the preaching in the wilderness and the prophet's fare of locusts and wild honey. But the hall was only the centre of a numerous group of buildings : a chapel, a gallery for portraits, a king's chamber and other reception rooms, an exchequer chamber, a treasury, a wardrobe, a pantry, a buttery, a larder, a scullery, a kitchen, a storehouse, a bakehouse, a brewery, a gardener's house and stables. The entrance gateway was flanked by a row of cottages for the reception of the company's poor almsmen.

Such a mansion was almost an exact replica of the house of the great noble who lodged his little army of retainers and held sac and soc within the city during the Middle Ages. Indeed, many of the wealthier companies began by taking over the mansion of a feudal magnate, or the buildings of a religious community which had an almost equally feudal character, and gradually adapting them to their own purposes. The Tailors themselves succeeded Sir Oliver de Ingham, who

ANCIENT DRAPERS' HALL

had held the high post of Seneschal of Gascony, and defended Bordeaux for Edward III. against the French. The Grocers took over the mansion of one of that famous FitzWalter family who, in earlier days, had held Baynard Castle, and had led the civic forces to the field by hereditary right. Skinners' Hall stands on the site of an old mansion known as Copped Hall, which met all their needs till the Fire. The Pewterers acquired a hall that had been part of the Nevilles' manor of Leadenhall. The great house and garden of Thomas Cromwell, Earl of Essex, was bought after his fall by the Drapers. The Mercers acquired the Hospital of St. Thomas of Acon ; the Leathersellers, St. Helen's Priory.

The Tailors and the Goldsmiths are the only crafts that are known with any certainty to have possessed halls before the close of the 14th century.*

Before the Tailors acquired the site of their present hall in Threadneedle Street in 1331, they occupied one "behind the Red Lion in Basing Lane in Cordwainer Ward." But the first record of actual building relates to the Goldsmiths' Hall, the site of which had been in the occupation of Sir Nicholas de Segrave, brother to the Bishop of London, in Edward II.'s reign, and had been transferred to the Goldsmiths in 1357. In 1364 their records speak of an assembly held in their "common place in the parish of St. John Zachary," and in the following year they spent £136, out of £168 which had accumulated in the hands of the wardens, on their common place for a hall, kitchen, pantry, buttery, and "two chambers with two beds." In 1380 a new parlour and cellar were added. The walls were of rubble and chalk, the roof of the parlour was leaded, the inside wainscotted with "planche bord" and painted in oil, and there were two chimneys. In 1447 the Livery raised a subscription towards rebuilding the parlour, and a member was admitted on the Livery for glazing the window. Other benefactors added a bay window to the hall, and the roof was surmounted with a lantern and vane in 1454. In 1467 the sum of £6 9s. 6d. was spent on "five benches of tapestry work with goldsmiths' arms and seven cushions for the same," and about the same time the hall was hung with red worsted and paved with tiles. A silver-gilt statue of

---

* The Fishmongers may have had one or more—Stow states they had as many as six—but the holding of a halimot does not imply the possession of a hall.

St. Dunstan, which stood above the screen, was broken up
and sold at the Reformation.

But perhaps the most interesting item in the Goldsmiths'
records relating to the furnishing of their hall, is the entry
which describes how three pieces of rich arras were procured
from Flanders in the reign of Henry VIII. A member of the
company who was entrusted with the commission sent over a
servant into Flanders to superintend the making of the arras,
which occupied him eleven weeks and a day, his travelling
expenses being £6. First of all, the life of St. Dunstan,
which was the subject to be illustrated, had to be translated
into Dutch, which cost 10s. Then four artists were employed
sixteen days at 1s. a day making a design in black and
white; and a boy was hired at 2d. a day to sharpen their
pencils. The cost of the actual making of the arras, which
measured 195 Flemish ells, was over £250. Ten shillings
were paid for the town seal of Brussels and for counsel; other
dues to Flemish officials amounted to over £3; a Spaniard
charged £2 for exchanging money, and the English custom
house levied another £10; so that by the time the arras was
hung behind the high dais it had cost the Goldsmiths as much
as would have built a hall for a smaller company.*

The Grocers, who had contented themselves for a long
time with meeting in the houses of their members, or in the
chamber which they had built for their chaplain, evidently felt
the great solemnity attaching to their first gathering within
walls of their own. Their record of it opens thus—

" In the Holy Name of Jesu, Amen. Remembrance made that
on Trinity Sunday and the third day of June in the year of King
Harry the VI. and the sixth year of his reign, was held the election
of chief governor and wardens which election was the first made in
our place of Coneyhoop Lane in the parlour . . . as the hall was but
little begun. . . . And in the said year . . . was performed the walls

* Herbert, II. pp. 222–226.

O

of our hall on both the sides up to the plate of the roof, and also the end of the said hall up to the half gable window at the dais and the other gable up to the window over the kitchen with other costs in the chamber and parlour, and every penny well and truly paid every Saturday to the last end of the year." *

Three more years were, however, spent in completing the work. Under date of 1431 we read—

" On July 1st was the first feast made in our fair hall, at the which feast was the mayor and many a worshipful person more, beside the whole craft, at the which feast was drunken two pipes of wine and nine barrels of ale with all the appurtenances that longeth therto . . . and more in our time the garden was made new with the fair Erber and all the new vines with all the new rails and a pair of fair new butts thereto." †

The company were minded to enjoy their new possessions in privacy. The wardens were instructed " not to allow men of Court or ' Courtyours ' nor none other Brotherhoods nor Fellowships to occupy our hall nor no part of our place, except the Brotherhood of St. Mildred in the Poultry. And also they shall not suffer no man to play at the tennis within the said place, except those that ben Freemen Shopholders." They were likewise to " suffer the grapes that come of the garden to hang still and ripe, to the intent that every man of the livery may daily send after two or three clusters home to their houses." ‡

During the years in which the Grocers' Hall was being built the Tailors were making extensive improvements to their buildings in Threadneedle Street. Repairs to the hall account for £31 in 1425, and for £35 in 1427. The kitchen was enlarged at an expense of £64 in 1430, and of £28 in 1432. Another £68 was spent in 1433. The Tailors sent a deputation to view the kitchen in Kennington Palace—on such an ambitious scale were their plans. §

---

* Kingdon, *Facsimile of Grocers' Records*, II. p. 174.   † *Ibid.*, pp. 193-194.
‡ *Ibid.*, I. 124.   § Clode, *Memorials*.

By this time halls were beginning to be built even by the lesser companies. The Saddlers had received a bequest from Thomas de Lincoln, on condition that they built a common hall for the use of the mistery within three years after his decease, and the fact that they obtained a charter entitling them to hold land in 1395 no doubt indicates that they began to build at that time.* The Brewers and the Carpenters built halls without waiting to be incorporated. The Carpenters had special facilities for building as the Brewers had for letting, and both companies seem to have the needs of others in view quite as much as their own. In the two years 1422–3, the Brewers let their hall to seventeen different fraternities, which, it may be assumed, had at this time no halls of their own. The Barbers hired it nine times, the Girdlers and the Clerks five times, the Dyers and the Armourers four times, the Point-makers and the Cooks three times, the Coopers twice, and the Butchers, the Smiths, the Ironmongers, the Founders, the Glaziers, the Galochemakers, and the Yeomen of the Cord-wainers, each once. In another list are found the Haber-dashers and the " Cotelers " ; and besides the fraternities of the crafts there were the Fraternity of the Cross and the Brotherhood of the Trinity, the Football-players, and the " Penny Brotherhood." The charge for a single occasion seems to have varied between 1s. 6d. and 2s. The Inquest of the Wardmoot paid 4d. The income derived in two years was £3 4s. 2d.† The Carpenters, whose hall was built in 1426, let it to sixteen different users in 1438, and raised the greater part of their income in that way.‡

By the middle of the 15th century the majority of the greater companies had come into full possession of their first halls. In several cases, those of the Skinners, the Vintners, and the Fishmongers, for instance, the site had been acquired at an earlier date, and passed on from one set of trustees to

---

* Sharpe, *Calendar of Wills*, II. 302.
† Brewers' first book, folios 84, 184.   ‡ Jupp, *Carpenters*, p. 16.

another by private arrangement, until a grant of incorporation
and the accumulation of bequests for the purposes of building
and of charitable endowment made it advisable for the company to assume full ownership.   Thus Richard Merivale, a
Vintner, by his will made in 1437, directed that if the Vintners
became incorporated within two years after his decease, his
feoffees in trust of certain houses and shops in the parish of
St. Edmund in Lombard Street " shall so arrange matters that
one of them should become solely seised of the property, so as
to be able to devise the same for the relief of the poor of the

VINTNERS' HALL AND BUILDINGS

mistery."   A few months later the company obtained its
charter, and in 1446 another vintner, Guy Shuldham, bequeathed more property on the condition that they should
convert to their own use a " large hall with parlour, counting
house, pantry, yard, etc. . . . and that they should bestow
thirteen little mansions lying together, parcel of the said lands
. . . upon thirteen poor and needy men or women of the
mistery," each receiving one penny a week out of the residue
of the property.*   The property thus converted to the
Vintners' use had been originally known as the manor of the

* Sharpe, *Calendar of Wills*, II. 487, 596.

Vintry, and had been held by Sir John Stodie, Vintner, who was mayor in 1357.*

The first Salters' Hall had a similar origin at about the same date. The Salters furnish the one clear instance of a livery company originating in a parish fraternity, that of Corpus Christi in the Church of All Hallows', Bread Street. In 1454 Thomas Beaumond, Salter, left to the wardens, brethren, and sisters of that fraternity, divers lands and tenements, comprising a parcel of land whereon a hall was in course of erection called Salters' Hall, and six houses newly erected in the same parish, in which six poor members of his art "were to be maintained as bedesmen, receiving a weekly sum of sevenpence." The wardens were also to distribute annually 20s. amongst the poor of the craft. By an earlier will he had left the fraternity other property—the White Bull in Bread Street and a house and garden in Pudding Lane—to provide a chantry for the souls of himself, his two wives, his friends, his parents, and all the faithful who should have died in the University of Oxford within seven years.†

In 1434 the Fishmongers' Company acquired possession, partly as a bequest, partly by lease, and partly to hold in trust for religious objects, of the site of their present hall, which had been occupied by distinguished members of their company, including John Lovekyn and Sir William Walworth, for many generations, but which was finally transferred to them by Sir John Cornwall, Lord Fanhope. When the two branches of the trade, the Fishmongers and the Stockfishmongers, which had been separated in 1505, were reunited in 1534, it was resolved to hold the meetings of the company "in the Fishmongers' Hall in the parish of St. Michael Crooked Lane and not in any other place, which hall is of the gift of Lord Fanhope" This probably implies that Lord Fanhope transferred the hall on specially favourable terms on condition of the Fishmongers observing his obit. In Richard III.'s reign the

* Stow, *Survey*, p. 240.   † Sharpe, *Calendar of Wills*, II. 534–535.

Fishmongers possessed two other halls, one in Old Fish Street, in the parish of St. Nicholas, Cole Abbey, and the other in Bridge Street, in the parish of St. Margaret.*

At the same date there existed, in addition to the halls that have already been mentioned, the Drapers' Hall, in St. Swithins by London Stone ; the Haberdashers' Hall, in the parish of St. Mary Staining, fast by Gutter Lane ; the Chandlers' Hall,

ANCIENT FISHMONGERS' HALL

fast by the Skinners' Hall in Wallbrook ; the Cutlers' Hall, in the parish of St. Michael Paternoster, fast by Ryal ; the Fullers' Hall, in Candlewick Street, within St. Martin's Lane ; the Bakers' Hall, in Warwick Lane ; the Barbers' Hall, in the parish of St. Olave, Silver Street; the Butchers' Hall, in "Mongell" Street, by Cripplegate ; the Dyers' Hall, in Anchor Lane, in the parish of St. Martin Vintry ; the Shearmen's Hall, in Mincing Lane ; the Cordwainers' Hall, in Distaff Lane ; the Girdlers' Hall, in Bassishaw ; the Tilers' Hall, in the parish of All Hallows', London Wall ; the Curriers', in the parish of St. Mary Axe by the Papey ; and the Armourers' Hall, in Coleman Street.†

* Herbert, *Livery Companies*, II.   † Harleian MSS., 541.

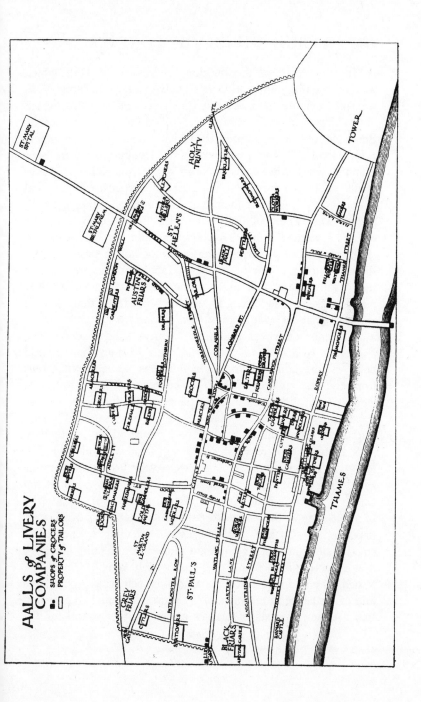

HALLS of LIVERY
COMPANIES

■ SHOPS of GROCERS
☐ PROPERTY of TAILORS

In the record of the building of Pewterers' Hall, which was proceeding during the first twelve years of Henry VII., we possess a detailed account of efforts and sacrifices which must have had their parallels in most of the other cases. Benevolences were raised, to which the poorest members contributed 4*d.*, the wealthiest £1. Deputations were sent round to view other halls so as to gather the latest improvements. The windows were glazed at the expense of individual donors, the less wealthy members undertaking a pane, or a half-pane. The ceiling of the parlour was furnished in the same way by seventeen members, who gave from four and a half to ten yards apiece. Others gave a table or half a table, a form, six joint stools, a pair of trestles, a table-cloth, an iron spit, a set of salt cellars, or a silver spoon—all which items are duly placed on record as " the giftys of such goodmen that be alive and they that be paste oute of this Worlde." *

Nothing could show more clearly how essential the possession of a hall was felt to be at this time than an old book of the Pinners' accounts, that has come down to us from the last quarter of the 15th century. The protectionist legislation of Edward IV. had seemed to be the Pinners' great opportunity, and they tried to take advantage of it by improved organization. They had managed to accumulate £18, though their fines and quarterages for two years yielded less than £6, and their expenses were very little short of this sum. They contributed 24*s*. 8*d*. to assist the other metal trades in procuring the Act of 1463, and paid 10*s*. for a copy of a mandate to the mayor to enforce its execution, which they deposited in Cutlers' Hall, besides expending a number of smaller sums in arresting foreign pinners, conducting searches, and executing a holocaust of the obnoxious pins in Cheapside. When they had met all the expenses of their legal proceedings and of boat-hire in journeys to Westminster Hall, had provided half a dozen trentals of masses at 2*s*. 6*d*. the trental for the

* C. Welch, *Pewterers*, I. 70–83.

souls of deceased members, paid the waxchandler, fee'd the sexton of Elsing Spital, and bestowed six hundred pins on the sisters of St. James' Hospital to secure their prayers, there was not much left to keep house on. So they contented themselves with hiring Girdlers' Hall at a cost of 2s. a year, and employing a beadle at a salary of 6s. 8d. Yet with all this economy they began to find after the first enthusiasm had passed away that their expenses were exceeding their income, and the £18 in hand, after rising to £22, fell to £12. A general slackness is visible in the accounts. No fines are levied. The elected officers borrow the cash in hand and put in I.O.U.'s.

It was at this seemingly unfavourable moment that the Pinners determined to have a hall of their own. No doubt some reformer thought that the best remedy for indifference was to have an object for which to make sacrifices. Debts were called in, and £12 12s. realized. A site, and probably a building, was rented at 20s. a year, and the Pinners proceeded to adapt it to their needs. They paid to the dauber and his man, 25s. ; to the carpenter, 15s. ; to the stainer, 31s. ; for brick, lime, and masons' work, 11s. 8d. ; for sprig, nail, and iron work, 15s. 6d. ; for lath and boards, 16s. 2d. ; for loam, sand, and gravel, 11s. 8d. Their furniture was of the simplest. A table and two trestles cost 4s., and four forms cost 16d. This heroic effort was made in 1480, and in 1497 the Pinners and the Wiremongers appeared before the Lord Mayor asking to be amalgamated, on the ground that " both fellowships were of so small number and in so great poverty and decay that they could not support their charges nor bear scot and lot separately." *

Of the permanent staff required by the hall the irreducible minimum was represented by the Beadle. Only the richer fraternities had chaplains on their staff, and in most companies the clerical work, which did not amount to more than the drawing up of an account every one or two years, was given

* Egerton MSS. in British Museum, 1142.

out to a scrivener.   But even before the acquisition of a hall
the beadle had been indispensable as a link between the
elected officers and the members.   He kept a list of members ;
summoned them to meetings, feasts, and funerals ; collected
quarterage, distributed alms, and attended searches.   When
the hall was acquired he became its caretaker, superintended
building operations, and tended the garden, whilst his wife
washed the linen.   In the wealthier companies, such as the
Tailors, who as early as 1399 paid their beadle £3 a year, the
more responsible of these functions were no doubt undertaken
by the Clerk, who, however, only received a salary of
£2 13s. 3d. and his table, which cost £2 12s., whilst some of
the lowlier duties were delegated to serving men.*   But in the
case of the Pewterers, who may be taken to represent the more
prosperous of the lesser companies, the beadle fulfilled every
function, from that of clerk of works downwards, until the
middle of the 16th century.   His salary, which had been
only 24s. in 1463, rose gradually to £4 in 1564.   His wife had
13s. 4d. for washing the linen, and he was to be allowed at the
master's dinner a boiled capon or a cock, half a goose, half a
pike, half a pie, half a custard, a rabbit, a dish of sturgeon, two
casts of bread and a gallon of drink, and to have a similar
allowance at the yeomanry dinner.   In 1679 his salary had
risen to £20 ; he had two-thirds of the sums paid for hire of
the hall for funerals, and he was allowed to farm the quarterage.   In addition to these sources of income he had always
had numerous small fees and house-room in the hall.†

Most of the greater companies had no doubt clerks of their
own—as we know to have been the case with the Tailors and
the Brewers—from the beginning of the 15th century, but
in the majority of the lesser companies the necessity for a
clerk was not imperatively felt till the middle of the 16th
century, when the weekly sittings of the Court of Assistants

---

* Clode, *Memorials of Merchant Tailors*, p. 66.
† C. Welch, *Pewterers*, I. pp. 20, 27, 29, 39, 248 ; II. 154.

began to require a regular record. The Barber-Surgeons promoted their beadle to the office in 1555 at a salary of £4. In 1603 this had become £10; but the fees the clerk was authorized to charge, such as 40s. for registering the accounts, 26s. for drawing a lease, 12d. for administering an oath or on the admission of a freeman, must have formed the chief part of his emolument. In 1648 his salary was raised to £30.* The Pewterers' Clerk, who had begun with a salary of £1, was receiving £20 in 1610, and when his house-room was required for extending the hall, an extra allowance was made, which grew to £12 in 1636.† The extensive financial operations in which many companies, including the Pewterers, were engaged at this time, rendered the position of the Clerk an important and responsible one. The Feltmakers, who paid £30 a year to their Clerk, in 1612 required him to invest £500 in their joint-stock enterprise, and the Farriers made a demise to their Clerk of his dwelling in the hall on condition that he would assist in raising monies on interest for the company when needful, and would be co-security with wardens and assistants. He was also to be bound in £50 to continue in their service.‡

The suits of livery from which the companies derived their names were as distinctly borrowed from feudalism as their halls. Originally "Livery" meant the allowance in provisions and clothing made to the servants and officers of great households, whether of baron, prelate, monastery, or college. Certain survivals of livery in this original sense still linger in the rations supplied to Fellows in the colleges of the older universities. The term was gradually restricted to the gift of clothing as a badge of service and of protection. The hired ruffian of the 14th or 15th century was as effectually sheltered under a great lord's livery as a priest was under benefit of clergy. The monastic orders had, moreover, early shown how

---

* Young, *Barber-Surgeons*, pp. 288 *et seq.*
† Welch, I. 154; II. 56, 76, 126, 156.
‡ Unwin, *Industrial Organization*, p. 163.

valuable a link of voluntary fellowship the adoption of livery
might be made, and at the time when the wearing of a
distinctive dress on special occasions was becoming common in
fraternities of all kinds, Edward III. instituted a new order of
nobility by granting the livery of the Garter. Livery of company
became fashionable.   Great lords wore one another's badges.
The factions at Court in which our party politics had their
origin distinguished themselves by their respective liveries.*

The numerous abuses to which the wearing of liveries lent
itself led to frequent demands in Parliament for their prohibition, and a long series of Acts were passed from the reign
of Richard II. onwards with that object, which had, however,
little effect in diminishing the evil till the Tudors began to
adopt more stringent measures.   These Acts were always
worded so as not to have reference to the liveries of fraternities,
but the petitions to Parliament expressly aimed at them also,
and the fear of being covered by one of these prohibitions was
no doubt what led some of the companies that were first to be
incorporated to procure an authorization of their livery in their
charters.

The livery of the fraternities consisted of two parts, the
gown and the hood, and in the earliest ordinances of some of
them we find the distinction made between those members
who only wear the hood and those who take the whole suit.
Before the middle of the 15th century there had grown up a
class of freemen in most of the companies who did not wear
the livery at all.   The Grocers in 1430 had 55 members in the
livery, 17 in hoods, and 42 householders not in the livery.
But suits of livery or hoods were plentifully bestowed by the
wealthier companies on outsiders, who were thus constituted
as honorary members.   Thus the Tailors in 1399, besides a
costly livery to the King and Prince, gave a less sumptuous
one to the Mayor, and hoods to the sheriffs, treasurer, recorder,
chamberlain and clerk, and seven robes and seven hoods to

* Stubbs, *Constitutional History*, III. 548.

others.* In 1415, and again in 1423, the Mayor, Aldermen, Sheriffs, or any other officers of the city, were forbidden to take any livery except that of the company to which they respectively belonged.

The less wealthy companies contented themselves with appointing a new livery every two, three, or four years. Where a fresh suit was given every year the member was required to keep each suit two years, so that he always had a second best for less solemn occasions. At the beginning of the 15th century a suit cost about 15s. or 16s., and the hood separately about 2s. 6d. The Brewers' Company, whose members were exceptionally numerous, spent in 1417 as much as £185 on one set of liveries, 39 of the wearers being women. The livery in early times was always of two colours, which varied with the fashion or taste of the company. The Grocers wore scarlet and green in 1414, scarlet and black in 1418, scarlet and deep blue in 1428, violet in grain and crimson in 1450. At first both gown and hood were parti-coloured, but fashions became soberer about the time of the Reformation.†

"But yet in London," says old Stow, "among the graver sort (I mean the liveries of companies), remaineth a memory of the hoods of old time worn by their predecessors : these hoods were worn, the roundlets upon their heads, the skirts to hang behind in their necks to keep them warm, the tippet to lie on their shoulder or to wind about their necks; these hoods were of old time made in colours according to their gowns, which were of two colours, as red and blue or red and purple, murrey, or as it pleased their masters and wardens to appoint to the companies ; but now of late time they have used their gowns to be all of one colour, and those of the saddest, but their hoods being made the one half of the same cloth their gowns be of, the other half remaineth red as of old time." ‡

* Clode, *Memorials of Merchant Tailors*, p. 65.
† Riley, *Memorials*, p. 612 ; Guildhall MSS., 110, fo. 154 ; Herbert, *Twelve Great Livery Companies*, I. 62.
‡ Stow, *Survey*, p. 446.

Besides the livery of their own company, it became the custom in the 15th century for some of the members of the greater companies to take the livery of the mayor and sheriffs. Those who wished for the mayor's livery sent in their names to the clerk of their company with 20s., and received four yards of cloth for a gown.*   In 1401 the Grocers, besides spending £67 on their own livery, laid out £6 more in providing those who were to ride with the Sheriffs with hoods of their livery, and in the same year bought 166 yards of motley and a large quantity of cloth of "colour verdubt," at a total cost of £43, for clothing the company against the coming of Queen Johanna, late Duchess of Brittany.†   On many of these special occasions the companies seem to have all worn the same colours, and to have been distinguished from each other by cognizances embroidered on their sleeves.

When the Mayor, Aldermen, and Commons rode out to meet Anne of Bohemia, the new queen, in 1382, the misteries of the city had it in charge that they should not have vestures of other colours than red and black.

"Notwithstanding," say the Goldsmiths' records, "as all the other misteries had divers cognizances, the Goldsmiths chose theirs, and did wear on the red of their dress bars of silver work and powders of trefoils of silver: and each man of the same mistery, to the number of seven score, had upon the black part five nouches (knots) of gold and silk: and upon their heads they wore hats covered with red and powdered with the said trefoils." ‡

The halls of the Livery Companies are associated in the popular mind mainly with feasting, and it is not generally realized that the daily work carried on in many of them represents a combination of the activities of a ducal estate-office with those of a charity organization society, and a department for technical education.   The administrative functions of the

---

* Herbert, 64.   † Kingdon, *Facsimile of Grocers' Records*, I. p. 90.
‡ Herbert, II. 217.

companies were of a different character in the age which immediately succeeded the first erection of their halls, and they were more closely connected with that great chamber which formed the centre of the group of buildings occupied by each of the companies. With the hall as the centre of the self-government of a community, and with the business judicial, financial, and administrative carried on there from week to week, we shall be concerned in subsequent chapters. But perhaps the social activities, and especially the feasts of the companies, may claim our first attention, since they, like the fabric of the hall itself, represent to a large extent a survival from earlier feudal times, from the traditions of the great household.

The companies had their feasts before they built their halls. When they had not, as the Grocers had, members with houses large enough for their accommodation, they met in the hall of a religious house, or in a tavern like the Mermaid in Bread Street. That a feast held under these conditions was not a mere fortuitous concourse of guests, but was permeated by a real family feeling, is sufficiently shown by the preservation amongst the Salters of a receipt for making a Christmas pie, which comes down from a period fifty years before the building of their hall, and which deserves quotation.

"Take fesaunt, haare and chykenne or capounne, of eche oone ; with ii partruchis, ii pygeonnes & ii conynggys ; & smyte hem on peces & pyke clene awaye therefrom alle the boonys that ye maye, & therwith do hem ynto a foyle (shield or crust) of gode paste, made craftely ynne the lyknes of a byrdes' bodye with the lyvours and hertys, ii kydneis of shepe, & farcys (forced meat) & eyren (eggs) made ynto balles. Caste thereto poudre of pepyr, salte, spyce, eysell (vinegar), and funges (mushrooms) pykled ; & thanne take the boonys and let hem seethe ynne a pot to make a gode brothe therfor, & do yt ynto the foyle of past, & close yt uppe faste, and bake yt wel & so serve yt forthe ; with the hede of oone of the byrdes stucke at the oone end of the foyle, and a grete tayle at the other, &

dyvers of hys longe fedyrs sette ynne connynglye alle about him." *

But as soon as they had halls of their own the fraternities began to take greater pride, if not greater pleasure, in their feasts, and to seek the honour of entertaining distinguished guests. As early as 1380 the books of the Goldsmiths record the fact that the wardens of that year, with the consent of their good people and commons, made a feast to which were invited " my very honourable lady Isabel, daughter of the King of England, and her daughter the Countess of Oxford, the Lord Latimer, the Grand Master of St. John's, Clerkenwell, and the Mayor, with six other good folks of the city, which put the wardens to great cost." †

Thus began the process by which the feasts of city merchants and traders were gradually assimilated in luxury, style, and expense to those of the greatest magnates in the land. The cost of keeping St. Dunstan's Day, which in 1357 had been only £4, was £10 in 1359, £16 in 1363, £21 in 1369, and £32 in 1495. In 1473, when £26 17s. 4d. was the total expense, the largest item was for comfits and spice, £5 17s. 6d., and the next for wine and beer, £4 10s. ; these items, with £3 4s. for minstrelsy, covered half the cost of the entertainment. Poultry accounted for another £3 ; fish for £2 11s. 6d. ; whilst butcher's meat only came to 14s. 5d., although it included 2 kids, 2 kid lambs, a sirloin of beef, 2 legs of mutton, 12 marrow bones, 4 pair of calves' feet, 3 knuckles of veal, a shoulder of veal, and a mouse piece of beef.‡

Feasting was not confined to the " greater " companies. Indeed, the Goldsmiths appear almost frugal by the side of the Brewers, who spent £38 on their feast in 1425, when 21 swans at 3s. 9d. each were provided, and the bill for poultry alone came to £8,§ including, besides the swans, 2 geese at 8d.,

* Herbert, II. p. 563.   † Ibid., p. 236.
‡ Ibid., p. 237.   § Ibid., I. 79.

40 capons at 6*d.*, 40 conies at 3*d.*, 48 partridges at 4*d.*,
12 woodcocks at 4*d.*, 12½ doz. smaller birds at 6*d.* the doz.,
3 doz. plovers at 3*s.*, 18 doz. larks at 4*d.*, 6 doz. little birds at
1½*d.* a doz. The Brewers, who were much harassed by the
famous Richard Whittington about this time on account of the
dearness of their beer, attributed the persecution solely to
the Mayor's jealousy of their swans, and of the great style of
their feasts. The cook who dressed their dinner was paid
23*s.*, and six turnspits and four assistants "from a tavern on
Fish St. end" received 3*d.* apiece. A hundred faggots and
four quarters of sea coal at 8*d.* the quarter were consumed.
Eighteen dozen of pewter vessels were hired at a cost of 10*s.* ;
rushes for the hall cost 8*d.*, lavender for the tablecloth 6*d.*, and
the players and two harpers and other minstrels received
£5 0*s.* 10*d.*

The smallness of the expense on butchers' meat is explained
by a passage in Harrison's *Description of Britain,* which,
though written in Elizabeth's days, is equally true of the
times of the earlier Tudors.

"The gentlemen and merchants," he says, "keep much about one
rate. . . . At such times as the merchants do make their ordinary
or voluntary feasts, it is a world to see what great provision is made
of all manner of delicate meats from every quarter of the country,
wherein besides that they are often comparable herein to the nobility
of the land, they will seldom regard anything that the butcher usually
killeth, but reject the same as not worthy to come in place. In
such cases also jellies of all colours, mixed with a variety in the representation of sundry flowers, herbs, trees, forms of beasts, fish, fowls,
and fruits, and thereunto marchpane wrought with no small curiosity,
tarts of divers hues, and sundry denominations, conserves of old
fruits, foreign and homebred, suckets, codinacs, marmalades, marchpane, sugar-bread, ginger-bread, florentines, wild-fowls, venison of all
sorts. . . . Of the potato and such venerous roots . . . I speak
not." *

* F. J. Furnival, *Elizabethan England,* pp. 91-92.

P.

The story told by the London chroniclers of how the
Mayor, Aldermen, Sheriffs, and Commons who had left the
Serjeant's feast at Ely Place in a huff because the Lord
Treasurer was placed higher than the Mayor within his own
city, and how they were afterwards found by the astonished
messengers, who came to apologize and to bring peace offerings,
feasting with equal magnificence in the Mayor's own house,
illustrates the equality in these matters which the city claimed
to hold in Tudor times.   There is a curious echo of this story
in the Drapers' records for the year 1521.   The Mayor, who
was a Draper, had attended the Serjeant's feast that year, and
though his rights of precedence were duly observed the Drapers
did not consider the banquet worthy of them.   " To show what
the fare was," says their record, " is but loss of time.   I suppose
that the worshipful citizens were never worse served." *

The Drapers may have had high notions, but they were
based on their own practice.   They dispensed hospitality on
a magnificent scale.   In 1516 they entertained seventy-eight
distinguished guests, amongst whom were the Bishop of
Carlisle, the Masters of St. John's Clerkenwell, and St.
Thomas' Acons, the Priors of Christ Church, Merton and
St. Mary Overy, the Lieutenant of the Tower, one of the
Barons of the Exchequer, the Mayor, Sheriffs, Chamberlain
and Recorder, Leland the antiquary, and a number of knights
and ladies.   The total number of those who sat down to
dinner must have been about two hundred, of whom about
thirty were at the chief table in the hall, and another hundred
at the two side tables.   Some forty ladies were seated at two
tables in the ladies' chamber, and twenty maidens in the
chequer chamber.   The guests at the chief table, and the
ladies, were served with brawn and mustard, capon boiled,
swan roasted, pyke, venison baked and roast ; jellies, pastry,
quails, sturgeon, salmon, wafers, and ippocras.   For the Livery
who sat at the side tables were provided " four sirloins of beef

* Herbert, I. p. 413.

throughout the ox," six sheep, and a calf. Forty gallons of curds were supplied by the milk-wife for this feast. The players and minstrels numbered about ten.

This being an election feast the ceremony of choosing the master and wardens followed the dinner. In all essentials it was the same as that described in connection with the Feste du Pui. The old master went with a garland on his head, and his cup-bearer before him, and designated his successor by delivering the garland to him, and the four wardens transferred their offices in like manner. The records at this time state that the ceremony was performed without minstrels, clearly implying that it had originally been performed to the sound of music as in the Feste du Pui. When the election had been completed, "all the company arose and went first to the master and after to such wardens as pleased them, and so from warden to warden after their minds," for the purpose evidently of drinking wine with them.

" Then the old masters bachelors presented a bill of eight names unto the old wardens, for the election of four new masters bachelors ; and out of the said eight by the assent of the foresaid old wardens and the old masters bachelors were chosen new masters bachelors without any garlands, minstrells, or other business : and then all the bachelors sat down at the said side table . . . where they had spiced bread, pears and filberts, wine and ale and *fit finis*."

That is, as far as the general company were concerned. For we learn from one of these accounts that the old wardens, their wives, the officers' and the wardens' servants, who no doubt had been too busy to do justice to the dinner, remained to supper, "and swans' puddings, a neck of mutton in pike broth, two shoulders of mutton roast, four conies, eight chickens, six pigeons, and cold meat plenty, and so departed." *

One of the most notable of these occasions was the election feast of the Merchant Tailors in 1607, which was attended by

* Herbert, I. pp. 444, 466, 469.

James I., Prince Henry, and a large number of the Court. The King and Queen were to dine privately in the King's Chamber, and in order that they might watch the young prince, who was to honour the feast in the Hall, a hole was made in the wall and a window provided for the purpose. Discreet men were appointed to make special search in and about all the rooms and houses adjoining the Hall to prevent all possibility of another Gunpowder plot, and the brick wall in the garden was raised "to take away the prospect of such as use to walk upon the leads of an adjoining tavern." The rulers of the Company were much exercised in their minds as to whether they ought to invite the Lord Mayor and Aldermen and their ladies. Various conceits and opinions were delivered. Some thought it would be an honour and grace to the company to see so many sit together in their scarlet robes. Others were of opinion that if the Lord Mayor and Aldermen were preferred to a principal table it would offend the nobles, who would reckon my Lord Mayor to be but an ordinary knight, and that, moreover, the Lord Mayor being a Clothworker might do his endeavour to cross the Company in the honour which the Prince intended to confer upon them. In the end it was considered safest not to send the invitations.

On the day of the feast the Company " made great haste to St. Helen's Church," to hear the sermon preached by the President of St. John's College, Oxford, who, with due regard to the occasion, had "finished in a very convenient time." The Mayor and Aldermen (albeit they were not invited, and some of them discontented therewith), came all in their scarlet and there stayed till his Majesty's coming, and then the Lord Mayor and the Master of our Company and some of the Aldermen went to the gate next the street, and the Lord Mayor delivered up his sword to the King, and the Master of the Company "did welcome his Majesty. . . . And at the upper end of the Hall there was set a chair of state where his Majesty sat and viewed the Hall, and a very proper child, well spoken, being clothed like an angel of gladness with a paper of frankinsense burning in his hand, delivered a short speech containing eighteen verses, devised by Ben Jonson the poet, which pleased his Majesty marvellously well, and upon either side of the Hall in the window were galleries or seats made for music, in either of which were seven singular choice musicians playing on their lutes ; and in the ship which did hang aloft in the Hall three rare men and very skilfull who sang to his Majesty. And over the screen cornets and loud music wherein . . . the multitude and noise was so great that the lutes nor songs could hardly be heard or understood. And his Majesty went up into the king's chamber where he dined alone . . . in which chamber was placed a very rich pair of organs, whereupon Mr. John Bull, Doctor of Music and a brother of this company, did play during all the dinner-time. . . . And the Prince did dine in the great Hall. . . . And the service to the King and Prince for the first course was carried up by the Knights, Aldermen, Masters, Assistants and Livery which were of the Company, the Livery having their hoods upon their shoulders. . . . And the Master did present his Majesty with a fair purse, wherein was a hundred pounds in gold. And . . . the Clerk did most humbly deliver unto his Majesty a roll in vellum which he had collected out of the ancient books and records of the Company," containing the names of seven Kings, one Queen, two Duchesses, five countesses, and two baronesses, seventeen princes and dukes, one archbishop, one and thirty earls, and a hundred other lords and gentlemen who had been honorary members of the Company.

The prince, to whom a similar roll along with a purse of fifty pounds was presented, said he would not only himself be free of the Company, but required all the lords present that loved him and were not free of other companies to follow his example, " whereupon three ambassadors, eighteen nobles, and some seventy gentlemen signified their willingness to do so. When the Master and Wardens went with garlands on their heads to publish the election, the Prince was graciously pleased to call for the Master's garland and put it on his own head, whereat the King who was watching through the window did very heartily laugh. After all which, his Majesty came down in the Great Hall, and sitting in the Chair of State did hear a melodious song of farewell sung by three men in the ship, being apparelled in watchet silk like seamen, which song so pleased his Majesty that he caused the same to be sung three times over. And his Majesty and the Noble Prince and Honourable Lords gave the Company hearty thanks and so departed." *

* Clode, *Memorials of Merchant Taylors*, pp. 147-160.

CHAPTER XIII

RELIGIOUS OBSERVANCES AND THE REFORMATION

OUR knowledge of the later history of the parish fraternities of London leaves very much to be desired. There is nothing to show that the majority of those we found existing at the end of the 14th century survived till the Reformation, or that, if they did so survive, their social and benevolent activities were brought to an end by the disendowment of chantries and obits. There were some eighteen London fraternities disendowed by the Act of 1547. Amongst them were most of those that had been endowed before 1389 —the Gild of St. Giles in St. Giles, that of Salve Regina in St. Magnus, that of St. Katherine in St. Mary Colechurch, that of Our Lady in St. Dunstan, and that of St. Fabian and St. Sebastian in St. Botolphs Aldersgate, along with several others dating from that same period which had not in 1389 acknowledged any endowment.

The large place occupied by religious observances in the life of the trade gilds has sometimes led to the not unnatural supposition that there must have been a complete break in their history at the Reformation. No such break is revealed in the records of the London companies, many of which had been expressly incorporated as fraternities, and all of which had become closely identified before the Reformation with a fraternity organization. Very considerable changes were, of course, effected in the disposition of their property, and in the nature and extent of their trusts, and the cessation of time-honoured customs must have been felt as a sore deprivation by the more conservatively pious members.   But the main current of the companies' activities flowed on without an interruption.   Their social gatherings, the administration of their charities, their regulation of industry and trade, were not disturbed; and even their religious observances, although reduced in importance and largely disendowed, were by no means entirely abolished.

The truth is that religious devotion had never supplied the primary motive for the establishment or maintenance of the craft gild.   At first it may have the most prominent of the subsidiary motives, but in course of time as the social and charitable activities developed, it lost this relative position. The really decisive change was, however, not so much one of motive as of policy.   Organization for religious objects under ecclesiastical sanction was at first the primary condition of voluntary association, but for a considerable time before the Reformation the trade gilds had ceased to be dependent on this condition, having secured a recognition from the Crown or from the municipality which covered all the various activities of their organization.   They might still put their religious observances in the forefront of their charters, but those observances no longer formed the vital essence of their association.   Some of the lesser gilds, it is true, continued to rest their existence on ecclesiastical sanction.   The Waterbearers' fraternity of St. Christopher held over its members the terrors of the great curse, but in most cases the fraternities collected their quarterage, and even enforced attendance at masses and funerals, by the authority of the royal charter or the grant of civic ordinances.   Whilst, however, the constitutions of most of the London trade gilds had been so far secularized as to be placed beyond danger of being affected by any merely religious change, the amount of property entrusted to them for those religious uses which were subsequently regarded as superstitious, *i.e.* the maintenance of chantries and obits for the dead, had not diminished but rather increased, and it was in regard to these endowments only that the fraternities of the crafts were affected by the Reformation.

The religious activities of the craft-gilds had not been of a simple or uniform character. At first the general tendency had been for them to attach themselves to one of the great religious houses rather than to a parish church. Perhaps the motive of this was a desire to secure greater freedom, since where a parish church was chosen it was often expressly stated that the fraternity was to be free to remove elsewhere whenever it pleased. In the same way the fraternities did not confine their patronage to a single religious house. Even a poor craft like the Pinners kept lights in both Elsing Spital and in the Hospital of St. James, and ordered its trentals of masses from the Whitefriars.* The Goldsmiths in their earliest records are found maintaining a light in St. James' and a standard in St. Paul's; later on, in 1354, besides paying the chaplain who officiated in the chapel of St. Dunstan in St. Paul's a salary of £4, they gave to the church of St. Peter in Cheap a donation of £20, to that of St. John Zachary £10, to St. Matthew, Friday Street, £6 13s. 4d., and to St. Vedast, Foster Lane, £1 6s. 8d.† These were the churches in the immediate neighbourhood of Goldsmiths' Row and Goldsmiths' Hall. Goldsmiths were their chief parishioners and benefactors, and were constantly making bequests to them for the observance of obits and chantries. In St. Vedast's there was a chancel dedicated to St. Dunstan. Now nothing was more characteristic of the mediæval testator than his anxiety lest his obit should be neglected. He generally named two sets of trustees, and sometimes three, in case the first set should fail in their duty. As the fraternities of the crafts gained a more assured corporate existence they began to

---

* Egerton MSS. in British Museum, 1142.
† W. S. Prideaux, *Memorials of Goldsmiths*, I. 1–5.

compete with the rectors and churchwardens for this position of trusteeship. A goldsmith who died in 1381 left bequests to St. Matthew in Cheap, to its ministers, to the Fraternity of St. Katherine in that church, to the old work of St. Paul's, and to the Wardens of the mistery of Goldsmiths, on condition that they observed his obit in St. Matthew.* Another goldsmith in 1391 left money for an obit to the Rector of St. John Zachary and the Wardens of the Goldsmiths jointly.† Down to the middle of the 15th century, however, the wardens of crafts were most usually named, if at all, in the second place, to act in case others failed to do so. After that date it became increasingly common to entrust them with the duty in the first instance.‡

By this time the corporations had been drawn into a closer connection with the parish churches. In some cases this connection had always existed. St. Michael's, Crooked Lane, had been almost exclusively endowed by the chantries of Stockfishmongers.' These seem to have been consolidated by the foundation of Walworth, and to have served as a basis for the Stockfishmongers' fraternity organization. The fraternity of Fishmongers at St. Peter's, Cornhill, was similarly based on the chantry of William de Kingston in that church. The Vintners' fraternity seems to have grown out of chantries in St. Martin Vintry, and Strype tells us there was a lawsuit between the parson of the church and the Vintners' Company over the site of the hall in Richard III.'s reign. The connection of the Salters with All Hallows', Bread Street, has already been noted. To these cases many additions were made by the transference of fraternities from religious houses. The Grocers left the monastery of St. Anthony for the parish church of the same saint, where one of their members built a chapel. The Drapers became connected with St. Michael's, Cornhill; the Skinners with St. John's, Walbrook; the Ironmongers found they had occupied the house of the leading

---

* Sharpe, *Calendar of Wills*, II. 227.   † *Ibid.*, 283.   ‡ *Ibid.*, 321.

parishioner of All Hallows', Staining, and that they were expected to replace him as a supporter of the parish church. The Tailors became possessed of the living of St. Martin, Outwich. The influence exercised by the companies as patrons and benefactors thus combined with their assured future as corporations to make them recipients of bequests for religious uses.

Another cause which operated in the same direction is strikingly exhibited in a document which was apparently displayed at St. Paul's in 1464 by way of advertisement, and which helps at the same time to account for the power which the Merchant Tailors possessed of attracting honorary members. The Master and Wardens of the Fraternity announce that " being possessed of ghostly treasure in which they are willing that all Christian people should be partners," they now make a declaration of all the indulgences, pardons and remissions which they had long since purchased in secret with a view to moving the readers and hearers to devotion. In the first place they had been admitted by the Prior of the Hospital of St. John into "a partnership of masses, mattins and other hours of prayers, fastings, almsdeeds, hospitalities, abstinences, watches, pilgrimages, ghostly labours, and of all other good deeds by the brethren of their religion done or to be done world without end;" and the Hospital of Our Lady of Rounceval at Charing Cross, the Monastery of Our Lady near the Tower, the Priory of Holy Trinity, the Hospital of Our Lady without Bishopgate, the Hospital of Our Lady of Elsingspital within Cripplegate, the Priory of St. Bartholomew, and the sisters and brethren of the monastery of St. Bridget of Zion, had admitted them to partnership on a similar footing.

Moreover, they had been admitted by Simon of Sudbury, Bishop of London, to the use of a chapel dedicated to St. John Baptist, on the north side of the mother church of St. Paul's, where they had appointed, by grant of the Bishop, priests to say masses daily and to pray for the souls of brethren and sisters of the fraternity; and Pope Boniface the Sixth had granted to "all Christian people that would put their hands to the making of the said chapel or to the maintenance of God's service within it, and to all those truly penitent and shriven that should visit it on certain feasts," a certain number of years of remission and of days of indulgence. Also the Archbishop of Canterbury and sixteen bishops had granted to "all those who put their helping hands to the laud of God in that chapel forty days of remission." *

Even this long list does not exhaust the spiritual privileges which a membership of the Merchant Tailors carried with it. The fraternity had a chapel adjacent to the hall which had been founded and endowed by some of its members, and in 1455 a special bull had been obtained from Pope Calixtus granting them permission to have masses celebrated, other divine services to be sung, with the ringing of bells and anniversaries to be performed.†

The business-like way in which the companies undertook the maintenance of chantries is amusingly illustrated by some negotiations recorded in the Drapers' Court-books. In August, 1515, the Court received a letter from Sir William Capel, containing a list of divers parcels of land and other things which he was minded to give to the fraternity for them to cause certain services to be done for his soul for ever, and wishing to know what money they would demand therefor in case they refused land. After some discussion the Court answered that they would accept the trust offered for 1000 marks immediate payment, or £14 yearly, and would add any further services he might wish further at that rate. They stipulated, however, that the chantry priest to be provided should assist in the company's religious services, and that their Clerk, Beadle, and almsfolk should have their portions of the coal to be distributed under the will; "and moreover," they

---

* C. M. Clode, *Memorials of Merchant Taylors*, pp. 49–52.
† *Ibid.*, pp. 44–45.

added, " we trust to have a special and kind brotherly token
of remembrance of plate, as basins, pots, cups, or other thing
of pleasure for a daily remembrance when it shall be seen, to
the intent that his soul may be thereafter remembered and
prayed for ; which we submit unto that honourable lady his
wife and to his worshipful executors."

The bargain thus struck was solemnly confirmed by the
whole company assembled in their hall to meet the Prior of
St. Bartholomew, in whose church the obit was to be kept, and
in the presence of the Mayor, Recorder, and several of the
Council. £600 were to be given to the company to purchase
land worth £15 7s. a year. Of this amount the salary of the
chantry priest absorbed less than half ; an almsman at 1s. a
week accounted for £2 12s. ; the yearly obit cost £1 ; the
potations for the drapers on that occasion, 6s. 8d. ; the parson,
priests, and clerk of the church received for ringing and potations, 3s. 4d. ; and 20d. was spent on a load of coals to be
given away in St. Bartholomew's parish. The Mayor and
Sheriffs received 6s. 8d. each, the Master of the Drapers 4s.,
each of the four Wardens 3s. 4d., the Clerk 1s., the Beadle 4d.
The sum total of all these payments was calculated to be £13,
so that the company would make a yearly profit of £2 on the
transaction.*

A great many arrangements of this kind might be cited
from the records of the greater companies, and most of them
belong to the fifty years preceding the Reformation. In the
year 1521, the Goldsmiths' Company found themselves already
engaged to attend twenty-five anniversary services at different
parish churches in the course of the year, to the great hindrance
and trouble of the wardens and all the livery. Even the fact
that a potation was provided for every obit did not make this
duty endurable, and arrangements were made for lumping the
obits together. Where the testator had provided a full endowment for a chantry priest to perform services all the year round,

* Herbert, *Livery Companies*, I. 408–409.

the company appointed the priest.* At the Reformation the Merchant Tailors had nine such livings in their gift.†

These trusts were clearly a source of considerable profit to the companies that had undertaken them. The expenses of the services always left an appreciable margin, and often they absorbed only a fraction of the amount bequeathed. No doubt this had been the intention of the testators, who were willing to add to the endowment of their fellowship as long as they could at the same time make some provision for the welfare of their souls, and secure the kindly remembrance of future generations. But the ambiguity of many of the bequests placed the companies in a difficulty when chantries and obits were abolished and their endowments seized into the hands of the king.

The first Act dealing with this matter—that passed at the close of the reign of Henry VIII. in 1545—did not condemn masses for the dead in principle, but only the abuse in practice of endowments for this purpose. Commissioners were appointed to inquire into cases of this kind, and to take into the king's hands all revenues that had been thus misappropriated. The companies were called upon to give an account of their stewardship. In one case we have the result fully recorded. The Merchant Tailors appointed a committee, who took legal opinion, and after discussing the situation several times over dinner, drew up a list of their charities and obits, and presented it to the Commissioners. A number of the obits had been connected with Grey Friars, and the Commissioners claimed as belonging to the king the endowments of these services for the half-dozen years since the dissolution of the monastery.‡

Two years later the first Parliament of Edward VI. "considering that a great part of superstition and errors in Christian religion hath been brought into the minds and estimation of

---

* Herbert, II. 206. † *Ibid.*, 434–435.
‡ *Ibid.*, II. 434 ; and Clode, *Early History*, p. 142.

men by reason of the ignorance of their very true and perfect salvation through the death of Jesus Christ, and by devising and phantasing vain opinions of Purgatory and Masses satisfactory to be done for them which be departed," and that the conversion of the revenues devoted to these uses " to good and godly uses as in erecting of Grammar Schools . . . the further augmenting of the universities and better provision for the poor and needy" could only be properly undertaken by the king, declared all Chantries, Hospitals, Colleges, Free Chapels, Fraternities, Brotherhoods and Guilds, with their lands and revenues, to be henceforth in the possession of the king.*

Taken by itself, this clause might be supposed to involve the abolition of those London companies that were incorporated as fraternities or gilds, but that this was not the intention of the Act is immediately made clear by another clause providing for the future payment as a rent-charge by all corporations, gilds, fraternities, companies or fellowships of misteries or crafts, of that part of their revenues that had been devoted to the purposes now condemned as superstitious, and it was expressly enacted that where but part of the revenues of any lands had been assigned to be bestowed in the maintenance of any anniversary or obit, or of any light or lamp in any church or chapel, the king was to receive an annual rent-charge to that amount only. All fraternities, brotherhoods and gilds other than such corporations, gilds, fraternities, companies and fellowships of misteries or crafts, were to be vested with all their possessions in the king.

As far as the London trade gilds were concerned there was nothing in this Act that can properly be described as confiscation of property. The purposes indicated in certain of their trusts having been declared illegal, they were simply required to pay the revenues of these trusts to the Crown. Twenty-nine of the companies had been holding property of an annual value varying from a few shillings to £150, and the total sum

* 1 Edw. VI. c. 14.

which the Crown derived from this source amounted to a little under a thousand pounds a year. But shortly after the passing of the Act the Government, being short of money, hit upon the device of compelling the companies to buy up the rent-charges on their trust property at twenty years' purchase. In this way the Government managed to raise £18,700 at the expense of their own future revenue, and the companies became owners of the property concerned, freed from the conditions of the original trust in so far as these were of a "superstitious" character. In order to find money for the purchase some of the companies were obliged to sell other portions of their property, but on the whole they do not appear to have suffered serious loss.*

The single apparent exception proves the rule. The Company of Parish Clerks suffered the confiscation of its hall and other property because it was not able to show to the satisfaction of the judges that it was a mistery or craft within the meaning of the Act. The matter was argued repeatedly before the highest legal authorities—the Lord Chancellor, the Justices of both benches, and the Privy Council—and it was four years after the passing of the Act before a decision could be arrived at. What seems to have been fatal to the claim of the Parish Clerks was the fact that the freedom of the city was not acquired through membership of their company. If the Parish Clerk was a freeman, as he no doubt often was, he had attained the rights of citizenship by being apprenticed or made free in another mistery. On this ground, and because their hall and other tenements were given to them for superstitious uses, the judges concluded that the company was not itself a craft but a new gild or fraternity given by the Act to the King's Highness. Much sympathy was felt in the city with the hard case of the Parish Clerks, who were, however, not long

* W. J. Ashley, *Introduction to Economic History*, Part II. 142-155; Herbert, *Twelve Great Livery Companies*, I. 111-117; Strype's *Stow*, Bk. iv. chap. xvi.

LEATHER-SELLERS' HALL (ST. HELENS PRIORY)

END OF EIGHTEENTH CENTURY

MERCHANT TAYLORS' HALL

IN SIXTEENTH CENTURY

in re-establishing themselves on a new footing. When Stow wrote his *Survey* they again had a hall of their own.*

The real troubles of the other companies began later on, in the middle of Elizabeth's reign, when they were accused of having "concealed" a considerable part of the revenues devoted to superstitious uses at the time when the amount of the rent-charge due to the Government had been fixed, so that the amount of trust property of which they had secured the full ownership was very much larger than that covered by the rent-charge they had bought up. Thus the Salters were said to hold lands given for religious purposes of an annual value of £82, whilst they had only declared and bought up rents to the value of £33 18s. 3d. Similarly the Drapers and the Vintners were accused of having declared and bought up only about a third of the rents actually received.

It is almost impossible at this distance of time to get at the real truth of the matter, as all the documents that have come down to us are statements of one side or the other. The informers who brought the charge belonged to the same class of men as the monopolists we shall have to deal with later. They were hangers-on of the Court who were always inventing some fresh scheme for raising money, ostensibly in the interests of the Crown. Rents in London had gone up very rapidly since Henry VIII.'s reign, and some of the property concerned was said to be worth three times its former yearly value. There can be little doubt that some of the lands held for superstitious uses had been actually concealed. But in most cases what had probably happened was that the company had interpreted the term "superstitious uses" so as to cover the minimum proportion of each bequest, whilst their accusers insisted on the maximum interpretation. Thus in the case already cited of a contract made for the provision of a chantry and an obit by the Drapers' Company, the company might consider that the salary of the chantry

* Christie, *Parish Clerks*, p. 90.

Q

priest and the actual fees paid for the obit, which accounted
for only about £8 out of a bequest of £15 a year, were
the only expenses incurred for superstitious uses, whilst the
informers might argue—as in fact they did in similar cases—
that the money spent in gifts and potations to members of
the company, in providing loads of coal for the poor or
continual support for an almsman, should all be included
under the same category, as the recipients were expected to
pray for the soul of the departed.

In many cases the companies seem to have been obliged
to make the best terms they could with the informers, though
some went to law and a few succeeded in repelling the attack.
In the reign of James I., after renewed attempts to extort
money on the same pretext, an Act was passed, by the same
Parliament that condemned monopolies, by which the king
renounced all claim to the property of the corporations on the
ground of concealments.

With the exception of the maintenance of chantries and of
obits, the religious observances of the companies remained
after the Reformation very much what they were before.
Attendance at funerals was still obligatory, except in cases
where the deceased had died of plague. In the year of
Elizabeth's accession the Pewterers order a fine of 6d. to
be imposed on any of the yeomanry "who slack themselves
to wait upon the Master and Wardens either to offerings or
burials," and they are to come "in cleanly apparel and without their aprons." A later order requires the journeymen to
come too, if they can be spared by their masters. Funeral
feasts were kept. Richard Manning, a Pewterer, on the
occasion of his wife's burial in 1570, gave 20s. towards a
recreation for the whole Livery, and it is accordingly "spent
at the Dolphin." But the provision thus made by the deceased
or his relatives seldom sufficed to meet the needs of the
occasion. At the funeral dinner, in 1567, of a Mr. Day, who
had left £3 for this purpose, each Assistant had to pay 1s.

and each member of the livery 16*d.* towards the further cost.* The great occasions when the generous foresight of the deceased rendered such contributions superfluous were deemed worthy of solemn commemoration. At a bountiful dinner provided by the gift of Mr. Swinnerton, a departed Master of the Merchant Tailors, there was openly pronounced " a grace or thanksgiving drawn by a learned Divine upon the Motion of a grave and Worthy ancient master of the Company intituled a Commemorable grace at a funeral dinner in the Hall for a good brother deceased." †

Attendance at church on the day of the election of Master and wardens was also still insisted upon. By the Cloth-workers' ordinances of 1587 and 1639, the election was fixed at eight in the morning, " and presently after the election, as well the Master, wardens and assistants as also the rest of the Livery, by two and two shall orderly and decently go in their livery from their hall into St. Dunstan's Church in the East . . . to hear divine service or some goodly sermon or both, and shall in like decent order return from thence to their Common Hall . . . there to do . . . such necessary business as to them shall seem meet, and so to dinner or drinking there, and not to depart thence without license of the Master and wardens till dinner or drinking be ended the same day."‡ The Grocers not only attended divine service at St. Stephen's, Coleman Street, before their election, but went on the following day to hear a solemn sermon, after which they took the sacrament.§ On Court-days at the Merchant Tailors' the chaplain of the company offered a prayer before business was proceeded with, and in 1578 the Master and wardens order a Bible to be set up in their Common Hall, so that those who

---

* Welch, *Pewterers*, I. 261, 272, 275.
† C. M. Clode, *Memorials of Merchant Taylors*, p. 137.
‡ Clothworkers' Ordinances.
§ Herbert, I. 193.

were waiting for their business to come on might have something wherewith to occupy their minds.*

This chapter cannot be concluded without some account of
the palls or hearse-cloths used by the companies at funerals.
These were often magnificent specimens of the embroiderer's
art, made in Lucca or Pisa, consisting generally of a breadth
of " baldakin " cloth, or cloth of gold, in the centre about 6
feet by 2 feet, to the sides and ends of which were attached
embroidered velvet flaps, rectangular in shape and about 10
inches in breadth.　The pall still in the possession of the
Saddlers' Company is of crimson velvet with a centre of
yellow silk.†　Those of the Vintners and the Ironmongers are
said to closely resemble in general arrangement and colour
one of the two still preserved by the Merchant Tailors.‡　The
design of this one is represented (by the kind permission of
the Company) in the accompanying illustration.　The centre-
piece is of cloth of gold, and measures 6 feet 4½ inches by
1 foot 10 inches.　The pattern is a huge red stalk running
from end to end with fruits and blossoms, chiefly of the
pomegranate.　The flaps at the sides and ends are of purple
velvet.　In the centre of the side-pieces, which are 10 inches
broad, is depicted the Baptism of Our Lord, on each side of
which are two representations of the Agnus Dei, and between
each pair is a figure of John the Baptist with the label, " Ecce
Agnus Dei."　Beyond these, on either side, is an angel
holding the head of John the Baptist in a charger, and at each
end is a pair of shears placed " saltierwise."　One of the shears
on one side has a tent between the blades.　The end-pieces
are of the same breadth as the sides.　On one of them is
represented the Decollation, and on the other the Entombment

---

* Clode, *op. cit.*, 127. The order appears to have been general in other
companies.

† Herbert, *Twelve Great Livery Companies*, I. 71.

‡ *Journal of Soc. of Antiquaries*, Vol. VI., Second Series, pp. 245–6 ; *Trans.
of London and Midd. Arch. Assoc.*, III. p. 491.

of the Saint, with an Agnus Dei in each case on either side. The pall is said to date from the last decade of the 15th century.*

The Fishmongers' pall is still one of the company's most treasured possessions. It consists of a centre slip about 12 feet long and 2½ feet wide, and two shorter sides each 8 feet 11 inches by 1 foot 4 inches. The pattern of the central part is a sprig or running flower-of-gold network bordered with red, on a ground of cloth of gold. On each of the end-pieces is wrought a picture in gold and silk of St. Peter seated on a throne, his head crowned with the tiara. One of his hands holds the keys, whilst the other is bestowing a benediction. St. Peter's vest is crimson raised with gold ; the inside of the sleeves of his outer robe, azure powdered with gold stars ; a golden halo encircles his head ; in his lap is an open book, in which are inscribed in black letter on a silver ground the first words of the Creed. On each side of the saint is a kneeling angel, whose wings are composed of peacocks' feathers in all their natural colours ; their outer robes are gold raised with crimson, their under vests white shaded with sky blue ; their faces are worked in satin of flesh colour, and they have long yellow hair. In the centre of each of the side-pieces is wrought a picture of Christ delivering the keys to Peter. The robe of Christ is crimson raised with gold, His inner vesture purple ; around His head is a jewelled and coronetted halo. With one hand He delivers the keys, with the other He upholds the golden mound of sovereignty surmounted with the cross, and from His mouth proceed the words, " Tibi Dabo Claves," etc. Those figures are placed in the arched recess of a Gothic building. On each side of this centre-piece the Fishmongers' arms are emblazoned, with a merman and a mermaid as supporters. The merman wears gold armour ; the mermaid's body is of white silk, her tresses of gold thread, and a jewel hangs

* C. M. Clode, *Memorials of Merchant Taylors*, 133.

from a gold chain round her neck. Her mirror reflects the head of Christ or Peter. The entire pall has a fringe of gold and purple 2 inches deep, and is lined with black silk. It dates from the period immediately preceding the Reformation.*

* Herbert, 72-3, note.

CHAPTER XIV

GOVERNMENT OF THE COMPANIES

THE form of government in the fully developed Livery Company of the 16th century was strictly oligarchical. The Court of Assistants, which was the deliberative body, was generally composed of those who had filled the position of Master or warden; its members held office for life, and recruited their numbers by co-option. The Master and wardens were changed every year, but they named their successors, or at most shared the choice with the ex-masters and ex-wardens who formed the Court of Assistants. The Master, Wardens, and Assistants named the freemen who were to be placed from time to time on the Livery, and in cases where the Yeomanry became a separate class from the freemen, they, too, were selected out of the freemen by the ruling body. A social hierarchy had thus come into existence, organized on the principle of selection from above. Such a formation was not peculiar to the Livery Companies. It was arising at the same period, not only in all the corporate boroughs of England, but in the colleges of the Universities, with their Masters, Fellows, Masters of Arts, and Bachelors, and in the Inns of Court, with their Treasurers, Benchers, Readers, and Inner and Outer Barristers.

It must not be assumed, in the case of the Livery Companies any more than in the other cases, that the oligarchy and the social hierarchy were the result of deliberate usurpation, or were erected on the ruins of a primitive democracy. It is true that in many, perhaps in most, of the original fraternities, the choice of executive officers had been vested in the general body of members. But the rules show that members shrank from the trouble and expense involved in holding office, and could only be induced to accept it by the prospect of a heavy fine in case of refusal. Moreover, in a number of the 14th-century fraternities, the retiring officers were called upon to select their successors, and were held jointly responsible with them for the gild's finances. In all cases the ex-officers seem to have formed an informal consultative body, and when consultation was made obligatory by special ordinance, it was quite as much with a view of limiting the discretion of the wardens as of encroaching on the rights of the commonalty, which had rarely been consulted at all.

The first appearance of a regularly appointed consultative body is in the Grocers' records for 1379, where it is ordered "that at the first congregation of the wardens there shall be chosen six of the company to be helping and counselling of the same wardens" for the year following.* The Shearmen's ordinances for 1452, after providing for the election of four wardens, add, "and then within fourteen days . . . the said wardens shall do call all the said brethren and sisters, and they shall make their election of twelve persons discrete and well avised . . . for to assist and counsel the said wardens." †

The Carpenters' ordinances of 1487 reveal the formation of a Court of Assistants in all but the name.‡ They provide that "weekly on Fridays the master and wardens shall call such of the said fraternity as they shall think convenient, for to assemble in their common hall for to have conversation, as well for the support and continuance of the good rules and ordering of the

---

* Herbert, I. 53.
† Ordinances of Clothworkers.
‡ Jupp and Pocock, *Carpenters*, p. 344 ; Livery Company Commission Report, II. pp. 5, 7.

said craft, as for the reformation, repressing and punishment of rebellious or misdoers against the rules."

But the completest account we possess of the formation of the Court is that given in the Mercers' records. Down to 1463 an informal committee of the wardens, ex-wardens, and aldermen free of the company, had been in the habit of preparing ordinances or other matter for the approval of a general court, but in that year a general court decided that it was "tedious and grievous to call so many courts and congregations of the fellowship for matters of no great effect," and that in future twelve sufficient persons should be yearly chosen to be assistants to the wardens, and that the fellowship would abide by all decisions of a majority of this body. The method of electing the assistants is not stated, but that is of secondary importance, as the choice had probably always been confined —as it was definitely stated to be in the ordinances of 1504— to "sad and discreet persons" such as had been wardens. In those ordinances seven was named as the quorum, and they were forbidden to put the common seal to anything without reference to a general court. Previously, in 1479, the assistants, who were known at this time as the Assembly, had acquired the right of nominating persons out of whom the wardens were to choose their successors. In 1505 this Assembly began to sit every Monday, and has continued to do so ever since.

In 1512, the Clerk of the Merchant Tailors records the fact that he transacted some business by the order of the master and wardens, "with the advice of the more part of the most substantial and discreet persons, assistants and counsellors of the fraternity." The charter of the Stationers' Company, granted in 1555, is said to be the first in which the Court of Assistants appears as part of the original constitution of a company; but before that date it had become an essential part of the administrative machinery of all the larger companies, and was no longer, as a rule, appointed by election of

the general body. The charters granted by Elizabeth, and the
disputes that arose out of them, indicate clearly the transition
through which the constitution of the typical livery company
was passing.   In the charter of the Broderers, granted in
1562, the freemen and livery are to assemble every quarter-day
to hear the ordinances read, and the annual accounts are to be
presented to the livery as well as to the assistants ; whilst in
the election of wardens the assistants are to nominate six, out
of which the livery may choose two.*   The Curriers' charter of
1587 provides for two meetings of the whole company every
year.   The wardens, with the consent of the assistants that
have been wardens, are to nominate freemen to the livery.
The three wardens are to be chosen by the wardens and the
fellowship.   A dispute arose in 1597 between the master,
wardens and assistants on the one hand, and the fellowship on
the other, as to the interpretation of this last provision, and the
Lord Mayor decided that the master and wardens were to
nominate two, one an assistant and the other not an assistant,
and that the fellowship were to choose the junior warden.†
The Joiners' charter of 1570 provides that the election both of
the twelve assistants and of the master and wardens is to be
by the majority of the commonalty, but before 1613 this had
ceased to be observed, and when a lawsuit was brought to
enforce them, it was decided that the election of master,
wardens, and assistants should be made, in the future as in the
past, by the assistants and the livery, out of the livery.‡   It is
clear that the control not only of the administration but of the
elections was passing into the hands of the Court of Assistants.
And in the charters granted by James I., or by subsequent
monarchs, the ruling body took care to have its powers placed
on a definite legal footing.   Hence these later charters are
reckoned the working charters of the companies.

The Court had become in fact the centre of the Livery

---

* Livery Company Commission Report, III. p. 197.
† *Ibid.*, p. 316.   ‡ *Ibid.*, p. 539.

Company's life. Besides its quarterly meetings, attended sometimes by the whole company, where quarterage was paid and routine business transacted, there were meetings every week or fortnight—the interval seems to have been often an irregular one—in which the multifarious questions arising out of the company's regulation of trade and industry, and its maintenance of order and discipline amongst its members, were dealt with as they arose. The number of courts held tended to increase with the expansion of the company's sphere of activity. The Barber-Surgeons' regular courts were monthly, but in 1557, 20 were held ; in 1572, 41 ; and in 1599, 46 ; the average attendance of assistants in 1572 being 12.

The Court books of most companies began to be kept about the middle of the 16th century, and there are very few aspects of the life of the citizen of that period that are not reflected in their records. Omitting such formal items as the registering of apprenticeships and the admission of freemen or of householders, perhaps the most constantly recurring class of item, is the record of disputes settled amongst members. Very often these have arisen out of hard words and insulting gestures. A pewterer named Wiltshire tells a fellow-craftsman named Scot that he "plays a Scot's part and has a Scot's heart," and Scot tells Wiltshire that he is a beggarly knave. One barber likens another to Æsop's dog. A tailor declares his fellow to be a prating boy. The disputants are bidden to be friends and bring the matter no more in question ; or a light fine is inflicted with the warning that if they mock or scorn each other henceforth it will be a more serious matter. Sometimes it is an apprentice that is to be admonished or chastised, for riotously wasting his master's substance, or for drawing blood from his mistress ; or a master is imprisoned for unlawfully breaking an apprentice's head. Sometimes a journeyman complains that he cannot get arrears of wages, or an employer wishes to have a workman who owes him money restrained from working for any one else till the debt is paid.

Small debts of various kinds are ordered to be paid by instalments.* Unsatisfactory bargains are revised. Ill-executed work is condemned. A barber-surgeon, who had undertaken to cure a client's wife " *de morbo Gallico* " and had not given satisfaction, is ordered to pay the customer 20s., or cure his said wife, and prefers to pay.†

Some of the Courts' decisions were concerned with the broader aspects of trade policy. In the second year of Elizabeth's reign an ingenious Venetian exhibited before the Court of the Clothworkers a certain gin devised for the rowing (shearing) of broad cloths, and offered to teach the company his feat of workmanship, on condition they would provide him his necessaries. Whereupon the master and wardens called the most expert men of the company and showed them the device, and gave them time to advise them; who, after deliberate advice taken, thought it would be a great decay unto the company. "So the master and wardens gave the stranger great thanks and also 20s. in money towards his charge and so parted."‡ The age of Watt and Arkwright was still two centuries off.

But the Court did not confine itself to deciding each case as it arose; it frequently made ordinances in general terms for the regulation of the trade, as when the Clothworkers' Court fixed the number of shears that might be occupied by the several classes of its fustian shearers,§ or the Pewterers decided that none of the company should lid stone pots for any one except a fellow-member at less than 2s. a dozen. Such ordinances were, however, only made as a rule at the request of the branch of the trade immediately concerned, and sometimes they were the result of an arrangement between the two classes within the company; as when the Pewterers order that none of the company shall give out spoons to be

---

* Unwin, *Industrial Organization*, pp. 228-229.
† Young, *Barber-Surgeons*, p. 427.
‡ Unwin, *Industrial Organization*, p. 117.   § *Ibid.*, p. 121.

made except to brethren of the company, on the strength of a promise made by all the spoonmakers in open court that they will work a gross of spoons for 20s.

Towards the end of the 16th century the Court of Assistants was often in the position of an Upper Chamber refusing to pass legislation demanded by a Lower Chamber composed of the Livery or Yeomanry or of both. An obvious way out of such a deadlock was to appoint a joint committee. The Pewterers' Court in 1583 thought good to choose twelve men, *i.e.* four of the assistants, four of the clothing, and four of the yeomanry, "to sit and determine as well of prices of wares as also any other matter which they shall find necessary and good for the company." *

Such compromises were not always so easily arrived at. Disputes between the different sections of a company, and rebellion against the authority of the Court of Assistants, were very common in the reign of Elizabeth. Some twenty years before the Pewterers appointed their joint-committee, a certain John Boulting addressed one of the rulers of the company in these words, "You have ruled a good while. I pray God you have not governed too long, and that the company have not occasion to curse you for your government." And in 1601 a Clothworker was put off the livery for saying to one of the assistants of the company, in the hearing of others, that the assistants of the company " were Pelicans and did suck out the blood of their dam and weed out the profit of the Company's lands, which of right belonged and was given to them of the handitrade of the company."

Several conflicts of this character have already been mentioned as having arisen about the proper interpretation of the charters and the right method of electing officers, and many others as having been brought about this time to the Mayor and Aldermen for settlement. Almost always, when details are given, the complaint of the commonalty against the

* Welch, *Pewterers*, I. pp. 289-290.

assistants is that they do not faithfully represent the industrial interests of the company, either because they are altogether outside the trade (many members of companies at this time owing their connection with it to inheritance), or because they were merchants who had no knowledge of the handicraft. It was less often the Livery than the Yeomanry who thus made themselves the champions of the industrial interest, and who in many cases headed a movement for secession which gave rise to a new set of incorporations. It is desirable at this point, therefore, briefly to consider the history of the yeomanry organization in relation to the Livery Company.

The status of the yeomanry within the companies has been a matter of some controversy, because of the apparent contradiction that arises when the yeomanry of one period are contrasted with the yeomanry of another. The yeoman of the end of the 14th century was a journeyman on strike. The yeoman or bachelor at the end of the 16th century was often a wealthy trader on his way to be Lord Mayor. The simple explanation is that the term "yeoman" is a relative one, and signifies a person in a period of probation and of subordination, one who is outside the ranks of the fully privileged. The growth of wealth and the differentiation of classes within the Livery Company had added many steps to the ladder of promotion, and however much the yeoman of the time of Gresham may have differed from the yeoman of Wat Tyler's day, he occupied the same relative position as one outside full membership of his company.

As to the social status of the yeomanry at the earlier period there cannot be the smallest doubt—they are invariably journeymen or serving-men. We hear, in 1396, of strife breaking out between the master saddlers and the serving-men called yeomen who have arrayed themselves in a new and like suit once a year, have held divers meetings at Stratford, attended Mass together and elected governors to rule their fraternity in honour of the Virgin Mary. The "yeoman" tailors, who are accused, in 1415, of wearing a livery and dwelling with one another in companies by themselves, and who ask leave to have their separate fraternity, are also described as serving-men and journeymen. The serving-men of the cordwainers, who conspired together against their wardens in 1387, and formed a fraternity at the Friars Preachers', were not then spoken of as yeomen ; but there can be no doubt that the yeomen cord-wainers, who still maintained their fraternity in 1423, and hired the Brewers' Hall for their feast, belonged to the same class.* The brotherhood of yeomen, whom we find admitted to a subordinate share in the Blacksmiths' fraternity in 1434, were servants who hired themselves for three years.† In all the cases met with of the use of the word " yeoman " in connection with a craft, down to the middle of the 15th century, the class referred to is clearly that of the journeyman or covenant servant working for wages.

But it must be noted that that class was then in a state of transition. Originally the serving-man had lived in his master's house, fed at his table and contracted himself for a year or a term of years, and remained unmarried. Hence the term " young man " or " bachelor " is often used synonymously with yeoman. But with the growth of a large class of serving-men who had no prospect of setting up as masters this arrangement was no longer possible. Serving-men and journeymen married, became householders, and took their work home. One of the offences of the yeoman tailors was that they lived apart by themselves ; and we find the Brewers attempting, in 1427, to get ordinances enforced forbidding any servant in their trade to hne himself out by the day as long as any one was willing to take him by the year, or to hold or occupy any chamber outside his master's house except he were a married man.‡ The Leathersellers' ordinances of 1482 complain that

---

* Riley, *Memorials*, pp. 542, 609, 653, 495.
† *London and Midd. Arch. Soc. Trans.*, IV.
‡ Brewers' first book, folio 37.

" when apprentices come out of their terms they will not serve masters but take upon them every one a mansion or shop having no goods nor ware of their own to put therein, and besides, each will have one or two apprentices having nothing to set themselves or apprentices at work . . . but are fain . . . to take other men's goods to occupy themselves." * There is abundant evidence that in all the larger industries of the city —amongst the weavers, tailors, clothworkers, goldsmiths, and pewterers—a new class of small masters, resident mostly in the suburbs, was being formed out of the journeymen who had created the yeomanry organizations.

The effects of this development are clearly to be discerned in another direction. Originally all the householders of the craft wore its livery. But before the middle of the 15th century a distinction had arisen between the householders who were of the Livery and the householders who were not, *i.e.* were *out of* the livery. Of the Grocers in 1430, 55 had the full livery, 17 wore the hood, and 42 householders were outside the livery.† An enumeration of the Pewterers shows 41 brethren that pay quarterage, 15 householders that pay quarterage but be no brethren (*i.e.* are not in the livery), 32 covenant servants and 94 apprentices.‡ The Goldsmiths in 1485 had 56 members in the livery and 73 young men out of the livery.§ The Founders in 1489 were divided into brethren of the clothing, brethren not of the clothing, and journeymen ;‖ and the Shearmen between 1452 and 1507 had developed a class of householders out of the clothing.¶

Now, although in some cases the householders who had not attained the livery were still reckoned as full brethren and remained distinct from the Yeoman or Bachelor Company, the natural tendency was for those excluded from one organization to gravitate towards the other. And this process was

---

* Black, *Leathersellers*.
‡ Welch, *Pewterers*, I. p. 30.
‖ Williams, *Founders*.
† Kingdon, *Grocers*.
§ Herbert, II. p. 135.
¶ Clothworkers' Ordinances.

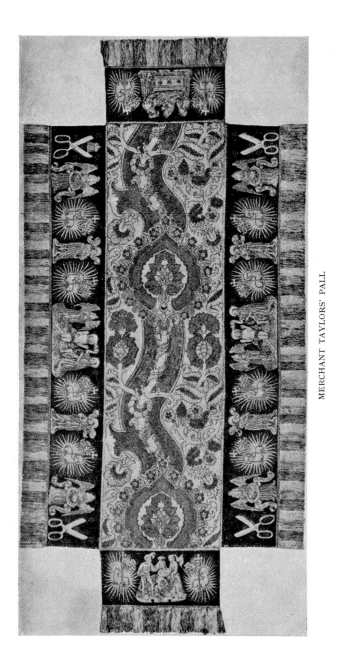

MERCHANT TAYLORS' PALL

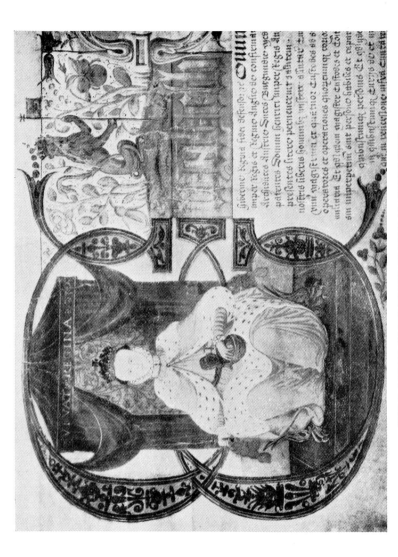

INITIAL LETTER OF ELIZABETH'S CHARTER TO CORDWAINERS

facilitated by the fact that the yeomanry organization, which at the beginning of the 15th century had been a prohibited association of rebellious journeymen, had before the end of the century been gradually transformed into a recognized but subordinate branch of the livery company. Sometimes the Yeomanry preserved a separate fraternity, sometimes they shared in the religious observances of the livery, but they generally possessed a box of their own and separate accounts. They had also separate officers, though these were often chosen or had to be approved by the executive of the livery.

It is probable that by the end of the 15th century nearly every livery company was supplemented by a yeomanry organization of this kind. We hear of the fellowship of the young men of the Carpenters in 1468. The Drapers have a bachelors' company numbering 60. In 1493 the yeomanry of the Ironmongers petitioned "the master, wardens and court of the livery that they might have license to choose two new rulers every year, to gather of every brother, covenant and other, the sum of 8*d.* a year, and to compel their members to attend the mass of Corpus Christi along with the Livery and to offer a penny each. . . ." The Fishmongers, the Merchant Tailors, the Haberdashers, the Leathersellers, the Armourers, the Clothworkers, the Founders and the Barber Surgeons, all possessed yeomanry organizations in the 16th century, and in fact there is scarcely a company whose history has been fully investigated in which such an organization has failed to be discovered.

But as there is no doubt that all the bodies of yeomanry met with in the first half of the 15th century were mainly composed of journeymen and serving men, so it is equally beyond question that the bodies of yeomanry of which we have any detailed account in the latter half of the 16th century were not mainly so composed, and in most cases scarcely represented the journeymen's interests at all. The rank and

R

file of the yeomanry at that period was made up of householders who were small employers or small traders, whilst the
wardens chosen to rule them were more prosperous members
of the company, who were expected to qualify for adoption on
the livery by accepting this inferior office.   The yeomanry
had in fact come to be generally identified with the main
body of freemen outside the livery.   Membership of it was
thus a stage through which all had to pass, and it was
therefore composed of two very different elements—those
who were destined for promotion to high office, and those who
were not.   It was the latter who constituted the yeomanry as
a continuous body with common interests, whilst it is the
former who appear in the company's records as holding office
amongst the yeomanry, or as contributing under the name
of the Bachelors' company a very large proportion of the
expense incurred by the company on great occasions.   It is
this class—the cadets of the ruling families of the company
or the wealthy members who desired admittance to the
oligarchy—who appear as Bachelors in " foins and budge "
on the exceptional occasions when a member of the company
has been chosen Lord Mayor.   With the yeomanry as a
permanent body with separate interests these birds of passage
had nothing to do.   And that that body had undergone such
a transformation as I have described in the course of the 16th
century is beyond all question.   In the records of the Tailors,
the Cordwainers, the Blacksmiths, the Ironmongers, the Clothworkers, the Pewterers, the yeomanry appear as journeymen
in the 15th and early 16th centuries, and as masters and
traders in the late 16th and 17th centuries.

The process of transition in the intervening period is
clearly enough marked in such full records as we possess.
From a report of a great variance and discord that arose in
1508 between the wardens and others of the livery of the
Founders on the one part and the yeomanry on the other
part, as to the custody of certain plate, napery, money and

jewels belonging to the craft, it might fairly be inferred that
all members not in the livery were in the yeomanry, and as
we know that there was a class of householders amongst the
Founders who were not in the livery, it follows that the
yeomanry was in part composed of them. The Mayor's
award was that the property in question should be kept in a
chest in St. Margaret's Lothbury, secured with four keys,
three of which were to be in the hands of the wardens, and
one in the hands of the yeomanry ; and on the annual
rendering of accounts the wardens were to call unto them six
of the yeomanry to hear them read, forasmuch as they be
members of the said fellowship.*

But the completest evidence of the transition is contained
in the Court Book of the Clothworkers. Under the date
1543, we read :—

"It is agreed that the wardens of the yeomanry now being shall
bring in their box with their money, their cloth and their torches,
and the master and wardens to choose four honest men being
journeymen, and they to be as wardens of the *journeymen only*, and
they to have the cloth and torches in their custody. And that there
be four journeymen yearly chosen to the said room by the master
and wardens for the time being."

It is quite clear from this entry (1) that the yeomanry had
been composed largely of journeymen, and (2) that it had
contained other members who can only have been small
householders. The existing organization proved too strong
to be altered from above. A month later we find it was
agreed that the wardens of the yeomanry shall choose new
wardens as they have done in times past and keep their old
order. In 1546 the wardens of the yeomanry brought in
£7 2s. 4d. which they had received the year before, and
£1 11s. 4d. increased in their time, and a box with four keys
was made to keep it in. £1 was to be granted to the

* Williams, *Founders*, p. 14.

wardens of the yeomanry when they kept a dinner, and 8*s.* when they kept only a drinking. In 1549 it was agreed that there should from henceforth be no more wardens of the yeomanry chosen nor no more quarterage gathered amongst the yeomanry. In December, 1552, the Court orders certain ordinances to be drawn for the good ordering of a yeomanry, to begin at Christmas next and so to continue as long as it shall be thought profitable for the house and for the worship of the company.*

These fluctuations of policy were not peculiar to the Cloth-workers. The Barber-Surgeons abolished their yeomanry in 1552, and set it up again with a new constitution in 1555.† With the broader economic causes underlying these changes of organization we shall have to deal in the next chapter. But another more immediate cause was at work in the period between the death of Henry VIII. and the accession of Elizabeth. An Act of 1547 had, as we have seen, placed the endowments of all chantries and obits and of all purely religious fraternities in the hands of the king, and the first question addressed by the commissioners appointed to carry out the Act to the companies, was whether or not they had any peculiar brotherhood or gild within their corporation. In some companies the yeomanry still constituted such a peculiar brotherhood, and in all cases where a yeomanry existed there was a danger that it might be so interpreted. Hence a new and pressing motive was supplied for the completion of that remodelling of the yeomanry in subordination to the livery company which had already been for some time in progress.

The Pewterers' yeomanry in this way ceased to be known as the Fraternity of St. Michael, but continued to exist as a mixed body of householders and journeymen with wardens of its own. In the rules made for the holding of the yeomanry

* Unwin, *Industrial Organization*, pp. 58-61.
† Young, *Barber Surgeons*, p. 278.

dinner in 1559, married householders and married journeymen are charged alike 16d. for man and wife, but a lone house-holder pays 12d. and an unmarried journeyman only 8d. Every man who has been married since the last feast must, according to old custom, give a cock or pay 12d. in addition. And every man is to pay as in times past a penny towards the play and a penny for his offering. But in the same year it was ordered that none of the yeomanry were to come to the audit supper but such as were householders, and such as were thought meet by the discretion of the Wardens of the Yeomanry.*

The Clothworkers' records for the reign of Elizabeth show that the journeymen were little more than an appendage to the remodelled yeomanry, which gradually came to be almost identical with the whole "handicraft," *i.e.* the manufacturing small masters as opposed to the mercantile interest of the ruling body. As the wardens of the yeomanry who were prospective members of the livery and court of assistants were also frequently merchants, eight assistants had to be appointed to execute their authority concerning the handicraft. The same situation arose in many companies. The yeomanry of the Haberdashers and Leathersellers were largely composed of the small master hatters and glovers, and householders of other crafts that had been absorbed by those companies ; and five feltmakers were appointed to assist the wardens of the Haberdashers' yeomanry in 1577. The story of the further conflict between the industrial interest as represented by the yeomanry, and the commercial or other interests represented by the court of assistants, belongs to another chapter.

Any account of the government of the livery companies in the period of their greatest activity and prosperity which failed to notice their relation to the Lord Mayor would be extremely misleading and incomplete. In spite of many fluctuations, the authority of the mayor over the companies

* Welch, *Pewterers*, I. p. 201.

had been steadily growing since the close of the 14th century, and may be considered perhaps to have reached its highest point in the reign of James I. when the Lord Mayor put forward the claim that he was master of all the companies. Several causes combined to favour the development of his authority at this time. In the first place, the growth of the city brought a need for new forms of regulation, administration, and defence to which the old machinery of the wardmote was inadequate, and for which the companies furnished the readiest organs. Secondly, the Crown also found it convenient to use the organization of the companies for revenue and police purposes, and thought it less invidious to do so through the instrumentality of the mayor. And thirdly, the disputes constantly arising within the companies themselves necessitated a great many voluntary references to his judgment, and so strengthened his hands for interference in cases where he was not called in.

In regard to all matters concerning the regulation of trade, and especially trade in victuals and drink, the mayor had, of course, from the first possessed and exercised most extensive powers of control, and the natural desire of the victuallers to have these powers exercised in a way conducive to their interests was one of the chief motive forces in London politics. The early records of the Brewers afford ample illustration of the importance that was attached by them to securing a friendly disposition on the part of the mayor. Indeed, it was a custom with them at one time to place on record the character of each mayor in this respect, and the means taken by them to improve it. One mayor was a good man, meek and soft to speak with, and the Brewers gave him an ox and a boar so that he did them no harm. Another refused their gifts with thanks, but promised to be just as kind as if he had taken them. The famous Richard Whittington they regarded as a sworn foe to the craft. During his term of office in 1419 he harassed them with domiciliary visits in person, selling up in one day by proclamation the stock (12 or 16 casks) of a brewer at Long Entry near the Stocks, and of others at the Swan in Cornhill, the Swan by St. Antony's, and the Cock in Finch Lane. Not content with this, he continued his crusade in the mayoralty of Robert Chichele three years later. The Brewers' description of their own experiences when twelve of them were called before the mayor and aldermen is worth quoting as one of the earliest pieces of English in the company's records.

" And whanne the forsaid Brewers comen before the Mayor and Aldermen, John Fray atte that tyme beyng Recorder of the said cite said to the Brewers yn this wise : Sires ye ben accused here that ye selle dere ale and sette your ale atte gretter pris thanne ye shold doo without live of this court ; and moreover ye be bounden yn this court yn a reconnsance of XX li, at what maner pris that malt is solde, ye sholen selle your best ale out of your houses to your customers for 9*d*. ob, that is a barell for xlii d and no derrer. And after this the mayor axed of Robert Smyth how he solde a barell of his beste ale and he answered for v s and somé barell for iiii s, x d. And on this manner seyden the moste parte of Brewers that were atte that tyme there present. And the Mayor shewed hem diverse ensamples of malt yn the same court to the which malt the Brewers answered that thei cowd make noo good ale thereof. . . . And the moste parte of the comones of the said citee seyden that hit was a fals thing to sell here ale so dere while they myghten have malt so good chepe, bote men seyden atte that tyme that Brewers were cause of the derthe of malt with ther ridinge yn to divers contrees to bie malt. . . . Then seide the Mayor and alle the Aldermen that they were condemned yn her bond of xx li, and the mayor ordayned . . . that the . . . maistres of Brewers craft . . . shold be kept yn the ward of the Chamberlayn. . . . And thus thei did abide . . . unto the tyme that the Mayor and the Aldermen weren goon hom ward to her mete and after this the seide maistres geden to the Chamberlayn and to John Carpenter to wete what thei sholde doo and the said Chamberlayn and John Carpenter dede commande hem to goon home to here houses. And so John Carpenter behight hem atte that tyme that thei shold no more harm have neither of prisonment

In þe zer of kyng Henry þe fifte þe seconde William Crowmer
mayr of london þe whiche William was a man of
gouernance for all þe comynalte of þe cite and and all þe
cite was well plesed with hym and also he was a good man
and belongynge to þe craffte of Brewers and yn his zer
he dede no dekk to þe seide craffte ne he wolde nevstyr
receyve no ziftes ne rewardes of þe same craffte yn all
his tyme but he dede thanke þe maistres of þe craffte goodly
with all his herte of þey goode chere þat þey made to hym as for
to have zove hym ziftes and also he thanked hem as meche as
þouȝ he hadde receyved hem and he made promys to be good
frende to hem be all his zer and so he was John mason Thomas
hatchey John Broke and Henry Tredewas maistres of þe seide
craffte of Brewers yn þe seide zer and þe same maistres dede
chesen serchers of þe seide craffte ffor heyr tyme þat is to sete
pers carpent William Welle Watt steyn þ zonger and John Hubey:—

The names of Brewers þat hadden barelles
and Tuberkyns þe whiche þey nons ha seled to þe
coupe marke yn þe tyme of þe seide Crowmer mayr of london

Henry Crowmer Hart q. Aleydyn þe nons he mor bon yn þe tene of Judgens Grygge
Aldermen yn þe Aley endof þe Chaffre yn Cornhill

EULOGY OF WILLIAM CROWNER, MAYOR
From the Brewers' first book

of her bodies ne of losse of xx li for wel thei wysten and knewen that alle the forsaid judgement of the mayor and the aldermen was not done at that tyme but for to plese Richard Whityngton."

After this it is interesting to find the Brewers' wardens entering £7 3s. 4d. into their accounts for the following year, "for two pipes of wine to Richard Whetyngton's butler, also money given to divers serjeants of the mayor for to be good friends to our craft." * The Brewers continued to get into trouble. They were called in question for obtaining their charter in 1438, and were fined £50 in 1461 for making ordinances prejudicial to the city's liberties. In 1551, by reason of their obstinate disobedience to the mayor, they were debarred for a time from membership of the Common Council.

In all this there was no new principle involved. But a more vigorous assertion of civic authority was called for, in the revision of ordinances which the crafts had drawn up by virtue of royal charters, than had formerly been needed when the crafts derived the sole authorization of their ordinances from the mayor and aldermen themselves. Nevertheless the city seems to have maintained a firm control over the crafts, whether incorporated or unincorporated. From the time of the accession of Edward IV., not only the victualling trades like the Brewers, Bakers, Butchers, Cooks, and Fishmongers, but most of the other greater and lesser companies had their ordinances revised, modified, or annulled by the Mayor and Aldermen.

A more unprecedented form of control—exercised as a rule only over the lesser companies—was constituted by frequent interference in the domestic concerns of the companies. No doubt the way for this was opened by the appeals of the rulers of companies against refractory members or *vice versâ*. Disobedience to the wardens was punished with

* Brewers' first book.

imprisonment or disfranchisement, and on the other hand we find the wardens of the Butchers discharged of their places for perjury, and others appointed in their stead. In 1461 an unwilling Girdler was enjoined to take on the livery of his company ; and in 1476 another Girdler was restored to the livery as having been unjustly displaced. In 1473 one of the junior wardens of the Butchers was dismissed and the other committed for disobedience to their " Ancients." The wardens of the Saddlers were ordered in 1549 to allow six of the eldest of the livery to be privy to the elections and the accounts. The method of electing officers in the lesser companies was frequently regulated during Elizabeth's reign by the Mayor and Aldermen. But the most striking case of intervention occurred in 1545, when the Lord Mayor and three Aldermen sitting in Bakers' Hall commanded all they that were not assistants to depart, "and then declaring the weakness of one that had been chosen, caused another to be chosen in his stead, and ordered that in future elections should be only by those that had been wardens." The powerful influence thus exerted by the civic authorities assisted very materially in the universal establishment of that oligarchical form of constitution in the companies which has already been described.

The city had always protested against the grant of corporate powers to the several companies, but, not being strong enough to prevent it, had compromised the matter by insisting that the companies should hold their charters in due subordination to the Mayor and Aldermen. When, however, some thirty companies, representing all the main branches of trade and industry, had gained incorporation, the vested interest thus established strengthened the hands of the city government in resisting any addition to their number. From the beginning of the 17th century onwards, it was necessary for a company to obtain licence from the city to sue for incorporation or even for a new charter. Licence was granted to the Musicians and the Turners in 1603, to the Founders in 1613, and to the Scriveners in 1615. On the other hand a charter sought by the Artisan Skinners was quashed in 1606, the master and wardens of the Plumbers were committed in 1614 for refusing to bring their charter to be enrolled,* and the Feltmakers, who had obtained incorporation without licence in 1604, were refused admittance into the freedom till the Commonwealth period, in spite of pressure from the king and an offer of £1500. Other companies, like the Basketmakers, and the Paviors, that sued for licence after the Restoration, never attained incorporation at all.

The administrative use which the Lord Mayor made of his authority over the companies was of gradual growth, and rested on dubious legal foundations. The companies derived their privileges from the exercise of the royal prerogative, and continued to hold and enjoy them by the sanction of the mayor. It would have been difficult, if not impossible, to maintain them as legal rights against the determined opposition of either city or king. When, therefore, a Tudor king issued commands to them through the mayor, resistance became a serious matter, and though there was frequent grumbling, and occasional protest, actual resistance did not become general till the reign of Charles I.

The mayor's " Precepts," as these decrees were styled, may be divided into two classes, though there is not always a clear line between them. Some were for purely civic purposes, and these were generally issued on the initiative of the Mayor himself or of the Common Council, whilst in others the Mayor was merely the mouthpiece of orders from the Crown. The municipal duties imposed on the crafts may be considered perhaps as originating in the semi-feudal relation they bore to the mayor and sheriffs, which was symbolized in the annual ridings to Westminster. The cost of providing men and

* Guildhall MSS., Vol. 110, contains a brief digest of the above-mentioned cases.

horses for these occasions, and also attending the Mayor when he rode to meet the king or queen, forms one of the main items of the budget of every craft in the 15th century ; and a requisition to attend the Midsummer watch, or to take part in cleansing the city ditch, may be reckoned in the same category.

The custom of raising loans from the companies for municipal purposes was not thoroughly established till the middle of the 16th century.   Most of these loans were for the provision of corn against times of scarcity.   Stow tells us that Stephen Brown, Grocer, who was mayor in 1439, sent into Prussia " causing corn to be brought from thence, whereby he brought down the price of wheat from three shillings the bushel to less than half that money," and that Simon Eyre, Draper, mayor in 1446, "built the Leadenhall for a common garner of corn for the use of this city."   After this it became usual, when scarcity was feared, for some provision to be made with the help of loans and contributions from the mayor, aldermen, and other prominent citizens.   In 1512, when supplies ran so short that the bread carts of Stratford were besieged by a hungry mob every morning, " the mayor, Roger Achley, in short time made such provision that the bakers were weary of taking it up. . . . The mayor also kept the market so well that he would be up at Leadenhall by four o'clock in the summer's mornings ; and from thence he went to other markets, to the great comfort of the citizens." *

The first loan demanded from the companies for this purpose was in 1521, when the Common Council determined that £1000 should be borrowed, and it was agreed that "in all goodly haste the said sum should be levied and paid by the fellowships of sundry misteries and crafts."   The Lord Mayor and Aldermen were to appoint what sum was to be

---

* Stow, *Survey*, 173.   The Bakers, however, complained in 1526 that they were compelled to take a musty supply of municipal corn at excessive prices : *Letters and Papers of Henry VIII*, iv. 2, No. 2749.

levied of each company, and the wardens were to assess the amount to be lent by every particular person. Officers called corn-renters collected the money and paid it in to the Bridge masters, who gave bonds for repayment. After 1543 precepts were issued for the raising of such loans nearly every year. In 1545 the assessments varied from £10 on the Fletchers to £100 each on the Grocers, the Mercers, the Drapers and the Merchant Tailors. The Pewterers, on whom £50 was assessed in 1561, levied £35 in sums varying from 5s. to 40s. on twenty-nine members of their livery, and £15 in sums varying from 5s. to 20s. on their yeomanry. The Iron-mongers in 1587 demanded from each person of the degree of an alderman £16 6s. 8d. ; from all that had been master, £10 ; from all that had been wardens, £6 13s. 4d. ; from the livery £3 apiece, and from the yeomanry £2.*

The Bridge House built over the two last arches on the Southwark side had long replaced the Leadenhall as the storehouse for the corn, and in accordance with an order of Common Council of 1559, mills were erected on sheds in front of the piers to grind it. Ten ovens were also erected, largely out of a bequest by a charitable sheriff, to bake bread for the relief of the poor, and a " fair brew-house " was added later for service of the city with beer. In the early part of Elizabeth's reign much discontent arose as to the irregular way in which the loans were discharged, and as the companies were not satisfied to receive mouldy wheat in repayment, it was finally arranged that they should administer the provision themselves, and the garners at the Bridge House were, in 1578, divided into twelve equal parts, which were assigned by lot to the twelve greater companies. In 1596, in consequence of an alarm that the Government might seize the Bridge House supply for the navy, the companies began to build granaries at their own halls, and it was the destruction of these by the Fire that finally put an end to the custom.

* Nichol, *Ironmongers*, 143.

The precepts issued by the Lord Mayor to the companies at the command of the Crown were far too numerous and varied to be dealt with here in any detail ; but they fell broadly under two heads—demands for money, and demands for men.* During the whole period of the Tudors and Stuarts, not omitting the interval of the Civil War and the Commonwealth, the city companies furnished one of the chief financial resources of the Government. Henry VII. exacted a benevolence of nearly £10,000 from the city, to which each company contributed a quota. Elizabeth raised a compulsory loan of £20,000 in 1579 for the suppression of the Irish rebellion, and Charles I. demanded a like sum in 1640 for his campaign against the Scots. Parliament borrowed so largely from the companies for the prosecution of the Civil War that in 1647 the Merchant Tailors claimed to have lent over £26,000 and the Ironmongers over £7000, of which sums only a trifling proportion had up to then been repaid. Participation in State lotteries was twice forced upon the companies by Elizabeth, and once by James I.† Another device for raising money was embodied in the arrangement by which the companies acquired their Irish estates in 1610. The Governor and Assistants of the New Plantation in Ulster were to pay the king £60,000 for the escheated lands of the Irish rebels. Each of the greater companies was to be responsible for one-twelfth of this amount, and was to draw lots for a twelfth of the land, which might be shared with such of the lesser companies as could be induced to enter the undertaking.‡ The Ironmongers made up their £5000 with the help of £700 from the Brewers, £570 from the Scriveners, £420 from the Coopers, £360 from the Pewterers, £350 from the Barbers,

---

* Precepts were also issued for assistance in erecting the Royal Exchange, in repairing St. Paul's, in providing work for the poor, in subsidising projects of discovery. See Herbert, I. 120, and Nichol's *Ironmongers*.

† Herbert, I. 151–154, 176–180.

‡ *Ibid.*, I. 220. For a fuller account, see *Concise View of the Irish Society ;* Nichol, *Ironmongers ;* and Heath's *Grocers*, app. 17.

and £300 from the Carpenters, so that their own actual venture was only £2300. The charter of the Irish Society was revoked and its lands resumed by Charles I., but both were restored under Charles II., and though some of the "manors" have changed hands, the companies still retain their lordship over the larger part of the Plantation. When Macaulay visited Londonderry for the purposes of his history, he found the country "enriched by industry, embellished by taste, and pleasing even to eyes accustomed to the well-tilled fields and manor houses of England," and could still discern the arms of the Fishmongers, the Vintners, and the Merchant Tailors on the old culverins and sakers which these companies had supplied for the defence of the colony.

The Government's demands for men were more frequent and probably scarcely less burdensome than their demands for money. The Coopers' accounts show that these levies were regularly made in Henry VIII.'s reign. They found four men for the wars in the North in 1537, at a cost of £10 8s. 1d.* When the city raised a force of 400 footmen and 100 horsemen to support the Lords of the Council against Protector Somerset in 1549, the Carpenters' four men cost £4 12s. 5d.† In 1559 the companies provided a muster of 1400 in Greenwich Park, "whereof 800 were pikemen all in fine corslets, 400 harquebuts in shirts of mail with morins, and 200 halberters in almain rivets . . . which made a goodly show before her majesty, the Emperor's and French King's ambassadors being present." ‡ To a levy raised by precept in 1562, the Grocers and the Merchant Tailors were each required to furnish 35 men, and the Ironmongers 19; in 1569, when the Grocers supplied 60, the Ironmongers sent 28. In 1572 the companies organized at the command of the Privy Council a regular force of 3000 for the defence of the city, in which the Merchant Tailors' contingent appears to have numbered 200, the Ironmongers' 111,

---

* Firth, *Coopers.*   † Jupp and Pocock, *Carpenters*, p. 49.
‡ Stow, *Annals.*

and the Carpenters' 24 (the equipment of the 24 cost £56).
In 1585, when the city militia was entrenched for a whole
week on Blackheath in expectation of a Spanish invasion, the
numbers were about 4000, the highest contingents—those of
the Grocers, Haberdashers, and Merchant Tailors—being each
composed of 395 men; whilst of the lesser companies the
Brewers and the Leathersellers each sent 100, the Saddlers
and the Cordwainers each 54, the Tallowchandlers and Dyers
each 40, the Stationers and Cutlers each 27. The cost of the
levy seems to have averaged about 30s. per man. For the
equipment of this militia each company maintained an armoury,
and generally kept an armourer at work.* An inventory of
the Coopers in 1570 shows that they then possessed 13 corslets,
19 calivers, 19 flax and touch boxes, 17 morions, 34 swords,
29 daggers, 31 girdles, 13 leathers for shot, and 15 pikes, some
of which were in use in the Low Countries.† From 1574
onwards each company was required to keep a store of gunpowder. When the Civil War broke out, Merchant Tailors'
Hall must have been as well provided for a siege as most
castles in the country. Its armoury contained 153 swords, 52
muskets, 70 pikes, 50 corslets, 32 halberds, 300 cwt. of bullets,
300 cwt. of match, and 40 barrels of powder.‡

* Strype's *Stow*, V. 451.   † Firth, *Coopers*, p. 124.
‡ Herbert, I. 127.

MASTERS OF STONE AND WOOD GIVING EVIDENCE OF SKILL IN THEIR CRAFTS BEFORE
THE CONSUL OF THE GILD AT FLORENCE

FOURTEENTH CENTURY

FIGURES IN LORD MAYOR'S PROCESSION, 1616

CHAPTER XV

INDUSTRIAL EXPANSION UNDER THE TUDORS

THE livery companies that have been so far dealt with have been those that had their origin and for the most part received their charters before the Reformation. But more than half the companies that now survive were incorporated after the Reformation. About a dozen of these, *e.g.* the Fanmakers, the Coachmakers, the Glass-sellers, the Gunmakers, and the Spectacle-makers, represent trades unknown in mediæval England, and not established in London till the 17th century. In other cases, such as those of the Feltmakers, the Glovers, the Pinners, the Stationers, and the Weavers, the technical and economic conditions of production had been so changed as to necessitate an entire re-organization of the industry. Only in a few cases did the companies incorporated in the 17th century represent a continuance of the conditions of mediæval craft. There was, in fact, a distinct pause between the earlier epoch of incorporation which closed in the first years of Henry VIII. and the later epoch which opened with the Stationers' charter in 1555 ; and the economic atmosphere which pervaded the 17th-century company was entirely different from that in which the 15th-century company had moved and had its being. If this marked difference does not appear in the constitutions of the livery companies as they have come down to our day, it is because the newer companies on the one hand modelled themselves on the old, whilst the older ones,

S

on the other hand, by obtaining fresh charters assimilated themselves to the new.

Perhaps the most significant difference between the earlier and the later charters lies in the extent of the area to which they apply. The earlier grants give powers of regulation and search over London and its suburbs, and in certain exceptional cases they give similar powers over England generally. These exceptional powers of national extent occur also in some later grants, but the main point of difference is in regard to the metropolis. In the great majority of charters granted after the accession of Elizabeth the metropolitan area to which the powers conferred extend is much wider than the city and its original suburb. The Broderers, who were incorporated in the third year of Elizabeth, obtained rights of regulation in the city and suburbs, also in the city of Westminster, in the borough of Southwark, and in St. Katherine's. The Joiners' charter of 1571 gives a two-mile circuit; the Blacksmiths' in the same year gives a four-mile circuit in addition to the city and suburbs. In subsequent charters the average area is a four- or five-mile circuit, and when a company gets a new charter the area covered by its powers is almost invariably increased. The Butchers obtained a one-mile area from James I., and a two-mile area from Charles I. Similarly the Carpenters and the Brewers increased their two miles to four. Under Charles II. the supervision of the Masons, the Plumbers, and the Poulterers extended to a seven-mile radius, and those of the Waxchandlers to a ten-mile radius. In short, the London over which the 17th-century company exercised its rights was already coming to be loosely identical with the greater London of our own time, and this expansion involved important social and economic consequences.

Mediæval London had embraced for purposes of industrial regulation, in addition to the area within the walls, only the small territory comprised in Portsoken ward and in Farringdon, Cripplegate, and Bishopgate wards Without. Its rights over Southwark were, until 1550, extremely restricted and of dubious application. Even within these narrow limits large subtraction must be made for the numerous exempted areas or liberties both within and without the walls, many of which, like Blackfriars', St. Martin's le Grand, and Holy Trinity Priory (afterwards Duke's Place) survived the Reformation. By the close of the 15th century, however, the movement had already begun by which almost all the industries of the city were gradually transferred to that ring of parishes out of which have arisen the metropolitan boroughs of Holborn, Finsbury, Shoreditch, Bethnal Green, Stepney, Bermondsey, and Southwark, some of which cover an area twice as large as that of the city, whilst all of them taken together contain a population more that thirty times as numerous.

The stream of population that fed this process of expansion was threefold. In the first place, there was a steady overflow from the city itself, all through the 14th and 15th centuries, of the poorer craftsmen who could not afford to set up shop within the walls and who were largely dependent for the sale of their wares on the city shopkeepers. At first they congregated in the wards "without," forming colonies outside Cripplegate and Bishopgate and along Fleet Street and Holborn; but soon they spread over the border into Westminster, Clerkenwell, Shoreditch, Whitechapel, Southwark, and Bermondsey. In the second place, the numbers of these emigrants were swelled by a constant stream of immigrants from the country, the "foreigners" from Hertfordshire, Essex, Kent, Surrey, Middlesex, or more distant counties, whose place of origin was marked in the 14th century by their names, as John of South Mimms, Richard of Reigate, etc. And thirdly, there were the alien strangers, as distinguished from the English foreigners. From the earliest times these had always contributed an influential part of the industrial population, and the influx steadily increased. Of some 1800 aliens to whom licences were given in 1437, 540 were resident in London, mostly in Southwark or the eastern suburbs.* In 1563 the aliens in the city, Westminster and Southwark, numbered 4534; in 1583 they were 5141, of whom 1604 were outside the city proper.†

There can be no doubt that the alien immigrants of the 15th and 16th centuries supplied the main factor in an industrial renaissance which had as much importance for the economic development of England as the literary and artistic renaissance had for its intellectual development. All branches of industry were affected by it ; old handicrafts were revolutionized, new ones were created. The native goldsmiths were kept in a condition of healthy emulation by the steady influx of aliens, whom we find being invited in 1464 to a friendly contest of skill, and many of whom settled in Westminster, Southwark, and in the liberties of St. Martin, St. Bartholomew, and St. Katherine. The London weavers were nearly all of alien extraction, and of a list of 70 master weavers who signed an agreement in 1456, only 33 resided within the city, whilst 7 lived in Southwark, 6 in the Bishop of Durham's liberty (in the Strand), 5 in Bermondsey, 5 in Whitechapel, 2 in the Strand, 2 in Charterhouse, and one each in Clerkenwell, Holborn, and Westminster.‡ These were woollen and linen weavers. Another wave of immigrants, who introduced silk-weaving in the 16th century, settled in Shoreditch and Spitalfields. A colony of feltmakers, mostly from the Rouen district, who displaced the native cap by the improved felt hat or the costly beaver, settled in Southwark alongside the Flemings, who introduced the brewing of beer with hops. The printers who followed Caxton from the Low Countries found it safer to set up at first as he had done, outside the city in Westminster and Clerkenwell. There was

---

* C. L. Kingsford in *English Hist. Rev.*, April, 1908, p. 363.
† Huguenot Society, *Returns of Aliens.*
‡ Facsimile of Weavers' Ancient Book.

a whole row of alien shoemakers in the liberty of St. Martin's, and another in Blackfriars, where they possessed a gild of their own. The trades of tanning and leather-dressing, also largely recruited by aliens, had already moved out to their present quarters in Bermondsey.

Whilst, therefore, the aliens were by no means solely responsible for the migration of industry, they took a sufficiently prominent share in it to attract to themselves the greater part of the ill-feeling which it occasioned amongst those whose interests were affected. And their unpopularity was increased by other causes. The aliens were not all industrialists, nor did they all settle permanently in London. Many were merchants engaged in importing a great variety of manufactured goods which were still better made on the continent than in England, or in exporting English cloth in a half-manufactured state so that it might be dyed and finished to the taste of the foreign consumer. Whether, therefore, as importers or as exporters, they were popularly regarded as taking the bread out of the mouth of the English craftsman, and the alien settlers who were helping to lay the foundations of England's industrial greatness were included in the same condemnation.

This feeling found a violent expression on Evil May Day, 1517. For some years before this a storm had been brewing. In 1514 the craftsmen of London had petitioned the Government against the freedom allowed to aliens, and in 1516 a handbill was posted up in the city which accused the King and Council of ruining England by favouring foreigners. Great efforts were made to discover the author, but in vain. The Spital sermons, which were annually preached in Easter Week before the mayor and aldermen, seemed to the agitators a good opportunity of urging the rulers of the city to take sides with the commonalty against the strangers. The first preacher who was asked refused, but the second consented, and took for his text, " The heaven of heavens is the Lord's, but the earth He has given to the children of men"; which he interpreted to mean—England for the English, and London for the Londoners.

"The Dutch," said the statement which was given him to read, "bring over iron, timber, leather, and wainscot, ready wrought as nails, locks, baskets, cupboards, stools, tables, chests, girdles, and points, saddles and painted cloths so that if it were wrought here Englishmen might have some work and living at it. . . . And, further, the strangers compass the city round about in Southwark, in Westminster, Temple Bar, Holborn, St. Martin's, St. John's Gate, Aldgate, Tower Hill, St. Katherine's, and forestall the market so that no good thing for them cometh to the market which is the cause that Englishmen want and starve. . . . And they (the aliens) keep such assemblies and fraternities together and make such a gathering to their common box that every brother will hold plea with the city of London." *

The story of the outbreak itself is too well known to need re-telling here. In almost every detail the disturbance was a mere repetition of what had happened a dozen times already in the history of mediæval London, but the rioters had to deal with a Tudor monarch who knew how to render both his severity and his clemency more impressive by the use of dramatic effect. Yet neither the hanging of a dozen apprentices before their own doors, nor the pardon of four hundred other rioters with ropes round their necks, were any more likely to remove the lasting causes of discontent than were the mob's onslaught on alien craftsmen and their pillaging of foreign merchants' houses. The real evil for which the innocent alien was made the scapegoat was one for which an adequate remedy cannot even yet be said to have been found—that massing of unorganized labour which is popularly known as the "sweating system."

A pamphleteer of the period has given us a brief glimpse into the beginnings of this social problem, all the more

* Hall, *Chronicle.*

striking because it occurs quite incidentally in the course of an argument against free imports.

"Before May Day," he says, "poor handicraft people which were wont to keep shops and servants and had labour and living by making pins, points, girdles, gloves, and all such other things . . . had thereof sale and profit daily, until thirty years ago a sort began to occupy to buy and sell all such handicraft wares called haberdashers . . . whereby many rich men is risen upon the destruction of the poor people, which poor people perceived themselves having no living and were bound prentices in London not able to keep no houses nor shops, but in alleys sitting in a poor chamber working all the week to sell their ware, on the Saturday brought it to the haberdashers to sell . . . which would not give them so much winning for their wares to find them meat and drink saying they had no need thereof; their shops lay stored full of [wares from] beyond sea." *

In a narrower sphere and under simpler conditions the craft gilds had aimed with some success at preventing evils of this kind, and the London companies now claimed that the true remedy in this case also was to extend their powers beyond the boundaries of the city so as to place the regulation of aliens in their hands. Their view obtained the sanction of Parliament in 1524, when "all aliens using any manner of handicraft in city or suburbs, the town of Westminster, the parishes of St. Martin's in the Fields, Our Lady of the Strand, St. Clement's Danes, St. Giles' in the Fields, St. Andrew's in Holborn, the town and borough of Southwark, Shoreditch, Whitechapel parish, St. John's Street, the parish of Clerkenwell, St. Botolph's parish without Aldgate, St. Katherine's, Bermondsey Street, or within two miles' compass of the city or the parishes aforesaid," were placed under the "search and reformation of the wardens and fellowships of crafts within the city with one substantial stranger being a householder of the same craft chosen by the wardens." †

* R. Pauli, *Drei Volkswirthschaftliche Denkschriften.*
† 14 & 15 Henry VIII. c. 2.

The interpretation of this Act having been disputed, a decree of the Star Chamber in 1528, ratified by a further Act the following year, decided that the aliens must contribute to the taxation borne by the city companies and must pay the quarterage levied by them, which in the disputed case of the Cordwainers was 6d. a quarter for a householder and 3d. for a journeyman.* All aliens were to swear allegiance to the king at the common halls of the companies representing their several trades. They were to assemble there if summoned by the officers of the company, and were not to hold assemblies anywhere else. None but those who had qualified as denizens were to set up shops. The effect of these measures in swelling the lower ranks of the companies is clearly marked in the records of the period. The Coopers, whose numbers in 1541 had only been 124, including 13 Dutchmen, increased by 1547 to 194, of whom 40 were in their livery, 43 were householders out of the livery, 32 were English free journeymen, 9 foreign free journeymen, 43 Dutch householders, 13 free denizen journeymen, and 12 " new come in" Dutch journeymen. The total number on their books had increased by 1553 to 267.† The Cordwainers in 1599 levied quarterage on 439 persons, of whom 28 only were in their livery. Of the rest, 152 belonged to their yeomanry, 85 were cobblers free of the company, and 32 were free cobblers in some other sense, 11 were cordwainers free of other companies, and 131 were foreigners or aliens living in the liberties or outside the city. The distribution of these outsiders is interesting. In St. Martin's le Grand there were 11, in St. Bartholomew's and St. John's Street 21, in Holborn, Chancery Lane, Temple Bar, and the Strand 29, in Blackfriars 20, in Creechurch (Duke's Place) 15, in St. Katherine's 14, in Whitechapel 2, in Southwark 17, in Westminster 2.‡ In 1583 the Weavers had 73 aliens among the free brethren of their

---

* Schanz, *Handelsgeschichte*, II. 598.   † Firth, *Coopers*, p. 115.

‡ Accounts of Cordwainers' Company for 1599.

company; and 80 journeymen and 100 strangers who lived outside the city were under the supervision of the Joiners.*

But it soon appeared that to place the aliens under the rule of the companies was no solution of the problems that had been raised. The real difficulty did not lie in the alien as such, but in the extension of the industrial area, the separation of the functions of craftsman and trader, and the inadequacy of the "craft" organization to the larger methods of production that were now becoming general. Even when the companies obtained by charter, as many of them did about this time, powers of search and regulation, covering the whole metropolitan area and including the English craftsmen of the suburbs as well as the aliens, their only way of using these powers was to enforce the rights of one of the divided interests against the others, and thus to emphasize the natural difficulties of the situation. The industrial records of Elizabeth, James I., and Charles I. are full of disputes arising in this way: (1) between the craftsmen of the city and those of the suburbs; (2) between two companies interested in the same industry; (3) between two classes representing the industrial and the commercial interests within the same company. Behind all these disputes lay this fundamental economic situation: that the craftsman was no longer in direct contact with the consumer, but was dependent on the capital of the middleman, whether as trader or as a direct employer, to find a market for his wares or his work. This dependence was an economic necessity, but it was bound to bear hardly on the craftsman until he had adapted his organization to the new conditions, and the difficulties of the transition stage were greatly increased when the traders in the companies used their powers of search so as to monopolize the market for themselves. Artificial monopolies were met by artificial remedies for monopoly. Instructive examples of the failure of both fill the statutes of the Tudors and the state papers of

* Huguenot Society, *Returns of Aliens.*

the Stuarts.   Only perhaps in this way could the ground be cleared for those broader conceptions of economic development which are or ought to be the commonplaces of to-day.

Nearly every session of a Tudor Parliament saw a fresh Act introduced to regulate the leather trades.   Every process in the making of a pair of shoes was defined by the legislator. The tanner, the currier, and the cordwainer were not only carefully restricted within the limits of their respective crafts, they were instructed as to what kind of leather they might buy, with what quality of grease they might curry it, at what point they might insert the knife, which hide they were to use for the inner sole and heel, and which for the outer sole.   At first sight it seems like the wise care of a paternal Government, intervening with technical omniscience and sublime impartiality to fill the place left vacant by the gild ordinances; but a little examination of the statutes removes this impression. There were five Acts passed between 1548 and 1558, and each legislated in the opposite sense to its immediate predecessor. Looked at a little more closely this violent fluctuation of national policy proves to be due to a struggle between the London Cordwainers and Curriers.   The wealthy traders connected with each of these companies wished to have the sole right of selling leather or giving out work to the poorer members of both crafts, and to the aliens or non-freemen in the suburbs.   In the preambles to the numerous Acts each company in turn appears anxious to rescue the poor craftsmen from the tyrannical monopoly exercised by the other.   While the Bills were before Parliament excitement ran so high that the Common Council found it necessary to restrict the number of Cordwainers and Curriers who might go "lobbying" together.   As the political pendulum swung to and fro, each craft secured the repeal of the Act passed in the last Parliament and replaced it by another.   The precise rules laid down for the conduct of business in each craft were therefore largely dictated by the mercantile interest of the hostile craft which happened for the moment to have gained the political ascendency.*

Thus while the Cordwainers' Company appears throughout the reign of Elizabeth as the champion of the small shoemaker and cobbler against the oppressive middlemen of the Curriers' Company, it was at the same time engaged in a constant struggle with the cordwainers of Westminster who refused to own any allegiance to Cordwainers' Hall. In 1576 the company sued the Westminster men in the Exchequer, and the Westminster men having raised a levy amongst themselves to obtain legal advice, exhibited a bill in the Star Chamber against the company. Whereupon the company indicted a number of them before the Justices of Middlesex for unlawful assembly. They also arrested a Savoy shoemaker for breach of the peace, and when the Westminster men's solicitor came to serve a subpœna on a city cordwainer, he was struck to the ground with a dagger.†

A compromise appears to have been arranged on this occasion, but in 1580 the disputants were again before the Star Chamber, and very probably the frequent recurrence of similar differences in other crafts was one of the chief motives for the grant of a charter to Westminster in 1585.

Almost an exact parallel to this situation can be traced at the same moment in every important London industry— amongst the clothworkers, the hat and cap makers, the pinners, the printers, the glovers, the skinners. The separation of those interested in the several industries into two distinct classes is everywhere described in the same terms. In the shoe-leather crafts there were on one hand a number of poor artificers not able to buy two or three hides or backs at one time, nor to pay ready money for them, and on the other

---

* Statutes of the Realm, 3 Hen. 8, c. 10 ; 5 Hen. 8, c. 7 ; 24 Hen. 8, c. 1 ; 2 & 3 Ed. 6, c. 9 ; 3 & 4 Ed. 6, c. 6 ; 5 & 6 Ed. 6, c. 15 ; 1 Mar. c. 8 ; 1 Eliz. c. 10 ; *Victoria Hist. of Surrey*, II. 331.

† Lansd. MSS. 26 ; Strype, *Stow*, V. 213.

a few rich men that were common engrossers of leather and had all the buying of leather and tallow in their hands.* In the same way the feltmakers were described as buying their wool in small quantities day by day from the rich haberdashers who held a monopoly of the supply, and therefore sold the worst refuse at the price of the best wool ; the workmen cutters of white leather (for gloves), over a thousand in number, were said to be constrained to buy all their skins from the leathersellers in London, who were but eight persons, and who put four bad skins in every dozen ; the great majority of the printers were obliged to take out work from the booksellers, who had monopolized all the best copyrights ; the small master fullers and shearmen were dependent for employment on the wealthy exporters of cloth who controlled the Clothworkers', Merchant Tailors' and Drapers' Companies ; the pinners depended partly on the girdlers for the purchase of their wire, and partly on the haberdashers for the sale of their pins ; † and within the companies of Goldsmiths, Skinners, Pewterers, and Armourers, there was the same opposition of interest between a ruling class of merchants and middlemen and a dependent class of small master craftsmen.

It has already been seen how the industrial element in the older companies came to be identical in most cases with the yeomanry organization, and it was through this organization that the craftsmen who were freemen of the city naturally first sought a remedy for their grievances. The feltmakers, who were part of the Haberdashers' yeomanry, were constantly petitioning the Court of that company to support them in carrying out a search amongst foreigners, in prosecuting unlawful intruders, in suppressing female labour and in enforcing the Statute of Apprentices.‡ The printers desired the Stationers' Company to ordain that no work should be given to foreigners, that the number of apprentices should be limited,

---

* I Mary, c. 8.   † Unwin, *Industrial Organization.*
‡ *Ibid.*

and that work should be properly paid for in money.* The fullers and shearmen urged the Clothworkers' Court to limit the number of apprentices and to enforce the law which forbade the export of unfinished cloth. There were two main obstacles to the granting of these requests. In the first place the companies' powers were limited. Over their own members they had considerable authority, and this had been extended in some degree so as to cover aliens and foreigners ; but over freemen of other companies who practised their calling their authority was dubious and could generally be successfully resisted. And secondly, even if the Court of Assistants had been able, it was not willing to carry out the industrial policy recommended by the yeomanry. It was not to the interest of the merchants and employers who composed the ruling bodies of the companies to suppress the activity or restrict the numbers of the suburban workers. The Stationers, for example, told the printers that if they refused to give work to "foreigners" their customers would themselves purchase paper and give out their printing direct to the strangers. Moreover, the interests of the rulers of the companies were more often mercantile than industrial. The haberdashers who imported large quantities of hats, caps and pins, the clothworkers who were mainly exporters of unfinished cloth, could not be expected strictly to enforce the execution of laws restricting imports or exports in the supposed interests of the craftsman.

The craftsmen seeing they could hope for no effectual remedy from their several companies naturally turned to the Government, and found it not indisposed to consider their grievances. The advisers of the Crown were just beginning to realize that the expansion of industry might afford them the very fiscal resource of which they stood in need. In France at this period industry was being declared by the Crown officials to lie within the King's domain, so that a

* Arber, *Transcript of the Stationers' Registers*, II. 881.

large part of the fees that had been paid to the gilds might flow into the royal exchequer.   In England so direct and sweeping a policy was not practicable, but indirectly the same results were aimed at.   The means adopted was the grant of letters patent to gentlemen about the court, by which the right to regulate trade and industry and to impose fines and fees was farmed out to them, or bestowed upon them in consideration of services rendered.   With the help of these patents the Government provided with lavish generosity for the needs of every class that had a grievance.   It granted special powers to enforce the law for the benefit of those who complained that it was a dead letter, and bestowed on the other hand special powers of dispensation for the benefit of those upon whom a law pressed too heavily.   In this way all the advantages of an active legislature were secured with a minimum of its evils.   Public opinion was gratified, local option was consulted, and a double opportunity was opened to the Exchequer.

During the reign of Elizabeth there was scarcely one of the London companies that was not affected by the grant of these patents.*   Sometimes, no doubt, the grants were made without any reference to the wishes of any section of the company concerned, but more often they were the outcome of an arrangement between the patentee and a discontented body of craftsmen, who sought to obtain in that way some form of regulation which they could not procure from their company or from the city authorities.   The " members of the handicraft" in the Clothworkers' Company petitioned the Privy Council in 1575 for the appointment of a "packer" to inspect the shipping of cloth and prevent the merchants from exporting it unfinished.   The feltmakers in 1579 organized

---

* Strype's *Stow*, Book V. chaps. 9-15 ; see under Grocers, Skinners, Haberdashers, Vintners, Clothworkers, Brewers, Leathersellers, Pewterers, Tallowchandlers, Cutlers, Cordwainers, Painters, Bowyers, Fletchers, Horners, Stationers, Upholders, Distillers, Feltmakers, Refiners.

an agitation in support of a patent to a certain Dr. Hector, to authorize him to search all wool supplied by the haberdashers and to see that it was properly cleansed and sorted.* In 1592 Mr. Edward Darcy took up the cause of the glovers and other workers in leather, and proposed to protect them against the oppression of the leathersellers by establishing a place of inspection at Smithfield for all skins sold to them, and stamping the genuine article, in return for a fee of 10*d.* a dozen on the lesser skins, and as much as 10*d.* each on some of the more costly ones. The craftsmen were to be bound in £40 not to deal in unstamped skins.

To this project the Leathersellers offered a stout opposition, in which they had the warm sympathy of the city. Darcy, who had spent £500 or £600 in procuring the patent, which was not the first (nor the last) he applied for, lost his temper and so far forgot himself as to strike an alderman in the Lord Mayor's presence during a discussion of the proposal. The insult was noised abroad, the city apprentices gathered, and Darcy would not have escaped with his life but for the protection afforded by the Lord Mayor. The patentee, however, with the support of the Government, persisted in his scheme, and as the Leathersellers were equally determined their four wardens were ultimately committed to prison. Their appeal to Burleigh, in spite of a touch of acerbity which leads them to speak of one of Darcy's agents as being lineally descended from a witch on his mother's side, breathes the finest spirit of puritanism, in which a fervent loyalty to the Queen was blended with an even stronger attachment to the laws and liberties of their country. All they desired was that Mr. Darcy's claim and their defence might be referred to the ordinary trial of the laws of the land, "which is," they said, "the chiefest inheritance that every mean subject is born unto, and the surest anchor hold by which the greatest subject in the realm doth enjoy all he hath." They spoke boldly of

* Unwin, *Industrial Organization*, pp. 122, 132.

the patents as being contrary to the laws of the land, and as a "great unnecessary taxing of all the commons in the realm and especially of the poorest sort whose chief wearing leather is." They protest that to allow the patentees' claims would be to break the oath they had taken to maintain the franchises of the city, and thus to defile their consciences with the stain of perjury, "from which," they piously conclude, "God preserve every good man and strengthen us with all constancy and patience to endure anything rather than by our own act to dispossess ourselves of that which hath been enjoyed by us and our predecessors, citizens of London, 300 years and more." They had no other choice, they assured the Lord Treasurer, but to endure imprisonment or to damn their own souls, and they ventured to remind Burleigh, and through him Elizabeth, of a saying attributed to Henry VIII., "that his mind was never to take anything of his commons that might sound to his dishonour or to the breach of his laws." * The wardens were released within a year and Darcy's patent withdrawn, but Elizabeth claimed £4000 from the city and the leathersellers in compensation.† The creation of offices of this kind and their subsequent abolition on payment of a large fine was a mode of extortion frequently practised by the French government on the *Corps de metier* of Paris.

It would, however, be unjust to give all the credit of opposing the patents to the merchants, and all the discredit of procuring them to the craftsmen. The journeymen and small master printers had been beforehand with the leathersellers in the struggle against monopoly in a still more unequivocal form. It is true patents obtained by members of the Stationers' Company, giving them the sole right to the production of many books in common use, were said by their apologists to have been granted for the protection of the printer against the dominance of the bookseller. The early printers had been

---

* Lansdowne MSS., Vol. 74, Nos. 42–51.
† *Analytical Index to Remembrancia*, pp. 179–182.

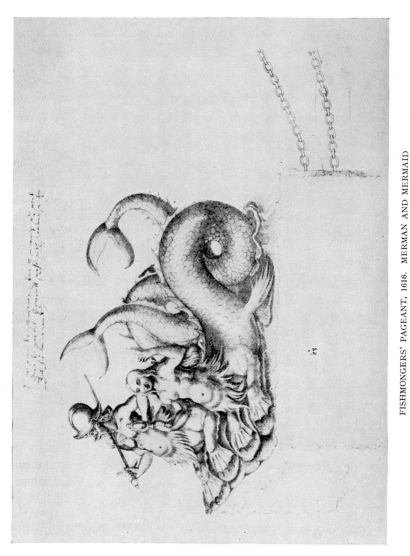

FISHMONGERS' PAGEANT, 1616. MERMAN AND MERMAID

FISHMONGERS' PAGEANT CHARIOT 1616

men of means who sold their own books and could afford to wait for the slow returns upon them, but as printing became general and printers increased in numbers, many of those who set up for themselves had not capital enough for this. They were obliged to sell their sheets as they came from the press to the stationers, who bound them up and disposed of them to the public. In this way the booksellers came into possession of most of the best copyrights, and the incorporation of the Stationers' Company in 1555, with full powers of control over the printing trade, was an indication of the ascendency which the trader had here as in so many other cases gained over the craftsman. But there were still a number of independent printers amongst the rulers of the Stationers' Company, and some of these, having represented to the Government how important it was that printers should not be tempted for want of regular work to print unlawful books, obtained various grants of monopoly for the production of Bibles, Prayerbooks, lawbooks, dictionaries, grammars, and other books in common and regular use. Each of these privileges involved of course a serious diminution in the freedom of all other printers and booksellers, and they were at first opposed by the company. Gradually, however, as the patentees increased in number to about a dozen, they contrived to capture the executive of the company, so that the monopoly became a joint concern, and all outside printers became much more dependent on the privileged members of their own trade than they had previously been on the booksellers.*

Infringement of the patents was under these circumstances inevitable. The booksellers supplied the poorer printers with paper, a skilled Frenchman was employed to counterfeit the patentees' trade-marks, and tens of thousands of A B C's and catechisms were produced, some of which were sent as far as Shrewsbury.† The eight or ten rulers of the Stationers'

* Lansdowne MSS., Vol. 48, No. 82.
† Arber, *Transcript of the Registers of the Stationers' Company*, II. 761.

T

Company found themselves confronted by an opposition composed of one hundred and seventy-five masters and journeymen, besides apprentices. They seized a printer named John Wolfe, who was not of their company but was free of the Fishmongers, and cast him in the Clink. This was an unfortunate move. A Swiss by extraction, Wolfe had been much abroad, and was a man of ideas. He saw that the printers ought to appeal to the growing public feeling against monopolies. He organized his campaign from the Clink, and when he was released he held meetings in his house in the Exchange and in the church of St. Thomas Acon. He appeared at the head of his followers in Stationers' Hall and boldly declared that it was lawful for all men to print all books. "Luther," he said, "was but one man and reformed all the world for religion, and I am that one man that must and will reform the Government in this trade." Thus it came about that just at the moment when several bodies of craftsmen were organizing support for patentees who were to deliver them from bondage to the middleman, the printers were raising a fund amongst themselves to resist a monopoly which had proved to be a worse infliction than the evil it was designed to remedy.

The rulers of the Stationers' Company thought it expedient to negotiate with Wolfe through one of their members, Christopher Barker, the Queen's printer, and though it would not be fair to Wolfe to accept unreservedly Barker's account of the interview, the conversation as reported by him is not only amusing but instructive. "Wolfe!" said Barker after much talk had passed between them, "leave your Machiavellian devices and conceit of your foreign wit which you have gained by gadding from country to country, and tell me plainly, if you mean to deal like an honest man, what you would have." *Wolfe:* "If I should come into your company I would have allowance of my five apprentices. I would be provided whereon to live if I could have the benefit which now I have in my own company." *Barker :* "Touching your five apprentices it is against our order, yet for quietness' sake I would be a mean as far as I can that you shall enjoy them. To provide you a living that is the work of God only, upon whose providence you must depend ; yet I dare promise you after a sort that being of our company you shall have good and gainful copies whereon you may live in measure, and yet not print other men's copies. Touching the loan of £20 which you have in your company, we Stationers are very poor and have no land but the house we sit in and our whole stock is under £100, yet I will do what I may to procure you £20 thereof upon your good security." *

The proposed transference of Wolfe (which seems to have been ultimately effected) from the Fishmongers to the Stationers, is an apt illustration of the working of the forces that were producing the new corporations. He was to desert a greater company for a lesser one, a wealthy corporation for a poor one, and to exchange a condition of comparative freedom from regulation for one of subjection to the rule of the men of his trade ; but, on the other hand, he was invited to leave a company where his membership gave him no influence in any trade for one in which he might hope to acquire a strong influence over his own trade, and he was promised a share in a monopoly of that trade which, with the sanction of the Government, was growing steadily more complete. No other company, it is true, ever attained the same degree of monopoly as that which the State thought it expedient to confer on the Stationers, but all the lesser companies made such a monopoly their aim. And it must be remembered that in a great majority of cases there was no such choice of alternatives as that which presented itself to Wolfe. Most of the members who were drawn into the new industrial companies had no privileges of membership to resign elsewhere.

We are now in a better position to take a brief survey of

* State Papers, Domestic, Eliz., Vol. 15, 37-40.

the industrial movement which was gathering to a head in the
reign of Elizabeth, and which found its full expression in the
reigns of the first two Stuarts. It was not confined to the new
corporations. Three distinct elements may be found blend-
ing within it. In the first place, a number of the lesser companies, incorporated in the 15th century, were endeavouring
to regain that connection with and control over the trade
they represented which always tended to slip away after
about a century of a company's existence. And secondly,
there were a number of fellowships of old standing, possessing
halls and liveries, but not yet incorporated, which were obtaining charters that gave them extended powers of regulation
over an area of several miles round London. Within both
these classes of companies there was a strong feeling that
the "custom of London," which enabled a citizen who had
obtained the freedom in any company (generally through
inheritance) to practise the trade of any other, and which
prevented any company from having a complete control over
the trade it represented, should be in some way reformed.
A petition of fourteen crafts (some of which—the Cutlers, the
Girdlers, the Cordwainers, the Carpenters, the Dyers, the
Tallowchandlers, the Coopers, and the Bakers—were old
incorporations, others—the Stationers and the Blacksmiths—
had been recently incorporated, whilst the rest—the Painters,
the Glaziers, the Horners, and the Upholders—were to receive
charters from Elizabeth or the Stuarts) was presented to the
Court of Aldermen in 1571, praying for a return to the condition of ancient times when each company had the sole
exercise of its art or handicraft, and things were "truly, substantially, and workmanly made." "By achieving this
reform," said the petitioners, "the aldermen would purchase
everlasting renown and immortal fame here on earth, with the
fruition of the immortal God in the world to come." *

But there was a third element in the movement that made

* Clode, *Early History of the Merchant Taylors*, I. 205.

more stir than either of the other two. This consisted of the craftsmen and retailers who formed the yeomanry of the greater companies, and of the Leathersellers' company which belonged economically to the same group. We have seen what a number of crafts had been absorbed in and subordinated to the greater companies during the first period of incorporation. That process was now to be reversed. Several of the subordinated crafts regained their independence, and achieved incorporation. The Feltmakers were freed after a prolonged struggle from the Haberdashers, the Apothecaries from the Grocers, the Glovers from the Leathersellers, the Pinners from the Girdlers—whilst other new companies were formed out of the members of the old; *e.g.* the Starchmakers and Distillers out of the Grocers ; the Gold and Silver wire-drawers out of the Goldsmiths ; the Tinplate-workers out of the Ironmongers ; the Gunmakers and the Clockmakers out of the Blacksmiths ; to represent industries that had not till then possessed a separate organization. Besides all these cases there were a number of efforts that failed, or only partially or temporarily succeeded. The attempts of the Artisan Skinners and the Artisan Clothworkers to obtain separate charters were defeated. The retailing Vintners succeeded in obtaining for a time an independent monopoly and separate powers of regulation.

The attitude of the ruling classes in the city was on the whole unfriendly to the movement. The predominant interest of London had always been commercial rather than industrial, and the "custom of London," while it secured the privilege of the citizen as against the "foreigner," left him free to transfer his capital from one trade to another. It was, in fact, just one of those compromises in which Englishmen have always delighted. The authority of each company to regulate its trade was nominally preserved, but its power to enforce its regulations depended upon circumstances, and if it came to be oppressive, could generally be evaded. This loose and vague arrangement met the practical needs of the situation better than a more logical settlement would have done, and, in spite of temporary and partial concessions to more logical principles, it was never really abandoned.

Nevertheless, the concessions made to the principle of the full control of each trade by a single company were sufficiently numerous during the Stuart. period to indicate the existence of a strong current of public opinion. When the Cooks received a new charter in 1605, an order was made by the Court of Aldermen obliging all cooks to be translated into the company, but this extreme concession was ·withdrawn in 1614.* In 1608 all cordwainers free of the Curriers and Embroiderers were ordered to make a "proof-piece" (specimen of their skill) at Cordwainers' Hall.† The glaziers free of other companies were required in 1615–17 to submit to the correction of the Glaziers' Company, and to bind their apprentices to a warden of that company, so that in time they might be free of that company,‡ and a similar rule was applied to the Clockmakers in 1637.§ Dyers free of other companies, although not compelled to bind their apprentices at Dyers' Hall, must take an oath for true dyeing and pay 4d. at the search.‖ The Silkthrowers,¶ the Brewers,** and the Bakers †† were in like manner authorized to impose an oath on members of other companies practising their trades. The Weavers ‡‡ and the Turners §§ also received power to regulate non-members.

The dominant idea of all this regulation was the preservation of the status of the master craftsman. With this object most of the industrial companies had limited the number of

---

* Journals, Low, 339.

‡ Jos. Jolles, 133 ; Jos. Bolles, 339.

§ Rep. Bromfield, 19, 20.

¶ Rep. Campbell, 4, 26.

†† Rep. Garway, 24.

† Rep. Weld, 24, 356.

‖ Rep. Whitmore, 32, 46.

** Rep. Deane, 266.

‡‡ Rep. Cockain, 526.

§§ Rep. Cotton, 151. I owe these references and a number of others to a valuable digest contained in Guildhall MSS., No. 108, fo. 166 *et seq.*

apprentices to three for one of their governing body, two for one of their livery and one for an ordinary member. A rule had also been made in 1555, with the sanction of the Common Council, that no apprentice was to be admitted as a freeman nor allowed to set up house till he was twenty-four years of age, and many companies required the aspirant to full master-ship to pass an examination in workmanship and to prove that he was possessed of sufficient capital to start for himself.* Rules of this character had existed in many of the crafts from the earliest times, but they were now made more definite and exclusive. It is not till the 16th century that we hear of the "masterpiece," or, as it was commonly called, the proof-piece, in connection with the London crafts. In the later stages of the French and German craft gild the master-piece played an important part, mainly as a device for exclud-ing new members. The aspirant for entrance to a trade was required to produce some elaborate and costly evidence of his skill, for which the ordinary journeyman could afford neither the money nor the time. It seems probable that the require-ment of the masterpiece had become general in London by the 17th century. The Weavers, the Saddlers, the Felt-makers, the Broderers, the Clockmakers, the Joiners, and the Tinplate-workers required it from their members,† and a dispute that arose amongst the Joiners in 1615 shows not only that it operated to some extent as a restriction in that craft, but also that it was common in other companies. Many journey-men had refused to make the masterpiece, which, they said, was an unlawful restraint on their entry into the trade and especially forbidden by an Act of 1536; whilst the Joiners' Company, on the other hand, claimed that the masterpiece was a thing that had hitherto been put in practice without controversy or refusal by all manner of craftsmen within the

---

* Welch, *Pewterers*, I, 194; Nichols, *Ironmongers*, 71-3.

† Unwin, *Industrial Organization*, p. 48; Sherwell, *Saddlers*, p. 190; Ebble-white, *Tinplate-workers*, p. 4.

city.* There can be little doubt that the masterpiece was used as a barrier against the flood of journeymen whom the masters desired to keep in the position of wage-earners.

Another feature of this renaissance of the crafts was the frequency of disputes as to the limits of the several trades. These were specially common in the building trades, and led the Carpenters and Joiners to appeal to the city authorities, in 1632, for an authorized schedule of the branches of wood-work belonging to each. The plasterers complained of the encroachments of the bricklayers, and the painters declared that the bricklayers, the carpenters, the wiremakers, the box-makers, the embroiderers, the turners, the joiners, the drum-makers, the coachmakers, the virginal-makers, the plumbers, the glaziers, the smiths, the armourers, the hotpressers, but more especially the plasterers, combined painting with their several callings. Disputes of this kind are common enough at the present day between the trade unions whose members work in close contact, but in the 17th century they had a different significance. What was complained of was, not that workmen of one trade undertook the work of another, but that capitalists of one trade set on the journeymen or small masters of another. The bricklayer or the carpenter included painting in his estimate of a job. The brewer furnished the timber and the workshop, and set on a number of coopers to make barrels. The demand of the incorporated crafts was that all work should be carried on under the direction of an independent capitalist. That demand proved incompatible with the economic development of industry, but it had an important influence on the formation of the monopolist corporations which have still to be considered.

* _Index to Remembrancia_, p. 99.

CHAPTER XVI

THE LORD MAYOR'S SHOW

L OVE of jousts and "guisings," of minstrelsy and plays, of shows and processions, was a characteristic of all towns and cities in the Middle Ages, and what it lost in some directions by the Reformation it gained in other directions by the Renaissance. Gogmagog and Corineus—who now enjoy a well-earned rest at the Guildhall, and whose wickerwork predecessors welcomed the victorious Henry V. after Agincourt, and presented the weary Elizabeth with the concluding moral, in Latin verse and English, of the endless pageantries of her first reception—belong to a prolific race of giants, and had kinsmen and kinswomen in many old English towns and in nearly all the cities of Flanders.* Of the processions and shows of Corpus Christi we have much fuller accounts in the records of York and Chester than any yet discovered in those of London. The celebration of May day and of Midsummer Eve were pagan survivals common to all Christendom.

Many of these festivals survived to the 16th century, to be recorded by the quickened imaginations of those who had seen them pass away. Stow's account of the Skinners' procession on Corpus Christi day has been already cited. He also speaks of the regular theatre having superseded in his own time the original stage plays such as that presented in

* Fairholt, *Gog and Magog*, p. 27.

1391 by the Parish Clerks of London at the Skinners' Wells beside Smithfield, which continued three days together, the king, the queen and nobles of the realm being present; "and another in the year 1409, which lasted eight days, and was of matter from the creation of the world." * Of the Midsummer watch, the earliest in origin of all the festivals, which had been abandoned in 1539, and the brief revival of which, in 1548, must have been one of the brightest of his youthful memories, Stow gives this glowing account:

"On the vigil of St. John the Baptist and on St. Peter and Paul the Apostles, every man's door being shadowed with green birch, long fennel, St. John's wort, orpin, white lilies, and such like, garnished upon with garlands and beautiful flowers, had also lamps of glass with oil burning in them all the night; some hung out branches of iron curiously wrought, containing hundreds of lamps alight at once, which made a goodly show, namely in New Fish St., Thames St., etc. Then had ye beside the standing watches all in bright harness, in every ward and street of this city and suburbs, a marching watch, that passed through the principal streets thereof, to wit, from the little conduit by Paul's Gate to West Cheap, by the Stocks through Cornhill, by Leadenhall to Aldgate, then back down Fenchurch St., by Grasschurch, about Grasschurch conduit, and up Grasschurch St. into Cornhill, and through it into West Cheap again. The whole way for this marching watch extendeth to three thousand two hundred tailor's yards of assize; for the furniture whereof with lights, there were appointed 700 cressets, 500 of them being found by the companies, the other 200 by the Chamber of London. Besides the which lights every constable in London, in number more than 240, had his cresset: the charge of every cresset was in light two shillings and fourpence, and every cresset had two men, one to bear or hold it, another to bear a bag with light, and to serve it, so that the poor men pertaining to the cressets, taking wages, besides that every one had a straw hat, with a badge painted, and his breakfast in the morning, amounted in number to almost 2000. The marching watch contained in number about 2000 men, part of them being old soldiers

* Stow, *Survey*, p. 119.

of skill, to be captains, lieutenants, serjeants, corporals, etc., whifflers, drummers and fifes, standard and ensign bearers, sword players, trumpeters on horseback, demi-lances on great horses, gunners with hand guns or half-hakes, archers in coats of white fustian signed on the breast and back with the arms of the city, their bows bent in their hands with sheaves of arrows by their sides, pikemen in bright corslets, burganets, etc., halberds, the light billmen in almaine rivets and aprons of mail in great number; there were also divers pageants, morris dancers, constables, the one half, which was 120, on St. John's Eve, the other half on St. Peter's Eve, in bright harness, some overgilt, and everyone a jornet of scarlet thereupon and a chain of gold, his henchman following him, his minstrels before him and his cresset light passing by him, the waits of the city, the mayor's officers for his guard before him, all in a livery of worsted or say jackets party-coloured, the mayor himself well mounted on horseback, the sword bearer before him in fair armour well mounted also, the mayor's footmen, and the like torchbearers about him, henchmen twain upon great stirring horses, following him. The sheriffs' watches came one after the other in like order, but not so large in number as the mayor's; for where the mayor had beside his giant three pageants, each of the sheriffs had beside their giants, but two pageants, each their morris dance and one henchman, their officers in jacket of worsted or say party-coloured differing from the mayor's, and each from other, but having harnessed men a great many, etc." *

The expense of the watch to the Carpenters in 1548, including the wages of eight cresset-bearers and three bag-bearers, the provisions of a bow, a sheaf of arrows, a bracer, a shooting glove and a coat for each of four archers, points and buckles for the harnessed men, cressets, lights and bags, was a little over £3.†

Each company furnished its proportion of men in harness, archers, cresset-bearers, and bag-bearers, and the companies to whom the mayor and sheriffs belonged provided their pageants, giants, and morris dances. The Drapers' giant was

* Stow, *Survey*, pp. 126–8.   † Jupp and Pocock, p. 43.

known as Lord Marlingspikes, and in 1521, when the mayor was of their company, they refurbished their old pageants to do him honour. One of these was the King of the Moors, wearing a turban of white feathers and black satin and shoes of silver paper; a canopy was borne over his head, and ·his progress was accompanied with a display of wild fire. The year after, when one of the sheriffs was a Draper, two pageants, one of the Assumption and the other of St. Ursula, were displayed. St. Ursula and her modest allowance of six virgins were presented by living children, and the Assumption was a stout piece of joinery that required fourteen porters to bear it, on which apparently were seated two harpers and two luters with wings and crowns, and four children in surplices singing.*

The Midsummer Watch seems to have been distinguished by a combination of all the elements of pageantry used on other great occasions, such as the ridings with the mayor and sheriffs after their election, and the reception of kings, queens, and foreign potentates. As regards the more elaborate displays prepared for these occasions—the pageants proper—there seems to have been a continuous following of tradition in the greater companies for many centuries. The Fishmongers' ship, which sailed up Cheapside in 1292 when Edward I. returned from defeating the Scots, and again in 1312 when Isabella bore a prince to Edward II., was still a leading part of their pageant at the Lord Mayor's Show of 1616. At the coronation of Richard II. the Goldsmiths' pageant consisted of a castle erected at the upper end of Cheap, with four towers on two sides of which ran wine, and from which four damsels clad in white blew on the king's face leaves of gold and strewed his path with counterfeit gold florins. When the king arrived at the castle, cups of wine were offered to him and his suite, and a golden angel descending from the top of the castle presented a crown. This pageant was reproduced five years later on the occasion of Richard's marriage, when it cost £35 including

* Herbert, *Twelve Great Livery Companies*, I. 455.

minstrels.* Once more in 1392, on the reconciliation of Richard with the city, the same machinery was erected in Cheapside, and though the poet who celebrated the king's entry does not attribute the pageants he describes to the various companies, this one was clearly prepared by the Goldsmiths. The "forest full of wild beasts" through which Richard passed at Temple Bar was still being displayed by the Skinners in 1689, when Sir Thomas Pilkington, Skinner, was mayor, and the pageant of St. John the Baptist and the Lamb, which is said to have softened the king's heart and completed the work of reconciliation, may be ascribed with no less certainty to the Merchant Tailors.† The Grocers' island of tropical fruits and spices, which was a permanent feature of their Lord Mayor's Shows in the 17th century, was doubtless an adaptation of the grove erected near the Great Conduit in 1432 on the return of Henry VI. from France, in which were inserted wells in honour of the mayor (John Wells, Grocer), from which Mercy, Grace, and Pity drew wine for the king, whilst the patriarch Enoch and the prophet Elias handed round the fruit, the varieties of which are recorded by Lydgate—

> " Oranges, almondys, and the pomegranade,
>   Lymons, dates, there colours fresh and glade,
>   Pypyns, quynces, chandrells to disport,
>   And the pom cedre, corageous to recomfort :
>   Eke other fruits whiche that more comown be,
>   Quenyngges, peches, costardes, and wardens,
>   And other manye ful faire and freshe to se." ‡

The Maiden Chariot of the Mercers was probably of equal antiquity, though the accounts we possess of it are derived from the end of the 17th century, by which period it had no doubt undergone a good deal of elaboration. The central figure was a young beautiful gentlewoman of good parentage,

* Herbert, II. 217.
† Wright, *Political Poems and Songs*, Rolls Series, Vol. I.
‡ Herbert, *Twelve Great Livery Companies*, I. 94.

religious education and unblemished reputation, selected by a
committee. Her dress was of white satin with a fringe of gold ;
on her dishevelled hair was placed a coronet of gold richly
set with emeralds, diamonds, and sapphires, and from her
shoulders hung a robe of crimson velvet. Her buskins were
of gold, laced with scarlet ribbons. In one hand she held a
sceptre, and in the other a shield with the Mercers' arms.
Surrounding the virgin in her Roman chariot of embossed
silver, adorned with angels and cherubims, sat Vigilance,
Wisdom, Chastity, Prudence, Justice, Fortitude, Temperance,
Faith, Hope, Charity, Loyalty, and the Nine Muses, while
Fame blew her trumpet on a golden canopy above. Eight
pages of honour in cloth of silver walked on foot, and Triumph
served as charioteer. This immense pageant, which was 22
feet high, was drawn by nine white Flanders horses, three
abreast, each mounted by an allegorical rider, and was attended
by eight grooms and forty Roman lictors. Twenty servants
bearing the company's trophies marched in front, and before
them went twenty savages or "green men," throwing fireworks.
A corps of wheelwrights and carpenters were at hand in case of
a breakdown. At the Lord Mayor's Feast the virgin, with
her retinue, dined in royal state at a separate table.*

The Lord Mayor's Show of later times absorbed these and
many other elements of pageantry, which, down to the middle
of the 16th century, are seldom heard of except in connection
with royal entries and with the midsummer watch. The
expenses recorded of early ridings before the mayor seem to
imply no more than a contingent from each craft on horseback,
accompanied by minstrels in hoods. In 1417 we hear "how
of old custom the crafts of the city have been used to ride with
the mayor to the palace of Westminster and from thence to
the city again, and that when they came in Cheap, every craft,
each by other holding, on horseback abode till the mayor rode
through them." These customary halting-places, which had

* Herbert, I. 256, 257.

already begun to be appropriated by the companies as of pre-
scriptive right, were replaced on greater occasions by wooden
stands, so many yards of railing being appropriated to each
company, the greatest having twenty-six yards and the least
three. Thus we read that on the entry of Elizabeth of York
to be married to Henry VII. in 1486, " all the streets through
which she should pass by were cleanly dressed and beseen with
cloths of tapestry and arras, and some streets, as Cheap, hung
with rich cloth of gold, velvet, and silk. Along the streets
from the Tower to Paul's stood in order all the crafts of London
in their liveries, and in divers parts of the city were ordained
well-singing children, some arrayed like angels and some like
virgins, to sing sweet songs as her Grace passed by." *

Early in the 15th century the river became the chosen
scene of some of the most effective pageantry. We know
from the accounts of various companies that processions of the
crafts in hired barges to Westminster had taken place thirty
years before the mayoralty of John Norman in 1453, who is
said to have established the custom by causing a barge to be
made at his own charge, in which he was rowed with silver
oars, " for joy whereof the watermen made a song in his praise,
beginning ' Row the boat, Norman. Row to thy leman.'" †
He is also said to have made the barge he sat in " burn on the
water," so that he may have been the originator of the foist or
fire-barge, which afterwards became a regular feature of all
pageants. On the entry of Elizabeth of York " the mayor,
sheriffs, and aldermen of the city, and many worshipful commoners chosen out of every craft in their liveries, in barges
freshly furnished with banners and streamers of silk richly
beseen with the arms and badges of their crafts, and in especial
a barge called the Bachelors' Barge, garnished and apparelled
passing all other, wherein was ordained a great red dragon
spouting flames of fire into Thames ; also many other gentle-
manly pageants, well and curiously devised, to do her Highness

* Leland, *Collectanea*, IV. p. 218. † Herbert, p. 100.

pleasure." * At the coronation feast of Anne Boleyn, when
the companies escorted the royal pair to Greenwich, the
mayor's barge and the bachelors' barge were quite distinct
from the foists, of which there were two, one containing
"terrible monstrous and wild men casting fire " as well as the
red dragon, and the other carrying a water pageant.†

Considerable expense was often bestowed on the banners
and streamers with which the crafts decorated their barges,
but it does not seem to have been usual for the companies to
own the barges themselves till the close of the 16th century.
The Goldsmiths, following "the example of some of the other
companies," had their first barge built in 1616, and another in
1656, which cost £100, and for which a barge-house, to be
shared with the Skinners, was built at Lambeth, and afterwards
removed to Chelsea.‡

As the midsummer watch ceased to be held, the Lord
Mayor's Feast came to be the one great civic pageant of the
year.   Before the accession of Elizabeth the processions on
land and water had acquired the essential form on which the
later elaborations of poetry and pageantry were only so much
embroidery.   The aldermen accompanied the mayor on horseback to the waterside to take barge for Westminster.   Before
the mayor's barge sailed the barge of his own company's
livery, then the bachelors' barge, then the barges of all the
companies in their order.   On their return the procession of
the crafts re-formed, and preceded the mayor through St. Paul's
Churchyard to the place of the feast.   The order of the land
procession in 1553 is described in Machyn's diary—

"First were two tall men bearing two great streamers of the
Merchant Taylors' arms, then came one with a drum and a flute
playing, and another with a great fife, all they in blue silk, and then
came two great 'wodyn' armed with two great clubs all in green and

---

* Jupp and Pocock, *Carpenters*, p. 36.
† Allen, *History of London*, I. p. 216.
‡ W. S. Prideaux, *Goldsmiths*, I. p. 126; II. p. 105.

FISHMONGERS' PAGEANT, 1616

PELICAN AND LEMON TREE

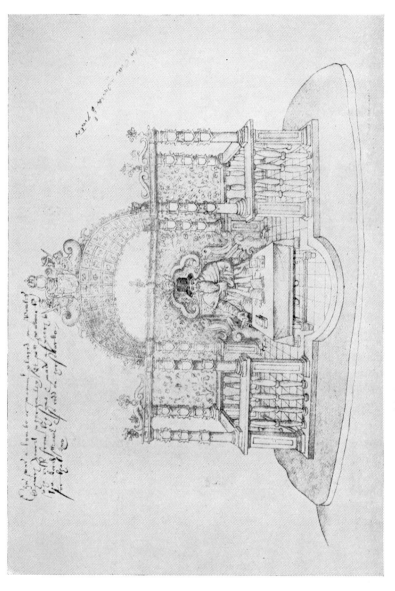

FISHMONGERS' PAGEANT, 1616. WALWORTH'S BOWER

with squibs burning, with great beards and side hair, and two targets upon their backs, and then came sixteen trumpeters blowing, and then came men in blue gowns and caps and hose and blue silk sleeves, and every man having a target and a javelin to the number of seventy, and then came a devil, and after that came the bachelors all in livery and scarlet hoods, and then came the pageant of St. John Baptist gorgeously with goodly speeches, and then came all the king's

GREEN MAN AND WILD MAN IN LORD MAYOR'S PROCESSION

trumpeters blowing and every trumpeter having scarlet caps, and the waits caps and goodly banners, and then the crafts, and then the waits playing, and then my Lord Mayor's officers, and then my Lord Mayor and two good henchmen." *

The elaborate form exhibited by the pageants of a later period, with their half-dozen different scenes, their numerous personages and long speeches, was a natural product of the Elizabethan age. The first libretto that has been handed down belongs to the mayoralty of Sir Thomas Rowe, Merchant Tailor (1568), and consists of a dozen verses spoken by four boys, one of whom personified John the Baptist—

> "I am that voice in wilderness
> That once the Jews did call,
> And now again am sent by God
> To preach unto you all."

* *Diary of H. Machyn*, Cam. Soc. Pub. 42, p. 47.

U

To which another replies—

> " Behold the Roe the swift in chase,
>   Yet stayeth still to hear,
> As soon as John begins to speak
>   The Roe doth yield him ear." *

The next recorded literature of the pageant shows a great advance on this.   Before 1585 several theatres had been erected in London, and the great age of the English drama had begun.   George Peele, who composed the device of a pageant to be borne before Sir Wolfstan Dixie, Skinner, in that year, was one of those who helped to make blank verse the subtle instrument it afterwards became in Shakespeare's hands ; as may be seen from the speech put into the mouth of one that " rid on a lucerne before the pageant apparelled like a Moor "—

> " From where the Sun doth settle in his wain,
>   And yokes his horses to his fiery cart,
>   And in his way gives life to Ceres' corn,
>   Even from the parching zone, behold, I come
>
> . . . . .
>
>   And offer to your honour good, my Lord,
>   This emblem thus in show significant.
>   Lo ! lovely London, rich and fortunate,
>   Famed through the world for peace and happiness,
>   Is here advanced and set in highest seat,
>   Beautified throughly as her state requires."

And so through fifty lines, the presenter describes each figure of the pageant : Magnanimity and Loyalty, the Country and the Thames, the Soldier, the Sailor, Science who represents the peaceful arts, and four nymphs ; after which the children who set forth these characters each repeat a rhymed verse of four or six lines.†

George Peele's second composition of this kind is entitled " Decensus Astræa, the device of a pageant borne before Mr. William Webb, Lord Mayor (1591), whereunto is annexed a

---

* Clode, *Memorials of Merchant Taylors.*
† Peele's *Works,* ed. Bullen, I. p. 351.

speech delivered by one clad like a sea nymph who presented a 'pinesse' on the water, bravely rigged and manned, to the Lord Mayor at the time he took barge to go to Westminster." Enthusiastic homage to Elizabeth is the dominant note of it.

> " Astræa, daughter of th' immortal Jove,
> Whose pure renown hath pierced the world's large ears,
> In golden scrolls rolling about the heavens ;
> Celestial sacred nymph that tends her flock
> With watchful eyes. . . .
> Honour attends her throne ; in her bright eyes
> Sits Majesty ; Virtue and Steadfastness
> Possess her heart. Sweet Mercy sways her sword ; "

Astræa is. attended by Euphrosyne, Aglaia, Thalia, Charity, Faith, Hope, and Honour; whilst Champion defends her against the plots of Superstition a friar, Ignorance a priest, and First and Second Malcontents. Fortune, Nature, and Time conclude the device by a reference to the mayor's name.

> " *Time.* I wind the web that Kind so well begins,
> And Fortune doth enrich what Nature spins." *

The reign of James I. was the Golden Age of the Lord Mayor's Show. The Court set an example by its masques, for which Ben Jonson wrote the words, Inigo Jones designed the pageantry, Thomas Giles invented the dances, Alfonso Ferrabosco, junior, composed the music, the Queen and her ladies supplied the acting, and the nation at large furnished the money. The youthful spirits of the Inns of Court willingly followed so congenial a fashion, and Inigo Jones had scarce got Dr. Thomas Campion's Court Masque for Shrove Tuesday, 1613, off his hands, when he had to set about producing another, written for the Middle Temple and Lincoln's Inn by George Chapman, and a third composed for Gray's Inn and the Inner Temple by Francis Beaumont. At the end of the same year there were two other masques performed before the Court, one on December the 26th—to celebrate the ill-fated

---

* Peele's *Works*, ed. Bullen, I. pp. 361-6.

marriage of James's favourite Somerset with the Countess of
Essex—and, three nights later, the Irish Masque of Ben
Jonson.*

Five pageants might seem enough for one year. But no ;
the city's emulation was fired, and in spite of the fact that
the triumphant conclusion of Hugh Middleton's great enterprise " The New River " had just been celebrated at Michaelmas
on the day of the election of Sir Thomas Middleton as Lord
Mayor, it was resolved that the pageantry of the mayor's
inauguration should surpass all previous displays in magnificence and even outshine the splendour of the Court. One
thing was certain, the city could better afford the expense.
Not more than £600 had been spent by the Queen on two
masques. The Grocers were prepared to spend nearly £900
on their show. The drapery alone, including blue gowns,
sleeves, and caps for 124 almsmen, would cost them over £200 ;
the 24 dozen white staves for the whifflers, and the 780
torches, large and small, would amount to £48, and the
mercery to another £67 ; whilst the poetry, scene-painting, and
general upholstery of the pageants was to be contracted for
by a minor dramatist for £282. Besides all which, there were
the 32 trumpeters, the 18 flourishers of long swords, the city
waits who stood on the roof of St. Peter Cheap, and last, but
by no means least, the 500 loaves of sugar, 36 lbs. of nutmegs,
24 lbs. of dates, and 114 lbs. of ginger to be cast abroad to
the expectant citizens by those who rode the griffins and
camels.

Such open-handed profusion was enough to inspire any
poet, and Thomas Middleton, the dramatist, who designed the
pageant and supplied the words, expresses in his preface a
strong sense of responsibility. The streams of art ought to
equal those of bounty. There is needed a knowledge that

* H. Morley's Introduction to his edition of Ben Jonson's *Masques*. See also
Humpherus' *Watermen*, I. 117, for a description of the water pageant of this
year.

may take the true height of such an honourable solemnity
which is miserably wanting in the impudent common writer ;
" and it would," he adds, " heartily grieve any understanding
spirit to behold many times so glorious a fire of bounty and
goodness offering to match itself with freezing art sitting in
darkness with the candle out, looking like the picture of Black
Monday." These unkind remarks seem to be directed at
Anthony Munday, the city laureate and continuator of Stow,
who had been the author of two earlier pageants.

The first scene of Middleton's pageant is at Soper Lane
end, where a Senate House has been erected on which are
musicians playing, and a solo is sung while the crowd waits.
Then trumpets are sounded, and enter the Lord Mayor,
whereon a Grave Feminine Shape, representing London,
attired like a reverend Mother with long white hair, and with
a model of steeples and turrets on her head, appears to
welcome her favourite son with a speech in blank verse, ere he
passes to the river, " on whose crystal bosom float five islands
artfully garnished with all manner of Indian fruits, trees, drugs,
and spiceries," and designed, no doubt, as a graphic prospectus
of the first great joint stock venture on which the ships of the
East India Company had sailed a year ago.

Arrived back from Westminster the Lord Mayor is met at
Baynard Castle by Truth's Angel, clad in white, and by Zeal,
in flame-coloured silk, armed with a scourge, who after more
verses lead him to St. Paul's Churchyard. There he is confronted by Error, in ash-coloured silk, with an owl on her head,
a bat on one shoulder, and a mole on the other, a mist hanging
at her eyes, and more blank verse in her mouth. With her
rides Envy on a rhinoceros, " attired in scarlet silk suitable to
the bloodiness of her manners, her left pap bare where a snake
fastens." As these dread apparitions are driven back by
Truth and Zeal, who arrive opportunely in a white satin
chariot with various allegorical birds and reptiles, the islands
heave into sight on trolleys, inhabited by the Five Senses,

accompanied by their symbolic beasts and birds—the eagle, hart, spider, ape, and dog—and after the islands a strange ship bearing the King and Queen of the Moors, having neither sailor nor pilot, but instead thereof an inscription (in Latin), "I am steered by truth." The whole procession now moves down Cheap, Truth driving Error before her, when lo! at Great Conduit appears a mountain whose top is involved in clouds but at whose four corners sit four disciples of Error armed with clubs. As Truth approaches, the clouds disperse, and behold London seated at the feet of Religion and surrounded by the cardinal virtues, whilst Perfect Love, standing up with a sphere in one hand and two billing turtles in the other, makes the final speech before dinner. After dinner the Lord Mayor and his company go to service in St. Paul's. "Then all returning home full of beauty and brightness," the Mountain and the Chariot of Truth are placed near the Lord Mayor's House at Leadenhall. London desires to express her gratitude to them—

> "That were at cost this day to make this shine
> And be as free in thanks as they in coin."

Time prepares to cut off the glories of the day with his scythe, when Zeal, whose head is now circled with strange fires, asks leave to destroy Error. At a sign from Truth a flame shoots from his head, which, fastening on Error's chariot, consumes it with all its freight of beasts, and with an outburst of fireworks the day's festivities come to an end.*

If the productions of Middleton in this kind, though amusing enough and not wanting in a certain lively imagination, do not indicate poetical genius of a high order, those of Anthony Munday, his rival, frequently fall below the level of tolerable journalism. Born in 1553, and apprenticed to a London stationer, Munday betook himself while yet a youth to a vagabond existence. His earliest efforts at writing professed to reveal the dark plots of the English Catholics which

---

* Heath, *Grocers*, p. 445.

he had discovered whilst enjoying the hospitality of the Roman Church at its headquarters, and later on he gained popularity by denunciation of Campion the Jesuit. To these services, no doubt, must be attributed his appointments as Messenger of the Queen's Chamber and as City Poet. But no kind of literary activity seems to have come amiss to him. He poured out plays whilst Shakespeare was at his best. His "Sweet Sobbes and Amorous Complaints of Shepherds and Nymphs" challenges, if it does not sustain, comparison with Spenser's "Shepherds' Calendar." He translated romances as long as the Arcadia, and undertook to complete the work of John Stow. In the midst of these multifarious labours he found time for what were no doubt the most lucrative of his engagements—the supply of the upholstery, poetry, and music for at least eight Lord Mayors' Shows. It is hardly surprising that his performances in fulfilment of the literary part of the contract should have been rather perfunctory, and we have other evidence than the gibes of Middleton to show that they failed to give satisfaction even to an uncritical city audience. The Ironmongers complained in 1609 that the children were not instructed in their speeches ; that the music and singing were wanting ; the apparel most of it old and borrowed ; and that the poet had not performed his speeches for the pageant on land ; and refused to give him the £5 which he had applied for in addition to the £45 for which he had originally bargained. There is, indeed, more than a suspicion of sameness about most of Anthony's brief programmes. The ship called the *Royal Exchange*, which formed the central feature in Lord Mayor Halliday's Show in 1605, where the master of the vessel bids the mate and the boy—

> "Take of our pepper, of our cloves and mace,
> And liberally bestow them round about "

may perhaps have served with a fresh coat of paint and new rigging for the triumphs of the golden Fleece in 1623 ; when "a beautiful and curious Argoe, shaped after the old Grecian antique manner," was supposed to have returned from Colchos purposely "to honour this triumphal day by the rare art of Medea the Enchantress that kept the Fleece through so long a time and wherewith she was now the more willing to part in regard of her affection to the Drapers' Company." The Argo was manned by Jason, Hercules, Telamon, Orpheus, Castor and Pollux, and six tributary Indian kings holding their several dominions of Medea. "This service," says the director of the pageant, "being performed on the water, the like is done on the land all the rest of the day following."

The one pageant with which Munday seems to have taken more than usual pains was that provided at the expense of the Fishmongers for Sir John Leman in 1616. The company still possesses the design for the eight pageants that composed the show. The first of these was the Fishing Buss which, as we have seen, had been exhibited by the company on great occasions for over three centuries. Three fishermen were on board, one casting a net, whilst the others held up live fish, which they bestowed bountifully amongst the people. The second pageant was the dolphin from the company's arms, with Arion on his back ; and the third was the king of the Moors gallantly mounted on a golden leopard, and hurling gold and silver everywhere about him, followed by the six tributary kings that were subsequently to own allegiance to Medea. This pageant was intended to show that the Fishmongers were not unmindful of their combined brethren the Goldsmiths. Next came a large lemon tree to represent the Lord Mayor, and a pelican feeding her young with her blood "to symbolize the cherishing love borne by the mayor to the citizens." Underneath the tree sat five children, dressed as the five senses, but also, by a somewhat embarrassing pluralism, figuring forth the flower, fruit, rind, pith and juice of the lemon. The fifth pageant consisted of six horsemen in armour, the first of whom bore Wat Tyler's head on a spear.

Behind these came a merman and a mermaid in heraldic costume as the companies' supporters, and represented as drawing the Fishmongers' Pageant Chariot, the central figure of which was Richard II., seated at the feet of his guardian angel and surrounded by eleven royal virtues.

The last pageant was intended to form the centre of the whole show when it gathered to a head, as was usual on these occasions, in St. Paul's Churchyard on the Lord Mayor's return from Westminster. It consisted of—

"a goodly Bower shaped in form of a flowery arbour, and adorned with all the scutcheons of arms of so many worthy men of the Fishmongers' Company as have been Lord Mayors. . . . In this bower is a fair tomb whereon in armour lyeth the imaginary body of Sir William Walworth. . . . Suppose his marble statue (after the manner of knightly burial) to be upon the tomb, and both it and the bower to be worthily attended by those five knights, in armour and mounted on horseback, that were knighted with Sir William in the field after he had slain the proud insulting rebel. Six mounted trumpeters and twenty-four halberdiers guard the tomb.

"London's Genius, a comely youth attired in the shape of an angel with a golden crown on his head . . . sits mounted by the bower with an officer at arms, bearing the rebel's head on Walworth's dagger."

As soon as the Lord Mayor approaches, the Genius strikes Walworth with his wand, "whereat he begins to stir, and coming off the tomb looks strangely about him." Having shed a few tears of natural joy at finding the office of Lord Mayor had lost none of its former lustre and (on a timely whispered hint from the Genius) complimented his successor on being the second unmarried mayor, Walworth proceeds to act as exponent of his own tomb.

> " And see my Lord this bower relates
> How many famous magistrates
> From the Fishmongers' ancient name
> Successively to honour came.
>
> . . . . . .

> Turke, Lovekin, Wroth, Pechie, Mordon,
> These before me were every one.
> Then I : next Exton, Ascham, Falconer,
> Michel, Parneis, Reinwall, Foster,
> Hulin, Hampton, Ostridge, Remington,
> Kneisworth, Coppinger. These being gone
> Succeeded Ameotes, Curteis, Allot,
> And now John Leman.

"Aldermen," adds Sir William, "we have had many more," and is about to apologize for their omission from the tombstone when the Genius interrupts with an impatient wave of his wand,

> "Walworth, here stay : we may do wrong
> And hold this worthy man too long."

In short, dinner is waiting, and lists of dead aldermen are out of place when a live mayor is hungry.*

But Munday's absurdities do not furnish a fair specimen of the Lord Mayor's Show at its best. A more serious attempt to realize the possibilities of imaginative retrospect afforded by the historic traditions of the greater companies is represented by the series of pageants designed by John Webster for the Merchant Tailors in 1629, the programme of which it will be well to give in the poet's own words, a little abbreviated, merely remarking that the last pageant of the series, the "Monument of Gratitude," was a tribute to the memory of that young Prince Henry whom we have already seen presiding at the Merchant Tailors' feast in 1609.

"I fashioned," says Webster, "for the more amplifying of the show upon the water, two eminent spectacles in manner of Sea-triumph. The first furnished with four persons : in the front Oceanus and Thetis ; behind them Thamesis and Medway, the two rivers on which the Lord Mayor extends his power as far as from Staines to Rochester. The other show is of a fair Terrestrial Globe, circled about in convenient seats, with seven of our most famous navigators ; as Sir Francis Drake, Sir John Hawkins, Sir Martin Frobisher, Sir Humphrey Gilbert, Captain Thomas Cavendish,

---

* *The Fishmongers' Pageant of* 1616, edit. J. G. Nichols.

Captain Christopher Carlisle and Captain John Davis. The conceit of the device to be, that, in regard the two rivers pay due tribute of waters to the seas, Oceanus in grateful recompense returns the memory of these seven worthy captains, who have made England so famous in remotest parts of the world. These two spectacles, at my Lord Mayor's taking water at the Three Cranes, approaching my Lord's barge, after a peal of sea-thunder from the other side of the water, these speeches between Oceanus and Thetis follow.

> *Thetis.* What brave sea-music bids us welcome ! Hark !
> Sure this is Venice and the day St. Mark,
> In which the Duke and Senates their course hold
> To wed our empire with a ring of gold.
> *Oceanus.* No, Thetis, you're mistaken ; we are led
> With infinite delight from the land's head
> In ken of goodly shipping and yon bridge :
> Venice had ne'er the like : survey the ridge
> Of stately buildings which the river hem,
> And grace the silver stream as the stream them.
> That beauteous seat is London. . . . "

" After my Lord Mayor's landing and coming past Paul's Chain, there first attends for his honour in St. Paul's churchyard, a beautiful spectacle called the Temple of Honour ; the pillars of which are bound about with roses and other beautiful flowers, which shoot up to the adorning of the King's Majesty's Arms on the top of the Temple. In the highest seat a person representing Troynovant or the City, enthroned in rich habiliments : beneath her, as admiring her peace and felicity, sit five eminent cities, as Antwerp, Paris, Rome, Venice and Constantinople : under these sit five famous scholars and poets [Chaucer, Gower, Lydgate, Thomas More, Philip Sidney].

" I present riding afore this temple Henry de Royal, the first pilgrim or gatherer of quarterage for this company, and John of Yeacksley, King Edward the third's pavilion-maker, who purchased our Hall."

Here follow the speeches of Troynovant and Sir Philip Sidney.

" These passing on, in the next place my Lord is encountered with the person of Sir John Hawkwood in complete armour, his plume and feather for his horse's chaffron, of the Company's colours white and watchet."

Sir John had begun life as an apprentice in the Tailors Company.

Sir John Hawkwood. My birth was mean, yet my deservings grew
To eminence and in France a high pitch flew :
From a poor common soldier I attained
The style of captain and then knighthood gained ;
Served the Black Prince in France in his wars ;
Then went in th' Holy Land ; thence brought my scars,
And wearied body which no danger feared,
To Florence where it nobly lies interred :

. . . .

"After him follows a Triumphant chariot with the arms of the Merchant Tailors. . . . In the chariot I place . . . eight famous kings of this land that have been free of this worshipful company. [All the kings from Edward III. to Henry VII.] The speaker in this pageant is Edward the third.

Edward the Third. View whence the Merchant Tailors' honour springs
From this most royal conventicle of kings.

. . . .

Let all good men this sentence oft repeat
By unity the smallest things grow great.
Chorus of Kings. By unity the smallest things grow great.

" . . . After this pageant rides Queen Anne, wife to Richard Second, free likewise of this company. . . . [Then follow two knights of St. John.]

"Next I bring our two Sea Triumphs ; and after that the Ship called the Holy Lamb, which brings hanging in her shrouds the Golden Fleece. . . . To second this follow the two beasts, the Lion and the Camel, proper to the arms of the Company ; on the Camel rides a Turk such as use to travel with caravans ; and on the Lion a Moor or wild Numidian.

"The fourth eminent Pageant I call the Monument of Charity and Learning ; this fashioned like a beautiful Garden with all kinds of flowers ; at the four corners four artificial birdcages with variety of birds in them. . . . In the midst of the Garden under an elm tree, sits the famous and worthy patriot Sir Thomas White : who had a dream that he should build a college where two bodies of an elm sprang from one root . . . and riding one day at the North Gate at Oxford, he spied on his right hand the self same elm . . . and in the same place built the College of St. John Baptist; and to this day the elm grows in the garden carefully preserved, as being under God a motive to their worthy foundation.

" . . . The chief person in this is Thomas White sitting in his eminent habit as Lord Mayor; on the one hand sits Charity with a pelican on her head; on the other Learning, with a book in one hand and a laurel wreath in the other: behind him is the college of St. John Baptist in Oxford, exactly modelled: two cornets which for more pleasure answer one another interchangeably; and round about the Pageant sit twelve of twenty-four cities (for more would have overburdened it) to which this worthy gentleman had been a benefactor.

[Here follows the speech of Learning.]

" The last I call the monument of Gratitude which thus dilates itself. Upon an Artificial Rock, set with mother of pearl and such other precious stones as are found in quarries, are placed four curious Pyramids, charged with the Prince's Arms, the Three Feathers; which by day yield a glorious show; and by night a more goodly, for they have lights in them, that, at such time as my Lord Mayor returns from Paul's shall make certain ovals and squares resemble precious stones. The Rock expresses the richness of the kingdom Prince Henry was born heir to; the Pyramids, which are monuments for the dead, that he is deceased. On the top of this rests half a celestial Globe; in the midst of this hangs a Holy Lamb in the Sunbeams; on either side of these an Angel. Upon a pedestal of gold stands a figure of Prince Henry with his coronet, George, and garter: in his left hand he holds a circlet of crimson velvet, charged with four Holy Lambs, such as our Company chose Masters with. In several cants [niches] beneath sits, first Magistracy tending a beehive, to express his gravity in youth and forward industry to have proved an absolute governor: next Liberality, by her a Dromedary, showing his speed and alacrity in gratifying his followers: Navigation with a Jacob's staff and compass, expressing his desire that his reading that way might in time grow to the practice and building to that purpose one of the goodliest ships was ever launched in the river: in the next Unanimity with a chaplet of lilies, in her lap a Sheaf of Arrows, showing he loved nobility and commonalty with an entire heart: next Industry, on a hill where Ants are hoarding up corn, expressing his forward inclination to all noble exercise: next Chastity, by her a Unicorn, showing it is guide to all other virtues and clears the fountain-head from all poison: Justice with her properties: then Obedience, by her an Elephant, the strongest beast but most observant to man of any creature: then Peace sleeping upon a Cannon; alluding to the eternal peace he now possesses: Fortitude, a Pillar in one hand, a Serpent wreathed about the other; to express his height of mind and the expectation of an undaunted resolution. These twelve thus seated I figure Loyalty as well sworn servant to this City as to this Company; and at my Lord Mayor's coming from Paul's and going down Wood Street, Amade le Grand delivers a speech unto him." *

The literature of the Lord Mayor's Show may perhaps be considered to have reached its highest point in the pageant which Thomas Dekker prepared for the Ironmongers' Company in 1629, under the title of "London's Tempe." The eulogy of iron which Jove addresses to Vulcan has quite a Shakespearean ring about it.

> "And what helps this but iron. O then how high
> Shall this great Troy text up the memory
> Of you, her noble Praetor, and all those
> Your worthy brotherhood through whose care goes
> That rare rich prize of iron to the whole land.
> Iron far more worth than Tagus' golden sand!
> Iron best of metals! pride of minerals
> Heart of the earth! hand of the world! which falls
> Heavy when it strikes home . . .
> Iron that main hinge on which the world doth turn!" †

It is interesting to compare this outburst with the effort of the gentle Heywood in 1636, when the Mayor was a Draper, to rise to the full height of his opportunity, and to celebrate fitly in heroic numbers the merits of the sheep.

* Clode, *Memorials*, Appendix.
† Nichol, *Ironmongers*, 232.

> "What beast or bird for hide or feather rare
> For man's use made can with the sheep compare?
> The horse of strength and swiftness may be proud,
> But yet his flesh is not for food allowed.
> The herds yield milk and meat (commodious both),
> Yet none of all their skins make wool for cloth.
> The sheep doth all. The parrot and the jay,
> The peacock, ostrich, all in colour gay,
> Delight the eye, some with their notes the ear.
> But what are these unto the cloth we wear?
> Search forests, deserts, for beasts wild or tame,
> The mountains or the vales, search the vast frame
> Of the wide universe, the earth, the sky—
> Nor beast nor bird can with the sheep comply."

Yet even this passage, though it reads like a prophetic parody on Dyer or Crabbe, preserves a flavour of literature which is scarcely to be found in any of Heywood's successors. John Tatham, for instance, in 1659, out of all the poetical possibilities offered by the romantic art of the grocer, could make no more than this—

> "Heart-pleasing cinnamon, cloves, mace, nutmegs are
> From famed Arabia brought. . . .
> Then Senna, Rhubarb, China roots that do
> Not only purify but strengthen too,
> Sarsaparilla. . . ."

And Thomas Jordan, who raises our expectations by the words he puts into the mouth of Apollo—

> "With Oriental eyes I come to see
> And gratulate this great solemnity
> With my refulgent presence,"

afterwards introduces "a Wilderness or Desart which," he explains, "doth consist of divers trees in several sorts of green colours, some in blossom, others laden with ripe and proper fruit and spices, as dates, pineapples, cloves, nutmegs, figs, raisins, large plums, vines, inhabited by tawny Moors, . . . also three pipers and several kitchen musicians that play upon tongs, gridirons, keys, etc., also birds native of that country, as parrots, popinjays, turtle-doves, wild-ducks, etc.," and crowns the whole with "a proper masculine woman with a tawny face, raven black long hair, several pearl necklaces, aurora-coloured silk stockings, silver buskins laced up to the calf with gold ribbons, bearing a banner with the Lord Mayor's family coat," causes this lady to enlighten the mystified onlookers with these opening words—

> "That I the better may attention draw,
> Be pleased to know I am America."

With Jordan the Lord Mayor's Show lost whatever share it had once possessed of the more serious atmosphere of the legitimate drama, and adapted itself to the taste of the Restoration period by combining in one entertainment all the ill-assorted attractions of the variety stage. The Show of 1677 (when Sir Francis Chaplin, Clothworker, was Mayor) was entitled " London Triumphs: illustrated with many magnificent Structures and Pageants ; on which are orderly advanced several stately Representations of Poetical Deities, sitting and standing in great splendour on several Scenes in proper Shapes, with pertinent Speeches, jocular Songs (sung by the City Musick) and Pastoral Dancing"; and that of 1681 in honour of Sir Patience Warde, Merchant Tailor, comprised "an illustrious description of the Sword, Triumphant Pageants on which are represented Emblematical Figures, Artful Pieces of Architecture and Rural Dancing with the Speeches spoken at each Pageant; also three new songs, the first in praise of the Merchant Taylors, the second the Protestant Exhortation, and the third the Plotting Papists' Litany, with the proper tunes." The Comic Countryman became a usual feature at this time, the absurd simplicity of the rural mind being rendered still more ridiculous to the refined urbanity of a cockney crowd by the use of the dialect of Somersetshire or Dorset.

As the element of literature declined, that of pure pageantry tended to grow more elaborate. The Skinners in 1671 added

to their traditional wilderness of wild beasts, a group of satyrs
dancing to the music of Orpheus, and a bear performing
on a rope; whilst in 1689 they introduced a number of live
dogs, cats, foxes, and rabbits, which being tossed hither and
thither amongst the crowd afforded great diversion. The
Drapers in 1679 exhibited the twelve months of the year
and numerous other allegorical personages, a golden ram
backed by a beautiful boy, a group of shepherds ·tending
flocks on Salisbury Plain, and a confused crowd of carders,
spinners, dyers, woolcombers, shearers, dressers, fullers,
weavers, who indulged in all such jovial actions and movements of agility as might express their joy and exultation
in their compliments to the new Lord Mayor. St. Katherine
(the patron saint of the Haberdashers), drawn by two large
Indian goats in a silver chariot with four golden Catherine
wheels, was followed in 1699 by Commerce seated on a rich
throne with milliners' shops serving as her footstool, whilst
screws of tobacco were thrown broadcast amongst the onlookers. In the Clothworkers' pageant of 1693 Jack of
Newbury was set off against Apollo, who since his service
with King Admetus was supposed to retain a lively interest
in the wool trade, and "a rich figure of a rising sun" above
ten feet in diameter appeared out of the back of the chariot,
whilst the sun-god was addressing the Lord Mayor. The
garden of the Hesperides with Jason and his golden fleece
were also exhibited on that occasion; a pageant, as the
designer remarks, entirely applicable to the honourable Clothworkers in more ways than one. "The dragon being a
watchful creature intimates the caution, industry, and vigilance" that are necessary for success in business. St. Dunstan
with a crosier in one hand, a goldsmith's tongs in the other,
and the devil beneath his feet, formed the centre of the
Goldsmiths' pageant; and St. Martin armed *cap-à-pie* on
a stately white steed, attended by twenty satyrs dancing
with tambors, ten halberdiers with rural music, and ten Roman

V

lictors, and followed by cripples and beggars, was the leading feature of the Vintner's show of 1702.* But these were special efforts vainly put forth to arrest the decay of an old tradition. As the 18th century advanced, the Lord Mayor's Show became a mere survival, and neither Clio nor Melpomene could by any stretch of the imagination be conceived of as presiding over it.

* Herbert, I. 199-211.

CHAPTER XVII

MONOPOLIES

THE simplest account that can be given of the monopolies is that they were a device of the Stuarts for raising money without the consent of Parliament, rendered more intolerable by the greed and unscrupulousness of the courtiers who suggested them and shared in the profits when there were any to share. This account explains why the monopolies were abolished ; and it is true as far as it goes, but it does not go far enough for our purpose. On the other hand, a fully adequate account which explained how the monopolies lasted as long as they did, would carry us too far from our subject. It would require us to deal with the origins not only of joint-stock enterprise and of co-operative production, but also of the permanent Civil Service, the Factory Acts, the adulteration laws, and of many other achievements of the modern state.

The monopolies were, in fact, a crude device for solving at one stroke a great many political, social, and economic problems which are not yet solved, and which could only be put on the way towards solution by being carefully separated from each other and dealt with each on its own merits. They were not only to provide the king with money, but also to furnish salaries, pensions, and rewards to his friends and servants ; whilst at the same time they were to encourage native industries, to check the evils of "dumping," to protect the small manufacturer from the domination of the capitalist, and to guarantee to the consumer a supply of sound and serviceable commodities at reasonable rates. If we can imagine a court favourite, who has been called in to form a Government, nominating his friends and relations to most of the chief posts in the Civil Service and providing for their remuneration by placing in their hands the regulation of the milk supply, the inspection of the meat markets, and the control of all the industries of the East End ; and if we further imagine that the Home Secretary or the Postmaster-General—encouraged thereto by a decree prohibiting the import of foreign matches and the export of English timber and phosphorus—had accepted at the earnest request of a deputation of Bryant and May's work-girls the chairmanship of a great Match Trust, and that the Companies Act was thereupon suspended to secure favourable conditions of flotation, and the metropolitan police instructed to arrest at sight all users of matches not bearing the official stamp—we shall have some notion of the many-sided operation of a Stuart monopoly.

What we are here concerned with is the relation of the monopolies to the London companies. A great number of the monopolies were closely connected from the first with that movement towards incorporation which has been described, and after the passing of the statute of monopolies in 1624 a corporation—generally a London company—was the only legal form of monopoly. Some of the historians of the companies have regarded them as the mere victims of oppression and extortion at the hands of the patentees. In regard to the older companies, this view may have a good deal of truth ; but the new companies seeking incorporation were, as we have seen, in many cases the allies of the patentees. They provided the patentees not only with ideas for their schemes, but also with a public opinion in support of them, and an organization through which to work them. If it had not been for the favouring conditions presented by the industrial movement, it may be safely said that one-half of the monopolies would never have been mooted. That this was so is made clear by the fact that the companies were not only the allies but also the rivals of the patentees, and had sometimes occupied the field before them. In order to obtain authority over those who exercised their trades in the suburbs, they were willing to serve as excise officers for the Government.

The Tallow Chandlers obtained from Elizabeth in 1576 letters patent authorizing them to be "searchers, examiners, viewers, and triers" of soap, vinegar, butter, hops, and oils, not only in the city, but in Southwark, St. Katherine's, Whitechapel, Shoreditch, Westminster, Clerkenwell, and St. Giles'. None was to sell these articles before they were searched, and for the payment of the searchers there was an imposition on every barrel of soap 2*d.*, on a tun of vinegar 8*d.*, on a barrel of butter 2*d.*, on a tun of Seville oil 8*d.*, on a sack of hops 8*d.* This scheme of taxation was naturally resisted by the Mayor and Aldermen as an encroachment on their own powers of search in the city, and on those possessed by the lords who held Courts Leet around the city. Their enumeration of these latter gives an interesting glimpse into the manorial conditions still prevailing in the industrial suburbs.

" In Southwark the Lord Mayor and Commons had a Leet or Law day, in Westminster the Dean and Chapter, in St. Katherine's the Master and Confrères, in Whitechapel the Lord Wentworth, in Shoreditch the Dean and Chapter of St. Paul's, in Clerkenwell the Queen, in St. Giles' and High Holborn the Lord Mountjoy, so that there was no place left where the Tallow Chandlers might exercise the office of search." *

It scarcely needs to be pointed out how easily the powers of inspection and of taxation sought by the Tallow Chandlers might pass into monopoly. The Retailing Vintners actually obtained a monopoly through the services of one of their members, Edward Lane. Lane was the author of an epistle

* Strype's *Stow's Survey*, V. 210.

to Burleigh almost mystical in its elaborate obscurity, in which
he set forth the degenerate condition of the London companies
and the necessity of their being reorganized by the Government.
His own practical contribution to this scheme of reform seems
to have been a disappointment. In return for the pardon for
past offences and the patent to legalize future monopoly which
he had procured for the Vintners, Lane was to have received
£1000 and his expenses. With a view to meeting these
obligations and exploiting their monopoly, the governing body,
consisting of some ten persons, had raised a stock within the
company; but, some eight or nine years later, Lane complained to Cecil that they had ever since retained and converted
to their own private use all the stock and the profits thereby
arising.*

These examples show that the projectors did not always
need to force their schemes on the companies. The spirit of
monopoly within many of the companies and the king's need
of revenue had in many cases already predisposed the two
parties to a bargain, and the patentee was only the broker
that brought them together. In the case of the Upholders'
Company we are fortunate enough to possess an account of
some negotiations of this kind. In 1585 a projector named
Cordel petitioned Burleigh for a patent to inspect the feathers,
down, etc., used by the Upholders, which were said to be
deceitfully mixed with "cow-hair, thistle-down, naughty flocks
that would breed worms," as well as with "lime, dirt, dust,
stones, and other rubbish." Burleigh sent his secretary Osbern
to test the feeling of the trade. But as soon as Osbern casually
let fall the suggestion of a search, the upholder with whom he
was talking declared that it would be their ruin.

"It is the merchants," said he, "and not we who are to
blame. . . . The real trouble is," he added, "that our company
is not a corporation, and we are not rich enough to buy a
charter. There are not more than half-a-dozen well-to-do

* Lansdowne MSS., Vol. 16, No. 9.

tradesmen in our craft. If £100 would be of any use, they might manage to raise it. But the less we hear of an outside searcher the better."

Osbern sent the upholder to see Burleigh, who recommended that the craft should secure their incorporation by arrangement with the projector. Let them collect what ready money they could towards the cost of their charter, and no doubt the patentee would find the rest on condition of receiving half the fees derived from the search.

There were acute differences of opinion amongst the Upholders as to the wisdom of accepting this advice. Some of the craftsmen, in their bitterness against the middlemen, who belonged to the Drapers', the Merchant Tailors', the Skinners', and Clothworkers' Companies, were eager to call in the patentee, as we have seen the Feltmakers and Glovers doing at this very time against the Haberdashers and Leathersellers. Others could see clearly that even a Government searcher would not enable them to do without middlemen, and that unless they secured the co-operation of some of the merchants they would be liable to find themselves in the position of the Feltmakers, who, after signing a petition for the appointment of a Garbler, had been sarcastically told, when they went to buy wool, that they could not have any till it was garbled. The merchants themselves pointed out the futility of the whole scheme, and it was apparently allowed to drop. The Upholders were not incorporated till 1626.*

It is not impossible that the Upholders had taken warning by the example of the Distillers. A certain Richard Drake had received a patent in 1593, giving him authority to correct the abuses existing in that trade, and to see that the makers of vinegar and aqua vitæ were provided with wholesome materials, instead of the "hog-wash, the washing of the cool-backs, and the brewers' dregs" which it was alleged had been hitherto supplied for that purpose. But after several years'

* Strype's *Stow*, V. 229-230.

The complaint of M, Tenter-hooke the *Proiector*, and Sir Thomas Dodger the *Patentee*.

I haue brought money to fill your Chest,
For which I am curst by most and blest.

Cry Amen Yea,
and thy Trapdore is kick at a clape.

Sir Thomas Dodgers Answer;

If any aske, what things these Monsters be,
'Tis a Proiector, and a Patentee.

trial it was found that the same "draggs, laggs, etc.," were used after this grant as before, "nay, far worse than before, and were allowed by the patentee . . . that the poor traders that bought and sold vinegar and those other commodities were compelled by threats and imprisonment to enter into bonds to buy of none but the patentee only, and to pay for the making of their own bonds 3s. a piece ; that they forced the brewers to sell unto them their grounds, which themselves before . . . had in very foul and odious terms named ' draggs,' etc. ; that they compelled the tradesmen to compound with them for 2d. the barrel, and would not permit them to buy where they would for their best ease and profit, as where they had best credit and might be assured of good and wholesome stuff, except they would pay 3d. a barrel, which would amount to a great sum by the end of the year, which payments being made the tradesmen might do what they listed." *

By this time, however, the outcry against the patentees was becoming general. The riot caused by the violence of Darcy and the imprisonment of the four Leathersellers for resisting his project, were still fresh in the minds of the Londoners ; and while the £4000 demanded by the Queen for the revocation of Darcy's patent was yet unpaid, respectable citizens and members of the Grocers' Company were being haled every month before the Privy Council for infractions of a starch monopoly, which had been bestowed on two courtiers to enable them to pay their debts. New patents had just been made out controlling the importation of steel, stone pots and bottles, and Spanish wool ; and the exportation of beer, horns, woollen rags, and tin ; most of them in the professed interests of some section or other of the industrial population. During the last ten years of Elizabeth the manufacture of paper, glass, salt, alum ; the mining of gold, silver, copper, quicksilver, lead, and coal ; the printing of books, the supply of unlawful games, were all in the hands of monopolists. When a list of monopolies

* Strype's *Stow*, V. 237.

was read in Parliament, a member ironically expressed surprise to hear that bread was not included. In spite of Elizabeth's promise of redress in 1597, the list continued to grow. The price of many articles was said to have been doubled. When Parliament met in 1601 the public indignation had risen to such a pitch that the Queen saw the necessity of graceful concession, and contrived to save her prerogative, "the chiefest flower of her garden and the principal and head pearl of her crown and diadem," by proclaiming the abolition of the most unpopular patents, and leaving the rest to the decision of the judges. A monopoly in playing-cards, obtained by Edward Darcy after the failure of the leather-searching project, was made the test case, and the patent was condemned as a dangerous innovation contrary to common law.*

This defeat of the monopolies was not final. All the social and political causes that had assisted to produce them remained in operation, and as soon as the discontent they had aroused had subsided they were certain to reappear. Until the fundamental matters at issue between Crown and Parliament were settled, monopolies in one disguise or another furnished the line of least resistance on which the Crown could attempt to solve the problem of finding a revenue adequate to its needs. Ultimately, no doubt, the monopolies roused resistance enough. But statesmen are usually the most short-sighted of mortals, and the only resistance which Stuart statesmen took into account was that which confronted them at the moment when the imposition was decreed. At that moment those who were to bear the burden of taxation were not consulted, whilst on the part of those who conceived they might benefit by it there was often what might be construed as a popular demand for the imposition. This is the real explanation of the extreme readiness with which grants of monopoly were made by James and Charles or their advisers. It was not merely that such grants seemed to afford

* W. H. Price, *English Patents of Monopoly*, 24.

the easiest way out of the Crown's growing financial difficulties. The spirit of corporate monopoly which pervaded all classes engaged in commerce and industry, from the richest to the poorest, made it possible, perhaps with sincerity, to represent the grants, not as a hateful but unavoidable expedient for raising money, but as part of a great and beneficent scheme of national policy.

With the accession of James I., that general movement towards incorporation which has already been described came to a head. Although James had been met at Hinchinbrook by would-be patentees anxious to forestall his favours, and had made indiscreet promises, he thought it wise on arriving in London to repeat Elizabeth's proclamation renouncing monopolies. The few months in which he adhered to this policy afforded a favourable opportunity to the companies, since the king would be likely to sell his grants on easier terms, while there were no individual patentees competing in the same field; and even when royal extravagance had led to a relaxation of principle, the desire to save appearances led projectors of monopoly to advance their schemes under cover of a petition for incorporation. Thus opened an epoch of company formation which lasted till the meeting of the Long Parliament, and in which every section of the population in the city and suburbs was involved. The merchants had already divided the known habitable world into spheres of monopoly. The Muscovy Merchants and the Eastland Company claimed Northern Europe, the Merchant Adventurers Central Europe, the Levant Company the Mediterranean, and the East India Company Asia. But they had to admit the intrusion of new bodies, some of which, like the Virginia Company and the Guinea Company, represented new fields of enterprise; others, like the companies trading to France and Spain, carved for themselves territories out of old fields nearer home; whilst a third class entered into direct rivalry with the older companies and made the Government better offers for the same privileges. Similarly, every branch, every interest in the industrial world was represented by the new corporations. Old crafts, like the Butchers, the Founders, the Horners, the Curriers, the Turners, the Upholders, the Fruiterers, the Bowyers, the Plumbers, the Shipwrights, and the Glaziers: old callings that bordered on professions like the Apothecaries, the Scriveners and the Musicians: and new bodies of manufacturers like the Spectaclemakers, the Tobacco-pipemakers, the Playing-cardmakers, the Gunmakers, the Combmakers, the Soap-makers, the Starchmakers, the Distillers, the Silkmen and the Silkthrowsters: clothed themselves in the same corporate privileges; whilst even the transport service—the Porters, the Watermen, the Carmen, and the Hackney coachmen—acquired rights of a corporate or semi-corporate character. In spite of the common element of incorporation and the now universal form of administration through a Court of Assistants, the social and economic character of these companies exhibited almost as great a variety as the occupations of their members. Many of them were the genuine products of an associative impulse; a few had been entirely promoted in the interest of monopolists; but in the great majority these two elements were blended in varying proportions, and contended with each other for the predominant influence.

The link between them was supplied by the new spirit of joint-stock enterprise which was then on the eve of some of its most signal achievements. By a natural transition the joint property of the companies had come in some cases to be used as joint capital. The Pewterers had made purchases of tin, the Horners of horns, the Clothworkers had made common provision of teasels, the Stationers had secured rights of copy with the avowed purpose of finding employment for poorer members. These operations were facilitated and encouraged by the prevalent idea which guided the legislator of the 16th century—that the craftsmen had the first right to the materials used in his calling. The exportation of hides, tin,

wool, undressed cloth, and other raw materials of industry was
prohibited in the supposed interest of the native craftsmen, and
further restrictions were laid on wholesale dealings in these
materials with a view to safeguarding the supply of the small
master. These laws had long remained ineffectual for want
of a strong organization to enforce them. It was, indeed,
mainly with a view to enforcing them that many bodies of
craftsmen had sought incorporation. The powers they had
thus acquired to exploit their legal monopoly made them
specially advantageous channels for the investment of capital ;
and as the capital of their own members was generally insufficient
for any large enterprise, there was a natural tendency to seek
the co-operation of outsiders.*

At that time a good deal of the accumulating wealth of the
upper and middle classes was seeking investment, and the
formation of that large class who nowadays live on the income
derived from invested capital was just beginning. The East
India Company gave them their first great general opportunity. To the million and a half invested in the voyage of
1617 there were nearly a thousand contributors, including 15
earls and dukes, 82 privy councillors, judges and knights, 13
countesses and ladies of rank, 18 widows and maiden ladies,
26 clergymen, 313 merchants, 214 tradesmen, and 25 merchant
strangers. But the East Indian venture did not stand alone.
From the year 1608 onwards the possibilities of various joint-
stock enterprises, in which the king took an eager interest,
must have been the common talk of the city. In that year a
precept was circulated to the companies conveying a strong
recommendation by the Privy Council for a project for colo-
nizing Virginia. The next year the scheme for the plantation
of Ulster was pressed even more earnestly, and led to the
establishment of the Irish Society whose achievements have
been already referred to. From 1611 to 1613, the great
enterprise of Hugh Middleton for supplying the city with

* Unwin, *Industrial Organization*, pp. 148-156.

water, in which the king had taken half the shares, was struggling to its triumphant completion, and in 1612 was undertaken the first voyage of the East India Company, for which the capital was supplied by a general joint stock.

It is not at all surprising, therefore, that some of the bodies of craftsmen, who had just paid or who were trying hard to pay a large sum for the privilege of incorporation, should have entertained the idea of furnishing themselves with the capital they so much needed by raising a joint-stock with the assistance of the investing public. A complete prospectus of a scheme of this kind drawn up for the Feltmakers casts a most welcome light on the aspirations of the working class in the Stuart period. The case of the Feltmakers was a typical one. Their struggle during Elizabeth's reign to free themselves from the control of the Haberdashers, their early success in obtaining a charter from James, and their difficulties in getting their newly acquired authority over their industry recognized by the city, had been watched with eager interest by thousands of suburban workers who were seeking similar remedies for the same evils.

The grievances of which they had been complaining to the Haberdashers for many years without redress were partly such as might be expressed by a trade union of to-day—the employment of women and boys, the non-enforcement of apprenticeship, and the intrusion of aliens—and partly of a kind associated nowadays with the home workers in the sweated industries, the oppressive profit made by the middleman, who supplied them with materials and bought their wares when finished. The fact that the middlemen who sold the wool and bought the hats were mostly Haberdashers, had led them to seek a separation from that company, but their new charter was of no use unless it enabled them to get the functions of the middleman performed in some more satisfactory manner. The Feltmakers therefore proposed to raise by themselves, and such as would venture with them,

£15,000, for the taking in and buying up of all the wares they made into their own hands: to form in fact something of the nature of a "trust." A hall was to be secured in some convenient part of the suburbs to which all feltmakers were to bring their hats, as they made them, to be valued by the experts of the company and paid for with ready money, and the merchants were to be compelled to seek their supply at that source. As an inducement to the Haberdashers to accept this arrangement, the Feltmakers engaged to refuse to serve country chapmen, so that they would be driven to buy from the city middlemen. The management of the enterprise was to be in the hands of a board of twelve or more directors, some of whom were to represent the outside shareholders. There were to be a number of agents or warehousemen, to value the wares when brought in and sell them out again to the profit of the stock, a cashier, and a register or clerk of the stock. "That this may be lawfully undertaken," concludes the prospectus . . . " it hath been resolved by learned counsel it may. . . . If, therefore, any may be desirous to join with them in adventure, here is security sufficient for his stock and an assured profit for his principal."

This bold scheme never seems to have gone any further, but it was replaced by a less ambitious plan which was actually tried, with disastrous results. A capital of £5000 was raised, mainly from outside investors, to be used in supplying wool to the Feltmakers. The Stockers were to constitute a separate concern from the company, but they hired the company's hall and agreed to allow the Feltmakers a penny in the pound on their profits. The Feltmakers never received this modest dividend, but they found when it was too late that their corporation had somehow been involved to the extent of £500, which the Stockers had borrowed from the company's clerk in the name of the company. When the enterprise collapsed, and one of the Stockers against whom the clerk had commenced an action had died in prison, the

clerk entered a suit against the company and got a verdict for
£750 in 1623. Some of the Feltmakers were imprisoned for
the debt, and the master of the company, when on his way to
present a petition to the Commons, was seized and cast in the
Fleet. The indignant Commons ordered the release of the
Feltmakers, but how they got rid of their creditor is not
stated.*

Since collective enterprise—owing to the weakness of the
law, the inexperience of investors, and the ease with which
fraudulent agents could shift their responsibility—was apt to
prove so disastrous, it is easy to understand that the alterna-
tive offer of the individual capitalist to finance an industry
had its attractions for the craftsmen. The Pinmakers, who
had obtained a charter, soon after the Feltmakers, which they
hoped would enable them to exclude foreign pins, had
procured capital for these purposes from a courtier, to whom
they engaged in return to pay fourpence for every 12,000 pins
made, for forty years. It did not, however, prove so easy, in
spite of the constant prosecution of importers, to keep the
Dutch pins out. The Haberdashers declared that the London
Pinmakers were not capable of supplying one-third of the
English demand, and the craftsmen had to content themselves
with a protective duty of sixpence per 12,000.†

These brief examples may suffice to illustrate the natural
development of the new corporations in the direction of
monopoly, with only a moderate degree of encouragement on
the part of the Government, and in face of the strong opposition of the city. After the dissolution of Parliament in 1611
without any settlement of the problem of taxation, a new
situation was created. The monopolies were no longer a mere
furtive source of pocket money for the king and his courtiers ;
they were fast becoming a necessity of state ; and as the state's
necessity is the capitalist's opportunity, there was soon found
a party in the city ready to lend them their support. Lionel

* Unwin, *op. cit.*, 156–164. † *Ibid.*, 164–166.

Cranfield, a mercer's apprentice, who had founded his fortunes by marrying his master's daughter, and whose adroitness and business capacity were to raise him to the highest offices of state, had already gained the ear of the king, and was giving advice which astonished even Bacon by its sagacity. Why should the raising of revenue take such universally unpopular forms? A tax on currants was resisted by the merchants, and everybody sympathized with the resisters. But a tax on manufactured articles would arouse so much enthusiasm amongst the craftsmen in the city that the discontent of the consumer, if it ever found expression, might be ignored. Moreover, high grounds of policy could be assigned to such a course, as being for the advantage of the kingdom and the disadvantage of the stranger, and as preventing a dangerous outflow of the precious metals. The new taxation might indeed be brought in this way within the constitutional prerogative of the Crown. It might be justified as a necessary act of retaliation on a foreign power, which could only be effective if done immediately, by royal authority, without waiting for the consent of Parliament.

The business experience and the more normal commercial interests of most city merchants remained opposed to these ideas ; but those who sincerely believed in them, and those who readily found their interest in any large manipulation of taxation, were warmly supported by the new corporations and by the industrial sections of the older companies. Above all, the courtiers, the titled ladies of limited means, the friends and relations of the reigning favourite, had a new field opened to their exploitation. Indeed, the competition amongst them became so keen, and the mind of the king so unsettled by conflicting claims, that the grants of monopoly, which were now part of the accepted policy, were transferred like so much scrip from one holder to another in rapid succession. The Earl of Northampton had received a grant of the starch patent valued at £4500 a year, and when this was taken from

W

him to give to Lord Hay, another patent was assigned to him valued at £4000. Lord Harrington, who had spent a fortune in acting as tutor to the Princess Elizabeth, was granted a monopoly in brass farthings to replace tradesmen's tokens; but before it could be put to use, the Duke of Lennox persuaded the king to let him share in it. The glass patent was granted to half a dozen different holders in succession, the rights of previous holders being generally ignored, until it came into the hands of Sir Robert Mansell, who held it till the Long Parliament deprived him of it. The monopolies in gold and silver thread, in soap, in alum, in tobacco-pipes, in pins, each passed through a succession of hands.*

The effect of these influences on the companies is clearly marked in every full set of records that has been preserved. In most of the greater companies, and many of the lesser, a division arose between a party—generally the yeomanry—who wished to take advantage of some offer of monopoly and industrial protection, and another party—generally the governing body—who opposed it. The artizan clothworkers found encouragement from those in high places to petition, in conjunction with the artizan dyers, that the exportation of all unfinished cloth might be prohibited. The artizan skinners supported a patent for the tanning of all coneyskins before export, which had been granted to one of Buckingham's brothers with a rent of £300 reserved to the king.† The Ironmongers had their trade restricted by the grant of a patent for cutting iron into rods, which nailers and smiths had been persuaded to support, because it was connected with a prohibition of Flemish iron.‡ The craftsmen of the Pewterers' Company, headed by the son of their late beadle, petitioned the king that the farmers of the tin monopoly should give out four score thousand weight of tin to be wrought into pewter

---

* Calendar of State Papers, Domestic, 1613-1618.   Index.
† *Ibid.*, pp. 352, 544.
‡ Nichol, *Ironmongers*, 177-180.

by them, and then taken back by the farmers " to be trans-
ported abroad or otherwise sold by them at their pleasures." *
The gold and silver wire-drawers belonging to the Goldsmiths'
Company desired to have that company's consent to their
obtaining a separate charter, which would enable them to work
under the shelter of Lady Bedford's monopoly.† The Grocers
engaged in a long struggle with the Apothecaries, the Sugar
Refiners, and the Starchmakers. The Haberdashers, unable
to prevent the incorporation of the Feltmakers, continued to
resist through two reigns their admission to the freedom of
London. The Leathersellers endeavoured to draw together
the leather merchants, who at that time mostly belonged to
other companies, so as to oppose the incorporation of the
leather workers of the suburbs (who had the assistance of
Lady Killigrew) under the name of the Glovers' Company.‡
The printers, who had now abandoned the hope of abolishing
the monopoly enjoyed by the rulers of the Stationers' Company, sought to alleviate their exclusion by supporting the
grant of another monopoly which was to be exercised in their
favour.§

The records of the Privy Council and the private correspon-
dence of ministers reveal a great variety of other consequences.
Having based its fiscal proposals on the necessity of encouraging native industries, and of finding work for the
unemployed, whilst at the same time protecting the vested
interests of each class of workers, the Government found itself
saddled with the responsibility of maintaining its principles
even where no fiscal fruit was to be gathered. The Privy
Council became the Court of Appeal for all the industrial
disputes of the metropolis. The year 1613 may serve as an
example. In that year the Council had quite enough fiscal
business to occupy its attention. One set of alum monopolists

---

* Welch, *Pewterers*, II. 58. † Prideaux, *Goldsmiths*, I. 120.
‡ *Leathersellers' Court Book*, 1637–1638.
§ *Index to Remembrancia*, p. 100.

had just become insolvent, and an elaborate arrangement was being made with another set, by which the Crown was to sink a great amount of capital without return, the consumer was to have a dear and insufficient supply of bad alum, and nobody was to gain anything except the astute Treasury official from Yorkshire, who floated the scheme off one rock and steered it direct for another.* The farm of the impost on French wines occupied much of the Council's attention. The Lord Mayor was anxious to have it. He had once before held it for twelve years, and had raised it from £6000 to £15,000. He offered the ruling favourite £1000 a year if he would procure for him the privilege of screwing an even greater amount out of the taxpayer. Others, however, accused the Lord Mayor of fraud, and argued that the king would gain from £15,000 to £20,000 by keeping the profits of the wine season to himself. Delicate negotiations were in progress in reference to the glass monopoly; the Crown was disposing of a privilege which it already had sold two or three times to a fresh set of enterprising capitalists. Another projector recommended the Government to do the same with the tobacco monopoly, and assured the Council that half-profits on the transaction, which he generously offered to relinquish, would amount to £15,000. Several different sets of patentees were disputing over the gold and silver wire monopoly, then only in its beginnings. Amongst the other petitioners were the Tallowchandlers. The patent they had obtained from Elizabeth had been bought up for a term of years by the city. The term had now expired, and they wanted it renewed to themselves. The artisan Clothworkers and the Dyers asked for the prohibition of the exportation of unfinished cloth. The Feltmakers obtained a proclamation against the importation of hats.

In the midst of this serious and pressing business the attention of the Council was claimed for more disinterested applications of the same great principles. The Plasterers'

* W. H. Price, *English Patents of Monopoly*, 869.

Company complained of the disorderly bricklayers who employed black-leg plasterers in the suburbs. The Painter-stainers came to explain why they had been guilty of getting their blue starch from abroad. Good blue starch had once been made in Southwark by an ingenious foreigner, but an Englishman, having stolen the secret of the manufacture, had procured a monopoly for it, and made it so badly that the Painters could not use it. The Shipwrights of Rotherhithe, who had recently been incorporated with powers extending over England, received power to imprison the shipwrights of Wapping, who took their stand on their rights as freemen of London. Perhaps, however, the most interesting application made in this eventful year to the Privy Council was that of the Watermen, great numbers of whom had been employed in carrying over the young gallants of the West End to the theatres on Bankside, of which no less than three—the Globe, the Rose, and the Swan—had often entertained full houses at the same time. It was now proposed to build a theatre on the north side of the Thames, and the Watermen petitioned that for the sake of their large families, and in the interests of the upkeep of the navy, no theatre might be allowed in Middlesex within four miles of London. The players poured ridicule on the petition by suggesting that the Royal Exchange, Paul's Walk and Moorfields should likewise be removed to Bankside for the benefit of the watermen. But the subtle intellect of Bacon enabled him to see the logical connection of the waterman's claim with the government's policy, and he delighted the heart of Taylor the water poet by observing with great gravity that "in so far as public weal was to be regarded before pastimes, or a serviceable decaying multitude before a handful of particular men, or profit before pleasure, so far was the watermen's suit to be preferred before the players." *

The dissolution of the Addled Parliament in June, 1614,

* Humpherus' *Watermen*, I.

finally committed the king to a policy of industrial monopolies at home, coupled with a system of retaliatory tariffs on imports. It was a policy naturally congenial to the king. His intellectual curiosity and versatility made him take delight in any project because it was a project, and he had no judgment to discern a good project from a bad one. From the very beginning of his reign the ambitious schemes of his neighbours, Henry of Navarre and Frederick of Wurtemberg, for planting foreign arts amongst their subjects and for placing the established industries under the care of inspectors and tax-gatherers, had stirred a royal emulation in him. In 1607, when he sent 10,000 mulberry plants for distribution to the Lords Lieutenants of certain counties with instructions for breeding silkworms, he informed them of the achievements of the French king, and asked them to assist him in " waining " his own subjects from " idleness and the enormities thereof. . . . All things of this nature," he added, " plantations, increase of science, and works of industry, are things so naturally pleasing to our own disposition that we shall take it for an argument of extraordinary affection." *

It was, therefore, with something like a childish pleasure that James threw himself and his kingdom into the arms of the projectors. The chief of these at that moment was Alderman Cockayne, the first Governor of the Irish Society, who along with other city capitalists had been at the back of the agitation amongst the artisan Clothworkers and Dyers. They were prepared to buy up all the cloth dyed and finished in England and to find a market for it abroad, on condition of receiving a monopoly of the whole export trade of cloth. The old Merchant Adventurers declared that the English white cloth which they had been accustomed to export could not be dyed and finished in England so as to be saleable abroad. Their charter was taken away, and their privileges transferred to Cockayne's syndicate under the title of the New Merchant

* Harleian Miscellany.

Adventurers. For a year and a half this body dictated terms to the Privy Council, which attempted to manipulate not only the foreign trade of the country, but also its principal manufacture, to suit the schemes of the projectors. The officers of the company were to sit at the Custom House, and no cloth was to be exported without their seal. The exportation of wool, fells, yarn, fullers' earth, was prohibited. All dealing in wool by middlemen was forbidden, and the country justices were required to act as a state agency for the supply of wool to the clothier.

The responsibilities of the Privy Council increased enormously as the logical consequences of this policy developed. No foreign ship was to be allowed to land its freight unless English goods, preferably dyed cloth, were taken in exchange. Foreign commerce could thus only be carried on by way of exception to the rules, and each exception had to be decided on its merits by the Privy Council. The prohibition of the middleman spread to other trades, and citizens of London were indicted for the enormity of supplying the metropolis with butter and cheese. The country gentlemen of distant counties were called up before the council for selling their wool without a licence. All this extra work might have been faced with cheerful patriotism by Bacon and his colleagues if success had seemed to come any nearer. But the astonishing perversity of the Dutch baffled all their calculations. No sooner had the English government, in pursuit of its great and beneficent scheme, forbidden English merchants to sell any unfinished cloth, than the Dutch government encouraged their merchants to " make a monopoly or unlawful confederacy whereby they bound themselves not to buy any English cloth that was finished."

The result of all these measures was that the price of wool went up, the price of cloth went down, half the looms in the West country were stopped, the number of the unemployed was doubled, and the customs on cloth declined to the extent

of £10,000 a year. In June, 1616, Alderman Cockayne had
feasted the king and exhibited the golden prospects of the
trade in a pageant of clothworkers, dyers, and Hamburgians,
with words by Ben Jonson. The entertainment had concluded
with the presentation of £1000 to the king in a basin and
ewer of gold.* Three months later he was called before the
distracted Council to find some remedy for the unexampled
stagnation in the cloth industry. The king was present, and
commanded Cockayne to say plainly whether his project were
impossible or not. Cockayne admitted that without more
foreign sales they could not go on buying, but hoped they
might hold out for a while. " For how long ? " said the king.
The alderman could not tell, and when pressed, asked leave
to call a court of his company. As he left the royal presence
James was heard to declare that he would call all the merchants
of England to the work rather than have it fail. For a time
this heroic spirit prevailed. Plans were made for imprisoning
the Merchant Adventurers till they consented to buy ; for
compelling all Londoners worth £10,000 to take £1000 in
cloth ; for making blue homespun the only wear at Court.
The Dutch were also to be severely dealt with. Their fisheries
were to be stopped ; their cheese, butter, and hops rejected ;
and a special care was to be taken to prevent English wool
crossing the sea in beer-barrels. But before the new year
opened the whole project was abandoned as hopeless. The
New Merchant Adventurers were dissolved and the old
company reinstated, and a royal proclamation was issued
declaring that " we intend not to insist and stay longer upon
specious and fair shows which produce not the fruit our actions
do aim at." †

This sudden access of wisdom does not seem to have been

---

* Calendar of State Papers, Domestic, James I., lxxxvii. 57.

† F. H. Durham, " Relations of the Crown to Trade under James I.," *Trans.
R. Hist. Soc.*, 1899 ; W. H. Price, *English Patents of Monopoly*, 102-6 ; Unwin,
Industrial Organization, 182-195.

available for wider application, and there was no abatement in the pursuit of other schemes of monopoly. About the time that Cockayne's project was started, the pinmakers were endeavouring to start a pin-trust amongst themselves. But a certain Sir Thomas Bartlett, who as Carver-in-ordinary to the queen had acquired a fortune of £40,000, had been nursing the pin-business for some years with a view to a profitable investment. On the last day of 1614 he offered Winwood, the king's secretary, £4000 to further his suit, and after two years' negotiations a bargain was struck. Sir Thomas bought out a previous patentee for £8000, and devoted the rest of his fortune to financing the monopoly. He was to supply the pinmakers with wire and take all the pins produced at fixed rates. The success of the enterprise depended on obtaining a control over the importation of foreign pins. After eighteen months' further struggle with those interested in a cheap supply, Sir Thomas procured from the Council a grant of the sole right of importation. But the attempt to enforce this right threatened to cause more trouble with the Dutch, whom the Council were now anxious to conciliate. Sir Thomas was accordingly thrown over. The pins came flooding in and the dearly bought monopoly was worthless. The ruined projector in his desperation made himself so disagreeable to the Government that he was committed to the Tower, and died shortly after.*

That Sir Thomas was sacrificed to expediency and not to principle, is clear from the fact that the whole authority of the Crown was at that moment being exerted to enforce two patents in which the brothers of the new favourite Buckingham were deeply interested; the patent for the licensing of inns, and the patent for the manufacture of gold and silver thread. The latter monopoly had already passed through several phases without coming nearer to success. The industry had been introduced in Elizabeth's reign by foreign immigrants

* Unwin, *op. cit.*, 167-168.

who asked for no exclusive rights, but as soon as it began to take root in this natural way it attracted the attention of courtiers on the look-out for a suitable subject of monopoly. It was easy for Lady Bedford to make out that the French-woman whom she had subsequently brought over was the first maker of the genuine article ; that this second introduction of the industry under her own distinguished patronage was the first that had any real chance of success ; and that therefore her nominees ought to be protected by royal letters patent from the competition of those who had nothing but their own ingenuity and perseverance to recommend them, and who had the additional unfair advantage of being already in the field. For the services thus rendered to industrial progress Lady Bedford was not to go unrewarded. The four patentees engaged to pay her £1000 out of the profits of the monopoly.

In spite of imprisonment and the seizure of their tools the original workers continued to resist the monopolists, and as the hearing of the case before the Council cast some doubts on the validity of the patent, a new grant was prepared to which the Chancellor Ellesmere, who had refused outright to pass the patent for inns, only fixed his seal in 1616 after seventeen months of hesitation. Bacon, who in 1617 succeeded him, had no such doubts, especially after it appeared that Sir Edward Villiers, the half-brother of Buckingham, had invested £4000 in the undertaking. In 1618, as the gold-smiths still maintained the illegality of the new patent, the manufacture was taken into the king's hands. Sir Edward Villiers was to receive a pension of £500 as interest on his £4000, and Christopher Villiers a pension of £800 in recognition of the interest he had kindly manifested in the business. The soundness of this arrangement was confirmed in a striking manner by a brilliant historical discovery made by the new Chancellor. Under a statute of Henry VII., which had hitherto been overlooked, not only by the goldsmiths but by the law officers, the making of gold thread was in itself an illegal operation. It was clear, therefore, that it could only be fittingly performed by the king himself or his agents.

As the goldsmiths and silkmen were not convinced by this reasoning, they were required to sign bonds to sell to none but the monopolists. Sir Giles Monpesson, one of the Commissioners employed to enforce these patents, declared that if they refused to sign "thousands should rot in prison." A beginning was made with six silkmercers, who were cast into the Fleet. The indignation of the city was roused. Four aldermen offered to stand bail in £100,000. The king released the mercers, but issued a proclamation confirming the monopoly. The ransacking of workshops, the seizure of thread, the imposition of bonds continued, and it was in the midst of the exasperation caused by this and a score of other patents that the Parliament of 1621 assembled. The three men who had taken the leading parts in suggesting the policy of the king—Bacon, Buckingham, and Cranfield—were each anxious to disavow the monopolies and shift the blame on each other; and Bacon's fall was not an excessive penalty for his own large share of responsibility. The Statute of Monopolies, passed in a later session of the same Parliament, declared that "all commissions, grants, licenses, charters and patents for the sole buying, making, working, or using of any commodities within the realm were contrary to law." †

Extremely important as the Statute of Monoplies was, both from the legal and from the political standpoints, it cannot be said to have settled the question it dealt with. It had not killed the snake, nor even scotched it very effectually. Not only were there half a dozen important monopolies specifically excepted, without the slightest justification, from the operation of the Act: a special proviso was made that it should not apply to any grant made to a corporation

---

* Gardiner, *History of England*, IV.
† W. H. Price, *English Patents of Monopoly*, p. 33.

of any trade, or to any company of merchants. Parliament cannot be absolved from all responsibility in this matter. Probably some of those who were loudest in their denunciations of individual patentees would have been far from willing to renounce their share in the corporate monopoly enjoyed

INITIAL LETTER OF CHARLES I.'S CHARTER TO CLOCKMAKERS

by the company of merchants or body of manufacturers to which they belonged. The results of this weakness of the law soon became evident. During the fifteen years that elapsed between the passing of the statute and the assembling of the Long Parliament there were more companies incorporated than in any previous reign; and the great majority of

them were established with the avowed intention of securing
a monopoly.

The effects produced on the inner life and structure of
the companies by the operation of these influences in the
reign of Charles I. were only a continuation or a natural
development of those already described. Since the reign
of Elizabeth there had been a tendency for the projector
of monopolies and the association of craftsmen or traders
to be drawn together on common ground. The Statute of
Monopolies encouraged this tendency. It compelled the
would-be monopolist to become a company promoter, and it
offered the strongest inducements to the would-be corporation to assume the form of a monopoly. The results in
either case are so similar that it is often difficult to tell whether
the individual or the collective interest predominated in the
origin of a company. The Tobacco-pipe makers obtained
a charter in 1619, and a year later they proceeded on the
strength of a royal proclamation to break into the houses of
those who infringed their monopoly. At the same time we
find the Mayor and Recorder trying to make friendly accord
between four courtiers who had been instrumental in obtaining
the charter and had sunk £3000 in the monopoly. Soon
after the accession of Charles I. this group of financiers found
their vested interests threatened by the intrusion of another
court favourite, and ultimately the old charter was declared
invalid, and a new one granted on condition of the payment
of £100 a year to the king.* The craftsmen were merely
pawns in the game. The pinmakers were in much the same
case. When the financial troubles of Charles made the pin
monopoly once more a business proposition, the heirs of the
unfortunate Sir Thomas Bartlett placed their rights in the hands
of a certain Mr. Lydsey, who sunk another £7000 in the concern,
but had to pay £500 a year to the Queen for a fresh grant.†

---

* State Papers, Domestic, James I., xcv. 53 ; cix. 160 ; cxv. 104 ; cxvi. 83 ;
Charles I., lxxxix. 12.   † Unwin, *Industrial Organization*, p. 168.

Sometimes the individual promoter does not appear so clearly on the surface of the records. A corporation of Beavermakers was authorized by special proclamation in 1638, at whose hall every beaver hat was to be stamped and to pay an excise of one shilling. The state papers contain long accounts of their struggles in 1638-9, to maintain their privileges against the opposition of the Feltmakers and the Haberdashers, in all of which there is nothing to indicate the existence of any individual interest behind the collective monopoly of the Beavermakers. But when petitions began to pour in upon the Long Parliament, it was the general body of the beavermakers who complained of the monopoly, in obtaining which, they asserted, only eight of their number had originally been concerned. These had persuaded another score to join them, and the body thus formed, as it contained most of the larger employers, had been able to compel another fifty to acknowledge the authority of the corporation and to pay its tolls. If this had been all, the procedure followed would probably not have differed much from the usual methods of establishing a corporation.* But the eight original members had not acted on their own initiative. The chief agent in procuring the charter was a certain Francis Spatchurst, and Spatchurst represented the interests of the Earl of Stirling, who had laid out considerable capital in promoting the beaver business and was to receive a rent out of the tax.†

It might seem to make very little difference whether a body of manufacturers made their own bargain with the Crown for the enjoyment of a monopoly, or were brought into relations with the king through the agency of a friend at court who had some capital to invest. And, as far as the burden laid on the consumer was concerned, the effect was

* Rymer, *Faedera*, Order xx. 230 ; and Carew, *Transcripts in Record Office*, fo. 52.

† State Papers, Domestic, Charles I., ccccxvii. 2 ; ccccxviii. 72.

much the same in either case. But a purely collective monopoly, administered and enjoyed by the whole body of the trade, had much more chance of conciliating public opinion than a monopoly engineered by an individual or by a group of financiers. The famous soap monopoly, which aroused violent opposition whilst it was worked under the second of these forms, contrived after it had passed into the hands of the trade to outlive the storms of the Long Parliament and to secure the approval of a judge under the Protectorate. The original soap patent was granted in 1623 to two nominees of Sir John Bourchier, who were supposed to have found a way of using the ashes of bean-straw and pea-straw, of inland kelp and English barilla, and thus of saving many thousands of pounds yearly spent on foreign commodities. But as the king was offered a diamond worth £35,000 and it was proposed to put a tax of £2 a ton with a view to producing £20,000 for the Exchequer, the economical use of pea-straw and kelp may be regarded as a negligible factor in the project. The London soap-boilers objected to the patent, and a test wash was ordered before a committee of aldermen and citizens. They reported that the washerwomen disliked the new soap, and that, though it would serve to wash coarse linen if applied with sufficient labour and skill, it was far inferior to the ordinary soap in " goodness, sweetness and merchantableness," and was not fit to be used on fine linen at all, as it fretted and consumed it.

When the monopolies began to be revived after Charles's breach with Parliament, a company was formed under the name of the Soapmakers of Westminster to buy up the soap patent. The king was to receive £4 a ton. The importation of soap or potash was prohibited, as also the exportation of tallow and ashes, and all soap was to be made with vegetable oils. Sixteen soapboilers of London were tried before the Star Chamber for infringing the patent, and fined sums ranging from £500 to £1500; two of them died in prison,

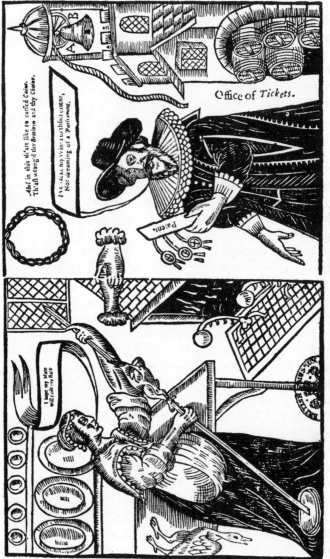

ALDERMAN ABEL AND HIS WIFE

Consumers were forbidden to make their own soap. Grocers, salters and chandlers were forbidden to buy or sell any but the patent soap. The king's tax was increased to £6 a ton, and the price raised in proportion. And, finally, the patentees were freed from the restrictions about vegetable oil which had been the main argument for the patent. When Laud became the leading influence in the Council he adopted the policy of conciliating the industry whilst retaining and even increasing the fiscal gains from the monopoly. The London soapmakers were allowed to buy out the patentees for £43,000, and an additional £20,050 for plant and material. The tax was raised to £8 a ton, and later governments found this excise too convenient to be abolished. The diffusion of the monopoly amongst the general body of manufacturers in London and Bristol seems to have disarmed the fiercest element of the opposition to it.*

When the Long Parliament met, the most unpopular of the patents was that for the retailing of wines. Some patriots might put up with the dearness of soap, but a serious rise in the price of wine was enough to cool the most ardent loyalty. The thrilling news of the execution of Strafford was accompanied by the glad tidings that canary had fallen to sixpence a pint. " Sixpence a pint," cries *Inquisitive* in a contemporary broadside, "and how comes that to pass ? " " This blessed Parliament," replies *Intelligencer*, "has pried into Alderman Abel's trickery, has made a confusion of his ticket office and laid him and his brother Kilvert in a house of stone." † Another broadside attempts to satisfy the natural curiosity of the public as to the personal appearance of Alderman and Mrs. Abel, their early life previous to marriage, and their methods of making a fortune at a tavern in Old Fish Street. A third professes to give a verbatim report of the conversation between Abel and Kilvert in which the scheme of a wine monopoly was first mooted.

* W. H. Price, *English Patents of Monopoly*, 119–128
† *Old news newly revived*, 1641.

X

Abel. "Those patents for casks and for tobacco and for cards and dice with divers others have already passed the seal. What new reach have you now by which to enrich us ? "

Kilvert. "You are a vintner, Mr. Alderman. What think you of a patent for wines and for dressing meat ? "

The alderman strongly approves of the project, and promises that if Kilvert will buy the freedom of the city he will get him elected on the Vintners' Court of Assistants. Kilvert then expounds his plan.

Kilvert. "Marry then ; we must first pretend both in the merchant and vintner some gross abuses, and these no mean ones either. And that the merchant shall pay to the king forty shillings for every tun ere he shall vent it to the vintner; in lieu of which, that the vintner may be no loser, he shall raise the price also of his wines. . . . Now to cover this our craft . . . because all things of like nature carry a pretence for the king's profit, so we will allow him a competent proportion of forty thousand pounds per annum ; when, the power of the patent being punctually executed, it will yield double at least, if not treble that sum and return it into the coffers of the undertakers."

Abel. "Mr. Kilvert, I honour thee before all the feasts in our hall. . . . Methinks I see myself in Cheapside upon an horse richly caparisoned and my two sheriffs to attend me ; and methinks thee in thy caroch drawn by four horses, when I shall call to thee and say, 'Friend Kilvert, give me thy hand !' "

Kilvert. "To which I shall answer, 'God bless your honour, my good Lord Mayor.'" *

This account is sufficiently accurate for the purposes of popular journalism, but a controversial literature of a more serious character provides the data for a more exact knowledge of the matter. The ruling body of the Vintners—the wholesale importers—disavowed all responsibility for the monopoly. As early as 1632, they declared, the Lord Treasurer Weston

* Herbert, I. p. 158.

had tried to force an imposition of £4 a tun upon them, and when they did not submit, the Star Chamber put pressure on them by prohibiting the retail vintners from dressing meat. In 1633 Lords Cottington and Dorset told the Vintners that it was folly to deny their purse to robbers against whom they had no defence. In 1634 the company paid £6000 to have their privileges confirmed and to be secured from the Star Chamber decree. But the Vintners' trade was too good a means of raising revenue to be left alone, and the offers and threats of the government were soon resumed. At this point Kilvert appeared on the scene. Through Alderman Abel, who was master of the company in 1637, he communicated a tempting offer to the retailing vintners. They were to be allowed to dress and sell victuals and to deal in tobacco, beer, sugar, etc., to be free from informers, and from outside competition, and to be authorized to add a 1d. and 2d. a quart to their prices—in short, they were "to be for ever a glorious company." In return for all these privileges the king was to impose a tax of 40s. a tun on all wines sold.

A general meeting of "all retailers of wines in London, Westminster and the confines thereof" chose a committee consisting of Alderman Abel, two wardens, and nine others to negotiate with the king. The authority of the Court of Assistants was thus set aside, and the majority, who were opposed to the project, seem to have regarded resistance as hopeless and to have stayed away. Subsequent proceedings were, however, carried on under the ordinary forms with the approval of a dozen Assistants. It soon became clear that it was not merely the retailing vintners who were to gain by the project. The most important part of the arrangement was the formation of a syndicate, to whom the king would grant the farm of the new excise on wines at £30,000. Such a delicate financial operation could not be left in the hands of the generality, even if they could find the requisite capital. A body of ten was chosen with Abel at its head. These were to co-opt a score of others, and each of the thirty was to furnish capital to the extent of £1000 in such instalments as were from time to time needed. In the hands of this syndicate of "farmers," whose numbers were afterwards increased to thirty-seven, was placed a monopoly of the wine trade throughout the whole country. The importers of French and Spanish wines were to sell to them alone, and they were bound in return to take a fixed quantity at set prices. The syndicate provided Abel with a spacious house in Alderman-bury to use as his "Ticket Office," and a salary of £500 a year. They also appointed a Secretary at a salary of £200 a year, and made a grant of £1000 to Kilvert for his services in floating the concern. In addition to this Kilvert received a grant of £500 a year out of the wine farm, in consideration, as he afterwards stated, of a debt previously owed to him by the King.*

The syndicate held together during the last four years of Charles's rule, but no one seems to have been satisfied with it, except perhaps the main projectors. The King complained that he did not get all the farm. The importers complained that the retailers bought from others. The retailers could not sell the wines supplied by the syndicate, and were cast into the Fleet for refusing to pay the excise. The feelings of the consumer have already been sufficiently indicated. A similar widespread discontent with a score of other monopolies must be reckoned amongst the more potent but less obvious causes of the great rebellion.

Nevertheless, the main difference between the monopolies of James and those of Charles lay in the greater degree of fiscal success attained by the latter. Nearly all were short-lived, it is true, and many of them were failures from the first, but considerable sums were raised from half a dozen of them during the last years of personal rule. The wine

* *A True Discovery of the Projectors of the Wine Project*, 1641 ; *The Vintners Answer to some Scandalous Pamphlets* (Guildhall Library).

monopoly yielded for a time £30,000 a year, and the soap monopoly about the same; tobacco brought in £13,000; so that the Government was in a fair way to make up its regular deficit of about £100,000 a year.* This comparative success served to make the monopolies more politically obnoxious than before. The despotism of James had been tempered by inefficiency. The reckless extravagance of Buckingham, and the philosophical opportunism of Bacon, were easier to bear than the incorruptibility and thoroughness of Laud and Strafford.

Regarded purely as taxation, the monopolies were in one sense justified by subsequent history. The money raised by them, and indeed much larger sums, had to be raised later in a similar manner by excise duties. It is possible to argue that the monopolies were the only way of accustoming the consumer to indirect taxation. But apart from the question of the consent of Parliament, the fatal defect of monopolies was their extreme wastefulness. The evidence of the leaders of both political parties and of the monopolists themselves, all goes to prove that for every pound that reached the Exchequer at least three or four pounds were paid by the consumer. The playing-card makers required a protective duty of 40s. a dozen to be laid on foreign cards, in order that they might pay the king 36s. on every gross made. The corporation of Brickmakers were to give the king 6d. a thousand, and charge the consumer an extra 1s. 6d. The retailing vintners, having bargained to give the king £2 a tun, were said to have raised the price £4, £8, and £12 a tun. But this did not represent all the waste by any means. In the case of many monopolies the king got nothing, and the patentee perhaps little or nothing, whilst the price was raised, the quality of the wares deteriorated, and the progress of the industry retarded by the restriction.

But whatever degree of fiscal success the monopolies may

* W. H. Price, *English Patents of Monopoly.*

have had, their social consequences were unmistakably bad. The alliance of the companies with the Government and their subordination to fiscal purposes was fatal for the time being to their character as voluntary associations. It destroyed their spontaneity of action, and thus disabled them from making any serious contribution to the social problems which were being raised by the new industrial conditions of the period. It deprived them of the power of devising some larger form of organization in which the diverging interests of the craftsman, the employer, and the merchant might have been to some extent harmonized by a spirit of mutual compromise. The natural tendency of the system of monopolies was towards a very crude kind of State-socialism. A number of industries, such as gold and silver wire-drawing, pinmaking, the manufacture of playing-cards and of alum, were actually taken into the hands of the king; and a plan was several times mooted for the nationalization of the cloth trade by the creation of county corporations, presided over by justices of the peace. To conceive of what England might have been if her social history had been worked out on these lines would be an admirable exercise for the imagination of the writer of Utopian romance. One thing seems certain. If such a system could have been maintained, the Industrial Revolution would never have happened.

CHAPTER XVIII

FROM GILD TO TRADE UNION

THE breakdown of the personal government of Charles I. was not an event of merely political significance ; its social consequences were probably even more far-reaching. The main road along which the solution of a great number of social problems had been sought was suddenly blocked up, and the seekers were obliged to turn in another direction. It had been the natural policy of the Tudors and of the Stuarts to take the part of the new industrial classes, whose emergence from below was the principal factor in the expansion of the nation. It was not the classes that inherited old rights and privileges, but the classes that were struggling for the recognition of new ones, that had most to gain from the Crown. There was, therefore, a real bond of interest between the Stuarts and the bodies of small master crafts-men who constituted the working-class of the 17th century. A less short-sighted statesmanship would no doubt have turned the connection to more account, but in spite of constant mismanagement and corruption it remained a factor of first-rate importance in the politics of the time.

A brief glance at the register of the Privy Council or at the Calendar of State Papers for the last two or three years before the outbreak of the Civil War is sufficient to show the truth of this. Every new proposal of monopoly brought forward to meet the growing financial difficulties of the

Government was backed by a body of small master craftsmen or retailers who wished for a grant of incorporation.
The Buttonmakers, in 1637, complained of being brought to
beggary by the intrusion of aliens and of many young people
"who lived loosely and lewdly and made false and counterfeit
buttons," and offered, in return for a charter bestowing "all
the lawful powers grantable to artists of like condition," to
pay into the Exchequer, through the hands of two Government
nominees, a list of excise dues as per schedule.* The Tobacco
manufacturers of Westminster made an exactly similar offer
in 1638 in conjunction with another projector.† About the
same time the Glovers were seeking a charter in alliance
with Lady Killigrew. Their petition claimed to represent
the wishes of 400 householders, and 3000 workers living in
the suburbs of the city, who suffered from the "great confluence
of both men and women from all parts of the kingdom," who,
having served little or no time to their trade, worked privately
in chambers and took many apprentices, and also from the
engrossing of leather into few men's hands, whereby the
petitioners were forced to buy bad leather at excessive rates.‡

The king's alliance with the craftsmen had in some cases
gone further than the mere grant of a charter. He had himself become a "model employer." The Privy Council Register
for March 18, 1640, contains a copy of an indenture by which
the king agreed to provide the pinmakers with merchantable
wire at £8 the hundredweight, to supply a capital of £10,000
out of which pins could be paid for week by week, and to
furnish them with a Hall. The fact that the king at the
same time arranged to hand over the fulfilment of these
engagements to an agent, does not lessen his responsibility.
The outbreak of the Civil War prevented the undertaking
from being carried out, but a similar scheme had been in

* State Papers, Domestic, Charles I., ccclxxii. 75.
† *Ibid.*, ccccxiv.
‡ Privy Council Register, April 29, 1638.

operation during three years for the benefit of the playing-card makers. They had complained in 1637 that the competition of foreign cards "compelled them to sell at such low rates that they could scarce get bread for their fainting bodies," and the king had graciously covenanted to buy a constant weekly proportion of good cards at specified rates, and "to such of the Company as were poor widows, aged men past labour or not able to maintain themselves, his Majesty out of his princely goodness had allowed a maintenance . . . for which they praised God and blessed his Majesty." As a modest return for his benevolence, the king had levied an excise of 36s. a gross, which was said to produce a revenue of at least £5000 a year.*

Sometimes, as in the case of the Watermen v. the Hackney coachmen, the benevolence of the Crown was distracted by competing claims. When the Hackney coach came upon the scene, in the reign of Elizabeth, the watermen were already in possession of the public. A kind of corporate existence had been conferred upon them by the Act of 1555, which authorized the Mayor to appoint eight overseers, and they claimed to be the greatest, i.e. the most numerous, company in London. At a later date their numbers were put at 40,000, but this figure, even if not an exaggeration, represented all who plied the craft from Gravesend to Windsor. There can be no doubt that there were several thousands of watermen in the neighbourhood of London. They were well organized, and they possessed an unusually effective spokesman in Taylor the Water Poet, who fulminated for twenty years in prose and verse against the introduction of the hated Hackney coach.

A brief specimen of each kind will suffice to indicate the feelings aroused in the waterman by the "upstart hellcart coaches."

"The first coach was a strange monster, it amazed both horse

* Unwin, *Industrial Organization*, 144-446, 236.

and man.   Some said it was a great crab-shell brought out of China ;
some thought it was one of the Pagan temples in which the cannibals
adored the devil. . . . Since Phaeton broke his neck, never land
hath endured more trouble than ours by the continued rumbling of
these upstart four wheeled tortoises.   Whence comes leather so dear?
By reason or against it of the multitude of coaches which consume
all the best hides in the Kingdom : when many honest shoemakers
are undone and many poor Christians go barefoot at Christmas." *

> " Caroches, coaches, jades and Flanders mares,
> Do rob us of our shares, our wares, our fares.
> Against the ground we stand and knock our heels,
> Whilst all our profit runs away on wheels."

At first the Government lent an ear to the watermen, of
whose services it often stood in need, and though Parliament
rejected a bill in 1614 against "outrageous coaches" the Star
Chamber continued to place restrictions on their use, especially after a patent had been granted in 1626 to Sir Sanders
Duncombe for the introduction of Sedan chairs, which claimed
to serve all the purposes of city locomotion without any of
that obstruction of the streets, breaking up of the roads and
appalling consumption of oats which were the main objections
to the hackney-coach.   At length, in 1634, a certain bold
adventurer named Captain Bailey, after failing to discover a
gold-mine in Guiana, conceived the brilliant idea of setting
four hackney-coaches to ply for hire in the streets of London
at fixed rates.   The watermen were furious, and the unwearied
Taylor set out on another of his campaigns.   He spent £34,
of which only £19, he tells us, was repaid him, and for the
moment prevailed upon the Star Chamber to forbid the hiring
of coaches except for three-mile journeys.   Next year, however, the hackney-coachmen to the number of a hundred made
a successful counter-move.   They pointed out to the Government that the evils complained of (consumption of oats, etc.)
were due to chandlers, innkeepers, and others who intruded
into the profession, and would be obviated by the grant of a

* Humpherus, *Watermen*, I. 142.

corporation for which the coachmen would pay £500 a year. The Government withdrew the restrictions and presumably pocketed the £500.*

There were cases, however, in which the intervention of the king or of his council on behalf of the craftsman had a more disinterested appearance. Perhaps we may reckon the regulation of the printing trade as one of these, although it was carried out under the authority of the Archbishop of Canterbury. The close restriction which the Government placed on the number of those who owned presses placed an insuperable bar in the way of journeymen becoming masters, and made them entirely dependent on the authorized printers for employment. It was only just, therefore, that the status of the workmen should be protected by authority. This had been done to some extent by a decree of the Star Chamber in 1586, and further complaints of the printers led to the drafting of a set of regulations conceived almost entirely in the spirit of an early trade union. All workmen not properly apprenticed were to be dismissed ; boys and girls were not to be employed in taking off sheets ; the number of books to be printed at one edition was limited, and type was not to be kept standing except in certain specified cases.† In like manner, the king's advisers, though unable for reasons of state to grant the request of the calkers that they might be made a separate corporation from the Shipwrights, insisted that the Shipwrights should give them representation on their ruling body and should admit them to take part in their surveys.‡

The first effect upon this class of petitioners of the political revolution which began its course in the winter of 1640, was to lead them to seek the same remedy as had been provided by the King from another authority. The Glovers, who had been petitioning the Crown for a corporation in 1638, and who had been complaining to the Privy Council in 1639 that the

---

* State Papers, Domestic, Charles I., cccxxvii. 121.
† *Ibid.*, ccci. 105.   ‡ *Ibid.*, cccliii. 87.

charter granted to them had no legal validity, transferred their plea to the Court of Aldermen, and asked " that they might be a brotherhood as anciently they had been and be empowered to search for deceitful gloves." * But it was the House of

A SEVENTEENTH-CENTURY BROADSIDE

Commons that succeeded to the greater share of responsibilities of the Stuart system. Petitions of much the same kind as those previously addressed to the Privy Council but more numerous and more audacious in tone were pouring in

* *Leathersellers' Court Book*, August 3, 1641.

upon Parliament throughout 1641. The apprentices of London, who claimed to number 30,000, took occasion to ask that the privileges of their order might be better respected. They were bound, they said, only to their masters, " yet of late their mistresses had gotten the predominancy over them also." They were the innocent scapegoats for every disturbance in the city, and when they came out of their time they found their living taken away by the thousands of Dutchmen, Frenchmen, and Walloons who crowded the tenements of the suburbs.* At the same time the playing-card makers begged the Long Parliament to continue to them the monopoly granted by Charles on the same profitable terms ; † and the printers asked that the monopoly which had gradually got into the hands of the booksellers might be restored to themselves who were the rightful possessors.‡

A parliament which had earned half its laurels by abolishing monopolies was not in a position to grant such favours. But the rapid development of political ideas was providing the discontented craftsmen with a new way of realizing their ambitions. At the very moment when the House of Commons was repudiating the authority of the House of Lords because it had no representative character, and when an influential member of the popular chamber was setting forth the view that " all power lies originally in the people, and that the community by virtue of its paramount interest may justly seize power and use it for its own preservation," § a large number of the generality of freemen of the Pewterers' Company appeared at a meeting of the Court of Assistants and claimed the right to take part in the government of the company and in the election of its officers.‖ A similar demand

---

* *Humble Petition of the Apprentices of London.* Thomason Tracts.
† Unwin, *Industrial Organization*, 144.
‡ Petition of master and workmen printers. British Museum, 669, fol. 4, 79.
§ G. P. Gooch, *English Democratic Ideas in the* 17*th Century*, 108.
‖ C. Welch, *Pewterers*, II. 105.

was gathering to a head amongst the rank and file of the Weavers, the Clothworkers, and the Stationers, and doubtless in many other companies.

Democratic theories of the origin and nature of government which had been slowly growing for nearly two generations amongst a small minority of religious enthusiasts now suddenly found a wide entry into the field of practical politics. It is scarcely surprising that some of those who had long cherished these ideas in secret should have been carried away by the conviction that the day of the Lord was at hand. From the earliest dawn of the Reformation the craftsmen and small tradesmen of the suburbs had furnished a strong contingent of political and religious idealists, some of whom had suffered martyrdom as Lollards in the 15th century. Since the days of Elizabeth there had been a small congregation of Independents in Southwark, and their principles had been gaining a wide acceptance in the decade that preceded the meeting of the Long Parliament.

Among the "swarm of sectaries" whose doctrines were ridiculed by royalist pamphleteers like Taylor the water-poet were Barebones the Leatherseller, Greene the Feltmaker, Spence the Horse-rubber, and Quartermine the Brewers' Clerk ; and a broadsheet published in 1647, entitled "These tradesmen are preachers in and about the city of London," displays a picture of twelve craftsmen of different trades at work, whilst underneath are enumerated the revolutionary and heretical ideas to the propagation of which they were supposed to devote their scanty leisure. Men of this earnest type must always have been in a minority, but the time was coming when the destinies of the nation would seem to lie in their hands. Their burning zeal and their firm convictions gave them the leadership in the inevitable struggle.

Foremost among the influences that were moulding the ideas of the industrial democracy at this period was the personality of John Lilburne. Born at Greenwich and apprenticed

A
SVVARME
OF
SECTARIES, AND
SCHISMATIQVES:

Wherein is difcovered the ftrange preaching (or prating) of fuch as are by their trades
Coblers, Tinkers, Pedlers Weavers, Sow-
gelders, and Chymney-Sweepers.

BY JOHN TAYLOR.

The Cobler preaches, and his Audience are
As wife as Moffe was, when he caught his Mare.

Printed luckily, and may be read unhappily, betwixt
hawke and buzzard. 1641.

to a city cloth merchant, he had scarcely reached manhood when he was compelled to fly to Holland. On his return in 1637, the Star Chamber had condemned him to be whipped from Fleet Street to Palace Yard for the publication of seditious literature. Thoughout the whipping he continued his work of propaganda, and disseminated tracts from the pillory. The Long Parliament in 1641 pronounced his sentence "bloody, violent, and cruel." He entered the army, rose to be lieutenant-colonel, and became one of the leaders of opinion in the "New Model." His personal experiences assisted in the logical development of a mind naturally radical. When the Lords committed him for attacks on his commanding officer, he appealed to the sovereignty of the Commons. When the Commons imprisoned him for a later attack on the king, he was led to attribute the supreme authority to the nation at large. Thoroughly impracticable in temper and as devoid of tact as he was incapable of compromise, he nevertheless possessed untiring pertinacity in the assertion of his ideas and unlimited resource in the defence of them, and was therefore peculiarly fitted to perform the important function of interpreting the popular mind to itself. The imprisonment of Lilburne called forth an address entitled "A remonstrance of many thousands of citizens . . . calling their Commissioners in Parliament to account how they in this Session have discharged their duties to the Universality of the People their sovereign Lord, from whom their power and strength is derived and by whose favour it is continued." *

That Lilburne had a large and enthusiastic following in the city as well as in the army cannot be doubted. The well-affected apprentices in the Ward of Cripplegate Without issued a thankful acknowledgment and congratulation to the " ever to be honoured Colonel John Lilburne, now a prisoner in the Tower," which concluded by urging their fellow-apprentices in every other ward to choose "four or six cordial

* Gooch, *English Democratic Ideas in the* 17*th Century*, pp. 144, 145.

active young men to be agitators, and forthwith to appoint
meetings for carrying on of the work." And the publication
of Lilburne's which led to his prosecution for high treason
by the Council of State was signed by six of these city disciples,
and was entitled "An outcry of the Young Men and Apprentices of London, or an inquisition after the lost fundamental laws of the people of England." *

It is not, therefore, surprising to find a widespread attempt
being made at this time to apply Lilburne's democratic principles
to the internal government of the companies. In the eight
eventful years that separated the battle of Naseby from the
dismissal of the Rump, the lower ranks of the Saddlers, the
Stationers, the Weavers, the Merchant Tailors, the Clothworkers, the Founders, the Goldsmiths, and the Clockmakers
were busily agitating, with some degree of temporary success,
for the reform of the constitution of their companies on
democratic lines.†

The Commonalty of the Weavers pointed out that their
charter was granted, not to so many particular men, but to the
whole society, and that "whatsoever any person or persons were
afterwards invested with must of necessity be by the consent
election, and approbation of the whole body." The Commonalty
of the Founders asked for nothing more than a "reducement
of themselves to their primitive rights and privileges, . . .
seeing that men in all ages have through their supine careless-
ness degenerated from the righteousness of their first principles."
Similar arguments on the part of the yeomanry of the Clothworkers led the governing body of that company to open their
Bibles, on the first page of which they found a striking confirmation of their own constitutional principles. On the first
day God created the light, and left it in a state of democratic
diffusion thoughout the universe. But on the fourth day He
"contracted it into those two great rulers of the world," the

* Thomason Tracts, 669, f. 14, 30.
† Unwin, *Industrial Organizations*, p. 209.

Y

Sun and Moon, the obvious prototypes of the Warden and Assistants of a Livery Company. Not only so, but He did this according to Ordinances. "They continue this day," says the Psalmist, "according to Thy ordinances." And as God in 2 Kings 17 complaineth "that 'they neither feared God nor did after their ordinances,' so (and not without cause) do the present Governors complain at this present of our dissenting brethren." *

Many of the rulers of the companies had been presbyterian, if not royalist, in their sympathies. The Founders declared that their Assistants were notoriously disaffected and had manifested their malignity in words and deeds, and had countenanced their Clerk, who was a mocker and a scoffer of all manner of godliness and holiness.† The Weavers complained that while they were fighting the battles of the Parliament the malignants who stayed at home got all the trade, so that hundreds of them had been driven to become porters, labourers, waterbearers, chimneysweepers, saltcryers, and small-coalmen. Parliament was obliged to lend an ear to its defenders, and intervened to some extent on their behalf. The Commonalty of the Weavers were empowered to elect 140 representatives to act for the whole body.‡ The "Council for the Advance of Trade," after frequent hearings of both parties, contrived to arrange a compromise between the governing body of the Clothworkers and their yeomanry.§ The Printers were conciliated for a time by the transference to them as a body of the monopoly in the printing of Bibles and Testaments, which had been enjoyed by the descendants of Christopher Barker.‖

Similar concessions to the demands of the popular party

* *The Government of the Fullers, Shearmen, and Clothworkers of London as proved by their Charters* (Guildhall and British Museum).

† Williams, *Founders*, 34–5.

‡ *Case of the Commonalty of Weavers* (Guildhall Library).

§ Clothworkers' Court Book, Dec. 19, 1648, to Oct. 6, 1651.

‖ Petition of Workmen Printers in 1659 (British Museum Library).

were made by the rulers of the city. The principle that every body of craftsmen following a distinct trade had a vested interest in their calling and a right to the corporate control of it was generally admitted. Committees of aldermen and councillors were constantly sitting to consider the advisability of enrolling some new company (the Feltmakers, the Combmakers, and the Hatbandmakers were admitted to the freedom about this time), or of strengthening the control of the older companies over their trades by obliging all freemen of other companies who followed that trade to be translated.* In 1653 the Carpenters, Joiners, Bricklayers, Weavers, Feltmakers, Plasterers and Hatbandmakers presented a joint petition to the Lord Mayor and Aldermen asking for an Act " enjoining all persons using their respective trades to present, bind and make free all their apprentices at their respective companies, and to be subject to the search and government of that company whose trade they use as hath been granted to the trades of Glaziers and Painter-stainers." † In 1659 petitions of a similar nature were presented by the Founders, the Scriveners, the Upholders, the Free-masons, the Clockmakers, the Carpenters, and the Gunmakers, which seem to have been favourably considered by the Court of Aldermen, until the Twelve Great Companies presented reasons on the other side which fully satisfied them that the Acts desired for the binding of apprentices should not be passed. " Howbeit," they added, " we think that some expedient as to view and search, and the limitation of persons free of other companies, . . . be thought on as well to the contentment of those companies as to the weal of the city and citizens." ‡

The existing looseness of the relation between the companies and the trades they represented was too deeply rooted in the " custom of London," and too much adapted to the practical

* Repertories, 60-70, *passim*. † Jupp and Pocock, *Carpenters*.
‡ Williams, *Founders*.

needs of the city, to be easily altered. Yet the anomalies produced by it were undeniable. The history of the Paviors' Company supplies an amusing instance. The Paviors, who became a recognized company in 1479, were still in the middle of Elizabeth's reign a small body numbering about a score and possessing some thirty shillings in their common box. About 1587 it so happened that one William Hanney, being at first a Waterbearer, came to marry a widow who had a son bound apprentice to a " foreign " pavior, and upon some hard measure offered that apprentice he was taken from that foreign pavior and bound to Hanney himself, who had become a freeman of the Goldsmiths. . . . " And ever after the said Hanney used the trade of a pavior and brought up four of his sons to that trade, and both father and sons used that trade only and got their living thereby ; and of that brood there are now sprung up " (says a Paviors' petition in 1637), " twenty free of the Goldsmiths but living merely and solely by paving, and now deny to pay quarterage or to conform themselves to the orders and government of the company." By the year 1671 the Goldsmith-paviors numbered thirty-nine as against fifty-two members of the Paviors' Company ; but in the meantime a compromise had been arrived at by which the Goldsmith-paviors agreed to acknowledge the authority of the company and to pay quarterage. In 1679 one of them was required to serve as warden of the Paviors or to pay a fine.*

There were thus, during the period of the Commonwealth and the Protectorate, two distinct movements for the reform of the companies. On the one hand it was sought to make the membership of each company identical with the membership of a particular trade, and thus to strengthen its control over that trade ; and on the other hand an effort was being made to secure adequate representation on the governing body of each company for all classes included in its membership. If both these movements had succeeded the result might have

* Paviors' Minute Books, Guildhall MSS. 182, vols. 1, 2, and 3.

been to forestall by a couple of centuries some of the most recent experiments in industrial organization. The series of " Alliances " between employers and workmen in many of the hardware trades of Birmingham which came into existence during the final decade of the last century with the object of securing "better profits to manufacturers and better wages to work-people," embody substantially the same ideals as those cherished by the 17th-century industrial companies of London.

But the most essential of the two movements—the attempt to democratize the companies—ended in failure. The advantages gained by the rank and file of the companies in this way proved to be of a very temporary character. Whatever share in the government of their company had been conceded to the commonalty of the Weavers was lost again at the Restoration. The liberty to print Bibles and Testaments had not been enjoyed a dozen years by the general body of printers when it was once more restrained in the interests of two stationers. The revived activity of the yeomanry, which seemed for a time to be about to make the companies fully representative of all the classes engaged in each industry, proved in most cases to be the final flicker that precedes extinction. Before the end of the 17th century the yeomanry in a number of companies was abolished or disappeared, and where the name survived it was generally used merely as a synonym for the body of free-men who had no influence whatever in directing the affairs of the companies. The older system of elections—with few exceptions strictly oligarchical—was restored where it had been altered, and remains unchanged at the present day.

The other movement achieved a considerable degree of success. During the latter half of the 17th century and the earlier half of the 18th, Acts of the Common Council were continually being passed with a view to making the membership of the lesser companies coincident with the membership of the trades they represented, and translations from one company to another with the same object became very common. The consequence of this was that as late as 1837 it was possible for nearly half the lesser companies to claim a real connection as far as membership was concerned with their several trades. In more than a score of cases half or two-thirds of the company followed the trade, and it was still usual for those who entered the trade to take up their freedom in the company. The Cutlers' Company, for instance, reported that though the byelaw requiring all persons exercising the trade of a cutler to be free of the company had not been enforced for many years, it was nevertheless common for working cutlers and dealers in cutlery to resort to the company for their freedom, and that fourteen of the Court were or had been cutlers.* The Bakers' Company stated that the great majority of the company were or had been practical bakers, that journeymen were desirous of coming into the company as the freedom was considered as conferring a certain degree of respectability, and that about three-fourths of the Court were or had been connected with the trade.† A similar condition of things was reported in the cases of the Barbers, the Brewers, the Butchers, the Saddlers, the Curriers, the Masons, the Plumbers, the Innholders, the Cooks, the Weavers, the Scriveners, the Apothecaries, the Stationers, and other companies.

But with remarkably few exceptions the control formerly exercised by the companies over their trades had been abandoned in practice before 1837. In most cases the search had been given up before the end of the 18th century. The Assize of Bread, which had been the earliest of industrial regulations, was one of the latest to be set aside. The Bakers' Company had been authorized "to view, search, prove and weigh" all bread made and sold within an area of twelve miles round the city, and in case of finding it unwholesome—or not of due assize—to distribute it to the poor of the parish where it was found, and these seizures had been made and the

---

* Second Report on Municipal Corporations: London and Southwark, p. 88.
† *Ibid.*, London Companies, p. 95.

fines imposed "to the great benefit," as the company asserted, "of the public and the protection of the fair trader, until the abolition of the Assize Laws by the Act of 3 George IV., when it was considered that the trade was entirely thrown open." *

The Saddlers' Company, also one of the earliest trade organizations, furnished perhaps the most interesting exception to this general abandonment of control. Nine annual searches were still made, as late as 1837, by the Committee of the Court of Assistants attended by the Beadles. No fees were charged, but if any defective goods were found they were taken to the Hall, and if the opinion of eight or ten respectable saddlers who had been called in to inspect the goods agreed with that of the Court, the articles were destroyed. The company claimed that the searches had the effect of raising the character of London-made saddles.†

As a rule, however, the reports of the companies to the Commission indicate that the search and other forms of industrial regulation had fallen into desuetude about half a century earlier. This final abandonment was the effect of causes that had been at work for at least a century before that. In 1685 the calculations of Sir William Petty had led him to the conclusion that the number of people residing in the 124 parishes of the London bills of mortality was about 696,000, a population much larger than that of any other European city and ten times as large as that of London itself at the end of the 14th century. A system of industrial organization that had been formulated at a time when London had some fifty thousand inhabitants could not be expected to maintain itself, even with extensive modifications, in a city whose population was rapidly nearing a million. It was not, however, so much the mere size of London that necessitated the change, as its position as the capital of the foremost industrial nation in the world. The first half of the 18th century saw the rise of the " great industry " in England. Throughout the country

* Second Report on Mun. Corp.: London Companies, p. 99. † *Ibid.*, p. 127.

districts the restrictions of the gild system had been for a long time largely ignored. The growth of London as an industrial centre was mainly due to a steady influx of craftsmen from the country. Under such conditions no artificial barriers could long avail to preserve the industrial privileges of the London craftsman. And indeed just at the very time (about the middle of the 18th century) when a great number of companies were procuring Acts of the Common Council which insisted that all those who entered their trade should become free of their company, they were openly abandoning the essential features of the gild system by abolishing all restrictions on the number of apprentices and the employment of foreigners.

Neither masters nor men had been willing to desert the old traditions which had almost become a part of the acknowledged legal custom of the city. The struggle to maintain them in face of adverse economic conditions is clearly marked by a constant stream of petitions against the employment of foreigners, which were generally dealt with by the civic authorities in a sympathetic spirit. The masters were exhorted to employ freemen wherever possible in preference to foreigners, and there can be no doubt that they were in many cases genuinely anxious to do so. But they were in a painful dilemma. They recognized that their own privileges and those of their journeymen rested on the same basis of gild-membership, and that both would probably be swept away if the new economic forces that surrounded their citadel were allowed to enter. Their disputes with their men were therefore often ended by an agreement to make common cause against the foreigner and to raise a joint fund for the prosecution of unauthorized masters. But at the same time the " fair trade " masters found it increasingly difficult to compete with suburban employers, who ignored all gild restrictions and who could draw on a large supply of alien and country labour at lower rates than the free journeymen were willing to take.

The struggle to maintain an industrial organization of the

gild type and the reluctant abandonment of it are best exemplified in those companies which had been most recently formed, and which had not had time to get out of touch with the trades they represented. The rank and file of the Clockmakers' Company, which had only been incorporated in 1631, complained in 1656 that though the exclusion of foreigners and the restriction of apprentices had been amongst the main objects of the charter, foreigners had been encouraged and apprentices multiplied till the trade was almost ruined. The search was no longer diligently carried out, and masters were made free without having demonstrated their skill by producing a proof-piece.* In the same year the Needlemakers were incorporated, and their byelaws, made when a new charter was obtained from Charles II. in 1664, exhibit the strictest gild type of organization. None but those who had served as rulers were to have two apprentices, and an ordinary freeman must have been a master three years before taking one. No woman except a master's widow was to follow the trade, and no master was to instruct even his son unless he was properly bound. The ordinances of the Feltmakers' Company, which received a new charter in 1667, forbad any workman to set up as a master or to take an apprentice till he had served three years as a journeyman, and made three proof-pieces. A master of three years' standing might take two apprentices, but no master was to have more, nor was any master to give out materials to be made up by domestic workers. At the same time a compact was made between the masters and the journeymen with a view to enforcing these ordinances and maintaining the gild system. The masters were not to admit foreigners except on the payment of £20, and the journeymen on their part agreed to work for certain piece-work rates, to pay for spoilt hats, and to give a month's notice.† The

---

* Atkins and Overall, *Clockmakers.*

† Unwin, *Industrial Organization*, pp. 245-7. The Tobacco-pipemakers and the Pattenmakers, who received charters in 1663 and 1670 respectively, both urged

regulations of the Wheelwrights, who were incorporated in 1670, were on similar lines. No apprentice was to be taken for the first five years and only one afterwards by the ordinary member ; only free journeymen were to be employed, and collections were made amongst the workmen for prosecuting refractory members.*

The records of the Tinplate-workers, also incorporated in 1670, exhibit the working of the gild system up to the time when it became practically extinct. Apprentices were required to produce a master-piece before being made free. Masters were fined for taking more than one apprentice, or for employing foreigners. General warrants were taken out against hawkers and illegal men. All tinplate-workers who had not taken up their freedom were prosecuted. Piece-work lists were regularly drawn up by the company, and as late as 1773 a search was still carried out in London Walk, East Walk, and West Walk, in the course of which £26 8s. 4d. was collected. For exactly a century there is no evidence of serious dispute with the journeymen, but in 1769 eighty of them complained of divers grievances and oppressions, and put forth a revised piece-work list which was rejected by the masters. Ten years later the company allowed each freeman to take an additional apprentice, and in 1787 all restrictions as to the number of apprentices were abolished.†

In many companies the break-down of the gild system had happened half a century earlier. Down to about 1720 the decisions of the Court of Aldermen were generally adverse to any departure from the traditional usages. In 1716, when a master blacksmith complained that he could get no freemen capable of doing his business and that he was prosecuted if he employed foreigners, the Court contented itself with

the necessity for limiting apprentices as a justification of the grants. The Printers obtained an Act of Parliament in 1663 with the same object.
* J. B. Scott, *Wheelwrights*, 54–8.
† E. A. Ebblewhite, *Tinplate-workers*, 4, 10, 12, 16, 19, 25, 26, 48, 50, 53, 56.

advising the free journeymen to be more accommodating.* A couple of years later we find it authorizing the Coachmakers, who had been complaining of a combination of their journeymen, to retaliate by repealing their byelaws in restriction of apprentices ; † but in 1731 it was still reluctant to allow the Clothworkers who were engaged in a similar dispute to call in foreign journeymen.‡

YOU are desired to accompany the Corps of Mr. *Thomas Moody*, from *Armourers-Hall* in *Coleman-Street*, to the Burying Ground on *Bun-Hill*, on *Friday*, *May* the 18th, 1716, by Five of the Clock in the Afternoon precisely.

And bring this Ticket with you.

By that time, however, it had been found impossible in many of the larger industries to reconcile the interests of the masters and the journeymen within the gild organization, and as with the advance of the Industrial Revolution this social cleavage became general, it gradually gave rise to the separate organizations of wage-earners known as trade unions, which

* Repertories, 121, fo. 349, 358, 394.
† *Ibid.*, 103, fo. 118 ; 122, fo. 170; 123, fo. 10.
‡ *Ibid.*, 136, fo. 21 ; 139, fo. 217.

in their turn, through a growing consciousness of common interests, produced the general movement known as Trades Unionism. The journeymen's clubs and "houses of call," which served as a basis for the trade union, had probably been in existence a long time, partly as an adjunct to the gild, but occasionally as a rallying point of opposition to it. We have seen how the numerous associations of journeymen which had arisen in London during the 14th and 15th centuries had been gradually transformed into bodies of small masters and subordinated to the livery companies   Whether the journeymen, as the yeomanry organizations passed out of their hands, formed new associations of their own we do not know.   In Germany, and to a less extent in France, the journeymen's associations maintained a chequered existence more or less in defiance of the secular authorities, and more or less under the protection of the religious orders from the 15th to the 18th centuries.   No doubt the withdrawal of the Church's protection made the survival of these associations more difficult in Protestant countries, and the custom of "wanderjahre" which enabled the journeymen of different towns to form a united body is not known to have been prevalent in England.*

It would be unsafe to conclude that journeymen's clubs had no existence in London during the 16th and 17th centuries, but they were probably weak and isolated institutions.   The new economic conditions already described called them into a vigorous activity.   It was by means of their clubs that the feltmakers organized a successful strike, or rather a series of strikes, in 1696–9.   In 1720 the master tailors obtained an Act of Parliament with a view to resisting the collective demands of their journeymen, who to the number of seven thousand and upwards were said to possess an organization

---

* G. Schanz, *Zur Geschichte der deutschen Gesellen-verbände*, ch. v.   L. Brentano, *On the History and Development of Gilds*, 89–92.   M. H. Hauser, *Le compagnonages d'arts et metiers à Dijon.*

centring round fifteen or twenty houses of call.*   In 1714
the journeymen wheelwrights established a club, and between
1718 and 1734 struck three times for higher wages and
shorter hours.   Before the middle of the 18th century the
bond of local privilege which had served to unite masters
and journeymen had ceased to be effective in most of the
larger interests of London.   A master feltmaker told a House
of Commons Committee in 1752 that he employed six
foreigners to one freeman, and that he did not hear of any
prosecutions likely to issue on that account.   Three years
later the restrictive ordinances relating to foreigners and
piece-masters were formally abolished by the Feltmakers'
Company.   From that time onwards, one company after
another abandoned the attempt to regulate an expanding
industry on gild principles, and by the end of the century the
interests of the manual workers had passed with few exceptions
from the hands of the gild to that of the trade union.

NOTE.—As the attack on the privileges of the companies by writ
of *quo warranto* in 1684, and the speedy restitution of 1688, left no
trace in their constitution, it has not been dealt with here.   A full
account will be found in Herbert, I. 212–220.   It may, however,
be added that the Government of Charles II. was here, as in other
instances, following the example of Louis XIV.

* F. W. Galton, *Select Documents illustrating the History of Trade Unionism.*
J. B. Scott, *Wheelwrights,* p. 24.   Unwin, *Industrial Organization,* p. 224.

CHAPTER XIX

SURVIVALS: GILDS OF TRANSPORT

THE most notable exceptions to the general development outlined in the last chapter were furnished by the gild organizations connected with transport—the Watermen, the Carmen, and the Porters. The Thames lighterman and the Billingsgate porter are perhaps the most picturesque, as they are certainly the most ancient, types of London industry. Their modes of work have varied very little during the twenty centuries which have elapsed since the Romans brought them—if indeed they did not find them —and there is nothing wildly improbable in the suggestion that they may have possessed some kind of organization continuously from the days of Claudius. As the *marchands de l'eau* are the earliest recorded, and the porters of the *Halles* the latest surviving of the Parisian gilds, so in London, Billingsgate is the first recorded scene of trade regulation, and the Watermen's Company is the one surviving body that still exercises all the powers of a gild. The Carmen's Company carried on its activities till towards the middle of the 19th century, and the Fellowship Porters were not finally disbanded till 1894.

None of these bodies was a livery company. None of them except the Watermen's Company at a late date possessed the powers of a corporation. Their recorded history begins with the 16th century, when they were recognized as fellowships by the city though they remained more under the oversight of civic authorities than the corresponding fellowships of craftsmen. The Lord Mayor and Aldermen were empowered by an Act of 1555 to select "eight of the most wise, discreet, and best sort of watermen being householders" to be overseers of all watermen and wherrymen rowing between Windsor and Gravesend; and the same authorities appointed twenty-four of the "saddest and ablest" of the Billingsgate Porters to act as a court of assistants to the Aldermen of Billingsgate, who acted *ex officio* as their Governor. The fares of the watermen and the rates charged by the Porters were likewise fixed by the city. But just at the time when the constitutions of the livery companies were losing the last vestiges of popular election, the Porters and the Watermen were struggling with some degree of success to introduce a democratic form of government into their companies. In the eventful year of 1641 the Watermen obtained an order from the mayor that in future the eight rulers should be chosen out of twenty persons nominated by fifty-five electors representing the towns and stairs between Windsor and Gravesend, and these fifty-five electors contrived to establish themselves as a court of assistants.* Important concessions were also made to the Carmen and the Porters during the period of the Long Parliament and the Commonwealth. The gilds of transport entered upon the most active period of their existence at a time when the gilds of handicraft were becoming obsolete.

The market supplied by the porter and the waterman, although it was rapidly expanding, was still a local market. They had not like the craftsmen to compete with the products of country labour, nor had they need of the merchant and the middleman to bring them into touch with a distant consumer. The problem of organizing their industry was a comparatively simple one. Since the civic authorities already

* Humpherus, *History of the Watermen*, Vol. I.

fixed the price of their labour and regulated in the last resort the entrance to their callings, the worst evils of monopoly were not to be feared, and their claim, therefore, to have their vested interests respected was one which a 17th-century government found it impossible to resist. Under these conditions the preservation by collective effort of a certain status of equality and the exclusion of the capitalist—the ends after which the 17th-century craft gilds had been vainly striving— were to prove more practicable in the case of the gilds of transport.

Even amongst the craftsmen the failures that have been recorded had not wholly extinguished the spirit of co-operative idealism. A certain amount of co-operative enterprise had been inherent in many of the crafts from the earliest times. Early in the 14th century the Cordwainers had bought their leather in groups, and a group of nine curriers had taken a lease of a workshop for joint use. The Horners' Company had made common purchases of horn, the Pewterers of tin, and the Stationers' Company still holds a valuable stock which was originally started as means of making the printer independent of the capitalist bookseller, but of which the poor printer even as early as 1637 found it difficult to enjoy any share.* Amongst the Painters the spirit of co-operation seems to have always been strong. Their ordinances of 1491 required a promise from every new member that he would help any brother craftsman to finish a piece of work, if need arose, at the request of the master of the company ; † and the superior class of artists who painted heraldic devices under the direction of the College of Arms for use at funerals, seem to have established in the 17th century a method of sharing the work amongst themselves in rotation. This plan was in operation in 1621, but towards the end of the reign of Charles II. it took a more elaborate and interesting form. A

* Calendar of State Papers, Domestic, for 1637, p. 210.
† Letter Book, L, 291.

workshop was hired near St. Paul's churchyard by twenty-two painters, seven of whom were described as seniors, eight as middles, and seven as juniors. A different set of seven or eight, drawn from all three classes, were to work together each week on a common account. A treasurer was elected out of the seniors, a book-keeper out of the middles, and a collector out of the juniors. On the last Monday in every month all the members met to make a reckoning and to receive a dividend, leaving enough for the purchase of materials. For every twelve pounds allotted to a senior, a "middle" received ten, and a junior eight. If a senior died, the eldest "middle" was promoted to be a senior and the eldest junior to be a middle, and the share of the lowest junior was to be assigned to the widow, on condition of her paying the wage of an able man to do the work. The recorded accounts cover several years, and the experiment seems to have been repeated after a short interval.*

The ideals manifested in this scheme were those fostered by, if seldom realized in, the gild, and they are still cherished by large numbers of manual workers to-day. But the trade unionist accepts the capitalist as an inevitable fact, and has adapted his organization to the pursuit of his ideals in the presence of the capitalist. The craftsman of the 17th century still hoped to exclude the capitalist, partly by legislative enactment and partly by raising a co-operative capital, and in that hope even the common labourer of the city had a share.

The Carmen's Company was erected by the city with a view to getting rid of the serious inconveniences caused by the sudden seizure of the carts of citizens for the king's use. On condition of supplying the king's needs on all occasions, the Carmen were authorized in 1516 to form a fraternity of St. Katherine the Virgin and Martyr, and were to enjoy a monopoly of plying for hire in the city. Carts coming into the city were to secure exemption from seizure by paying the

* Harl. MSS. 1058, fo. 53.

Z

Carmen a composition fee.   The Carmen undertook to keep
the streets clean and to carry goods at rates fixed by the city.
In the reign of Elizabeth stands were appointed for the cars
in different parts of Cheapside and other main thoroughfares,
and rules were made to prevent carmen driving at a trot or
taking to fisticuffs as they met in the narrow parts of Thames
Street.

At the end of the century the number of licensed cars was
fixed at 400, of which 100 were to be in Southwark, 100 on the
woodwharves, and 200 in the outer regions of the city.   The
right to one of these 400 stands or car-rooms, as they were
called, came to be regarded as the chattel of the holder.   He
disposed of it like the goodwill of a shop, and when he died
it passed by his will to his son or other successor.   The city,
however, was unwilling to admit this complete freehold of the
carmen, and placed them in a kind of feudal relation to the
Governor of Christ's Hospital, who became entitled to a
yearly rent for each licence and a fine when it was transferred.
After a struggle the carmen submitted to this reduction of
their status from freeholders to copyholders.   A still more
serious attack on their privileges followed.   The Woodmongers, who were the chief employers of the cars on the
wharves, managed to procure a charter in 1606 which drew
the carmen under the rule of their corporation, and not only
used their power over the carmen as a means of strengthening
their monopoly in coal and other fuel, but claimed that on the
death of a licence-holder the licence passed into the hands
of their company.†   The dispute between the Carmen and
the Woodmongers lasted through the whole Stuart period.
The Star Chamber decided in favour of the Woodmongers in
1624.   A Committee of the Long Parliament in 1649 reported

---

* Letter Book, N, 38.
† *Index to Remembrancia*, 56–60.   The Woodmongers had previously, in
1580, procured an order of the Court of Aldermen to this effect.   Humpherus,
Watermen, I. 134.

in favour of the Carmen. The Mayor who welcomed back
Charles II. was a woodmonger by trade, and procured an Act
of Common Council giving the Woodmongers the disposal of
the car-rooms. In 1665 the outcry against the coal monopoly
led the Common Council to place the car licences once more
in the hands of Christ's Hospital, and in 1668 the Carmen
regained their independence as a fellowship with three
wardens, twenty assistants, a clerk, and a beadle. Hence-
forward until 1832 their monopoly was never disputed, except
when the city in 1694 allowed the Woodmongers to employ
an additional 120 cars over and above the 420 then granted
to the Carmen. On that occasion the Carmen offered, in
addition to the £400 paid annually to Christ's Hospital, to
pay £400 to the city and to make and maintain a cartway up
and down Tower Dock if the city would withhold the extra
cars asked for by the Woodmongers. At a later date the
Carmen again undertook the dust collection of the city. The
right of the individual carman in his car-room was restored,
and once more he could transmit that right by his will. In
one case a car-room passed through a succession of heirs from
1672 to 1832. In 1717 a car-room sold for £150. But as
the privileges of the carmen did not extend beyond the city,
the value declined with the expansion of the port. In 1814
a car-room was worth £48. In 1837 it had little or no value.
But the value, whether little or much, was only secured to the
individual owner through his membership of the company.
An outsider who inherited or acquired a car-room must, even
if already a freeman of London, take up his freedom in the
Carmen's Company and pay as much as £100 before he could
use the privilege.†

The ideal which the carman of the 17th century shared with
the porter and with the small master craftsmen in every trade

* Strype's *Stow*, V. 226–228 ; Lansdowne MSS. 162, fo. 196 ; Harleian MSS.
6842, fo. 256.
† Second Report on Municipal Corporations, 1837 ; London Companies, 342.

had thus been attained. The carman had made himself independent of outside capital ; but he had done so by becoming a capitalist on his own account. A carman whose licence was worth £100 would be almost certain to set a hired man to drive his car. The Fellowship Porters had attempted a more democratic solution of the problem. They had become co-operative capitalists. Collectively they were the possessors of £10,000, whilst individually they still followed the humble calling of a labourer. By permitting a deduction of a penny in the shilling from their wages—known as the shift—they had provided a fund, part of which (54 per cent.) went to pay the Shifters, who organized their industry, whilst the rest furnished the capital out of which weekly wages might be advanced for work not yet completed or paid for. In 1832 this wages fund amounted to £7000 ; but besides this the Fellowship Porters had £2700 in the 3½ per cents., and distributed £1500 a year in pensions, gratuities, and clothing to their poor and aged members. This prosperous condition, however, was the result of long years of slow accumulation. Originally the Fellowship Porters had been partly dependent on capital furnished by the Shifter, who when appointed to his lucrative office by the city had been obliged to enter into a bond for £10,000.*

The Billingsgate or Fellowship Porters represented only one of several branches of their profession, each of which had from early times claimed a vested interest in its own department of work. Indeed, this seems to have been true from the 15th century onwards of every class of unskilled labour. The Waterbearers were not only organized as the fraternity of St. Christopher, but possessed through the greater part of the 16th century a hall of their own. The labourers who served the building trades had been combined in the reign of Henry VII.† in a brotherhood of the Holy Trinity. This, like other of the poorer fraternities, seems to have suffered temporary eclipse

* Second Report, etc., 1837, London and Southwark, p. 179.
† State Papers, Domestic, Eliz., cxcv. 105.

during the Reformation period. But the necessity of meeting the labour legislation of Elizabethan parliaments called it once more into active existence, and after much agitation it was again duly recognized by the city in 1605. A register was to be kept of all authorized labourers, and no newcomer was to enter the calling until the rulers of the brotherhood had given security to the Chamberlain that he would not become chargeable to the city. He then was to pay fourpence for a tin badge bearing a pair of crossed shovels on one side and his own name on the other, and sixpence as an entrance fee, and was to undertake to contribute fourpence a quarter to the benevolent funds of the brotherhood. The society had twelve rulers, two of whom were to attend every morning in Cheap to superintend the making of contracts with employers, and who along with twelve assistants were empowered to make rules for the labourers, subject to the approval of two aldermen specially appointed.*

The porters no doubt regarded themselves as being of a superior class to the labourers, and their organization was certainly of greater antiquity. The thirty men who are described in the 13th-century customs of Queenhithe as being under the directions of the Corn and Salt Meters must have represented along with their fellows at Billingsgate an old-established branch of the municipal service.† Their successors continued to be known as the Corn and Salt Porters, the Billingsgate Porters, or the Fellowship Porters, and retained the sole right to handle measureable commodities down to the middle of the 19th century, when they numbered nearly three thousand ; whilst the coal-porters, who had originally formed part of their body but who had moved out of the jurisdiction of the city, had grown into an additional thousand by the middle of the 18th century. The other main branch of the profession were the Street or Ticket Porters who handled

---

* Repertories, xxvii. 98.
† Liber Albus, translated by Riley, 212.

weighed commodities, and whom we find bargaining collectively with the Grocers' company at the end of the 14th century for the rates at which alum, madder, almonds, cinnamon, flax, pepper, black soap, and dried fruit should be carried into the city from the wharves, and engaging to have a gang of six men always ready in Sopers Lane and Bucklersbury.* But besides these two bodies there were two others—the predecessors of the modern stevedores—who worked on the wharves and in the vessels lading and unlading; one section being employed by the Tackle House Porters appointed by the twelve great companies to handle the goods of English merchants, and the other section being under the direction of the Packer appointed by the city to superintend lading and unlading of the goods of foreign merchants.†

The disputes of these various classes of porters amongst themselves and with their employers were endless. During the 17th century a committee of the Court of Aldermen was nearly always sitting to settle some difficult point of professional honour, or to delimit some disputed boundary between the several occupations. All sections objected alike to the intrusion of the foreigner. But as London was being built up mainly of foreigners, the porters were not able to keep them out—there existed at one time a separate brotherhood of foreign porters—and accordingly, after many complaints of unauthorized men being at work, there took place every now and then a wholesale whitewashing of "black-legs" by which the necessities of the labour market were met and the rights of the freemen formally respected.‡

No doubt each section of the porters had its own fraternity organization. We know this was the case with the Fellowship or Billingsgate Porters. We find them in the reign of Mary bringing their religious ordinances, which since the Act of 1547 had probably become of doubtful legality, for confirma-

---

* Kingdon, *Facsimile and Transcript of Grocery Records*, I. 55.
† Strype's *Stow*, V. 415–421.   ‡ Repertories, xix.–xxxvii. *passim.*

tion by the Court of Aldermen, who approve of them "saving
that they should not have more than two tapers of two pounds
apiece at the burial of a brother." * The ordinances authorized
ten years later exhibit all the original features of the religious
fraternity except the provision of masses for the souls of the
dead.† The annual mass is replaced by a goodly sermon at
the church of St. Mary at Hill, which was continued till about
thirty years ago, accompanied by such picturesque observances
as to stir the regret that it should not have survived to our
own day.

"The next Sunday after Midsummer day," says the historian of the
Watermen,‡ "a sermon was preached to them in the parish church of
St. Mary at Hill. The Fellowship furnished the merchants and
their families about Billingsgate with nosegays overnight, and in the
morning went from their Common Hall in good order, each having a
nosegay in his hand : they walked through the middle aisle to the
Communion table, where were two basins, and every one offered
something to the relief of the poor and towards the charges of the
day, and after they had all passed the deputy, the merchants, their
wives, children, and servants all went in order from their seats and
bestowed their offerings also. The charge of the nosegays cost them
in one year near twenty pounds."

Though the porters were paid by a piece-work rate they
have always worked in gangs, and the co-operative arrangements that are now found amongst the Millwall dockers, the
"Orange gang" of Billingsgate, and the Coal-porters, must
have their roots in extreme antiquity. The simplest form of
common action is indicated by two early rules to the effect
that when members of the Fellowship are working together
the first man shall help to "heave the last man away," and
that the last man shall take up the money from the merchant
and pay every man who has been engaged according to their
turns or courses without deceit or craft. The main object

* Rep., xiii. 255.   † Letter Book, V. 23-6.
‡ Humpherus, *Watermen*, I. 198.

of the porters' organization has always been to avoid the
necessity for a middleman by providing collectively for the
distribution of work and of payment.   For this purpose
the city allowed rulers to be selected out of the men themselves, who ultimately became the salaried servants of the
Fellowship and who had " full authority to send as many of
the company to any work (be it much or little) as by their
discretion they shall think meet, having regard that they
show favour as much as may be to ease the old and ancient
and weaker persons." *

But the chief need of the Fellowship was capital.   The
average individual power of abstinence in the porter class has
always been small.   The coal-porter of the present day is
said frequently to begin the day by borrowing 1s. on account
of wages, though he is paid daily and may have received 10s.
the night before.   In consequence of this weakness the porter
has generally been in bondage to the publican or small trader,
who give him credit or cash his wage-tokens on extortionate
terms.   The formation of a collective " wages-fund," out of
which the workers might be paid whilst the task on which
they were engaged was still in progress, was a need that would
become more urgent in proportion as the tasks undertaken
grew larger with the increasing size of ships.   The nucleus
of such a fund was formed by the contributions levied for
benevolent purposes.   In 1589 each member was required to
carry two turns in every week in corn, salt, or sea-coals, which
would amount to 1d. a week, for the relief of the lame, sick,
or impotent,† and under the Commonwealth we find the city
authorities increasing the rate of pay with the express idea of
encouraging the Fellowship to raise a stock.‡   Some years
before this the advisability of allowing an incorporation of the
porters had been under discussion in the Court of Aldermen,§
but nothing came of the suggestion, and after the Restoration

---

* Letter Book, V. 23 ; *ibid.*, 268 ; and Guildhall MSS. 444.
† Letter Book, etc., 268.   ‡ Guildhall MSS. 444   § Rep. xlvii. 34.

the prevailing opinion in the Court of Aldermen grew more distinctly adverse to new incorporations. If old-established companies like the Basketmakers and the Paviors were not allowed to acquire corporate powers, it was not likely that the aspirations of the sawyers and the porters would receive much countenance. The carpenters, joiners, and shipwrights who employed the sawyers resisted their incorporation on the ground that it would give legal sanction to a combination of wage-earners. The object of the sawyers, they pointed out, was to exclude all those sort of labourers who daily resort to the city of London and parts adjacent, and their success would be an evil precedent, all other labourers to masons, bricklayers, and plasterers having the same reason to allege for incorporation.*

In spite, however, of the want of a royal charter and a common seal, the Fellowship Porters continued to enjoy in practice many of the powers and privileges of a corporation, and their status was an object of emulation to other bodies of London labourers. The coal-porters, who owing to the removal of their trade from the city had become a separate body, petitioned the House of Commons in 1699 for a Bill to establish them "a Fellowship under such Government and rules as shall be thought meet after the manner of the Watermen, Carmen, Porters and Coachmen." † At what period the Billingsgate Porters established the rule of levying a penny in the shilling out of all wages is not clear, but in 1837 they had acquired all the characteristics of an aristocracy of labour. Applicants had often to wait three years for admission, and the entrance fee was £5, of which £3 4s. went to increase the common stock. After long service as a salt-porter a member was raised to the more dignified position of a corn-porter, and might look forward to ending his days as one of the 200 clothed pensioners of the Fellowship.

---

* Jupp, *Carpenters*, 307, 315 ; Unwin, *Industrial Organization*, 212.
† *House of Commons Journals*, XIII. 69. After agitating for half a century

The unique position of the Watermen's Company is due to the combined operation of many causes. From the 16th to the 18th centuries the company was the main recruiting agency for the navy, and the Government, therefore, whilst it favoured the maintenance of the company's privileges, was not likely to encourage any restrictions upon its membership. The amalgamation in 1700 of the watermen (who carry passengers) with the lightermen (who carry goods) was indeed accompanied by a more than usually strict limitation of apprentices, but the employers of the lightermen were soon complaining that these rules were producing an absolute decrease in numbers, and in 1706 they were set aside altogether, with the result that a year later 2400 fresh apprentices were said to have been bound, many of them under twelve years of age. From that time to this there has been a continual conflict between the rulers of the company and the main body of its working members on this question. Separate societies have grown up to represent the special interests of the employers, the foremen, and the workmen ; yet the Watermen's Company still retains the allegiance of all the members of all these associations, which have as one of their main objects the maintenance of the statutory powers of the company. This resultant harmony in spite of discordant interests is due primarily to the breadth of the company's base. The position of a freeman is accessible to all, and every freeman may by taking apprentices (whom he turns over to a capitalist employer) have a small share in the vested interests of his profession. The existence of these

---

the coal-porters obtained an Act of Parliament in 1758, which, however, was recognized as having been ineffective and repealed to make way for another enactment in 1770. In the interval had occurred the terrible riots of the coal-heavers in 1768, which, together with the similar disturbances amongst the Spitalfields weavers in 1765 and 1770, represent the climax of the transition from the old industrial conditions to the new. The Act of 1770 was allowed to lapse after three years. Second Report on Municipal Corporations, 1837 ; London and Southwark, 181.

nominal small masters along with the more genuine "masters of craft" who are still characteristic of the waterman's ancient calling, preserve a low centre of gravity in the company and give it an unusual degree of stability.* But probably from the first the Watermen's Company was more of a federation than a single gild, having many local associations, each preserving its own religious usages, its own friendly benefits, and in some cases its own co-operatively owned ferry.

* Booth, *Life and Labour of the People of London*, vii. 367-384.

APPENDIX A

I. List of Parish Gilds (see Map on p. 120).

Most of the references are to Dr. Sharpe's *Calendar of Wills enrolled in the Court of Husting.*

Church.	Dedication of Gild.	Date.	Reference.
Portsoken Ward—			
St. Botolph, Aldgate	Holy Trinity		
St. Katherine	St. Barbara	1518	Strype's *Stow*, II. 6.
	St. Katherine	1379	*Wills*, II. 209
Tower St. Ward—			
All Hallows, Barking	St. Nicholas	1381	*Wills*, II. 226
St. Dunstan	St. Mary	1389	Certificates
Aldgate Ward—			
St. Katherine, Cree	St. Mary	1378	*Wills*, II. 209
St. Katherine, Colman	St. Katherine	1381	*Wills*, II. 220
Bishopsgate Ward—			
St. Botolph	St. Mary	1473	*Wills*, II. 569
	St. John Baptist	1473	*Wills*, II. 569
Broad St. Ward—			
All Hallows by the Wall	All Hallows	1379	*Wills*, II. 209
	St. Mary	1361	*Wills*, II. 33
St. Christopher	St. Christopher	1361	*Wills*, II. 27
Cornhill Ward—			
St. Michael	St. Anne	1388	*Wills*, II. 266
St. Peter	St. Peter		

Church.	Dedication of Gild.	Date.	Reference.
Langbourne Ward—			
St. Mary, Woolnoth	St. Mary	1373	*Wills*, II. 159
All Hallows, Staining	All Hallows	1378	*Wills*, II. 209
Billingsgate Ward—			
St. Andrew, Hubbard	St. Katherine	1468	*Wills*, II. 563
St. Botolph	St. Mary	1390	*Wills*, II. 285
Bridge Ward—			
St. Magnus	Salve Regina	1343	Certificate
St. Benet, Gracechurch St.	St. Mary	1372	*Wills*, II. 150
St. Leonard	St. Mary	1386	*Wills*, II. 257
Candlewick St. Ward—			
St. Mary, Abchurch	Holy Trinity	1384	*Wills*, II. 244
Walbrook Ward—			
St. Mary, Woolchurch	St. Mary	1381	*Wills*, I. 226
St. John	St. John Evang.	1484	*Wills*, II. 587
Dowgate Ward—			
All Hallows, Haywharf	St. Katherine	1386	*Wills*, II. 260
Vintry Ward—			
St. Thomas	St. Eligius	1452	*Wills*, II. 522
St. James	St. James	1375	Cert., Smith, *English Gilds*
Cordwainer St. Ward—			
St. Mary, Bow	St. Mary	1361	*Wills*, II. 61
St. Antholin	St. Anne	1353	*Wills*, I. 653
Cheap Ward—			
St. Lawrence, Jewry	Holy Cross	1370	Certificate
	St. Anne	1372	Strype's *Stow*, III. 49
St. Martin, Pomery	St. Katherine	1388	*Wills*, II. 271
St. Mary, Coneyhoop	Corpus Christi	1443	*Wills*, II. 501
St. Mary, Colechurch	St. Katherine	1338	Certificate
St. Mildred, Poultry	Corpus Christi	1349	*Wills*, I. 576

Church.	Dedication of Gild.	Date.	Reference.
Coleman St. Ward—			
St. Stephen	St. Mary	1368	Strype's *Stow*, IV. 62
	St. Nicholas	1369	Strype's *Stow*, IV. 63
	Holy Trinity	1384	Certificate
Bassishaw Ward—			
St. Michael	St. Mary	1361	*Wills*, II.
Cripplegate Ward—			
St. Giles	St. Mary	1348	*Wills*, I. 504
	St. John	1361	*Wills*, I. 34
	St. Giles	1361	*Wills*, I. 34
	St. George	1368	*Wills*, I. 106
	St. Eloy	1437	*Wills*, I. 483
Aldersgate Ward—			
St. Botolph	Holy Trinity	1378	Smith's *English Gilds*
	St. Fabian and St. Sebastian	1381	Smith's *English Gilds*
	St. Katherine	1378	*Wills*, II. 217
Farringdon Ward (within)—			
St. Paul	St. Erkenwald	1378	*Wills*, II. 203
	St. Katherine	1352	
	All Souls	1379	
	Resurrection	1372	*Wills*, II. 157
St. Augustine	St. Austin	1387	
St. Owen	St. Anne		
St. Vedast	Holy Cross	1393	*Wills*, II. 302
St. Martin, Ludgate	St. Mary	1379	*Wills*, II. 209
St. Michael le Quern	St. Hilda	1369	*Wills*, II. 133
Bread St. Ward—			
All Hallows	Corpus Christi	1349	*Wills*, II. 547
St. John Evangelist	St. John	1484	*Wills*, II. 587
St. Matthew	St. Katherine	1365	*Wills*, II. 65
	St. Mary	1345	*Wills*, I. 685

Church.	Dedication of Gild.	Date.	Reference.
Castle Baynard Ward—			
St. Mary Magdalen	St. Mary	1361	*Wills*, I. 32
Farringdon Ward (*without*)—			
St. Bride	St. Bride	1375	
	St. Mary	1390	*Wills*, I. 285
St. Dunstan	St. Dunstan	1376	
St. Andrew	St. John	1380	*Wills*, I. 221
	St. Osythe	1394	*Wills*, I. 311
St. Sepulchre	St. Katherine	1361	*Wills*, I. 45
	St. Stephen	1376	Certificate

II. TRANSCRIPT AND TRANSLATION OF THE ENTRY IN THE BREWERS' RECORDS (reproduced on p. 167).

A list of the names of all the crafts exercised in London from of old, and still continuing in this ninth year of King Henry V., and here set down in case it may in any wise profit the hall and Company of Brewers.

Mercers	Plasterers	Hatters	Bookbinders
Grocers	Carpenters	Cofferers	Writers of texts
Drapers	Pewterers	Pointmakers	Stationers
Fishmongers	Plumbers	Wiredrawers	Poulters
Goldsmiths	Joiners	Cardmakers	Clockmakers
Vintners	Founders	Pinners	Chapemakers
Skinners	Leathersellers	Whittawyers	Sheders
Tailors	Bakers	Leather-dyers	Malemakers
Saddlers	Shearmen	Stainers	Tablemakers
Ironmongers	Lorimers	Hostillers	Lockyers
Girdlers	Waxchandlers	Cooks	Fourbours
Cordwainers	Tallowchandlers	Piemakers	Burlesters
Haberdashers	Tanners	Bellmakers	Lateners
Cutlers	Curriers	Corsours	Potters
Armourers	Pouchmakers	Chariotmakers	Stuffers
Weavers (wool)	Bowyers	Brothmakers	Fruiterers
Weavers (linen)	Fletchers	Jewellers	Cheesemongers
Fullers	Horners	Paternosters	Stringers
Dyers	Spurriers	Turners	Basketmakers

Barbers	Hurers	Carvers	Bottlemakers
Brewers	Woodmongers	Glasiers	Marblers
Butchers	Writers of Court letters	Felmongers	Netmakers
Tapicers	Limners	Woolmen	Potmakers
Broderers	Leches	Cornmongers	Glovers
Painters	Ferrours	Blacksmiths	Hosiers
Salters	Coppersmiths	Ropers	Orglemakers
Brasiers	Upholders	Lanternmakers	Soapmakers
Smiths	Galochemakers	Haymongers	

III. LIST OF COMPANIES KEEPING THE WATCH, 1518.

Letter Book L., p. 79 : *Mem.* "That att a court of Aldermen holden on the VIIIth day of June, Anno regis Henrici octavi Xth, it was agreed that yerely from henceforth on the vigils of St. John and St. Peter these number of Bowmen underwritten shall be provided and founde by the occupations undernamed to awayt upon the mayre in the watch every of the said nights."

Goldsmiths, VIII	Carpenters, VI	Cordwainers, II
Mercers, VIII	Plumbers, IIII	Innholders, VI
Drapers, VIII	Painters, Stainers, IIII	Armourers, IIII
Fishmongers, VIII	Pewterers, IIII	Masons, II
Skinners, VI	Cutlers, IIII	Bowyers, IIII
Tailors, VIII	Saddlers, IIII	Fletchers, IIII
Haberdashers, VIII	Barbers, IIII	Joiners, II
Salters, VIII	Waxchandlers, IIII	Pastelers, II
Ironmongers, IIII	Woolpackers, II	Coopers, IIII
Vintners, VI	Poulters, II	Woodmongers, II
Shearmen, VI	Broderers, II	Weavers, II
Dyers, IIII	Tilers, II	Spurriers, II
Brewers, VI	Fullers, II	Wiresellers, II
Bakers, VI	Girdlers, IIII	Carters, II
Leathersellers, VI	Curriers, IIII	Blacksmiths, II
Tallowchandlers, VI	Butchers, IIII	

A A

APPENDIX B

THE list of sources is designed to serve as a guide to the study of those companies whose histories have not been fully written Where a satisfactory history already exists, few, or no other, references have been given. A large number of pamphlets and broadsides relating to the companies, which can easily be found in the catalogues of the British Museum and Guildhall Libraries under the heading " London Livery Companies, Apothecaries, etc.," have also been omitted. The references to my own earlier work cover an additional list of sources, there published in an appendix.

APOTHECARIES.

Barrett, C. R. B., *History of the Society of Apothecaries*, 1905.

Harleian MS., 1454. An apothecary's account book, beginning 1594, and containing the accounts of Essex, Southampton, the Lady Arabella, Edward Herbert, and many other of the leading personages of that time. " Tobacco and pipes " one of the main items. The last half of the book has been used by the Painter-Stainers.

Lansdowne MSS., 457, fo. 358.

ARMOURERS AND BRAZIERS.

Riley, *Memorials*, 145.

Calendar of Letter Books, G, 44, 172; H, 44, 59, 62, 69, 152, 160; M, 127 (Union with Bladesmiths, 1506).

Guildhall MSS., 108, fo. 693; 110, fo. 682.

Liv. Comp. Comm., 1884. III. 13. Copies of charters of 31 Hen. VI. 1 Eliz., etc.

Repertories, XXII. 163, 435 (Dispute with Cutlers, 1590–2).

P. C. R., April 3, May 22, June 4, 1635. "Artisan *v.* Trader."

Morley, T., *Some Account of the Worshipful Company of Armourers and Braziers*, 1878.

Ellis, H. D., *A Short Description of the Silver Plate, etc.*, 1892.

Ffoulkes, C. J., " The Armourers Company of London and the Greenwich School of Armourers," in *Archaeologia*, vol. lxxvi, 1927.

Ffoulkes, C. J., *Some Account of the Worshipful Company of Armourers and Braziers*, 1927.

Pitt, S. H., *Some Notes on the History of the Worshipful Company of Armourers and Braziers*, 1930.

Wills, H. W., *The Worshipful Company of Armourers and Braziers*, 1917.

BAKERS.

Bateson, M., "A London Municipal Collection," *English Historical Review*, October, 1902, p. 18.

Liber Albus (trans. Riley), 231, 309, 313.

Riley, *Memorials*, 36, 162, 323, 423.

——, *Chronicles of Old London*, 43, 150, 240, 251.

Calendar of Letter Books, A, 120–1, 213, 217; B, 243–4; C, 57; D, 243; E, 7, 116, 261; G, 57; H, 43, 107, 183–4, 194, 207, 260–1, 373.

Plea and Mem. Rolls, A 1, Roll 2, Dr. Sharpe's MS. Calendar.

Letter Books, K, fo. 198 (Brotherhood of Journeymen); L, fo. 81, 122, 192, 227; N, 166, 210–14, 280; P, 115; V, 195; X, 2, 26; Etc., 178.

Young, S., and Buchanan, H. H., *A Catalogue of Books and Records at Bakers' Hall*, 1895.

Thrupp, S., *A Short History of the Worshipful Company of Bakers of London*, 1933.

BARBER-SURGEONS.

Lambert, G., in *Lond. and Midd. Arch. Soc. Trans.*, VI. 123.

South, J. F., *Memorials of Surgery.*

Young, Sidney, *Annals of Barber-Surgeons.*

Shoppee, C. J., *Description of Pictures and other objects in the Hall*, 1883.

Guildhall MSS., 1108–9, 1117. Collections relating to Barbers' Company.

BASKET-MAKERS.

The rules, orders, and regulations made by the Court of Aldermen, 1569, 1585, and 1610. Printed, 1827. Reprinted, 1886.

Journals, XIV. 133, 158.

Repertories, X. 135; XV. 513; XVI. 60, 106, 112, 149, 176, 471, 492–5, 499–502; XXV. 181.

Bobart, H. H., *Records of the Basket Makers Company*, 1911.

BLACKSMITHS.

Riley, *Memorials*, 361, 537.

Calendar of Letter Book, H, 369, 388.

Repertories, X. 161; XV. 49; XXX. 396; XLII. 147; LIII. 60, 289; LIV. 57.

Liv. Comp. Comm., 1884. III. 110. Charters of 1571, 1604, 1639, 1685.

Index to Remembrancia, 217–8.

Noble, *Ironmongers' Company*, pp. 61–74, 1889.

Adams, A. J., *The History of the Worshipful Company of Blacksmiths from Early Times until the year 1647*, 1937.

BOWYERS.

Calendar of Letter Books, H, 6, 11n, 43, 292, 389, 414, 416.

Letter Books, K, 636; L, 261 (Light in Chapel of St. Thomas on Bridge, 5 Hen. VII.).

Liv. Comp. Comm., 1884. III. 117. Charters of 1621 and 1668.

Repertories, X. 28; XII. No. 1, 222; XIII. 144; XIV. 252; XXIX. 94; XLI. 276.

BREWERS.

Liber Albus, 233, 307.

Riley, *Memorials*, 36, 225.

Calendar of Letter Books, A, 216, 220; C, 7; D, 237, 299; E, 71, 77; F, 27–9, 178, 189, 245; G, 52, 76, 172, 332; H, 43, 107, 122, 183–4, 201, 293, 373.

Herbert, *Twelve Great Livery Companies*, pp. 66–8, 78. Makes use of Brewers' first book, which begins 6 Hen. V., and contains material of great value for the topography of mediæval London.

Letter Books, K, 161; L, 30 (Beerbrewers' ordinances); 182 (ordinances, 22 Edward IV.), 195a, 303b.

Add. MSS. in British Museum, 36, 761, fos. 15, 19 *et passim*.

Journals, III. 11; VII. 95; VIII. 59, 172; IX. 4, 10; XVI. 104–7; XVIII. 92, 271–5.

Repertories, VII. 155–9; XV. 152, 381–8; XVI. 407–8, 435.

BRODERERS.

Liv. Comp. Comm., 1884. III. 197–8, 201–3, charters of 1561 and 1609 and ordinances.

Repertories, V. 128; VII. 107; XI. 290–4; XIII. No. 2, 343.

Letter Books, K, 89b (ordinances of 9 Hen. VI.); L, 315b (ordinances of 11 Hen. VII.).

BUTCHERS.

Daw, Joseph, *Early History of Butchers*, 1869.

Liber Albus, 230, 239, 243.

Liber Custumarum, I. 411.

Riley, *Memorials*, 141, 179, 214, 222, 226, 339, 356, 426, 599.

Calendar of Letter Books, D, 281–2; E, 137, 233, 258; F, 84, 123, 125, 208; G, 31–2, 43, 127–8, 139. 171, 173–4, 188, 207–8, 262, 332–3; H, 61, 108, 257, 372, 375, 376, 392, 394.

Letter Book L, 201b (ordinances 2 Rich. III.).

Liv. Comp. Comm., 1884. III. 208–14 gives a good account of the Butchers' records.

Journals, VIII. 82–90; XIII. 271, 376–9, 428, 434; XIV. 13–5, 320.

Repertories, IX. 10, 17–24, 46–49, 69–71, 86, 190; XIII. 38, 72, 85, 448–52; XXVII. 317; XXXV. 55; XXXVIII. 115.

Pearce, A., *The History of the Butchers Company*, 1929.

CARMEN.

Letter Book, N, 38.

Index of Remembrancia, 57–9, 475.

Second Report on Municipal Corporations, 1837, p. 342.

Orders for the establishment of the Company of Carmen, 1674 (Guildhall Library).

Strype, *Stow*, V. 226–8, 285–6.

Nef, J. U., *The Rise of the British Coal Industry*, 1932.

CARPENTERS.

Jupp, E. B. and Pocock, W. W., *An Historical Account of the Worshipful Company of Carpenters*, 1887.

Marsh, B., *The Records of the Worshipful Company of Carpenters*, 1913.

Welch, C., *The " Boke " of the Ordinances of the Brotherhood of Carpenters of London, 7 Edward III*, 1912.

CLOCKMAKERS.

Atkins, S. E. and Overall, W. H., *Some Account of the Worshipful Company of Clockmakers*, 1881.

Charters and byelaws, 1631, Guildhall Library, 1825.

Overall, W. H., *A Catalogue of Books, MSS., Specimens of Clocks, etc., deposited in Guildhall Library*, 1875.

Repertories, XLIV. 243; LI. 19, 20.

Atkins, C. E., *The Register of the Apprentices of the Worshipful Company of Clockmakers*, 1931.

CLOTHWORKERS.

Charters, etc., 1480–1688, published by the Company, 1881.

Ordinances, 1480–1639, published by the Company, 1881.

The Government of the Fullers, Shearmen, and Clothworkers of London, as proved by their charters and ordinances, 1650.

Unwin, G., *Industrial Organization in the Sixteenth and Seventeenth Centuries*, pp. 44–5, 57–60, 112–25, 198–9, 201–2, 228–34, 254–5.

Friis, A., *Alderman Cockayne's Project and the Cloth Trade*, 1927.

James, M., *Social Problems and Policy during the Puritan Revolution*, 1930.

COACHMAKERS AND COACH HARNESSMAKERS.

Second Report on Municipal Corporations, 1837, II. pp. 326–330.

Liv. Comp. Comm., 1884.   III. 248–58.

Guildhall MSS., 108, vol. iii., 1040–1051.

Repertories, XLVI. 142; XLVII. 87.

Rosedale, H. G., *Some Materials for a history of the Worshipful Company of Coach and Coach Harness Makers*, 1923.

Eland, G., *A History of the Worshipful Company of Coachmakers and Coach Harnessmakers of the City of London*, 1937.

COOKS.

Second Report on Municipal Corporations, 1837, II. 180.

Letter Books, L, 109b, 320; O, 225.

Repertories, III. 188; VIII. 14; XII. No. 1, 139–147, No. 2, 304, 307, 314, 327; XIV. 78, 289; XVII. 257, 266; XVIII. 41, 304; XXI. 2, 431; XXXII. 97; XXXIV. 312.

Guildhall MSS., 108, vol. iii., 1154–1223.

Phillips, F. T., *A History of the Worshipful Company of Cooks*, 1932.

COOPERS.

Firth, J. F., *Coopers' Company: London; Historical Memoranda, etc.*, 1848.

Repertories of Court of Aldermen, XXII. 199, *re* apprenticeship.

Hist. MSS. Comm. Report, vol. iii. 8, 19. "Coopers *v.* Brewers."

Elkington, G., *The Coopers; Company and Craft*, 1933.

Jackson, J., *Notes of the History and Antiquities of the Worshipful Company of Coopers*, 1914.

CORDWAINERS.

Liber Horn, CCCXXXIXb, transcribed in Guildhall MSS. 108, vol. i. fo. 393.

Liber Custumarum, I. 83.

Riley, *Memorials*, 54, 391, 420, 482, 495, 539, 570–1.

Calendar of Letter Books, E, 233; F, 118, 124–5, 128; G, 14, 172; H, 18, 20, 23, 43, 59; Etc., 311, 425, 432–3.

Letter Books, K, 78; L, 98b, 132a; S, 278; V. 129.

Journals, III. 16, 17; IX. 112.

Repertories, XXIX. 24, 356.

Unwin, G., *Industrial Organization*, 255.

Mander, C. H. W., *A Descriptive and Historical Account of the Guild of Cordwainers of the City of London*, 1931.

CURRIERS.

Calendar of Letter Books, C, 79; G, 171; H, 43.

Letter Books, K, 167b; L, 261b, 305, 322; P, 148; Q, 247; Z, 199; Etc., 125–8.

Unwin, G., *Industrial Organization*, 255.

Liv. Comp. Comm., 1884. III. 316–20.

Repertories, X. 23, 26; XI. 291, 458; XII. 29; XII. No. 2, 349–354; XIII. 143; XIII. No. 2, 323; XIV. 179; XV. 108, 255; XVIII. 191; XIX. 35, 40; XX. 190; XXI. 87, 375, 425, 465; XXIII. 519; XXV. 103; LIII. 151.

Burkitt, E. H., *A Short History of the Worshipful Company of Curriers*, 1923.

CUTLERS.

Riley, *Memorials*, 438, 567, 568, 597.

Calendar of Letter Books, E, 233; F, 57, 110; G, 172, 194, 299; H, 13, 44, 140.

Letter Books, K, 175; L, 210, 259b; V, 21, 46, 307.

Journals, IX. 199–202; XII. 39, 45.
Repertories, XIII. 349; XXVII. 207–25; XXIX. 232; XXXIII.
   272; XXXV. 213; LIII. 68.
Unwin, G., *Industrial Organization*, 255.
Guildhall MS. 660.
Welch, C., *A History of the Cutlers Company of London*, 1916–23.

DRAPERS.
   Johnson, A. H., *A History of the Worshipful Company of Drapers
   of London*, 1914–22.

DYERS.
   Riley, *Memorials*, 309, 364.
   Calendar of Letter Books, C, 52; F, 110, 192; G, 6, 7, 114, 140,
      293, 295; H, 43, 337, 370, 389, 403, 417.
   Letter Books, K, 133b; M, 25b, 71; N, 243; O, 266.
   Journals, X, 277–9.
   Repertories, IV. 162–80; VI. 82–9; VIII. 234; XIII. 274–6;
      XLVI. 32, 46.
   Unwin, G., *Industrial Organization*, 255.
   Robins, E. C., *Some Account of the Dyers*, in *Lond. and Midd.
   Arch. Soc. Trans.*, V., 441.

FANMAKERS.
   Second Report on Municipal Corporations, 1837, 340.

FARRIERS.
   Riley, *Memorials*, 292.
   State Papers, Domestic, Jas. I., XLI. 56.
   Entry Book in Record Office, XXXVI. fo. 175.
   Repertories, XXV. 28; XXXIII. 150; XLI. 183, 206.

FELLOWSHIP PORTERS.
   Strype's *Stow*, V. 414–20.
   Second Report on Municipal Corporations, 1837, I. 179–82.

FELTMAKERS.
   Unwin, G., *Industrial Organization*, 130–6, 145–6, 156–64,
      196–7, 215–25, 240–52, 256.
   Hawkins, J. H., *A History of the Worshipful Company of the Art
   or Mistery of Feltmakers of London*, 1917.

FISHMONGERS.
   Herbert, W., *History of Twelve Great Livery Companies*, II.
      1–120.

The last incorporation . . . to which is annexed several of the most particular byelaws, 1780.

Towse, J. W., *A Short Account of Portraits, etc.,* 1907.

FLETCHERS.

Riley, *Memorials,* 348, 556.

Letter Books, K, 6a, 196b; L, 196b (City ordinances, 1 Rich. III.).

Repertories, V. 81; XI. 240, 237, 358; XXII. 439.

FOUNDERS.

Williams, W. M., *Annals of the Founders' Company,* 1867.

Stahlschmidt, J. E. C., *Notes from an Old Account Book, Arch. Jour.,* XLII.

Hibbert, W. N., *A History of the Worshipful Company of Founders of the City of London,* 1925.

FRAMEWORK KNITTERS.

Overall, H. C., *The Framework Knitters,* 1879.

Liv. Comp. Comm., 1884. Charter of 1663.

Repertories, LXIII. 443-6; Browne, 249.

Chambers, J. D., *The Worshipful Company of Framework Knitters, 1657-1778,* in *Economica,* No. xxvii, 1929.

Wells, F. A., *The British Hosiery Trade,* 1935.

FRUITERERS.

Letter Books, L, 18a, 220; N, 18; R, 219; Etc., 161.

Journals, VIII. 88; IX. 120; XI. 241.

Repertories, XI. 9, 11, 12.

Gould, A. W., *A History of the Worshipful Company of Fruiterers of London,* 1912.

GARDENERS.

Welch, C., *History of the Worshipful Company of Gardeners,* 1900.

Guildhall MSS., 108, vol. iv., 1361-1426.

Repertories, XXVII. 106, 302; XXXIII. 74; XLVII. 138; XLIX. 261; LXXIV. 87.

Crosweller, W. T., *The Gardeners Company,* 1908.

GIRDLERS.

Smythe, W. Dunville, *An Historical Account of the Worshipful Company of Girdlers,* 1905.

Letter Books, K, 157 (ordinances of Hen. VI.); L, 69, 131b; V. 48.

Journals, VIII. 165.

Repertories, LXIII. 176.

GLASS-SELLERS.

The Worshipful Company of Glass-sellers, 1898.

Liv. Comp. Comm., 1884. III. 478, charter and byelaws of 1664.

Young, S., *The History of the Worshipful Company of Glass Sellers of London,* 1913.

GLAZIERS.

Letter Books, L, 103a; O, 125; Q, 48; X, 107; Y, 52.

Unwin, G., *Industrial Organization,* 257.

Journals, XXX. 132, 339.

Repertories, X. 222, 235, 239; XI. 252, 329, 394; XIX. 44; XV. 267; XXXII. 259; XLVIII. 455; LII. 53, 134; LVII. Pt. 2, 21.

Ashdown, C. H., *A History of the Worshipful Company of Glaziers of the City of London,* 1919.

Knowles, J. A., *Additional Notes on the Worshipful Company of Glaziers,* in *The Antiquaries Journal,* vol. vii, 1927.

GLOVERS.

Riley, *Memorials,* 245, 249.

Calendar of Letter Books, G, 172; H, 21, 132, 171, 346, 356, 417.

Letter Books, K, 251b; L, 185b; M, 13.

Unwin, G., *Industrial Organization,* 79, 129, 211, 257.

Repertories, XXXIV. 372; XLVI. 300; LV. 225; LVII. 239; LIX. 104–7.

GOLD AND SILVER WIREDRAWERS.

Stewart, H., *History of the Gold and Silver Wire-Drawers,* 1891.

Gardiner, S. R., *History of England,* 1603–42, vol. iv. pp. 33–5.

Unwin, G., *Industrial Organization,* 257.

Abrams, M. A., *The English Gold and Silver Thread Monopolies, 1611–21,* in *The Journal of Economic and Business History,* vol. iii, 1931.

Knight, A. C., *A List of the Masters, Wardens, [etc.] with a short history of the Company and the craft it represents,* 1922.

GOLDSMITHS.

Prideaux, Sir W. S., *Memorials of the Goldsmiths' Company,* 1896.

Herbert, W., *History of Twelve Great Livery Companies*, II. 121–298.

Unwin, G., *Industrial Organization*, 257.

Heal, Sir A., *The London Goldsmiths, 1200–1800*, 1935.

James, M., *Social Problems and Policy during the Puritan Revolution*, 1930.

GROCERS.

Heath, J. B., *Some Account of the Worshipful Company of Grocers*, 1854.

Kingdon, J. A., *Facsimile, Transcript and Translation of MSS. Archives, 1345–1463*, 1883–6.

Ravenhill, W., *A Short Account of the Company of Grocers*, 1689.

Repertories, VI. 75.

Rees, J. A., *The Worshipful Company of Grocers*, 1923.

Thrupp, S., *The Grocers of London* in Power, E. and Postan, M. M., *English Trade in the Fifteenth Century*, 1933.

GUNMAKERS.

Guildhall MSS., 108, vol. iv., 1480–1527.

Repertories, LIV. 87.

HABERDASHERS.

Herbert, W., *History of Twelve Great Livery Companies*, II. 531–553.

Unwin, G., *Industrial Organization*, 44, 79, 81, 106, 108, 127, 129–35, 145, 157, 165–7, 196–8, 240–5, 258.

Riley, *Memorials*, 91, 354.

Calendar of Letter Books, H, 43, 250, 273, 366, 416.

Letter Books, K, 246b; L, 258, 266b; M, 28a.

Eagleton, J., *Notes on the Worshipful Company of Haberdashers*, 1911.

HORNERS.

Compton, C. H., *History of the Worshipful Company of Horners*, 1882.

Guildhall MSS., 108, vol. iv. 1528–1546.

Letter Books, K, fo. 276b (ordinances, Henry VI.); L, 116a (ordinances, Edward IV.).

Lansdowne MSS., vol. 73, No. 15, and vol. 86, No. 12.

Repertories, XI. 244; XXIV. 140, 290, 297; XXXVIII. 213; L, 87.

Fisher, F. J., *A Short History of the Worshipful Company of Horners*, 1936.

INNHOLDERS.

Matthews, J. Douglas, *History of the Innholders' Company*, in *Lond. and Midd. Arch. Soc. Soc. Trans.*, new series, vol. i. 151–176.

Letter Books, L, 191b; M, 227, 253; V, 205.

A History of the Worshipful Company of Innholders, 1922.

IRONMONGERS.

Nichol, J., *Some Account of the Worshipful Company of Ironmongers*, 1866.

JOINERS.

Calendar of Letter Book, H, 43, 451.

Letter Books, K, 46b; R, 118, 119–121.

Jupp and Pocock, *Carpenters' Company*, appendix.

Journals, XVI. 124.

Unwin, G., *Industrial Organization*, 108, 212, 258.

Repertories, VII. 235; XI. 142; XII. No. 2, 364; XVII. 303; XXI. 437; XXIX. 191; XXXIII. 377; XXXVII. 233; XLVIII. 38.

Phillips, H. L., *Annals of the Worshipful Company of Joiners*, 1915.

LEATHERSELLERS.

Black, W. H., *History and Antiquities of the Worshipful Company of Leathersellers*, 1871.

Unwin, G., *Industrial Organization*, 127–30, 142, 211, 258.

LORINERS.

Latchford, Benjamin, *The Loriner*, 1871.

Guildhall MSS., 108, vol. iv. 1558–1602.

Letter Books, L, 270; M, 182; X. 16.

Repertories, XLVIII. 461.

MASONS.

Conder, E., *The Hale Craft and Fellowship of Masonry*, 1894.

Knoop, D., and Jones, G. P., *The Mediaeval Mason*, 1933.

——, *The London Mason in the Seventeenth Century*, 1935.

MERCERS.

Herbert, W., *History of Twelve Great Livery Companies*, I.

Watney, Sir J., *Some Account of the Hospital of St. Thomas of Acon*, 1892.

Selby, W. D., *The Charters, Ordinances, and Byelaws of the Mercers' Company*, 1881.

Brabrook, E. W., *The Worshipful Company of Mercers*, 1889.

Carus-Wilson, E. M., *The Origins and Early Development of the Merchant Adventurers* in *The Economic History Review*, vol. iv, 1933.

Lyell, L., *Acts of Court of the Mercers' Company, 1453-1527*, 1936.

Watney, Sir J., *An Account of the Mistery of Mercers of the City of London*, 1914.

MERCHANT TAILORS.

Clode, C. M., *Memorials of the Guild of Merchant Tailors*, 1875.

——, *Early History of the Guild of Merchant Tailors*, 1888.

Fry, F. M., and Sayle, R. T. D., *The Charters of the Merchant Tailors Company*, 1937.

Hopkinson, H. L., *Report on the Ancient Records of the Merchant Tailors*, 1915.

James, M., *Social Problems and Policy during the Puritan Revolution*, 1930.

Sayle, R. T. D., *The Lord Mayor's Pageants of the Merchant Tailors Company in the 15th, 16th, and 17th centuries*, 1931.

MUSICIANS.

Repertories, XV. 144; XVIII. 179, 232; XXV. 219, 223; XXVI. Pt. 2, 301; XLIX. 253; LII. 132.

Liv. Comp. Comm., 1884. III. 593. Charter of 1604 and byelaws of 1606.

Statutes, Laws and Ordinances of the Worshipful Company of Musicians, 1790-1825.

The Worshipful Company of Musicians; Charters, Byelaws, etc., 1902-3.

Repertories, XXVI(2). 301.

NEEDLEMAKERS.

Price, J. E., *An Account of the Worshipful Company of Needlemakers*, 1876.

Liv. Comp. Comm., 1884. III. 600, charter of 1664 and extracts from byelaws of same date.

Index to Remembrancia, 104-5.

Repertories, L. 145; LXV. 68.

PAINTER-STAINERS.

Crace, J. G., *Some Account of the Worshipful Company of Painters*, 1880.

Pitman, W. H., *The Worshipful Company of Painters*, 1906.

Liv. Comp. Comm., 1884. III. 613, City ordinances of 1467, charter of 1581.

Byelaws of 1582; charter of 1685; some extracts from records.

Lansdowne MSS., 20, fo. 9; 22, fo. 47; 106, fo. 58; 487; fo. 441.

Harleian MSS., 1099, 1506, 6815, 1454.

Journals, V. 225.

Letter Book, M, 36 (17 Hen. VII. United with Stainers).

Englefield, W. A. D., *The History of the Painter-Stainers Company of London*, 1923.

PARISH CLERKS.

Christie, Jas., *Some Account of Parish Clerks*, 1893.

Ditchfield, *The Parish Clerk*, 1907.

Ebblewhite, E. A., *The Parish Clerks Company and its Charters*, 1932.

PATTERNMAKERS.

Lambert, G., *The Worshipful Company of Patternmakers*, 1890.

Second Report on Municipal Corporations, 1837, 314.

Guildhall MSS., 104, vol. iv. 1603–1691.

Fitch, C., *The History of the Worshipful Company of Patternmakers*, 1926.

PAVIORS.

Welch, C., *An Account of the Worshipful Company of Paviors*, 1889.

Guildhall MSS. 178–83.

Welch, C., *A History of the Worshipful Company of Paviors of the City of London*, 1909.

PEWTERERS.

Welch, C., *History of the Pewterers' Company*, 1903.

Unwin, G., *Industrial Organization*, 153–6, 259.

PLASTERERS.

Letter Books, M, 37b (17 Hen. VII. City ordinances); M, 70 (charter enrolled); N, 228; Etc. 133.

Unwin, G., *Industrial Organization*, 260.

Legends of the Worshipful Company of Plasterers, 1886.

Journals, XXXI. 233.

Repertories, IV. 143; X. 29; XI. 460; XIII. 201; XIII. No. 2, 313, 333-6; XXVI. Pt. 2, 398; XXVIII. 164-6; XXX. 112, 116, 179, 194, 200; XXXIV. 271, 285.

PLAYING-CARD MAKERS.
State Papers Domestic, Charles, 1, CIV. 62; CLXXXV. 18; CCCCLXXVII. 64.
Privy Council Register for 1631, fo. 46.

PLUMBERS.
The Plumbers' Company in Ancient and Modern Times, 1902.
Riley, *Memorials*, 321, 355.
Calendar of Letter Books, H, 41, 44.
Letter Book, L, 252.
Repertories, XXVIII. 135; XXXII. 107; XL. 381; XLI. 346; XLII. 58, 60, 61, 96, 99.
Guildhall MSS., 108, vol. iv. 1693-1754.
Unwin, G., *Industrial Organization*, 206.
Waldo, F. J., *A Short History of the Worshipful Company of Plumbers of the City of London*, 1921.

POULTERS.
Riley, *Memorials*, 220-2, 300, 312, 389.
Jones, P. E., *A Short History of the Worshipful Company of Poulters of the City of London*, 1938.
Letter Books, M, 137b, 185, 201; N, 163; Q, 77; R, 75; S, 277; Z, 207.
Repertories, XII. 207; XIV. 320, 323.
Add. MSS., in British Museum, 36,761 (ordinances, 4 Edward VI.).
Second Report on Municipal Corporations, 1837, 174.
The Charters of the Worshipful Company of Poulters: its Orders, Ordinances, and Constitutions, etc., 1872.

SADDLERS.
Letter Book, L, fo. 208a.
Sherwell, J. W., *The History of the Guild of Saddlers of the City of London*, 1937.

SALTERS.
Gillespie, T., *Some Account of the Worshipful Company of Salters*, 1827.

Herbert, W., *History of Twelve Great Livery Companies*, II. 555–65.

Repertories, XXVII. 363.

SCRIVENERS.

Liv. Comp. Comm., 1884. III. charter of 1617; long report on position of Company in 1748.

Letter Books, K, 182; Y, 324.

Harleian MSS., 2295, 1–20, *re* incorporation.

Repertories, XV. 151; XVI. 64; XX. 242; XXII. 152; XXXII. 320, 348.

SHIPWRIGHTS.

Sharpe, R. R., *A Short Account of the Worshipful Company of Shipwrights*, 1876.

Guildhall MSS., 108, vol. ii. 634–761.

Unwin, G., *Industrial Organization*, 270.

Repertories, XXXI(1). 197; XXXIV. 412–3.

Ebblewhite, E. A., *The Worshipful Company of Shipwrights*, 1925.

SKINNERS.

Wadmore, J. F., *Some Account of the Worshipful Company of Skinners*, 1902.

Letter Books, K, 129b; L, 303.

Unwin, G., *Industrial Organization*, 183, 202, 361.

Herbert, W., *History of Twelve Great Livery Companies*, II. 298–382.

Journals, XXVII. 176.

Repertories, XXVIII. 6, 21, 25, 27.

Lambert, J. J., *The Records of the Skinners of London, Edward I to James I*, 1933.

SPECTACLE MAKERS.

Second Report on Municipal Corporations, 1837, 274.

Repertories, XLII. 252; XLVIII. 284; XLIX.

Champness, W. H., *A Short History of the Worshipful Company of Spectacle Makers*, 1930.

STATIONERS.

Arber, E., *Transcript of the Register of the Company of Stationers*, 1554–1640. A large number of documents relating to the printing trade are inserted in the five volumes which constitute the best history of the company.

Nichols, J. G., *Historical Notices of the Worshipful Company of Stationers*.

Rivington, C. R., *The Records of the Worshipful Company of Stationers*, 1883.

Eyre, G. E. B., and Rivington, C. R., *A Transcript of the Registers of the Worshipful Company of Stationers, 1604–1708*, 1913–14.

Greg, W. W., and Boswell, E., *Records of the Court of the Stationers Company, 1576–1602*, 1930.

SURGEONS.

Wall, C., *The History of the Surgeons' Company, 1745–1800*, 1937.

TALLOW CHANDLERS.

Monier-Williams, M. F., *Records of the Worshipful Company of Tallow Chandlers*, Pt. i. 1, 1897.

Calendar of Letter Book, H, 43, 402, 416.

Letter Book, L, 81.

Repertory, XV. 334.

Knight, A. C., *The Tallow Chandlers' Company*, 1918.

TINPLATE WORKERS.

Ebblewhite, E. A., *A Chronological History of the Worshipful Company of Tinplate Workers*, 1896.

Berry, C. W., *The Worshipful Company of Tinplate Workers*, 1926.

Brown, A., *The Worshipful Company of Tinplate Workers*, 1914.

TILERS AND BRICKLAYERS.

Riley, *Memorials*, 254, 308.

Letter Books, L, 56, 158; M, 89; N, 37; V, 105; Z, 44, 265.

Unwin, G., *Industrial Organization*, 262.

Repertories, XI. 474; XIII. No. 2, 352; XXIX. 92; XXXIII. 111; XLIII. 204; XLVII. 11.

TURNERS.

Riley, *Memorials*, 78, 234.

Letter Books, K, 151b; L, 149a (City ordinances, 19 Edward IV.).

Repertories, XXVII.(2). 299; XXIX. 74. 85; XL. 151 (*re* charter and search); XLIV. 144.

Stanley-Stone, A. C., *The Worshipful Company of Turners of London*, 1925.

UPHOLDERS.

Letter Books, L, 103b; M, 5.

B B

Repertories, XXXI. Pt. 2, 313; XXXII. 150; XXXIX. 59; LI. 54.
Strype, *Stow*, V. 229.

VINTNERS.
Herbert, W., *History of Twelve Great Livery Companies*, II. 625–642.
Milbourn, T., Nichols, J. G., and Overall, W. H., Articles in *Lond. and Midd. Arch. Trans.*, vol. iii.
Egerton MSS., 1143; Lansdowne MSS., 76, No. 43; 251, Nos. 7 and 9; Harleian MSS., 1219. See references in pp. 323–6.

WATERMEN.
Humpherus, H., *History of the Company of Watermen and Lightermen*, 1874–86.
Broodbank, J. C., *The History of the Port of London*, 1921.

WAX CHANDLERS.
Riley, *Memorials*, 300, 358.
Calendar of Letter Books, H, 44, 76, 97.
Letter Books, L, 255b; M, 241; V, 228.
Index to Remembrancia, 147, 149.
Journals, III. 16; IX. 46, 163, 192.
Repertories, VII. 72, 80, 116, 137; XV. 34.

WEAVERS.
See references in Chap. IV. of this book.
Unwin, G., *Industrial Organization*, 28–30, 262.
Facsimile of ancient book of Weavers' Company.
Calendar of Letter Books (see indices).
Letter Books, I, 64; K, 193–4; L, 295 and 345.
Journals, III. 99; IV. 26, 28, 34, 57; X. 113.
Repertories, XVI. 208; XXI. 19, 202; XXIII. 513; XXIV. 208; XXXIV. 526; XXXV. 11; XLI. 288; XLV. 74–79; LIV. 147-150; LVII(2). 201; LVIII. 206.
Journals, XL. 37b., 290, 293.
Consitt, F., *The London Weavers' Company*, 1933.
Waller, W. C., *Extracts from the Court Books of the Weavers' Company*, 1931.

WHEELWRIGHTS.
Scott, J. B., *A Short Account of the Wheelwrights' Company*.
Repertories, XLV. 105; XLVI. 142; XLVII. 87.

WOODMONGERS.

Letter Books, O, 142–5; P, 71; Q, 258; T, 188; X, 392; Z, 381.

Index to Remembrancia, 57, 58, 59, 160.

Strype, *Stow*, V. 226–8.

Act of Common Council relating to cars and carts, 1665, Guildhall Library.

Lansdowne MSS., 162, fo. 196; Harleian, 6842, fo. 266.

See tracts under headings " Woodmongers " and " Carmen," in Guildhall and British Museum.

Dale, H. B., *The Fellowship of Woodmongers*, 1923.

Nef, J. U., *The Rise of the British Coal Industry*, 1932.

WOOLMEN.

Calendar of Letter Book, E, 233.

Letter Book, L. 263b.

INDEX